Interactive Information Retrieval in Digital Environments

Iris Xie
University of Wisconsin-Milwaukee, USA

T0325040

IGI PUBLISHING

Hershey • New York

Acquisition Editor:	Kristin Klinger
Development Editor:	Kristin Roth
Senior Managing Editor:	Jennifer Neidig
Managing Editor:	Jamie Snavely
Assistant Managing Editor:	Carole Coulson
Copy Editor:	Lanette Ehrhardt
Typesetter:	Jeff Ash
Cover Design:	Lisa Tosheff
Printed at:	Yurchak Printing Inc.

Published in the United States of America by
　　　　IGI Publishing (an imprint of IGI Global)
　　　　701 E. Chocolate Avenue
　　　　Hershey PA 17033
　　　　Tel: 717-533-8845
　　　　Fax: 717-533-8661
　　　　E-mail: cust@igi-global.com
　　　　Web site: http://www.igi-global.com

and in the United Kingdom by
　　　　IGI Publishing (an imprint of IGI Global)
　　　　3 Henrietta Street
　　　　Covent Garden
　　　　London WC2E 8LU
　　　　Tel: 44 20 7240 0856
　　　　Fax: 44 20 7379 0609
　　　　Web site: http:/www.eurospanbookstore.com

Product or company names used in this book are for identification purposes only. Inclusion of the names of the products or companies does not indicate a claim of ownership by IGI Global of the trademark or registered trademark.

Library of Congress Cataloging-in-Publication Data

Xie, Hong, 1965-
　Interactive information retrieval in digital environments / Hong (Iris) Xie.
　　　p. cm.
　Summary: "This book includes the integration of existing frameworks on user-oriented information retrieval systems across multiple disciplines; the comprehensive review of empirical studies of interactive information retrieval systems for different types of users, tasks, and subtasks; and the discussion of how to evaluate interactive information retrieval systems. "--Provided by publisher.
　ISBN-13: 978-1-59904-240-4
　ISBN-13: 978-1-59904-242-8 (e-book)
　1. Information retrieval. 2. Information storage and retrieval systems. I. Title.
　ZA3075.X54 2008
　025.04--dc22
　　　　　　　　　　　　2007041359

British Cataloguing in Publication Data
A Cataloguing in Publication record for this book is available from the British Library.

All work contributed to this book is original material. The views expressed in this book are those of the authors, but not necessarily of the publisher.

Interactive Information Retrieval in Digital Environments

Table of Contents

Preface vii

Acknowledgment xxii

Chapter I. User-Oriented IR Research Approaches 1
The Divide between System-Oriented and User-Oriented Approaches 1
User-Oriented Approaches 2
   Taylor's Levels of Information Need Approach 3
   Belkin's ASK Hypothesis 5
   Dervin's Sense-Making Approach 8
   Kuhlthau's Information Search Process (ISP) Approach 10
   Wilson's Information Seeking Context Approach 12
   Cognitive Work Analysis 15
Summary 18

Chapter II. Interactive IR in OPAC Environments 29
Overview of OPAC Environments 29
   History and Background 29
   Definition and Types of OPACs 30
   Current Developments 33
   Challenges for Users 34
Research Overview 35
Interaction Studies 36
   User Goals and Their Impact 37
   Strategies/Behaviors and Affecting Factors 38
   Effect of Knowledge Structure on Search Success 40
   Evaluation Studies and Usability Testing 41
   Intermediary Studies and Their Implications 42
   Research Methods for Interaction Studies 43
Summary 45

Chapter III. Interactive IR in Online Database Environments..**53**
Overview of Online Database Environments..53
   History and Background...53
   Definition of Online Databases and Major Elements of the Online Industry.................................54
   Current Developments 56
   Challenges for Users 58
Research Overview 60
Interaction Studies 61
   Tasks and Their Impacts 61
   Levels of Search Strategies 63
   Shifts in Search Strategies/Stages/Foci..65
   Users' Knowledge Structure..66
   Searcher Characteristics/Cognitive Styles/Search Styles...68
   Ease of Use vs. User Control...70
   Evaluation Criteria for Interactive Online IR Systems..71
Summary 72

Chapter IV. Interactive IR in Web Search Engine Environments **83**
Overview of Web Search Engine Environments...83
   History and Background...83
   Definitions and Types of Web Search Engines 84
   Current Developments 85
   Challenges for Users 87
Research Overview 89
Interaction Studies 90
   Levels of User Goals/Tasks...90
   Usage Pattern: Patterns of Query Formulation and Reformulation....................................93
   Patterns of Multimedia IR..96
   Information Search Behaviors/Strategies of Different User Groups 97
   The Impact of Knowledge Structure..99
   Criteria for the Evaluation of Web Search Engines..101
   Comparison with Other Online IR Systems 103
Summary 105

Chapter V. Interactive IR in Digital Library Environments **116**
Overview of Digital Library Environments 116
   History and Background..116
   Definitions and Types of Digital Libraries...118
   Current Developments 120
   Challenges for Users 121
Research Overview 122
Interaction Studies 124
   Tasks/Goals and Their Impact 124
   Usage Patterns...126
   Online Help...127
   Usability Studies 130
   Organizational Usability...133
   Interactive Multimedia Information Retrieval..134
   Evaluation Criteria for Digital Libraries 136
Summary 139

Chapter VI. TREC and Interactive Track Environments...**153**
Overview of TREC 153
   History and Background..153
   Types of Tracks...154
Overview of Interactive Track...156

Types of Interactive Studies...158
    The Impact of Searchers' Knowledge vs. the Impact of the Dimensions of Tasks 158
    Query Formulation and Reformulation: Relevance Feedback and Query Length......................160
    Search Tactics and Strategies 165
    Results Organization Structure and Delivery Mechanism..166
    Comparison of Different Retrieval Models and Evaluation Methods.......................................170
    Interactive Multilingual/Cross-Language Information Retrieval (CLIR) 171
Summary: Impact and Limitation of TREC Interactive Track Studies 174

Chapter VII. Interactive IR Models..183
Three Major Interactive IR Models 183
    Ingwersen's Cognitive Model and Applications..184
    Belkin's Episode Model of Interaction with Texts and Applications..188
    Saracevic's Stratified Interaction Model and Applications...192
    Applications and Implications of the Three Interactive IR Models 195
    Limitations of the Three Models 196
Microlevel of Interactive IR Models and Approaches 197
    Ellis' Model of Information-Seeking Behavior 197
    Bates' Berrypicking Approach 198
    Vakkari's Theory of the Task-Based IR Process...199
    Spink's Model of Interactive Feedback..201
    Hert's IR Interaction in Relation to the Information-Seeking Process 201
    Wang, Hawk, and Tenopir's Multidimensional Model of User-Web Interaction 203
    Pharo's Search Situation and Transition Method 204
Summary: Major Components of and Limitations of Existing Macro- and
    Micro-Level of Interactive IR Models..204

Chapter VIII. Interactive IR Framework...215
Nature of IR and Interactive IR in Digital Environments 215
Planned-Situational Interactive IR Model...216
    Overview of the Planned-Situational IR Model 216
    Levels of User Goals and Tasks and Their Representation 217
    Relationships Between Levels of User Goals and Tasks...218
    Dimensions of Work Tasks and Search Tasks...220
    Personal Information Infrastructure...223
    Social-Organizational Context 225
    IR Systems 226
    Dimensions of Information Seeking Strategies 228
    Information-Seeking Strategies: Products of Plans and Situations...236
    Dimensions of Plans and Situations 241
    Shifts in Current Search Goals and Information-Seeking Strategies...243
    Factors Affecting Shifts in Current Search Goals/Search Tasks 250
Summary 252

Chapter IX. Illustration and Validation of the Interactive IR Framework.........................263
Overview of the Empirical Study 263
    Objective of the Study 263
    Methodology 264
Levels of User Goals and Tasks and their Representation..265
Personal Information Infrastructure..267
Social-Organizational Context 270
IR Systems 271
Types of Information-Seeking Strategies..273
Dimensions of Plans and Situations 278
    Dimensions of Plans 278
    Dimensions of Situations 280

Shifts in Current Search Goals and Information-Seeking Strategies...281
    Types of Current Search Goal Shifts..281
    Types of Interactive Intention Shifts..283
    Types of Retrieval Tactic Shifts..285
Factors Affecting Shifts in Current Search Goals/Search Tasks and Information-Seeking Strategies....286
    Planned Aspects...286
    Situational Aspects..288
Summary..290

Chapter X. Implications of the Planned-Situational Interactive IR Model..............................**294**
Theoretical Implications: The Understanding of the Nature of IR..................................294
    Clarification of Important Concepts..294
    Nature of Interactive IR: Products of Plans and Situations.....................................296
Practical Implications: Implications for Interactive IR System Design...........................298
    Supporting Multiple Types of Information-Seeking Strategies..................................298
    Balancing Ease-of-Use and User Control..302
    Creating Interactive Help Mechanisms...306
Implications for Interactive IR System Evaluation: Multi-Dimensional Evaluation Framework.......313
    Evaluation of Interactive IR System Performance...313
    Evaluation of Interface Usability and Organizational Usability................................316
    Evaluation of the Interactive Process between User and System................................318
    Integrating Multi-Dimensional Criteria for the Evaluation of Interactive IR Systems...............320
Summary..322

Chapter XI. Conclusions and Future Directions...**334**
Conclusions and Contribution of the Book..334
Unsolved Problems and Further Research Directions...338
    One-Size-Fits-All Model?...338
    The Gap between Users-Oriented Study and System-Oriented Design.......................339
    Complexity of Interactive Multimedia IR and CLIR..340
    The Evaluation of Interactive IR Models..341
    Further Research Directions and Related Questions...342

About the Author...**348**

Index...**349**

Preface

Different aspects of context are essential for the understanding of information seeking and retrieving (Cool & Spink, 2002). The emergence of the Internet has created a variety of digital environments, permitting millions of users to search for information by themselves from anywhere in the world and at any time of day or night. On the one hand, users have diverse backgrounds with different levels of knowledge and skills; they also have different tasks at hand when they are searching for information. On the other hand, different types of online IR systems are designed with different interfaces that focus on different collections. In digital environments, therefore, it can be a challenge for users to effectively find the information they need in order to accomplish their tasks. This preface offers background information about information seeking and retrieving in digital environments and explains why this book is needed.

Information Retrieval (IR) Systems and Different Digital Environments

Information retrieval is never an easy task. The problem with IR is that document representation, either by index terms or texts, cannot satisfy user need representation, which is dynamic and complicated. Moreover, traditional IR systems are designed to support only one type of information-seeking strategy that users engage in: query formulation. The new digital environments redefine online IR systems in terms of their design and retrieval.

IR and IR Systems

What is information retrieval? According to Meadow, Boyce, and Kraft (1999), information retrieval has been defined as "finding some desired information in a store of information or a database" (p. 2). Selectivity is the key for information retrieval. IR is not just a system activity; instead, it is a communication process between users and the system. The central problem of information retrieval is how to match, compare, or relate users' requests for information to the information that is stored in databases. Information retrieval can also be labeled as information-seeking, information searching, and information accessing. These terms can be considered as synonyms for information retrieval although their focus might be different (Chu, 2003). Wilson (2000) defined the differences between information seeking behavior and informaiton searching behavior. *Information-seeking* refers to purposive behavior involving users' interactions with manual information systems or computer-based systems in order to satisfy their information goals. *Information-searching* behaviors refers to the mirco level of behavior when interacting with a variety of information systems. However, in the literature on IR, researchers have used these terms to represent similar concepts. In this book, information-seeking and information-searching are used interchangeably with information retrieval, following Wilson's definition as well as other researchers' expressions when their works are cited.

Information retrieval can be mainly classified into the following types:

- Subject search: look for items with common characteristics.
- Known item search: find an item when a user knows particular information about that item, such as author, title, and so forth.
- Specific information search: look for exact data or fact.
- Update information: browse to enhance the existing knowledge structure of a subject area.

What is an information retrieval system? IR systems have been developed to enable users to find relevant information stored in a database(s). The typical components of an IR system include:

- User query input mechanism
- User query analysis mechanism
- Document selection/updating mechanism
- Document analysis mechanism
- Document storage mechanism
- Matching mechanism for documents and queries
- Interface for user input and system output

Why is it so difficult to find desired information? The main problem in the field of information retrieval is that the representation of documents in a database does not match the representation of user needs. Users' anomalous state of knowledge (ASK) creates cognitive uncertainty that prohibits users from adequately expressing their information needs, and their levels of need require that they can only gradually have more focused ideas about what information they need (Belkin, 1977, 1978,

1980; Taylor, 1968). Users' information needs can only be clarified in the process of interacting with IR systems along with interacting with information stored in the systems. The dynamic process of representation of information need cannot be compared with the static representation of documents.

Online IR Systems and Different Digital Environments

The development of the Internet has brought changes to existing online IR systems, such as online public access catalogs (OPACs) and online databases; at the same time, the Internet has also given birth to new online IR systems, such as Web search engines and digital libraries. How, then, to define online IR systems? Online IR systems differ from nononline systems and have their own characteristics. Walker and Janes (1999) identified the uniqueness of online IR systems: First, online searches are conducted in real time. Users can search and obtain results almost immediately. Second, online IR systems offer remote access. Users can search at any location as long as the there is an Internet connection. The typical online IR systems can be classified into the following four types: (1) online public access catalogs (OPACs), (2) online databases, (3) World Wide Web search engines, and (4) digital libraries. What are the characteristics of these online IR systems?

OPACs contain interrelated bibliographic data of collections of a library; more importantly, they can be searched by end users. OPACs were implemented in the mid1980s when they began to replace card catalogues. OPACs became the first type of IR system built for end users, and online costs are no longer an issue (Armstrong & Large, 2001; Chu, 2003). The first generation of OPACs followed either online card catalog models, emulating the familiar card catalog, or Boolean searching models, emulating online databases, such as DIALOG or MEDLINE. Second-generation OPACs integrated these two design models and added advanced features for searching and browsing, as well as display options. Third-generation OPACs enhanced advanced search features and offered ranked retrieved results (Borgman, 1996; Hildreth, 1985, 1997). The new generation of Web OPACs allows users to access resources of libraries, publishers, and online vendors (Guha & Saraf, 2005). Today, users can access an OPAC from anywhere in the world, even from the palm of their hand. The new generation of OPACs also incorporates advanced search features and new designs from other types of IR systems, such as allowing users searching OPAC and online databases via Web OPAC interface.

Online databases began to develop in the 1960s. The first major online dial-up service was MEDLINE in 1968, and the online version of MEDLARS. In 1972, DIALOG (Lockheed) and ORBIT (SDC) offered commercial online services (Walker & Janes, 1999). The first commercial system that allows searching for full-text documents was developed in 1972 by the Data Central Corporation, the ancestor of the present LEXIS/NEXIS system (Meadow, Boyce, & Kraft, 1999). Traditional online searchers are information professionals who serve as intermediaries between users and online databases. In the 1990s, online vendors began to move their services to the World Wide Web, and as a result, end users became searchers of online databases. For the past 30 years, the online industry has experienced considerable change. The number of databases, publishers, producers, vendors, and, more important, searchers has increased dramatically. An increase of full-text databases in text databases and an increase of multimedia-oriented databases are two characteristics in recent years

(Williams, 2006). New online database services pay more attention to customization, interactivity, and offering expert systems of online database services.

The creation of World Wide Web in 1991 by using a hypertext model brought millions of users to search for online information. Web search engines are the crucial tools that help users navigate on the Web. According to Nielsen//NetRatings (Sullivan, 2006), by October 2005, search queries reached more than 5.1 million. Four types of search engines have been developed to enable users to accomplish different types of tasks:

- Web directories with hierarchically organized indexes that facilitate users' browsing for information,
- Search engines with a database of sites assisting users' searching for information,
- Meta-search engines permitting users to search multiple search engines simultaneously, and
- Specialized search engines creating a database of sites for specific topic searching.

One unique aspect of Web search engines is their ranking capability for presenting the search results, which is based on the properties of term frequency, location of terms, link analysis, popularity, date of population, length, proximity of query terms, and proper nouns (Liddy, 2001). The new design of Web search engines takes into consideration interactivity, personalization, and visualization. New "community" search engines have been developed for users to share search results among themselves. Many of the Web search engines extend their services from Web search to desktop and other types of search applications.

The emergence of digital libraries provides more opportunities for users to access a variety of information resources. There are different definitions in terms of what constitutes a digital library available in the literature. Chowdhury and Chowdhury (2003) place them into two major categories based on Borgman's (1999) discussion of competing visions of digital libraries. One approach focuses on access and retrieval of digital content; the other focuses on the collection, organization, and service aspects of digital resources. Digital libraries incorporate information retrieval systems, although they are not equivalent insofar as digital libraries provide additional services such as preservation, community building, and learning centers. It has been argued that some approaches that have been taken in IR system design and evaluation are valid for digital libraries as well (Saracevic, 2000). Pre-Web digital library efforts began at the end of the 1980s and beginning of the 1990s (Fox & Urs, 2002). The Digital Library Initiative 1 & 2, funded by the National Science Foundation (NSF), the Defense Advanced Research Projects Agency (DARPA), the National Aeronautics and Space Administration (NASA), and other agencies, play a leading role in U.S. research and development on digital libraries in terms of both their technical and their social and behavioral aspects. Digital libraries can be hosted by a variety of organizations and agencies, either for the general public or for a specific user group. Interactivity, personalization, visualization, and designing for different types of user groups are the new trends in the development of digital libraries.

Different types of IR systems in digital environments are interrelated. Online databases are named "original search engines," and current search engines are influenced by online databases (Garman, 1999). At the same time, Web search engines offer more than Web pages (Hock, 2002). Wolfram and Xie (2002) identified two IR contexts that are related to online database systems and Web search engines: traditional IR and popular IR. Traditional IR is characterized by selective content inclusion from published and unpublished sources and by more sophisticated search features. In addition, it is generally used for search topics of a nonpersonal nature. In contract, popular IR creates a context that permits easy user access to and use of a variety of full-text information resources. The popular IR context has been criticized for lacking credibility in its content and sophistication in its resource organization and retrieval. Digital libraries represent a hybrid of both traditional IR, using primarily collections similar to those provided in online databases, and popular IR, exemplified by Web search engines. Information retrieval in digital environments is strongly affected by the IR system, the user, the information, and the environments.

In addition, information retrieval experimentation is an ongoing research activity. In recent years, the Text REtrieval Conferences (TREC), sponsored by the U.S. National Institute of Standards and Technology (NIST), the U.S. Department of Defense, the Advanced Research Projects Agency (DARPA), and the U.S. intelligence community's Advanced Research and Development Activity (ARDA) and other agencies, held every year since 1992, is a major joint effort to evaluate participants' own experiments with IR systems. More than 15 tracks had been created by 2005. Among them, the Interactive Track investigates how users interact with IR systems and how to evaluate interactive IR systems. The TREC Interactive Track creates a general framework for the investigation of interactive information retrieval, and for the evaluation and comparison of the performance of interactive IR systems (Dumais & Belkin, 2005). However, the restrictions of the setting, assigned tasks, convenience sample, data collection methods, TREC assessors, and short cycle contribute to the limitation of TREC results.

The Impact of Digital Environments and the Challenges of IR

In the past, searching for information is a privilege of information professionals. Now ordinary people become end-users. The emergence of the digital environments brings changes on IR systems, on users, information, and the environments that users interact with systems. That also poses challenges for users to effectively retrieve information to accomplish their tasks/goals.

Impact on IR Systems and the Challenges for Users

In digital environments, users have to face a variety of online IR systems. However, they are not all designed by taking into consideration of users, which hinders the effectiveness of user-system interactions (Dillon, 2004). From the system side, traditional IR is supported by the two core processes: representation and comparison. The core of information retrieval is the comparison between the representation of documents and the representation of user need (Salton & McGill, 1983; van Rijsbergen, 1979). In that sense, only one search strategy is supported: query formulation. In digital environments, term match—rather than concept match or problem match—is still a critical issue even though the search mechanism has been enhanced. IR systems in digital environments do provide a variety of browsing mechanisms for users to explore information, but the query box is still the main channel for users to express their information needs. Users are limited by the search box, and most of the searches contain only one or two terms (Jansen & Pooch, 2001). While users engage in multiple information-seeking strategies in digital environments (Fidel et al., 1999; Marchionini, 1995; Vakkari, Pennanen, & Serola, 2003; Wang, Hawk, & Tenopir, 2000), online IR systems still focus on support searching-related strategies while offering some help with browsing.

Interactivity is a fundamental characteristic of searching in digital environments. Users are able to interact with online IR systems, as well as their collection via multiple avenues. The inherent interactive nature of Web-based IR systems poses a challenge for users. While users praise the ease-of-use of interfaces of online IR systems, they are also concerned with the lack of control in interacting with these systems. The simplified design of Web search engines has been transferred to other types of IR system design. Researchers have paid more attention to ease-of-use of interface design and far less to user control. The existing online IR systems do not support both ease-of-use and user control (Xie & Cool, 2000; Xie, 2003). Accordingly, the design of online IR systems needs to be clear about user involvement and system role to facilitate user-system interaction (Bates, 1990; White & Ruthven, 2006; Xie, 2003)

All types of online IR systems have some commonalities in their design, such as a search box. However, there is no standard in the design of online IR systems. Different types of IR systems have different interface designs and different search mechanisms. Even within one type of IR system, interface design and search mechanism are not same. To make things worse, the commands for search are different in different IR systems. This has limited users' abilities to interact with these systems and their collections. In the past, users searched for information in libraries or information centers. Digital environments provide opportunities for users to search for information in their own environments, such as at home and in the work place. Their institutional/organizational work tasks or their home settings might affect their information retrieval process (Cool & Spink, 2002). Most important, while users enjoy the convenience of looking for information at any time they need, they also lose the benefits of getting help from intermediaries when they encounter problems.

Moreover, digital environments have shortened the distance between the system and user. At the same time, they also make it difficult or impossible for users to get any training. Users can only seek help from the Help function of each system. However, users rarely access Help because of the inadequate design of implicit as well as explicit Help in IR systems. In addition, users need help in every stage of their information retrieval process, but they cannot always specify their help-seeking situations or needs (Cool & Xie, 2004; Trenner, 1989; Xie & Cool, 2006). Finally, as noted by Jansen (2005), for the most part, Help mechanisms have been construed only as assistants in the query formulation process rather than as ongoing partners during the information retrieval process.

Impact on Users and the Challenges for Users

In digital environments, any human being is potentially an end user. For any given IR system in the digital environment, universal access is an objective. Users could represent diverse user groups with diverse backgrounds. They could be heterogeneous in terms of their age, language, culture, subject knowledge, system knowledge, and information-seeking skills. One user could have no knowledge of the IR system or even have computer phobia; another could construct a complicated query and customize the system. One user could have no knowledge about what he or she is going to search while another is the expert in the area. Users could also have different types of search tasks, for example, look for fact information, look for items with common characteristics, update information, and so forth. Even though they might look for the same information, different search problems might lead them to retrieve information that requires different results to solve their problems. Users might also exhibit different types of search strategies and behaviors, for example, search, browse, and so forth. The question is how to support end users of online IR systems who have different familiarity with the system environment, different information-seeking skills, different domain knowledge, different search tasks/goals, and different information-seeking strategies. In sum, how an online IR system be designed to support the diverse needs of diverse user groups?

In digital environments, users are able to access OPACs, Web search engines, and digital libraries for different types of information. Their past experience and background affect the way they interact with different types of IR systems. They might be expert users of one type of IR system but novice users of another. They bring their individual mental models and search strategies for one type of IR system to another one (Wang, Hawk, & Tenopir, 2000). Further, the new generation of Web users expects OPACs and other types of IR systems to have the same design and features as Web search engines (Novotny, 2004; Yu & Young, 2004). Simultaneously, experienced online searchers are accustomed to traditional online databases with a certain level of search sophistication, and they are unsatisfied with the inefficiency of Web-based IR systems (van Brakel, 1997; Bates, 1997).

Another change for users has to do with their expectations. The emergence of the Internet creates an illusion that users can find all the information they need within a short time. People lose patience when searching for information. Researchers have begun to compare the similarities and differences between Web searching and traditional information retrieval. These studies have found that while Web search engines follow the basic principles of IR systems, Web users show very different patterns of searching from those found in traditional IR systems, such as online databases and OPACs. For example, most Web users did not have many queries per search session, and each query tended to be short. Boolean operators were seldom used. Many users submitted only one query and did not follow up with successive queries (Jansen & Pooch, 2001; Silverstein, Henzinger, Marais, & Moricz, 1999; Spink, Wolfram, Jansen, & Saracevic, 2001).

Impact on Information and the Challenges for Users

Traditionally, relevance has been the main concern for users when they evaluate retrieved information. Before the emergence of Internet, users had no doubt about the authority and quality of the information retrieved from traditional IR systems. In digital environments, interaction with results has become a major component of information retrieval interaction. Users interact with results to find information to solve their problems; these results lead them to search for needed information or to find new ideas to reformulate their queries if the results fail to provide relevant information.

However, in digital environments, anyone can be a publisher of information on the Web by simply uploading documents. There is no one to review and approve the content of the information on the Web. As a result, users have to make judgments for themselves about the quality and authority of Web information. Moreover, the Web offers a different searching environment for users; it contains a variety of information in content, format, and organization (Fidel et al., 1999; Jansen, Spink, & Saracevic, 2000; Wang, Hawk, & Tenopir, 2000). When users interact with the retrieved results, they not only have to make relevance judgments but also have to make authority and quality judgments. However, users are only willing to devote a small amount of time to evaluate results. In Xie's (2006) study of users' evaluation of digital libraries and Rieh's (2002) evaluation study of the Web, most users think it is a challenge for them to make judgments about quality and authority because there is generally no quality control mechanism for the Web. Even though some IR systems do have authority control systems, users want to have a way to make their own judgments.

Another challenge for users is the overwhelming amount of information available in digital environments, which causes cognitive overload (Bilal, 2000). The problem is two-fold: on the one hand, although most IR systems try to increase the size of their collections, they only index a small portion of the available information; on the other hand, the IR algorithms were created for small and coherent collections, but the digital collections of Web-based IR systems are dynamic and diverse (Arasu, Cho, Garcia-Molina, Paepcke, & Raghavan, 2001). To make things worse, many of the electronic materials are multimedia and in different languages. The uncertainty and complexity of multimedia and cross-language IR pose more challenges for users to effectively retrieve multimedia and foreign language information, in particular in evaluating and interpreting information during their interactions with IR systems (De Vries, 2001; Downie, 2003; Gey, Kando, & Peters, 2005; Goodrum & Spink, 2001; Oard, 2001; Peters, 2005; Smeaton, 2004). In addition, electronic materials have been converted from their printed or physical formats. In the conversion process, these artifacts' content and context might be missing (Mi & Nesta, 2005).

The Need for an Interactive IR Framework

One way to deal with the challenges of IR in digital environments is to develop an interactive IR framework. According to Marchionini (1995), human existence is a series of interactions with the environment. Interactivity is a basic human characteristic, and the complexity of modern society forces people to interact increasingly with institutions and systems. However, electronic systems are beginning to replace human as the interactants. The evolving interactions in digital environments pose more challenges and problems.

Nature of IR as Interaction

Because IR is an interactive process, uncertainty and interactiveness are the two major characteristics of information retrieval. Taylor's (1968) classic work on question negotiation proposes four levels of information need that users go through in accomplishing their information-seeking tasks. The need comes from an unformulated question based on a user's uncertainty. The significance of Taylor's work is that it postulates a particular psychological state of mind of the user that may lead to an expressed request. Wersig (1979) uses the concept of problematic situation in which knowledge and experience may be sufficient to resolve the doubt. He identifies an explicit account of precursors to information-seeking behavior based on an individual's knowledge, beliefs, and situation. Belkin's "anomalous state of knowledge" (ASK) hypothesis (1977, 1978, 1980) is an extension of Taylor's model. ASK is similar to Taylor's "visceral need" and Wersig's "problematic situation," which indicates that the user's knowledge is insufficient for dealing with a specific situation. ASK provides a framework in which the reasons that users seek information could be explicitly represented and used for information retrieval. According to Taylor's "visceral need," Wersig's "problematic situation," and Belkin's "ASK," if users are not capable of recognizing their state of knowledge/problem space, they may end up in a state of uncertainty. They need to interact with information, systems, and the environment to clarify their information problems.

Ingwersen's (1992, 1996) cognitive model, Belkin's (1996) episode model of interaction with text ,and Saracevic's (1997) stratified model are the most-cited interactive IR models; all three describe general interactive information retrieval and its major components. While Ingwersen's model focuses more on the cognitive aspect of interactive information retrieval, Belkin's model emphasizes users' interaction with text (the information-seeking process); Saracevic's model concentrates on understanding the interplay among different levels of users and systems. All three models agree: 1) information problem/need is dynamic, and it changes during the information-seeking and retrieving process; and 2) information problem/need can be clarified by interactions.

The Need for an Interactive IR Framework

These three interactive IR models create a foundation for interactive IR research in digital environments. Ingwersen and Järvelin (2005) further proposed an integrated IS&R research framework with the model of interactive information-seeking, retrieval, and behavioral processes. However, these models only illustrate interactive IR at the macrolevel, and they cannot account for the specific process or issues that emerge in the interactive IR process, nor can they connect factors influencing IR interaction with users' information-seeking strategies or behaviors in digital environments. Most important, an interactive IR framework needs to be derived from empirical studies of different users with a variety of tasks interacting with different IR systems in digital environments. As Saracevic (1996) points out, "IR interaction is a complex process that is very much situation or context dependent: it starts from and relates to users, their tasks or problems, competencies, knowledge states and intents on the one hand, but it also involves characteristics and capabilities of the system, the information resources, and the interface, on the other hand" (p. 5). Mantovani (1996) further claims that understanding interaction is difficult, because what keeps changing in interaction are not just things in the world or things in the actor, but the very structure of their connection. In order to develop an interactive IR framework in digital environments, we need to explore user-centered approaches, characteristics of different IR digital environments, and empirical studies of interactive IR in digital environments as well as existing interactive IR models and approaches.

Overview of the Book

Objective of the Book

The objective of this book is to develop a theoretical framework for information retrieval (IR) interaction and to further discuss its implications in the design and evaluation of IR systems in the digital age. This book builds on the author's award-winning dissertation titled *Planned and Situated Aspects in Interactive IR: Patterns of User Interactive Intentions and Information Seeking Strategies* awarded by the Association for Library and Information Science Education (ALISE) in 1999. It provides an opportunity for the author to synthesize her 10 years of research and other researchers' work in this important and unique area.

Structure of the Book

This book can be divided into four sections. The first provides an overview and foundation for the book. The preface provides the background for the book and answers the question why this book is needed. Chapter I starts with the discussion of the divide between system-oriented and user-oriented approaches, and further presents a variety of user-oriented approaches that are essential for understanding interactive IR.

The second section offers an overview of various IR environments and a comprehensive review of empirical studies of interactive IR in these environments. Chapter II through Chapter V focus on interactive IR in OPAC, online database, Web search engine, and digital library environments. The overview of the IR environment presents history and background of IR systems, definitions and types of the IR systems, current developments on each type of IR systems, and the challenges to users. The review of empirical studies on interactive IR is classified by the key issues derived from empirical studies, including tasks/goals and their impact, levels of information-seeking strategies, users' knowledge structure, online Help, usability studies, evaluation of interactive IR systems, and so forth. In addition, Chapter VI summarizes the Interactive Track of TREC environment and different types of Interactive Track studies, in particular the contributions and limitations of the Interactive Track. This chapter also discusses relevant works on interactive cross-language information retrieval research mainly in the interactive track of Cross-Language Evaluation Forum (iCLEF).

The third section highlights the development of the interactive IR framework. Chapter VII reviews the macro- and micro-levels of interactive IR models developed in the field, and further discusses the strengths and limitation of these models. Chapter VIII is the heart of the book, in which the author's interactive IR framework—the planned-situational interactive IR model—is presented. The discussion of the model consists of an overview of the model, a discussion of the levels of user goals and tasks and their representations, relationships between levels of user goals and tasks, dimensions of work and search tasks, users' personal information infrastructure, the social-organizational context, IR systems, dimensions of information-seeking strategies, shifts in current search goals and information-seeking strategies, and factors affecting those shifts. Chapter IX illustrates and validates the planned-situational interactive IR model by reporting and discussing the results of a pilot of a large-scale study that focuses on the investigation of how people seek and retrieve information in their research proposal writing process.

The fourth section discusses the implications of the interactive IR framework for the design and evaluation of interactive IR systems. Chapter X discusses the theoretical and practical implications of the framework for designing and evaluating interactive IR systems, especially making suggestions for how to support multiple types of information-seeking strategies, how to balance ease-of-use and user control in terms of system role and user involvement, how to create interactive Help mechanisms, and how to develop a multidimensional evaluation framework to evaluate interactive IR systems. Finally, Chapter XI summarizes the contributions of the book, discusses future research directions, and raises questions for further research on interactive IR.

Targeted Audiences

This book is intended for researchers, designers, teachers, graduate and undergraduate students, and professionals who are interested in interactive information retrieval, IR system design, and IR system evaluation in digital environments. The theoretical framework and the comprehensive literature review on theory and practice will provide a foundation for new research on interactive information retrieval and can also serve as part of the curriculum for courses related to information retrieval and IR system design. The discussion of implications will offer guidance for designers and other professionals to design and evaluate new interactive IR systems for the general public as well as for specific user groups.

Members of the following associations would be the primary readers for the proposed book: (1) American Society for Information Science and Technology (ASIST), (2) Association for Computing Machinery (ACM), (3) Institute of Electrical and Electronics Engineers, Inc. (IEEE) Computer Society, (4) Association for Library and Information Science Education (ALISE), and (5) a variety of library associations, such as the American Library Association (ALA), Special Library Association

(SLA), and so forth. The secondary audience could be researchers and practitioners from other related disciplines (e.g., psychology, communication, computer science, engineering, health, education, etc.) who are interested in interactive IR, IR system design and evaluation.

References

Arasu, A., Cho, J., Garcia-Molina, H., Paepcke, A., & Raghavan, S. (2001). Searching the Web. *ACM Transactions on Internet Technology, 1*(1), 2-43.

Armstrong, C. J., & Large, A. (2001). *Manual of online search strategies* (3rd ed., Vol. 3). Aldershot: Gower Publishing.

Bates, M. E. (1997). Knight-Ridder on the Web: A brave new world for searchers? *Searcher, 5*(6), 28-37.

Bates, M. J. (1990). Where should the person stop and the information search interface start? *Information Processing and Management, 26*(5), 575-591.

Belkin, N. J. (1977). *A concept of information science.* Unpublished doctoral dissertation, University of London.

Belkin, N. J. (1978). Progress in documentation. *Journal of Documentation, 34*(1), 55-85.

Belkin, N. J. (1980). Anomalous states of knowledge as a basis for information retrieval. *Canadian Journal of Information Science, 5,* 133-143.

Belkin, N.J. (1996). Intelligent information retrieval: Whose intelligence? In J. Krause, M. Herfurth, & J. Marx (Eds.), *Harausforderungen an die Informationswirtschaft. Informationsverdichtung, Informationsbewertung und Datenvisualisierung, Proceedings of the 5th International Symposium for Information Science (ISI '96),* (pp. 25-31). Konstanz: Universitätsverlag Konstanz.

Bilal, D. (2000). Children's use of the Yahooligans! Web search engine: I. Cognitive, physical, and affective behaviors on fact-based search tasks. *Journal of the American Society for Information Science, 51*(7), 646-665.

Borgman, C. L. (1996). Why are online catalogs still hard to use? *Journal of the American Society for Information Science, 47*(7), 493-503.

Borgman, C. L. (1999). What are digital libraries? Competing visions. *Information Processing and Management, 35*(3), 227-243.

Chowdhury, G. G., & Chowdhury, S. (2003). *Introduction to digital libraries.* London: Facet.

Chu, H. (2003). *Information representation and retrieval in the digital age.* Medford, NJ: Information Today.

Cool, C., & Spink, A. (2002). Issues of context in information retrieval (IR): An introduction to the special issue *Information Processing and Management, 38*(5), 605-611.

Cool, C., & Xie, H. (2004). How can IR help mechanism be more helpful to users? In L. Schamber & C. L. Barry (Eds.), *Proceedings of the 67th ASIST Annual Meeting,* (Vol. 41, pp. 249-255). Medford, NJ: Information Today.

De Vries, A. P. (2001). Content independence in multimedia databases. *Journal of the American Society for Information Science and Technology, 52*(11), 954-690.

Dillon, A. (2004). *Designing usable electronic text* (2nd ed.). London: CRC Press.

Downie, J. S. (2003). Music information retrieval. *Annual Review of Information Science and Technology, 37*, 295-340.

Dumais, S. T., & Belkin, N. J. (2005). The TREC interactive tracks: Putting the user into search. In E. M. Voorhees & D. K. Harman (Eds.), *TREC: Experiment and evaluation in information retrieval* (pp. 123-152). Cambridge, MA: The MIT Press.

Fidel, R., Davies, R. K., Douglass, M. H., Holder, J. K., Hopkins, C. J., & Kushner, E. J., et al. (1999). A visit to the information mall: Web searching behavior of high school students. *Journal of the American Society for Information Science, 50*(1), 24-37.

Fox, E. A., & Urs, S. R. (2002). Digital libraries. *Annual Review of Information Science and Technology, 36*, 503-589.

Garman, N. (1999). The ultimate, original search engine. *Online, 23*(3), 6.

Gey, F. C., Kando, N., & Peters, C. (2005). Cross-language information retrieval: The way ahead. *Information Processing and Management, 41*(3), 415-431.

Goodrum, A., & Spink, A. (2001). Image searching on the World Wide Web: Analysis of visual information retrieval queries. *Information Processing and Management. 37*(2), 295-311.

Guha, T. K., & Saraf, V. (2005). OPAC usability: Assessment through verbal protocol. *The Electronic Library, 23*(4), 463-473.

Hildreth, C. R. (1985). Online public access catalogs. *Annual Review of Information Science and Technology, 20*, 223-285.

Hildreth, C. R. (1997). The use and understanding of keyword searching in a university online catalog. *Information Technology and Libraries, 16*(2), 52-62.

Hock, R. (2002). A new era of search engines: Not just Web pages anymore. *Online, 36*(5), 20-27.

Ingwersen, P. (1992). The user-oriented IR research approach. *Information retrieval interaction* (pp. 83-122). London: Taylor.

Ingwersen, P. (1996). Cognitive perspectives of information retrieval interaction: Elements of a cognitive IR theory. *Journal of Documentation, 52*(1), 3-50.

Ingwersen, P., & Järvelin, K. (2005). *The turn: Integration of information seeking and retrieval in context.* Heidelberg: Springer.

Jansen, B. J. (2005). Seeking and implementing automated assistance during the search process. *Information Processing and Management, 41*(4), 909-928.

Jansen, B. J., & Pooch, U. (2001). A review of Web searching studies and a framework for future research. *Journal of the American Society for Information Science and Technology, 52*(3), 235-246.

Jansen, B. J., Spink, A., & Saracevic, T. (2000). Real life, real users, and real needs: A study and analysis of user queries on the Web. *Information Processing and Management, 36*(2), 207-227.

Liddy, E. (2001). How a search engine works. *Searcher, 9*(5), 38-45.

Mantovani, G. (1996). Social context in HCI: A new framework for mental models, cooperation, and communication. *Cognitive Science, 20*, 237-269.

Marchionini, G. (1995). *Information seeking in electronic environments*. New York: Cambridge University Press.

Meadow, C. T., Boyce, B. R., & Kraft, D. H. (1999). *Text information retrieval systems* (2nd ed.). San Diego, CA: Academic Press.

Mi, J., & Nesta, F. (2005). The missing link: Context loss in online databases. *Journal of Academic Librarianship, 31*(6), 578-585.

Novotny, E. (2004). I don't think I click: A protocol analysis study of use of a library online catalog in the Internet Age. *College and Research Libraries, 65*(6), 525-537.

Oard, D. (2001). Interactive cross-language information retrieval. *SIGIR Forum, 35*(1), 1-3.

Peters, C. (2005). Comparative evaluation of cross-language information retrieval systems. *Lecture Notes in Computer Science, 3379*, 152-161.

Rieh, S. Y. (2002). Judgment of information quality and cognitive authority in the Web. *Journal of the American Society for Information Science and Technology, 53*(2), 145-161.

Salton, G., & McGill, M. (1983). *Introduction to modern information retrieval*. New York: McGraw-Hill.

Saracevic, T. (1996). Modeling interaction in information retrieval (IR): A review and proposal. In S. Harden (Ed.), *Proceedings of the 59th ASIS Annual Meeting,* (Vol. 33, pp. 3-9). Medford, NJ: Information Today.

Saracevic, T. (1997). The stratified model of information retrieval interaction: Extension and applications. In C. Schwartz & M. E. Rorvig (Eds.), *Proceedings of the 60th ASIS Annual Meeting,* (Vol. 34, pp. 313-327). Medford, NJ: Information Today.

Saracevic, T. (2000). Digital library evaluation: Toward an evolution of concepts. *Library Trends, 49*(2), 350-369.

Silverstein, C., Henzinger, M., Marais, H., & Moricz, M. (1999). Analysis of a very large Web search engine query log. *SIGIR Forum, 33*(1), 6-12.

Smeaton, A. F. (2004). Indexing, browsing and searching of digital video. *Annual Review of Information Science and Technology, 38*, 371-407.

Spink, A., Wolfram, D., Jansen, B. J., & Saracevic, T. (2001). Searching the Web: The public and their queries. *Journal of the American Society for Information Science and Technology, 52*(3), 226-234.

Sullivan, D. (2006). Nielsen/NetRatings search engine ratings. *Search Engine Watch.* Retrieved January 2, 2008, from http://searchenginewatch.com/reports/print.php/34701_2156451

Taylor, R. (1968). Question-negotiation and information seeking. *College and Research Libraries, 29*(3), 178-194.

Trenner, L. (1989). A comparative survey of the friendliness of online "help" in interactive information retrieval systems. *Information Processing and Management, 25*(2), 119-136.

Vakkari, P., Pennanen, M., & Serola, S. (2003). Changes in search terms and tactics while writing a research proposal: A longitudinal case study. *Information Processing and Management, 39*(3), 445-463.

van Brakel, P. A. (1997). Online database vendors: Will they transform to pull technology? *South African Journal of Library and Information Science, 65*(4), 234-242.

van Rijsbergen, C. J. (1979). *Information retrieval* (2nd ed.). London: Butterworths.

Walker, G., & Janes, J. (1999). *Online retrieval: A dialogue of theory and practice* (2nd ed.). Englewood, CO: Libraries Unlimited.

Wang, P., Hawk, W. B., & Tenopir, C. (2000). Users' interaction with World Wide Web resources: An exploratory study using a holistic approach. *Information Processing and Management, 36*(2), 229-251.

Wersig, G. (1979). The problematic situation as basic concept of information science in the framework of the social sciences. *Theoretical problems for informatics: New trends in informatics and its terminology* (pp. 48-57). Moscow: International Federation for Documentation.

White, R. W., & Ruthven, I. (2006). A study of interface support mechanisms for interactive information retrieval. *Journal of the American Society for Information Science and Technology, 57*(7), 933-948.

Williams, M. E. (2006). The state of databases today. *Gale directory of databases 2006*. Detroit, MI: Gale Research.

Wilson, T. D. (2000). Human information behaviour. *Informing Science, 3*(2), 49-56.

Wolfram, D., & Xie, H. (2002). Traditional IR for Web users: A context for general audience digital libraries. *Information Processing and Management, 38*(5), 627-648.

Xie, H. (2003). Supporting ease-of-use and user control: Desired features and structure of Web-based online IR systems. *Information Processing and Management, 39*(6), 899-922.

Xie, H. (2006). Understanding human-work domain interaction: Implications for the design of a corporate digital library. *Journal of the American Society for Information Science and Technology, 57*(1), 128-143.

Xie, H., & Cool, C. (2000). Ease-of-use versus user control: An evaluation of Web and non-Web interfaces of online databases. *Online Information Review, 24*(2), 102-115.

Xie, H., & Cool, C. (2006). Toward a better understanding of help seeking behavior: An evaluation of help mechanisms in two IR systems. In A. Dillon & A. Grove (Eds.), *Proceedings of the 69th ASIST Annual Meeting* (Vol. 43). Retrieved January 2, 2008, from http://eprints.rclis.org/archive/00008279/01/Xie_Toward.pdf

Yu, H., & Young, M. (2004). The impact of Web search engines on subject searching in OPAC. *Information Technology and Libraries, 23*(4), 168-180.

Acknowledgment

This book is not only the product of my research for 10 years in the library and information science area, but it also reflects contributions from many of the researchers in the field. Of course, I could not have written the book without the help of my family members, friends, and colleagues. Although I am not able to name everyone who deserves to be thanked because of space limitations, I would like to say thank you here to those who have been most supportive of my work.

First, I would like to thank every researcher's work that inspired my book. Among them, Marcia Bates, Nick Belkin, Raya Fidel, Carol Hert, Peter Ingwersen, Carol C. Kuhlthau, Nils Pharo, Amanda Spink, Tefko Saracevic, Pertti Vakkari, and Peiling Wang, who either sent me their original models or suggested how to obtain them. I would like to specifically thank Nick Belkin for offering his constructive suggestions for the structure of the book, Peter Ingwersen and Pertti Vakkari for their valuable comments on the early version of the planned-situational interactive IR model, and Marcia Bates and Andrew Dillon for their stimulating discussion of the model and its implications for IR system design at the CoLIS6 Conference.

I am indebted to the University of Wisconsin-Milwaukee for granting me the sabbatical leave that made it possible for me to write this book. I also received much support from my colleagues and students, in particular Dean Johannes J. Britz and Dietmar Wolfram at the School of Information Studies. In addition, I would like to thank Marilyn Antkowiak, Yang Zhuo, and Abby A. Von Arx for their assistance in finding relevant literature and checking references.

I would like to express my appreciation to Kristin Roth and Deborah Yahnke from IGI Global for answering my questions and supporting me at every stage of the book writing process, as well as the three anonymous reviewers for their insightful comments and suggestions. As a nonnative speaker of English, I have learned that writing a book takes extra effort. I owe my gratitude to Carolyn Kott Washburne for her editing of the book, and in particular for offering timely service.

Finally, I would like to dedicate this book to my husband, Charlie, and my daughter, Vivian, for their support, encouragement, and patience along the journey. Hopefully, by finishing this book, I can play a better role as a wife and mother. My daughter won't imitate my working on computer in her daycare, saying "Give mommy 5 more minutes" anymore. I'm also indebted to my parents for their unconditional love and support.

Iris Xie
University of Wisconsin-Milwaukee, USA

Chapter I

User-Oriented IR Research Approaches

The Divide between System-Oriented and User-Oriented Approaches

There exist two approaches in IR system design and research: system-oriented and user-oriented. The system-oriented approach has played the dominant role in the design of IR systems in the past. Only in recent years have system designers begun to accept the need to take the human, socio-technical approach. They recognize that technically-oriented designs cannot satisfy user needs, and as a result, these designs have not succeeded in the market (Shackel, 1997). The traditional model of information retrieval as a match between a request or a query and a set of documents is no longer working. The emergence of the cognitive approach in IR signified a shift from document representation to the representation of the cognitive structure of users (Vakkari, 2003). The new concept is to consider the user as an essential component of the system (Beaulieu, 2000; Robertson & Hancock-Beaulieu, 1992). At the same time, Wilson (2000) also noted the shift from a system-centered approach to a person-centered approach accompanied by a shift from quantitative methods to qualitative methods.

User studies have been conducted over the years. However, most of the suggestions of these studies are not implemented into system designs. In Borgman's popularly cited article (1996) "Why Are Online Catalogs Still Hard to Use?" she pointed out that online catalogs continue to be difficult to use because their design does not incorporate sufficient understanding of searching behavior. Research on searching behavior studies has not influenced online catalog design. The same can be said of other types of IR system design. The design of most IR systems assumes that users formulate a query that represents a fixed goal for the search, while users might engage in multiple types of information-seeking strategies in their retrieval process (Belkin, Cool, Stein, & Theil, 1995). Saracevic (1999) well summarized the relationship between the two approaches. While the user-centered approach criticized the system-centered approach for paying little attention to users and their behavior, user-centered research does not deliver tangible design solutions. Simultaneously, designers taking the system-centered approach do not care about user studies and their results in their design of IR systems.

Norman (1988) presented the criteria for user-centered design:

- Make it easy to determine what actions are possible at any moment (make use of constraints).

- Make things visible, including the conceptual model of the system, the alternative actions, and the results of the actions.

- Make it easy to evaluate the current state of the system.

- Follow natural mappings between intentions and the required actions; between actions and the resulting effect; and between the information that is visible and the interpretation of the system use. In other words, make sure that (1) the user can figure out what to do and (2) the user can tell what is going on (p. 188).

In order to take a user-oriented design approach, we first need to apply user-oriented research approaches to understand how users seek and retrieve information in different contexts and how they interact with different types of IR systems.

User-Oriented Approaches

In this section, the author introduces six well-known user-oriented approaches: Taylor's levels of information need approach, Belkin's anomalous state of knowledge (ASK) hypothesis, Dervin's sense-making approach, Kuhlthau's information search process (ISP), Wilson's information-seeking context approach, and Cognitive Work Analysis (CWA) introduced and applied to information-seeking and -retrieving research by Pejtersen and Fidel.

Here are the main reasons for the selection of these six approaches: 1) These are the most cited approaches that have had a significant impact on IR research, in particular on interactive IR research. Based on *Social Science Citation*, these approaches have been widely cited in IR research as theoretical frameworks and for practical guidance. 2) These approaches can be applied to general information-seeking/retrieval/searching situations even though they might be originally derived from a specific user group. They are further validated and enhanced either by the original creator or other researchers in the field. Detailed discussions of each approach and their implications are presented in the following subsections. 3) These approaches are not isolated; instead, they are interrelated. In general, the approaches that were developed earlier became the theoretical basis for the approaches developed later. They are also frequently co-cited by researchers in the field. 4) Finally, most important, these approaches are closely related to the theme of this book, interactive information retrieval. These approaches have influenced the development of the macro- and micro-level interactive information retrieval models discussed in chapter 7. Of course, not all the well-known user-oriented approaches are presented here. Some of them will be introduced in chapter 7; for example, Ingwersen's cognitive approach (1992, 1996) and Saracevic's (1996b, 1997) stratified approach will be discussed in detail in chapter 7 as the most influential macrolevel interactive information retrieval models. Ellis' (Ellis, 1989; Ellis & Haugan, 1997) model of information-seeking behavior and Bates' (1989) berrypicking approaches will be discussed in chapter 7 as microlevel interactive information retrieval models. Other approaches are not discussed here because they are not directly associated with interactive information retrieval.

Taylor's Levels of Information Need Approach

Taylor's 1968 article about levels of need is one of the most cited articles in the literature of the area. According to this article, in the process of question negotiation in using libraries, a user's negotiation might take two forms: (a) working through an intermediary, that is, the reference librarian, or (b) working himself or herself by interacting with the library and its contents. Taylor (1968) identified users' four levels of information need in the question negotiation process:

- **Visceral need:** Unconscious; actual but inexpressible need
- **Conscious need:** Conscious within the brain but undefined and undescribed need

- **Formalized need:** Rational and formal statement of question
- **Compromised need:** Question tailored to internal and external constraints, for example, experience, language, expectations of information systems.

At the visceral need level, a user might have a vague information need but it is not clear enough for him/her to articulate the need. At the conscious need level, a user might have a mental description but cannot define it. At the formalized need level, a user might be able to describe his/her need. At the compromised need level, a user might state his/her need in the form that he/she thinks a system could understand. From level 1 to level 4, a user gradually has a more focused idea about what information he/she needs even though at the fourth level a user has to compromise his/her needs.

Here is an example that can illustrate the four levels of information need. A student needs to write a paper for a class related to information science. She first thought about all the possible ideas that she might focus on and the potential information she might need, but she could not express herself. At the second level, she started to have some ideas of what information she needed. She thought about the poor Help features provided in IR systems and the fact that she and many of her friends did not like to use the Help in IR systems. However, she still could not make a statement of her information need. On the third level, she could make a statement that she needed information about why people do not use current help in IR systems and how that impacts on users' perception of the ease-of-use of IR systems. At the fourth level, she had to compromise her need to a query, "Help and IR systems and impact and use," and presented it to an IR system.

Although Taylor discussed levels of information need in the context of users' use of libraries, especially how they went through a reference interview, the implication of the identification of levels of information need has significant impact on research in information retrieval, in particular the user-oriented research approach. Taylor's levels of needs reveal the problem of information retrieval systems that only match users' compromised needs to representations of documents stored in the databases. It also raises the issue of how to design IR systems to assist users to clarify their visceral needs.

Taylor's work has set up a foundation for most of the user-oriented approaches in IR research. For example, Belkin and his associates extended Taylor's ideas to information retrieval and defined a fundamental element "anomalous state of knowledge" (ASK), which information need is derived from. Ingwersen (1992, 1996) built his cognitive model of IR interaction based on cognitive information-seeking and retrieval theory represented by Taylor's information need formation. Kuhlthau (1991) developed the information search process (ISP) by connecting levels of information need and stages of information search.

Taylor's work has also been applied to guiding studies of user needs. Many of the studies focus on examining the information needs of different types of users. For example, Cole, Leide, Large, Beheshti, & Brooks (2005) investigated the problem of information need identification for the domain novice user, and suggested a conceptual design to solve the problem. Bruce (2005) formulated five propositions that elaborate on the concept of personal and anticipated information need. Shenton and Dixon (2004) investigated young people's information needs and methods for studying them based on previous research, including Taylor's work on clarification of information needs. Applying the diagnostic tool based on Kuhlthau's and Taylor's concept of "focus" to assess undergraduates' information needs, Kennedy, Cole, and Carter (1997) connected online search strategies with information needs.

In addition to end-user studies, another type of application studies is related to mediated information searching. For example, Nordlie (1996) compared mediated and unmediated OPAC searches by analyzing patterns of interactions between users and librarians. He applied the "filters" in information interaction originally suggested by Taylor (1968) and modified by Lynch (1977) to classify the elicitations of the intermediary. Markey (1981) proposed a model to represent levels of question formulation in the negotiation of information need by analyzing online presearch interview data. In addition, the influence of Taylor's levels of information need and query articulation and negotiation is also extended to system design. For example, Meghabghab and Meghabghab (1994) presented an Intelligent Negotiating Neural Network (INN) design model that serves as an electronic information specialist learning to negotiate a patron's query and translates it into a well-formulated statement before he/she accesses an OPAC.

Belkin's ASK Hypothesis

Building on Taylor's (1968) levels of need and Wersig's (1979) "problematic situation," Belkin (1977, 1978, 1980) developed the "anomalous state of knowledge" (ASK) hypothesis. When encountering a problematic situation, users cannot solve the problem by applying existing knowledge, and their anomalous state creates cognitive uncertainty that prohibits them from adequately expressing their information need. They need additional information to clarify their thoughts. The driving force of information retrieval is the users' problem that leads to recognition of their inadequate knowledge to specify their information need. Simultaneously, users evaluate the information retrieved from an IR system related to the problematic situation, and that might also determine their Anomalous State of Knowledge. In other words, Belkin identified the ASK underlying users' information needs. Information needs and information retrieval are dynamic, and they change along a user's cognitive structure. Figure 1.1 presents a cognitive communication system for information retrieval (Belkin, 1980, p. 135).

Figure 1.1. Belkin's cognitive communication system for information retrieval. From "Anomalous states of knowledge as a basis for information retrieval" by N. J. Belkin, 1980. Canadian Journal of Information Science, 5, p. 135. Copyright 1980 by University of Toronto Press. Used with copyright permission.

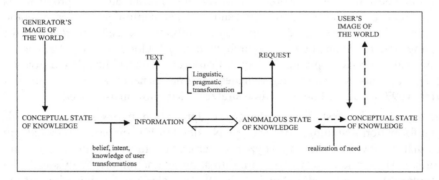

Belkin, Oddy, and Brooks (1982a, 1982b) further applied ASK to information retrieval system design. Based on the assumptions that (1) users cannot specify their information needs and (2) there are classes of ASKs that an IR system needs to be built on, Belkin, Oddy, and Brooks (1982a, 1982b) developed an ASK-based information retrieval system. The system was designed to ask a user to describe the ASK instead of specifying the need as a request to the system. The system was based on the cognitive viewpoint that human interaction is mediated by people's state of knowledge. In addition, the researchers considered the IR situation as a recipient-controlled communication system, as suggested by Paisley and Parker (1965). An ASK-based information retrieval system design was suggested as follows (Belkin, Oddy, & Brooks, 1982a):

1. User's problem statement

2. Structural analysis of problem statement

3. Choice of retrieval strategy according to type of ASK

4. Abstract presented to user simultaneously with explanation of why text was chosen

5. Structured dialog between system and user to infer user's evaluation of

    a. Method of choice

    b. Suitability of document to problem

    c. Whether need has changed

6. Modifications according to evaluation or finish

7. Return to 2 or 3 as necessary (p. 69).

ASK hypothesis has been widely cited as a theoretical basis for research on informa-tion retrieval, especially interactive IR research. It sets the foundation for the major interactive information retrieval models, such as Ingwersen's (1992) cognitive model, Ingwersen and Järvelin's (2005) integrated IS&R research framework, Belkin's (1996) episode model, and Saracevic's (1996b, 1997) stratified model. A predomi-nant characteristic of research in information retrieval in recent years has been the adoption of a "user-centered" approach to the design of IR systems. Belkin's ASK hypothesis was credited for the shift in emphasis. According to Lima and Raghavan (2004), this shift began primarily after Belkin proposed his ASK hypothesis.

Research has been conducted in terms of how to represent ASK. By analyzing the problem statements of users, Oddy, Palmquist, and Crawford (1986) were able to represent the anomalous state of knowledge for the creation a top-down, across-domain IR system. Cole et al. (2005) investigated the anomalous state of knowledge hypothesis in a real-life problem situation by studying how history and psychology undergraduates sought information for a course essay. They identified the importance of Belkin, Oddy, and Brooks' ASK papers. First, the ASK hypothesis creates a frame-work for dealing with a user's unknown information need without asking the user to specify it. Second, an interoperable structural code can be built into IR systems to connect the user's ASK to the relevant documents in the IR system. Wu (2005) examined elicitation during retrieval interaction as microlevel information-seeking (MLIS). She enhanced the dialogue structure derived from the ASK hypothesis by identifying the differences between patrons' and intermediaries' elicitation behaviors in terms of frequency and timeframe, and further revealed that intermediary elici-tation is preplanned and patron elicitation is situational. Liddy, Oddy, and Bishop (1988) applied the conceptual framework of ASK to problem statements, and they identified four major components: user traits, subject traits, information traits, and position in the problem-solving process.

Belkin (1993) extended the research of ASK to information-seeking strategies, and further developed the episode model of interaction with text in which interaction is the central process. Belkin and his associates conducted a series of studies to establish relationships between information-seeking strategies and users' informa-tion-seeking goals and problematic situations. For example, Belkin, Cool, Stein, and Theil (1995) developed four dimensions of information-seeking strategies: method of interaction, goal of interaction, mode of retrieval, and resource considered. Xie (1997, 2000, 2002) identified the patterns between users' interactive intentions and information-seeking strategies and further explored their shifts in information-seeking strategies. Lin and Belkin (2005) modeled multiple information-seeking episodes by analyzing eight types of information problems and their relationships with multiple searching episodes.

Dervin's Sense-Making Approach

The sense-making approach was developed in 1972 as an alternative approach to the study of the human use of information and information systems (Dervin, 1992). According to Dervin (1983), "In the most sense, sense-making (that which is the focus of study in the Sense-Making approach) is defined as behavior, both internal (i.e., cognitive) and external (i.e., procedural), which allows the individual to construct and design his/her movement through time-space. Sense-making behavior, thus, is communicating behavior" (p. 3). Information seeking and use are considered as constructing activities as individuals make sense for themselves. People's every need is associated with their information seeking and use (Dervin, 1976).

The development of the sense-making approach, which is rooted in American communication research, inspired research in library and information science, in particular the studies of information needs and use (Savolainen, 1993), specifically Bruner's (1973) cognition work about how people construct meaning and Carter and his associates' (Carter, 1980; Carter, Ruggels, Jackson, & Heffner, 1972) situational, constructivistic approach, which views the communication behavior as gap-bridging behavior.

The model of situation-gap-use is the foundation for the sense-making approach. The elements of this model are:

- Situations refer to the time-space contexts in which sense is constructed.
- Gaps refer to the information needs or questions that people have when they make sense in the time-space contexts.
- Uses refer to how the information derived from internal or external source help or impede bridging the gaps.

Among the three components, gap-defining and gap-bridging are essential for the sense-making approach.

Dervin's sense-making approach is one of the few approaches that not only offers a theoretical foundation for the understanding of information-seeking and use but also provides a systematic way to conduct studies. Dervin developed four techniques for the analysis of information-seeking and use (Dervin, 1983, 1992):

- The micromoment timeline interview is the most important and most frequently applied technique for the sense-making approach. It asks a person a series of step-by-step questions regarding a situation. For each step, the user is asked what the problem is, what can help make sense of the situation, and so forth.

- Help/hurt chaining mainly solicits information about information use. It requests information about how certain piece of information has facilitated or blocked a user's information use.

- The closed-ended sense-making interview is designed for hypothesis testing. Respondents are instructed to describe a real-life situation and justify the situation. Then they are asked to rate their situations, specific questions related to the situations, and specific helps needed.

- The message Q/ing interview is to collect information regarding sense-making during printed message reading. Respondents are instructed to read a message and stop at any time that they have a question. The analysis focus on each question asked relates to situations, questions, and the answers to the questions that help or hurt.

Dervin's sense-making approach has significantly contributed to build the theoretical framework as well as conduct empirical studies for information retrieval research. Applying the sense-making approach and other interdisciplinary research, Itoga (1991) presented an alternative framework focusing on how to understand a person's information needs. The alternative framework is represented by the personalization of information, insharability of information needs, and reflexivity of information provision. Spink and Cole (2006) proposed an integrated model to represent human information behavior and information use by examining and combining the everyday-life information-seeking sense-making approach, the information-foraging approach, the problem-solution perspective, and a theory of information use together.

In many cases, the sense-making approach has been widely used to explore the information needs of different types of users and different information-seeking environments. The sense-making approach was employed to investigate how engineers seek and use information to complete their projects. Seven information-seeking and -using situations were identified, and associated information strategies were discussed (Cheuk, 1998). Solomon (1997) explored people's information-seeking behavior in a public agency in terms of the sense-making of their work planning. The study focused on how people make sense of their situations, specifically on their cognitive, affective, and conative styles. Guided by the sense-making theory of information-seeking, Wicks (1999) investigated the information-seeking behavior of pastoral clergy and found that the interaction of their work worlds and work roles affect whether their information-seeking behavior is open or closed.

In addition, Savolainen and Kari (2006) applied the sense-making approach to analyze the new search environment that people face in Web searching and how they bridge gaps in the Web searching process. By videotaping searches, they identified gaps and search tactics. Three major factors—problematic content of information, insufficient search competence, and problems caused by the search environment—created the gaps for the searchers. Search tactics were employed in gap-bridging.

The sense-making approach provides relevant conceptual tools for investigating the dynamic nature of Web searching. Undergraduate students' sense-making in searching a full-text database was also investigated (Jacobson, 1991). In addition, sense-making research was used to explore the concept of narrative intelligence and its applicability to the ways in which people make sense of digital video (Wilkens, Hughes, Wildemuth, & Marchionini, 2003).

Sense-making has been cited as a paradigm, a theory, as well as a methodology. Applying the micromoment timeline interview technique, Baker (1998) studied the information needs of people with multiple sclerosis. The results found gaps in their knowledge about physical symptoms, emotions, and drugs, and unveiled different types of barriers to obtaining information. Dervin's timeline method was also employed to develop a user-process model for user interface design. The events, gaps, and uses elicited from each subject were within each user's situation, and merged across all subjects. The master timeline matrix illustrated the use of the features of the software. The results of the study led to the implementation of a new interface for usability testing (Ju & Gluck, 2003, 2005). In order to examine how public libraries used online community networks to facilitate the public's information-seeking and use in everyday situations, Pettigrew, Durrance, and Unruh (2002) collected data from online surveys and the follow-up interviews that were constructed based on the sense-making approach.

Kuhlthau's Information Search Process (ISP) Approach

By incorporating Kelly's (1963) phases of construction, Taylor's (1968) levels of information need, and Belkin et al.'s ASK hypothesis (1982a), plus a series of five studies examining how users search information in different information-seeking situations, Kuhlthau (1991) proposed a model Information Search Process (ISP). The model was developed based on a small-scale study (Kuhlthau, 1983), tested in two longitudinal studies, and verified in two large-scale field studies.

The ISP model presented physical actions taken, cognitive thoughts gone through, and affective feelings shown by users in the search process. Kuhlthau (1991, 1993) identified six stages in the ISP.

- The first stage is "initiation," where a person recognizes a need for information.

- At the "selection" stage, a user tries to identify a general topic or an approach in order to search for information.

- During "exploration," a user tries to explore information on the general topic.

- When coming to the "formulation" stage, a user tries to come up with a focused idea based on the information gathered from exploration.

- "Collection" is the time that a user tries to find information on the focused idea.

- Finally, at the "presentation" stage, a user completes the search process and prepares for the findings.

Table 1.1 (as shown in Kuhlthau 1991, p. 367) presents the stages in the ISP, feelings common to each stage, action common to each stage, and appropriate tasks according to Kuhlthau's model.

The major contribution of Kuhlthau's ISP model is its identification of the stages of ISP and the integration of physical actions, cognitive thoughts, and affective feelings that are related to the stages. Moreover, Kuhlthau's ISP model can be applied to any context, and it corresponds to the search process, not the context. The ISP model is one of the most frequently cited models in information-seeking and -retrieving research. Based on the ISP model, Vakkari (2001a, 2001b) validated the stages of task performance, and he refined the model in the domain of IR, such as search tactics, search terms, relevance feedback, and so forth. He further developed a theory of task-based information searching. The ISP model was also validated in

Table 1.1. Kuhlthau's information search process. From "Inside the search process: Information seeking from the user's perspective" by C. C. Kuhlthau, 1991. Journal of the American Society for Information Science, 42, P. 367. Copyright 1991 by John Wiley & Sons, Inc. Used with copyright permission.

Stages in ISP	Feelings common to each stage	Thoughts common to each stage	Actions common to each stage	Appropriate task according to Kuhlthau model
1. Initiation	Uncertainty	General/Vague	Seeking background information	Recognize
2. Selection	Optimism			Identify
3. Exploration	Confusion/ Frustration/ Doubt		Seeking relevant information	Investigate
4. Formulation	Clarity	Narrowed/ Clearer		Formulate
5. Collection	Sense of direction/ Confidence	Increased interest	Seeking relevant or focused information	Gather
6. Presentation	Relief/ Satisfaction or Disappointment	Clearer or focused		Complete

a study regarding how novice learners sought information in a hypertext system (Yang, 1997).

The ISP model has been tested in different environments. For example, Swain (1996) investigated the model in a college environment. The results show that Kuhlthau's model was followed. However, the model needs to be enhanced, such as changing the order of the tasks, iterating and combing steps, revising the search goals, and so forth. Another study explored the relationship between undergraduates' epistemological beliefs and their information-seeking behavior based on Kuhlthau's ISP model. The results demonstrated that epistemological beliefs also affected several stages of the ISP model: topic selection, prefocus formulation, focus formulation, and collection (Whitmire, 2003). Hyldegard (2006) explored Kuhlthau's ISP model in a group-based educational setting. The author found that although group members demonstrated cognitive experiences similar to those of the individuals in the ISP model, these experiences resulted not only from information-seeking activities but also from work task activities and intragroup interactions. Hyldegard (2006) suggested an extension of the ISP model to group process, which also addressed the impact of social and contextual factors on the individual's information-seeking behavior.

Kuhlthau's ISP model has also been applied to test devices in information retrieval systems and as teaching tools for users' information-seeking process. For example, Cole (2001) tested an uncertainty expansion IR device and an uncertainty reduction IR device in naturalistic settings. The devices were given at different stages of Kuhlthau's ISP, helping undergraduates perform the task of researching and writing a term paper. Cole found the timing of the device interventions is crucial to its potential effectiveness. In addition, Kuhlthau's ISP model was used as a teaching tool to assist users in their information-seeking process. Kracker and Wang (Kracker, 2002; Kracker & Wang, 2002) investigated the effects of a 30-minute presentation of Kuhlthau's ISP model on students' perceptions of research and research paper anxiety. The quantitative data showed positive trends as a result of the ISP model. The qualitative data confirmed Kuhlthau's ISP model and revealed additional affective and cognitive aspects related to research and writing.

Wilson's Information Seeking Context Approach

Wilson has developed several information behavior models across time. The emergence of new contexts, such as information-seeking on the Web, collaborative information-seeking, the role of information-seeking behavior in teams, and so forth, leads to the integration and modification of old models. Focusing on the context of information need, Wilson's 1996 model of information behavior is shown in Figure 1.2 (Wilson, 1999, p. 257). This model is a major revision of his 1981 model (Wilson, 1981) by integrating research in decision-making, psychology, innovation, health communication, and consumer research. The uniqueness of the model is that it incorporates other theoretical modes of behaviors, such as stress/coping theory, risk/reward theory, and social learning theory, to enlighten the relationships between needs and information-seeking behavior, information resource usage, and self-efficacy. In addition, it also identifies several modes of search, for example, passive search, active search, ongoing search, and so forth. More importantly, this model can relate to other information-seeking models. The models of Ellis and Kuhlthau are the expansion and illustration of the active search mode of information-seeking behavior (Wilson, 1999).

In order to provide an integration of models of information-seeking and information-searching, Wilson (1999, p. 266) proposed a problem-solving model of the information- seeking and -searching process (Figure 1.3). Inspired by Saracevic's (1996a) comments on uncertainty as the basic notion of IR theory and practice, Wilson explored uncertainty in communication theory; he found that uncertainty might lead to increased communication activity in the form of information-seeking and exchange. Schutz and Luckmann's (1974) problematic situation provides an answer for the solution of the problem of uncertainty. The problem-solving model focuses on the following information-seeking and -searching process:

Figure 1.2. Wilson's model of information behavior. From "Models in information behavior research" by T. D. Wilson, 1999. Journal of Documentation, 55, p. 257. Copyright 1999 by Emerald Group Publishing Limited. Used with copyright permission.

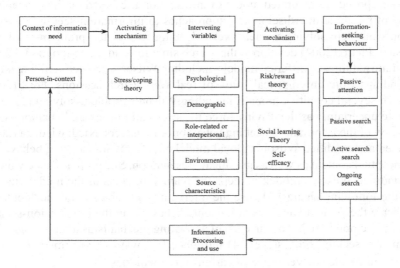

Figure 1.3. Wilson's problem-solving model. From "Models in information behavior research" by T. D. Wilson, 1999. Journal of Documentation, 55, p. 266. Copyright 1999 by Emerald Group Publishing Limited. Used with copyright permission.

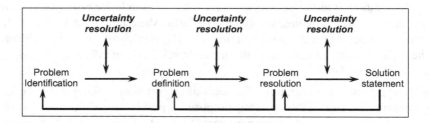

- Problem identification refers to finding out the type of problem.
- Problem definition refers to describing the specific problem.
- Problem resolution refers to identifying the answers to the problem.
- Solution statement refers to presenting the answers to the problem.

The model emphasizes that if uncertainty fails to resolve at any stage, it may lead to a feedback loop to a previous stage. By applying this model, Kuhlthau's ISP can be seen as reiterated steps that may occur between each stage (Wilson, 1999).

Wilson's models have been tested and enhanced by researchers in the field. In order to have a better understanding of information-seeking behavior, Spink and Cole (2006) proposed an integrated model of information use based on the conceptualization of the three interdisciplinary approaches to information-seeking in which Wilson's problem-solving model takes a leading role in the problem-resolution approach. Pharo (2004) developed the search situation and transition model based on literature studies of different models, including Wilson's problem-solving model and findings from an empirical study of real Web search sessions. Ford (2004) reviewed several cognitive models, including Wilson's problem-solving model, to illustrate uncertainty as the driving force for information-seeking behavior. Based on a study of the information-seeking behavior of managers, Niedźwiedzka (2003) criticized and modified Wilson's global model of information-seeking behavior in its conceptual content as well as graphical presentation. She proposed a new model that modified Wilson's model; it keeps the main constructs of the model but suggests the following changes: 1) use the intervening variables to define "context"; 2) indicate the context variables influencing behaviors in the information-seeking process; 3) emphasize the occurrence of activating mechanisms at all stages of the information-seeking process; and 4) introduce two ways of information-seeking with end-users themselves or using various intermediaries.

Wilson's model has also been applied to examine different user groups' information-seeking behavior. Guided by this model of the problem-solving process, Wilson, Ford, Ellis, Foster, and Spink (2002) studied the mediated search between a professional search intermediary and faculty and research students engaged in either personal or externally supported research projects. The article demonstrated that the problem-solving model serves as a useful framework in understanding information-seeking behavior. Drawing information-seeking strategies from Wilson's model, Thivant (2005) analyzed information-seeking and information use in a professional context, in particular the information-seeking behavior of economists and business analysts. This study demonstrated that the professional context and the activity itself can influence information-seeking behaviors. Citing Wilson's model, Zach (2005) identified the information-seeking and information-stopping behavior of senior arts administrators in the process of achieving their management tasks. The author further discussed the potential for applying the results of the study to confirm and expand existing models of information-seeking behavior.

Cognitive Work Analysis (CWA)

The Cognitive Work Analysis (CWA) approach (Rasmussen, Pejtersen, & Goodstein, 1994; Vicente, 1999), which focuses on the human activities and work context in which an information system is used, can offer guidance for analyzing human-information interaction. General systems thinking, adaptive control systems, and Gibson's ecological psychology are the theoretical foundations for the CWA framework. Strictly speaking, CWA is work-centered, not user-centered, and it analyzes the constraints and goals that define information-seeking behavior in the work place. Multiple dimensions need to be studied at the same time, including the environmental, organizational, social, activity, and individual (Fidel & Pejtersen, 2004).

The cognitive work analysis approach analyzes the complex interaction between activities of work domains and end users' cognitive activities, social activities, and subject preferences (Rasmussen, Pejtersen, & Goodstein, 1994; Vicente, 1999). CWA is commonly viewed as the analysis, modeling, design, and evaluation of complex socio-technical systems (Sanderson, 2003). It is generally done by field studies that involve systematical investigation of work domains, actors, and their interactions. It is a powerful approach for analyzing the complexity of interactions instead of just describing them because it facilitates an in-depth examination of the dimensions of a context (Fidel & Pejtersen, 2004).

The CWA approach has been widely applied to the design, development, and evaluation of variety of information systems. Vicente (1999) illustrated the five phases of CWA and various classes of systems design interventions:

1.   Work Domain
   a.   What information should be measured? (sensors)
   b.   What information should be derived? (models)
   c.   How should information be organized? (database)
2.   Control tasks
   a.   What goals must be purposed and what are the constraints on those goals? (procedures or automation)
   b.   What information and relations are relevant for particular classes of situations? (context-sensitive interface)
3.   Strategies
   a.   What frames of reference are useful? (dialogue modes)
   b.   What control mechanisms are useful? (process flow)
4.   Social-organizational
   a.   What are the responsibilities of all of the actors? (role allocation)
   b.   How should actors communicate with each other? (organizational structure)
5.   Work competencies
   a.   What knowledge, rules, and skills do workers need to have? (selection, training and interface form) (p. 120)

Pejtersen, Fidel, and their associates wrote a series of articles that applied CWA to library and information science, especially system design. Book House, one of the first interactive multimedia online public access catalogues (OPACs), was designed based on the CWA approach (Pejtersen, 1992). Guided by the same approach, the Design Explorer project, which supplemented the Book House project, specified requirements for an information system that effectively enabled design team members to interact more effectively in the design process. This framework is the basis for the specification of a digital library system supporting access to a wide network of heterogeneous databases and resources (Pejtersen, Sonnenwald, Buur, Govindaraj, & Vicente, 1997; Pejtersen & Fidel, 1998). It was also applied to analyze how to design systems to support engineers' searching for people in addition to searching for documents because they rely on people as sources of information (Hertzum & Pejtersen, 2000). Recently, it was introduced to investigate the collaboration in European film archives for the potential development of a distributed multimedia film collaboratory that supports the preservation, analysis, indexing and retrieval of films (Hertzum, Pejtersen, Cleal, & Albrechtsen, 2002). In addition, the CWA approach has been shown to be a powerful tool for the evaluation of system designs (Naikar & Sanderson, 2001).

The CWA approach has also been used to understand human-information interaction. Sonnenwald and Pejtersen (1994) developed a conceptual representation of information space based on field studies of relationships in cognitive work dimensions and communication networks for the design of information retrieval systems. The CWA approach was applied to study high school students' problems in Web searching and offer recommendations for design (Pejtersen & Fidel, 1998; Fidel et al., 1999). The cognitive work analysis framework has guided the field study to investigate situations where members of a work team seek and use information collaboratively to further design systems to support collaborative information retrieval (Fidel et al., 2000). Directed by the CWA framework, Fidel, Pejtersen, Cleal, and Bruce (2004) examined the design engineers' collaborative IR events, in particular the multiple dimensions underlying collaborative IR: the cognitive dimension, the specific task and decision, the organization of the teamwork, and the organizational culture. CWA has been also applied to the comparison of two design teams' collaborative IR behavior (Bruce et al., 2003).

Pejtersen and Fidel (1998) and Fidel and Pejtersen (2004)) developed a framework for Cognitive Work Analysis as shown in Figure 1.4 (Fidel & Pejtersen, 2004, http://informationr.net/ir/10-1/paper210.html). This framework illustrates the invariant properties of human-work interaction in which the technology is embedded to support work. These invariant properties highlight the stability and regularity of dynamic work environments, and they greatly help designers to characterize and further predict actors' information-seeking behaviors. They conducted a case study of high school students searching the Web for their homework to illustrate the model and its application for the improvement of Web design.

The following components and their properties are the essential parts of the model: 1) work environment, 2) work-domain analysis, 3) task analysis, 4) organizational analysis, 5) decision analysis, 6) strategies analysis, and 7) users' resources and values analysis. The work environment investigates the environments in which the work takes place. Work domain analysis identifies the current and future means and ends of a work place, which includes the goals and constraints, priorities, general functions, work processes, and physical objects. Task analysis focuses on specific tasks that the actors have to accomplish. Organizational analysis involves work allocation and social organization. Decision analysis offers detailed analysis of individual decisions related to specific tasks. Strategy analysis selects appropriate strategies to fulfill specific tasks and decisions. Users' resources and values analysis focuses on the knowledge and preferences that are related to information-seeking.

Adapted from the CWA framework, Xie (2006) further examined the dimensions and relationships of these interaction activities to study how people seek and retrieve information at a corporate setting. This study also discussed the applications of the results for the design of a digital library. After analyzing data collected from a Web survey, diaries, and telephone interviews, the author presented the characterizations of actors and work domain; more important, she identified three dimensions for

Figure 1.4. Fidel and Pejtersen's dimensions of cognitive work analysis. From "From information behavior research to the design of information systems: The cognitive work analysis framework" by R. Fidel and A. M. Pejtersen. Information Research, 10, (http://informationr.net/ir/10-1/paper210.html). Copyright 2004 by Raya Fidel and Annelise Mark Pejtersen. Used with copyright permission.

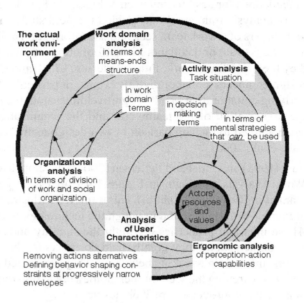

each of the four interactive activities involved in human-work interaction and their relationships: task activities (nature of task, types of task, time frame), decision activities (what to do, how to do it, when to stop), collaborative activities (types of collaborators, types of interactions, types of channels), and strategy activities (types of behaviors, types of resources, types of shifts). She enhanced the model by incorporating three dimensions for each of the interaction activities.

Summary

Table 1.2 summarizes the user-oriented approaches introduced above. These user-oriented approaches contribute significantly to the research in library and information science. The pioneering work of Taylor's levels of information need and Belkin's ASK identify tasks/problematic situations as the driving force for people to look for information, yet people have difficulty in expressing their information needs.

These approaches reveal the problems of IR systems that only match user query with document index, and they call for the need to design IR systems to enable users to clarify their information need. These authors began the shift from a system-oriented approach to a user-oriented approach. Dervin's sense-making approach provides an alternative approach for studying the human use of information and information systems. The major contribution of this approach is that it views information being constructed internally in order to fill in the gap in users' lives as well as provides a methodology that offers guidelines for studying situations involving information use and communication.

The uniqueness of Kuhlthau's ISP approach is that it not only specifies the stages of the information-seeking process, but it also connects them to users' cognitive thoughts, affective feelings, and physical actions Integrating previous models in information-seeking and -searching, Wilson's problem-solving model highlights uncertainty as the driving force for information-seeking, and considers the information-seeking process as a problem-solving process. Both Wilson's general model and his problem-solving model can be related to other models of information-seeking and -searching. The cognitive work analysis approach (CWA) goes beyond user studies, further analyzing human-information interaction in the actual work environment. It investigates user information use and system use from a broader view. It analyzes not only user characteristics, but also the organization, the work domain, and related activities. Just as Wilson (1999) concluded about models of information behavior, these approaches represent different aspects of the overall problem, and they are complementary.

While we praise the contributions of these user-oriented approaches, we also have to admit their limitations, which is why each approach has been further enhanced based on new studies and new situations. First, new digital environments and diverse user groups pose challenges for all the user-oriented approaches. None of the approaches can account of all types of information retrieval situations, and there is no one-size-fits-all approach. Second, these approaches focus more on the user side, in particular users' cognition changes or how users can make sense to themselves in the information-seeking and -retrieving process. Although the intervening variables, the environment, and the context are considered in some of these approaches, these approaches themselves cannot fully represent the dynamic information-seeking and -retrieving process that is affected by users' interactions with the environment, the system, or information. In particular, these approaches cannot further identify patterns of changes in users' tasks/problematic situations and changes in their behaviors/strategies. Third, one critical issue for these approaches is that research that takes the user-oriented approach is rarely applied to real system design, especially commercial IR system design. Saracevic (1997) argued that we need an integration of human-centered and system-centered approaches in both research and practice. In order to integrate and transcend the user-oriented and system-oriented approaches, an interaction framework needs to be adopted for IR (Beaulieu, 2000).

Table 1.2. Summary of user-oriented approaches

Types of approaches	Theoretical basis	Focus	Context	Major contributions
Levels of need	Psychology and cognitive science.	Levels of information need, especially the process from unconscious to compromised need.	Users' use of library.	Clarifies users' levels of information need; Indicates the problem of IR systems that only match user's compromised need to representation of documents.
ASK	Taylor's information need; Wersig's problematic situation.	Anomalous state of knowledge.	Information use and system design.	Identifies the ASK underlying users' information need; Sets up the foundation for models of interactive IR.
Sense-making	Bruner's cognition work; Carter's situational constructivistic approach.	Situations, gaps, and uses.	Information-seeking and use in everyday life.	Considers information-seeking and use as constructing activities; Offers methodology to study information-seeking and use in everyday life.
ISP	Kelly's phases of construction; Taylor's information need; Belkin's ASK hypothesis.	Stages in the information-seeking process.	Information-seeking and search process, independent of context.	Identifies stages of ISP; Integrates cognitive thoughts, affective feelings, and physical actions with stages of ISP.
Model of information behavior	Decision-making; Psychology; Innovation; Health communication; Consumer research.	Context of information need; Barriers, intervening variables, and information-seeking behavior.	General information behavior context.	Incorporates other theoretical models of behaviors; Identifies modes of search.
Problem-solving model	Communication theory; Schutz and Luckman's problematic situation.	Uncertainty and problem solving process.	General information-seeking and searching.	Integrates previous models of information-seeking and searching; Considers information-seeking process as problem-solving process driven by uncertainty.
CWA	General systems thinking; Adaptive control systems; Gibson's ecological psychology.	Human-information interaction in the work environment.	Human activities and work context.	Offers a unique approach for analyzing the complex interaction between work domains and end users' cognitive activities, social activities, and subjective preferences.

References

Baker, L. M. (1998). Sense making in multiple sclerosis: The information needs of people during an acute exacerbation. *Qualitative Health Research, 8*(1), 106-120.

Bates, M. J. (1989). The design of browsing and berry-picking techniques for the online search interface. *Online Review, 13*(5), 407-424.

Beaulieu, M. (2000). Interaction in information searching and retrieval. *Journal of Documentation, 56*(4), 431-439.

Belkin, N. J. (1977). *A concept of information science.* Unpublished doctoral dissertation, University of London.

Belkin, N. J. (1978). Progress in documentation: Information concepts for information science. *Journal of Documentation, 34*(1), 55-85.

Belkin, N. J. (1980). Anomalous states of knowledge as a basis for information retrieval. *Canadian Journal of Information Science, 5*, 133-143.

Belkin, N. J. (1993). Interaction with texts: Information retrieval as information seeking behavior. In G. Knorz, J. Krause, & C. Womser-Hacker (Eds.), *Information Retrieval '93: Von der Modellierung zur Anwendung* (pp. 55-66). Konstanz: Universtaetsverlag Konstanz.

Belkin, N.J. (1996). Intelligent information retrieval: whose intelligence? In J. Krause, M. Herfurth, & J. Marx (Eds.), Harausforderungen an die Informationswirtschaft. Informationsverdichtung, Informationsbewertung und Datenvisualisierung. *Proceedings of the 5th International Symposium for Information Science (ISI '96),* (pp. 25-31). Konstanz: Universitätsverlag Konstanz.

Belkin, N. J., Cool, C., Stein, A., & Theil, U. (1995). Cases, scripts and information seeking strategies: On the design of interactive information retrieval systems. *Expert Systems with Applications, 9*(3), 379-395.

Belkin, N. J., Oddy, R. N., & Brooks, H. M. (1982a). ASK for information retrieval: Part I. Background and theory. *Journal of Documentation, 38*(2), 61-71.

Belkin, N. J., Oddy, R. N., & Brooks, H. M. (1982b). ASK for information retrieval: Part II. Results of a design study. *Journal of Documentation, 38*(3), 145-164.

Borgman, C. L. (1996). Why are online catalogs still hard to use? *Journal of the American Society for Information Science, 47*(7), 493-503.

Bruce, H. (2005). Personal, anticipated information need. *Information Research, 19*(3), 232.

Bruce, H., Fidel, R., Pejtersen, A. M., Dumais, S., Grudin, J., & Poltrock, S. (2003). A comparison of the collaborative information retrieval behaviour of two design teams. *The New Review of Information Behaviour Research: Studies of Information Seeking in Context, 4*(1), 139-153.

Bruner, J. (1973). *Beyond the information given.* New York: W.W. Norton.

Carter, R. F. (1980, December). *Discontinuity and communication.* Paper presented at the East-West Center Conference on Communication Theory. East West Center, Honolulu, HI.

Carter, R. F., Ruggels, W. L., Jackson, K. M., & Heffner, M. B. (1972). Application of signaled stopping technique to communication research. In P. Clarke (Ed.), *New models for mass communication research* (pp. 5-44). Beverly Hills, CA: Sage Publications.

Cheuk, W. Y. B. (1998). Exploring information literacy in the workplace: A qualitative study of engineers using the sense-making approach. *International Forum on Information and Documentation, 23*(2), 30-38.

Cole, C. (2001). Intelligent information retrieval: Part IV. Testing the timing of two information retrieval devices in a naturalistic setting. *Information Processing and Management, 37*(1), 163-182.

Cole, C., Leide, J., Beheshti, J., Large, A., & Brooks, M. (2005). Investigating the anomalous states of knowledge hypothesis in a real-life problem situation: A study of history and psychology undergraduates seeking information for a course essay. *Journal of the American Society for Information Science and Technology, 56*(14), 1544-1554.

Cole, C., Leide, J., Large, A., Beheshti, J., & Brooks, M. (2005). Putting it together online: Information need identification for the domain novice user. *Journal of the American Society for Information Science and Technology, 56*(7), 684-694.

Dervin, B. (1976). The everyday information needs of the average citizen: A taxonomy for analysis. In M. Kochen & J. Donohue (Eds.), *Information for the community* (pp. 19-38). Chicago: American Library Association.

Dervin, B. (1983, May). *An overview of sense-making research: Concepts, methods and results to date.* Paper presented at the International Communication Association Annual Meeting, Dallas, TX.

Dervin, B. (1992). From the mind's eye of the user: The sense-making qualitative-quantitative methodology. In J. D. Glazier & R. R. Powell (Eds.), *Qualitative research in information management* (pp. 61-84). Englewood, CO: Libraries Unlimited.

Ellis, D. (1989). A behavioural approach to information retrieval system design. *Journal of Documentation, 45*(3), 171-212.

Ellis, D., & Haugan, M. (1997). Modeling the information seeking patterns of engineers and research scientists in an industrial environment. *Journal of Documentation, 53*(4), 384-403.

Fidel, R., Bruce, H., Pejtersen, A. M., Dumais, S., Grudin, J., & Poltrock, S. (2000). Collaborative information retrieval. *The New Review of Information Behaviour Research, 1*, 235-247.

Fidel, R., Davies, R. K., Douglass, M. H., Holder, J. K., Hopkins, C. J., Kushner, E. J., et al. (1999). A visit to the information mall: Web searching behavior of high school students. *Journal of the American Society for Information Science, 50*(1), 24-37.

Fidel, R., & Pejtersen, A. M. (2004). From information behavior research to the design of information systems: The cognitive work analysis framework. *Information Research, 10*(1). Retrieved January 2, 2008, from http://informationr. net/ir/10-1/paper210.html

Fidel, R., Pejtersen, A. M., Cleal, B., & Bruce, H. (2004). A multi-dimensional approach to the study of human-information interaction: A case study of collaborative information retrieval. *Journal of the American Society for Information Science and Technology, 55*(11), 939-953.

Ford, N. (2004). Modeling cognitive processes in information seeking: From Popper to Pask. *Journal of the American Society for Information Science and Technology, 55*(9), 769-782.

Hertzum, M., & Pejtersen, A. M. (2000). The information-seeking practices of engineers: Searching for documents as well as for people. *Information Processing and Management, 36*(5), 761-778.

Hertzum, M., Pejtersen, M., Cleal, B., & Albrechtsen, H. (2002). Analysis of collaboration in three film archives: A case for collaboratories. In H. Bruce (Ed.), *Emerging Frameworks and Methods: Proceedings of the 4th International Conference on Conceptions of Library and Information Science,* (pp. 69-84). Greenwood Village, CO: Libraries Unlimited.

Hyldegard, J. (2006). Collaborative information behaviour: Exploring Kuhlthau's information search process model in a group-based educational setting. *Information Processing and Management, 42*(1), 276-298.

Ingwersen, P. (1992). *Information retrieval interaction.* London: Taylor Graham.

Ingwersen, P. (1996). Cognitive perspectives of information retrieval interaction: Elements of a cognitive IR theory. *Journal of Documentation, 52*(1), 3-50.

Ingwersen, P., & Järvelin, K. (2005). *The turn: Integration of information seeking and retrieval in context.* Heidelberg: Springer.

Itoga, M. (1991). Meaning and understanding in human information uses: A critical study of information needs based on the sense-making concept. *Library and Information Science, 29*, 1-19.

Jacobson, T. L. (1991). Sense-making in a database environment. *Information Processing and Management, 27*(6), 647-657.

Ju, B., & Gluck, M. (2003). Developing a user-process model for designing menu-based interfaces: An exploratory study. In B. J. Bates & R. J. Todd (Eds.), *Proceedings of the 66th ASIST Annual Meeting* (Vol. 40, pp. 398-406). Medford, NJ: Information Today.

Ju., B., & Gluck, M. (2005). User-process model approach to improve user interface usability. *Journal of the American Society for Information Science and Technology, 56*(10), 1098-1112.

Kelly, G. A. (1963). *A theory of personality: The psychology of personal constructs.* New York: W. W. Norton & Co.

Kennedy, L., Cole, C., & Carter, S. (1997). Connecting online search strategies and information needs: A user-centered, focus-labeling approach. *RQ, 36*(4), 562-568.

Kracker, J. (2002). Research anxiety and students' perceptions of research: An experiment: Part I. Effect of teaching Kuhlthau's ISP model. *Journal of the American Society for Information Science and Technology, 53*(4), 282-294.

Kracker, J., & Wang, P. L. (2002). Research anxiety and students' perceptions of research: An experiment. Part II. Content analysis of their writings on two experiences. *Journal of the American Society for Information Science and Technology, 53*(4), 295-307.

Kuhlthau, C. C. (1983). *The library research process: Case studies and interventions with high school seniors in advanced placement English classes using Kelly's theory of constructs.* Unpublished doctoral dissertation, The State University of New Jersey, Rutgers.

Kuhlthau, C. C. (1991). Inside the search process: Information seeking from the user's perspective. *Journal of the American Society for Information Science, 42*(5), 361-371.

Kuhlthau, C. C. (1993). *Seeking meaning: A process approach to library and information services.* Norwood, NJ: Ablex.

Liddy, E. D., Oddy, R. N., & Bishop, A. P. (1988). *Use of document frame-structure clues in negotiating ill-formed information needs: Final report to U.S. West Advanced Technologies.* New York: Syracuse University, School of Information Studies.

Lima, G. A. B., & Raghavan, K. S. (2004). Information retrieval and cognitive research. *Knowledge Organization, 31*(2), 98-105.

Lin, S.-J., & Belkin, N. J. (2005). Validation of a model of information seeking over multiple search sessions. *Journal of the American Society for Information Science and Technology, 56*(4), 393-415.

Lynch, M. J. (1997). *Reference interviews in public libraries.* Unpublished doctoral dissertation, The State University of New Jersey, Rutgers.

Markey, K. (1981). Levels of question formulation in negotiation of information need during the online pre-search interview: A proposed model. *Information Processing and Management, 17*(5), 215-225.

Meghabghab, G. V., & Meghabghab, D. B. (1994). INN–an intelligent negotiating neural-network for information systems: A design model. *Information Processing and Management, 30*(5), 663-685.

Naikar, N., & Sanderson, P. M. (2001). Evaluating design proposals for complex systems with work domain analysis. *Human Factors, 43*(4), 529-542.

Niedźwiedzka, B. (2003). A proposed general model of information behaviour. *Information Research, 9*(1). Retrieved January 2, 2008, from http://informationr. net/ir/9-1/paper164.html

Nordlie, R. (1996). Unmediated and mediated information searching in the public library. In S. Hardin (Ed.), *Proceedings of the 59th ASIS Annual Meeting,* (Vol. 33, pp. 41-46). Medford, NJ: Information Today.

Norman, D. (1988). *The design of everyday things*. New York: Doubleday.

Oddy, R. N., Palmquist, R. A., & Crawford, M. A. (1986). Representation of anomalous states of knowledge in information retrieval. In J. Hurd (Ed.), *Proceedings of the 49th ASIS Annual Meeting,* (Vol. 23, pp. 248-254). Medford, NJ: Information Today.

Paisley, W. J., & Parker, E. B. (1965). Information retrieval as a receiver-controlled communication system. In L. B. Heilprin, B. E. Markuson, & F. L. Goodman (Eds.), *Proceedings of the Symposium on Education for Information Science,* (pp. 23-31). Washington, DC: Spartan Books.

Pejtersen, A. M. (1992). New model for multimedia interfaces to online public access catalogues. *The Electronic Library, 10*(6), 359-366.

Pejtersen, A. M. (1998). Semantic information retrieval. *Communications of the ACM, 41*(4), 90-92.

Pejtersen, A. M., & Fidel, R. M. (1998). *A framework for work-centered evaluation and design: A case study of IR on the Web.* Paper presented at the MIRA Workshop, Grenoble, France.

Pejtersen, A. M., Sonnenwald, D. H., Buur, J., Govindaraj, T., & Vicente, K. (1997). The design explorer project: Using a cognitive framework to support knowledge exploration. *Journal of Engineering Design, 8*(3), 289-301.

Pettigrew, K. E., Durrance, J. C., & Unruh, K. T. (2002). Facilitating community information seeking using the Internet: Findings from three public library-community network systems. *Journal of the American Society for Information Science and Technology, 53*(11), 894-903.

Pharo, N. (2004). A new model of information behaviour based on the Search Situation Transition schema. *Information Research, 10*(1). Retrieved January 2, 2008, from http://informationr.net/ir/10-1/paper203.html

Rasmussen, J., Pejtersen, A. M., & Goodstein, L. (1994). *Cognitive systems engineering.* New York: Wiley.

Robertson, S. E., & Hancock-Beaulieu, M. M. (1992). On the evaluation of IR system. *Information Processing and Management, 28*(4), 457-466.

Sanderson, P. M. (2003). Cognitive work analysis. In J. Carroll (Ed.), *HCI models, theories, and frameworks: Toward an interdisciplinary science.* New York: Morgan-Kaufmann.

Saracevic, T. (1996a). Relevance reconsidered'96. In P. Ingwersen & N. O. Pors (Eds.), *Information Science: Integration in Perspective: Proceedings of the Second International Conference on Conceptions of Library and Information Science,* (pp. 201-218). Copenhagen: Royal School of Librarianship.

Saracevic, T. (1996b). Modeling interaction in information retrieval (IR): A review and proposal. In S. Hardin (Ed.), *Proceedings of the 59th ASIS Annual Meeting* (Vol. 33, pp. 3-9). Medford, NJ: Information Today.

Saracevic, T. (1997). The stratified model of information retrieval interaction: Extension and applications. In C. Schwartz & M. Rorvig (Eds.), *Proceedings of the 60th ASIS Annual Meeting* (Vol. 34, pp. 313-327). Medford, NJ: Information Today.

Saracevic, T. (1999). Information science. *Journal of the American Society for Information Science, 50*(12), 1051-1063.

Savolainen, R. (1993). The sense-making theory: Reviewing the interests of a user-centered approach to information seeking and use. *Information Processing and Management, 29*(1), 13-28.

Savolainen, R., & Kari, J. (2006). Facing and bridging gaps in Web searching. *Information Processing and Management, 42*(2), 519-537.

Schutz, A., & Luckmann, T. (1974). *The structures of the life-world.* London: Heinemann.

Shackel, B. (1997). Human-computer interaction: Whence and whither? *Journal of the American Society for Information Science, 48*(11), 970-986.

Shenton, A. K., & Dixon, P. (2004). The nature of information needs and strategies for their investigation in youngsters. *Library and Information Science Research, 26*(3), 296-310.

Solomon, P. (1997). Discovering information behavior in sense making. III. The person. *Journal of the American Society for Information Science, 48*(12), 1127-1138.

Sonnenwald, D. H., & Pejtersen, A. M. (1994). Towards a framework to support information needs in design: A concurrent engineering example. In H. Albrechtsen & S. Ørnager (Eds.), *Knowledge organisation and quality management* (pp. 161-172). Frankfurt/Main: Indeks Verlag.

Spink, A., & Cole, C. (2006). Human information behavior: Integrating diverse approaches and information use. *Journal of the American Society for Information Science and Technology, 57*(1), 25-35.

Swain, D. E. (1996). Information search process model: How freshmen begin research. In S. Hardin (Ed.), *Proceedings of the 59th ASIS Annual Meeting* (Vol. 33, pp. 95-99). Medford, NJ: Information Today.

Taylor, R. (1968). Question-negotiation and information seeking. *College and Research Libraries, 29*(3), 178-194.

Thivant, E. (2005). Information seeking and use behaviour of economists and business analysts. *Information Research, 10*(4), 234.

Vakkari, P. (2001a). A theory of the task-based information retrieval process: A summary and generalization of a longitudinal study. *Journal of Documentation, 57*(1), 44-60.

Vakkari, P. (2001b). Changes in search tactics and relevance judgments when preparing a research proposal: A summary of the findings of a longitudinal study. *Information Retrieval, 4*(3-4), 295-310.

Vakkari, P. (2003). Task-based information searching. *Annual Review of Information Science and Technology, 37*, 413-464.

Vicente, K. J. (1999). *Cognitive work analysis*. Mahwah, NJ: Lawrence Erlbaum.

Wersig, G. (1979). The problematic situation as basic concept of information science in the framework of the social sciences. In *Theoretical problems for Informatics: New trends in informatics and its terminology* (pp. 48-57). Moscow: International Federation for Documentation.

Whitmire, E. (2003). Epistemological beliefs and the information-seeking behavior of undergraduates. *Library and Information Science Research, 25*(2), 127-142.

Wicks, D. A. (1999). The information-seeking behavior of pastoral clergy: A study of the interaction of their work worlds and work roles. *Library and Information Science Research, 21*(2), 205-226.

Wilkens, T., Hughes, A., Wildemuth, B. M., & Marchionini, G. (2003). The role of narrative in understanding digital video: An exploratory analysis. In J. B. Bryans (Ed.), *Proceedings of the 66th ASIST Annual Meeting* (Vol. 40, pp. 323-329). Medford, NJ: Information Today.

Wilson, T. D. (1981). On user studies and information needs. *Journal of Documentation, 37*(1), 3-15.

Wilson, T. D. (1999). Models in information behavior research. *Journal of Documentation, 55*(3), 249-270.

Wilson, T. D. (2000). Human information behavior. *Information Science Research, 3*(2), 49-54.

Wilson, T. D., Ford, N., Ellis, D., Foster, A., & Spink, A. (2002). Information seeking and mediated searching: Part 2. Uncertainty and its correlates. *Journal of the American Society for Information Science and Technology, 53*(9), 704-715.

Wu, M. M. (2005). Understanding patrons' micro-level information seeking (MLIS) in information retrieval situations. *Information Processing and Management, 41*(4), 929-947.

Xie, H. (1997). Planned and situated aspects in interactive IR: Patterns of user interactive intentions and information seeking strategies. In C. Schwartz & M. Rorvig (Eds.), *Proceedings of the 60th ASIS Annual Meeting,* (Vol. 34, pp. 100-122). Medford, NJ: Information Today.

Xie, H. (2000). Shifts of interactive intentions and information-seeking strategies in interactive information retrieval. *Journal of the American Society for Information Science, 51*(9), 841-857.

Xie, H. (2002). Patterns between interactive intentions and information-seeking strategies. *Information Processing and Management, 38*(1), 55-77.

Xie, H. (2006). Understanding human-work domain interaction: Implications for the design of a corporate digital library. *Journal of American Society for Information Science and Technology, 57*(1), 128-143.

Yang, S. (1997). Information seeking as problem-solving using a qualitative approach to uncover the novice learners' information-seeking process in a Perseus hypertext system. *Library and Information Science Research, 19*(1), 71-92.

Zach, L. (2005). When is "enough" enough? Modeling the information-seeking and stopping behavior of senior arts administrators. *Journal of the American Society for Information Science and Technology, 56*(1), 23-35.

Chapter II

Interactive IR in OPAC Environments

Overview of OPAC Environments

History and Background

Online catalogs are types of interactive computer systems; they can also be called "interactive catalogs" because a user interacts with the computer to find relevant information. The interaction is the main difference between Online Public Access Catalogs (OPACs) and other types of library catalogs (Hildreth, 1982; Matthews, 1985). Online catalogs are regarded as real-time interactive retrieval systems for libraries (Fayen, 1983). According to Peters (1991), the development of online catalogs can be characterized by three decades of development. In the 1960s, the development of online catalogs was led by the development of computer technology and the library community's desire to increase efficiency in finding library materials. In the 1970s, commercial vendors started to replace large university libraries as the principal developers of computer-based library systems. In the 1980s, local libraries expand their control of the library catalog systems.

Specifically, Yee and Layne (1998) highlighted some of the key developments of OPAC systems. In the late 1950s and early 1960s, the first computer-output micro-fiche catalog was created. During the 1960s and 1970s, many universities developed local library automation projects to support processing materials in the library. In 1967, Online Computer Library Center (OCLC) launched the first successful online library automation project. In 1968, the Library of Congress published the United States MAchine-Readable Cataloging (USMARC) format, which was the first standard structure for machine-readable data. The USMARC format permits record transferring without conversion. OPAC systems, which are designed specifically for public access, emerged in 1980s; they include MELVYL (University of California System) and MSU/PALS (Minnesota State University System) systems. In 1980, CLSI (Computer Library Services International, Ltd.) installed the first OPAC at the Evanston Public Library in Illinois. Another operational OPAC system is the Universal Library Systems (ULISYS) online catalog (Matthews, 1985). Three main benefits resulted from the availability of OPACs: reduced costs to provide a library catalog, improved access to the collection, and immediate access to location and status information (Kochtanek & Matthews, 2002).

Definition and Types of OPACs

An OPAC is defined, by Library of Congress at the Dartmouth conference sponsored by the Council on Library Resources in the 1980, as "an access tool and resource guide to the collections of a library or libraries, which contains interrelated sets of bibliographic data in a machine-readable form and which can be searched inter-actively on a terminal by users" (Fayen, 1983, p. 4). Saffady (1999, p. 218-222) summarized the general characteristics of OPACs:

- Organized, machine-readable collection that represents a library's holdings.
- Can be accessed from any locations by authorized persons equipped with compatible terminals.
- Can be updated in real time.
- Most of OPAC modules are menu-driven.
- Recent development supports OPAC searches by microcomputers equipped with Web browsers.
- In additional to the traditional retrieval functionality of card catalogs, many systems support unique record identifiers, such as library of Congress Card Number (LCCN) or International Standard Book Number (ISBN), and so forth.

- Keyword searching of designated fields is permitted in some systems, and some support proximity commands, wildcard characteristics that are commonly associated with full-text retrieval systems.
- Increasingly incorporate external information resources into OPAC searches.
- The NISO Z39.50 is widely supported for access to OPACs.

The development of OPAC goes through a long process. Large and Beheshti (1997) described the three generations of OPACs. The first generation requires character-by-character matching between user query and bibliographic record. The second generation has more advanced features, such as keyword search for known item search, use of Boolean operators, browsing capabilities, and online Help. The third generation provides enhanced search techniques and ranked retrieved results based on relevance. Hildreth (1991) summarized criteria for the second generation of OPAC:

- Subject access
- Keyword access
- Boolean searching
- Index term browsing
- Shelf list review/scan
- Full standard bibliographic records
- Multiple display formats
- Two or more dialogue modes
- Interactive search refinement/modification
- Search results display/print manipulation
- Help facility, context-sensitive
- Informative error messages
- Action and "how to" option prompts
- Search term approximate match routines (p. 22)

The second generation of OPACs was designed based on a tradition model that assumes that users can express their information need and know how to formulate and reformulate queries. After discussing the problems of the second generation of OPACs, Hildreth (1991) further suggested the E³OPAC concept, which would have enhanced usability, expanded collection coverage, and extended access. The third generation OPAC represents models of user information-seeking behaviors.

He summarized the third generation OPAC functionalities including second generation functionality plus:

- Natural language query expressions
- Automatic term conversion/matching aids
- Closest, best-match retrieval
- Ranked retrieval output
- Relevance feedback methods
- Intelligent navigation aids
- Integration of keyword, controlled vocabulary, and classification-based search approaches
- Expanded coverage and scope
- Extended access range via linkages and networks (p. 37)

Interestingly, many of the functionalities outlined by Hildreth have not been implemented in OPAC systems but have been incorporated in Web search engines and online databases. Guha and Saraf (2005) suggested that the new and fourth-generation OPACS emerged during the late 1990s. They are represented by interactive Web-OPACs which enable users to access the resources of libraries, publishers, online vendors, and so forth.

Technology change in microcomputers and the emergence of the Internet has influenced the design of OPAC interfaces. Yee and Layne (1998) identified five types of OPAC interfaces:

- Command-based interface offers users speed and flexibility but requires time to learn.
- Menu-based interface assists users in finding specific types of document more accurately, but users do not have the same speed and flexibility when they use command-based interfaces.
- Form fill-in interface is easy to use, but it does not have the flexibility and power of command-based interfaces.
- Client-server interface allows users to choose or customize their interfaces on existing systems but requires the client to have a powerful computer and be networked to the server.
- Graphical user interface facilitates human-computer interaction, but it is more difficult to design a GUI to represent the search process. In addition, there are no standard icons.

- Web interface facilitates universal access and multimedia material access, but it does not accommodate patterns of OPAC uses.

Because interfaces are the main channels by which users interact with OPAC systems, the design of an interface affects the success or failure of interactions. Each type of interfaces has its advantages and disadvantages. Ongoing research is needed to design an interactive interface to facilitate effective interactions between users and OPAC systems.

Current Developments

In the late 1990s, Web-based OPACs started to emerge. They enhanced traditional OPACs in terms of remote access and the potential to integrate library collections with different formats into one interface. Ramesh Babu and O'Brien (2000) characterized the features of Web OPACs: 1) graphical user interface (GUI), 2) standard features of traditional OPACs, 3) availability of hypertext links through bibliographic records, 4) emulation of search engines in terms of appearance and search features, 5) availability of full-text, and 6) one interface to search all electronic information.

The emergence of Web-based OPACs also highlights the need to integrate multiple online systems and online resources. Rogers (2001) pointed out that while the concepts of uber-OPACs have been discussed for several years, the technology to support the idea has just started. Sirsi and The Library Corporation are marketing their products iBistro and YouSeeMore. WebFeat, which offers simultaneous searching of OPAC and databases, goes a step further. It has been implemented in several corporate settings and public facilities.

OPACs play an essential role in helping librarians manage and track their inventories, which contain books, journals, videos, electronic journals, and so forth. According to McCracken (2003), electronic journals account for 86.5% of the journals provided at associate-degree-granting institutions, 83.3% at baccalaureate institutions, and 71.3% at master's institutions. There is a need to expand the ways to include different electronic resources in OPACs if librarians want OPACs to be the central source of their collection of all formats. Vendors and libraries have worked on solutions for incorporating e-journals into OPACs. With the development of e-journal management services, librarians have used A-to-Z lists of journals available through database aggregators as a way of managing their access to these journals. However, these lists cannot offer the same access points as an OPAC does. Serials Solutions combines aggregator title lists with CONSER MARC records to improve access to e-journals. Adding records to the OPAC for electronic journals confirms that the OPAC is the single system for locating all subscriptions of libraries regardless of their formats (McCracken, 2003). For example, the Ewell Sale Stewart Library of the Academy of Natural Sciences has used a Web OPAC with image files attached to bibliographic records to deliver digital collections (Mathias, 2003).

Because digital libraries, Web search engines, and OPACs have their own unique collections and design features, these co-existing online IR systems unavoidably impact each other. For example, the Cheshire II online catalog system, which was designed to address the problems of existing OPACs, serves as a bridge between existing online catalog technology and the growing digital libraries with full-text and multimedia collections. The objective of the system is to develop a new generation of OPACs incorporating advanced search features by applying new technologies (Larson, McDonough, O'Leary, Kuntz, & Moon, 1996).

Google's plan to make library books searchable posed a challenge for OPAC searching. Most of the OPACs still default to a last-in, first-out display order. Overall users are not satisfied with current OPAC systems compared to Web search engines. Pace (2005) introduced some innovations for the development of OPACs; for example, RedLightGreen ranked records in order of relevance to the search term and based on how many copies of a title exist in libraries. It can also cluster various editions of a work into a single display. The AquaBrowser's library system helps users search by using associations in providing results. Endeca has one of the impressive refining tools, consisting of name, subject, format, or locally defined fields.

The development of new technologies has not only influenced the design of OPACs but also the access to OPACs. Today you can put an OPAC in the palm of your hand. There are combination palm/bar code scanners for professional use. Embrey (2002) introduced 3M's Digital Library Assistant or "Palm-on-a-Stick," which is a good example of such a device. It can locate items in the stacks when you put Radio Frequency Identification (RFID) tags into the books. This can be used for checking circulation data, shelf-reading, and weeding.

Challenges for Users

OPACs are the first type of IR systems that allow ordinary citizens to become end users. That unavoidably poses challenges for users. Borgman (1996) identified three layers of knowledge required for OPAC searching:

- Conceptual knowledge of the IR processes—how to convert an information need to a query.
- Semantic knowledge of how to implement a query in a given system—how to use system features to facilitate the searching process.
- Technical skills in executing the query—how to construct queries.

Another type of knowledge is also important for any information retrieval: domain knowledge. Users are not always experts on the topics they are searching. They need domain knowledge to assist them in coming up with query statements. The lack of domain knowledge might affect the effectiveness of OPAC searching.

When 21st century users meet a 20th century OPAC, users who are accustomed to Internet searching also need to be effective searchers of OPACs (Theimer, 2002). The popularity of the Web has influenced users' mental models, their expectations, and their behaviors when using a Web-based OPAC interface (Yu & Young, 2004). Novotny (2004) found that many of the participants expected OPACs to operate as Web search engines based on a protocol analysis of a Web-savvy generation of library users searching an online catalog. After analyzing the results of transaction logs at one university, Yu and Young (2004) suggested that the meta-searching, relevance-ranked results, and relevance feedback offered by Web search engines were expected by users searching OPACs, and this should be incorporated into the design of OPACs.

Research Overview

The objective of OPAC research is to gather information that enables more effective OPAC systems to be designed and implemented in libraries (Large & Beheshti, 1997).

A national study of user behavior on requirements of existing online catalog systems was conducted by OCLC and sponsored by the Council on Library Resources (CLR). Ten OPAC systems from 10 organizations were compared. After analyzing written documentation and accessing each OPAC system, researchers compared the systems' capabilities and experiences with human communication. The success of the interaction between users and OPAC systems is determined both by the willingness of users to interact with systems as they normally do with humans and by OPACs, especially the interactive interfaces that facilitate the interaction. There is a need for improved dialogue design (Hildreth, 1982). The OCLC/CLR study agreed with Hayes, Ball, and Reddy (1981) that users of interactive systems are frustrated with their communication experience with these systems because the existing systems are not very good at communicating with their users.

Another national survey of OPAC use, sponsored by the Council on Library Resources (CLR), focused on the interaction between human users and the online catalogs. By analyzing the survey of users and nonusers of online catalogs in the United States, Matthews, Lawrence, and Ferguson (1983) identified six categories that affect the usage of online catalogs: the user, the task, the organizational interface (the library), the online system, the database, and the human-online interface. Subject searching is a major aspect that affects users' search satisfaction. The survey suggested that OPACs should implement keyword searching for subjects, and allow users to browse the subject index or thesaurus.

There are a series of review articles on OPAC research. Hildreth's (1985) comprehensive review of OPAC research presented an overview of OPAC design, development, and use. In particular, he reviewed OPAC research studies published before 1985. He pointed out that "online library catalogs are a class of interactive information retrieval systems, and user interaction with them is a form of human-computer interaction" (p. 272). In that sense, much of the research on information retrieval and human-computer interaction can be applied to the design and evaluation of OPACs. Hildreth identified problems of OPAC searching revealed by previous research: failed searches, nonrelevant results, high expectations from users, lack of using controlled vocabulary, and so forth. He also suggested further research and design directions. Lewis (1987) reviewed research on the use of OPACs in early online catalog studies, the CLR OPAC studies, and other studies of online catalogs. He further discussed the implications of these studies for library practice. He argued that current subject retrieval capabilities are not adequate and need to be enhanced even though users like online catalogs.

Seymour (1991) reviewed research methodologies applied in OPAC user studies from March 1986 through November 1989. She concluded users could not understand OPAC structure and subject organization, and they rarely used online and off-line Help. She discussed the problems in applying a variety of methods to OPAC user studies, especially experimental statistical methods. Yee (1991) reviewed the current research on specific user interfaces to online catalogs. She pointed out that in-depth research on user needs of online catalogs is required in order to design effective interfaces for OPACs. Large and Beheshti (1997) provided an overview of OPAC studies since 1990. They focused on the crucial problems of OPAC research: users, library settings, search strategies, systems, and, in particular, relevance. They found that most of the OPAC studies had concentrated on subject searching, a challenge for OPAC users. OPAC systems and their enhancements and developments were also reviewed by O'Brien (1994). In conclusion, it is clear that OPAC studies cover a wide range of areas, from user studies to system evaluation and comparison.

Interaction Studies

After reviewing the research on interactive IR in OPAC environments, the author identified the following types of interaction studies: 1) user goals and their impact, 2) strategies/behaviors and affecting factors, 3) effect of knowledge structure on search success, 4) evaluation studies and usability testing, 5) intermediary studies and their implications, and 6) research methods for interaction studies.

User Goals and their Impact

User goal is an important component of OPAC interaction studies because it is the objective of IR interaction. It is important to understand user goals and their relationships with both search strategies and information-seeking behaviors. By employing questionnaire surveys, semistructured interviews, transaction logs, and unobtrusive observation, Belkin, Chang, Downs, Saracevic, & Zhao (1990) identified design principles for the third generation OPACs through an understanding of the intentions and behaviors of people as they interacted with information in different types of libraries. They classified the goals, behaviors, and intentions associated with interaction with information, and further identified relationships among goals, behaviors, and intentions. Analyzing the same data, Chang (1995) identified the underlying common dimensions of browsing: scanning, resource, goal, and object. Based on these four dimensions, she discovered five themes and nine patterns of browsing. Goal is one key dimension that determines the browsing patterns.

Although researchers agree that user goals have an impact on users' interactions with IR systems, there is a disagreement on whether users change their goals during their interaction with IR systems. Hert (1996, 1997) defined user goal as what a user attempts to accomplish during the interaction. She further developed the notion of information-seeking interaction as "situated action" in an investigation of information interactions of OPAC users. After analyzing videotapes, transaction logs, and interviews, the results of her study indicated that user goals were not greatly modified during their information interactions. Users' actions were not completely predetermined; instead, elements of the situation, such as elements associated with the respondent, elements associated with the problem or project, and elements associated with the system response, affect users' interactions with OPAC systems. She further suggested that system design should build on dynamic user models and focus on feedback mechanisms.

Using Daniels' (1986) classification of goals, Xie (2000, 2002) constructed four types of user goals and eight types of subgoals, interactive intentions based on users' interactions with OPACs in different types of libraries. However, contrary to Hert's findings (1996, 1997), she found that users did not change their long-term goals and leading search goals, but they did change their current search goals, which correspond to the user goals, as defined by Hert (1996, 1997), and the interactive intentions in the process of achieving their leading search goals. She identified patterns between interactive intentions and information seeking strategies, and investigated the shifts in current search goals, interactive intentions and information-seeking strategies. This study demonstrated that interactive information retrieval is the product of plans and situations, and suggested that the design of interactive IR systems should support multiple types of information-seeking strategies and shifts in levels of goals and types of information-seeking strategies. It is important to further investigate whether users change their different levels of goals for a variety of tasks in different settings, and under what circumstances they shift their levels of goals.

Slone (2002) investigated the influence of user mental models and goals on search patterns during Web interactions, including interactions with OPAC systems. She found that elements of situational goals, along with users' experience, motivation, and mental models, affected how they searched for information. Different types of user goals led to different search approaches. Users who intended to accomplish job-related or educational goals were more highly motivated than those who tried to fulfill recreational or personal goals. Users with job-related or educational goals used a variety of tools or Web online catalog, or off-line sources depending on their Internet experience. Users with recreational or personal use goals conducted more searches by serendipity.

There are still unanswered questions about user goals. For example, what are the relationships among user goals, tasks, and problems? Do user goals change in their interactions with OPACs? Large and Beheshti (1997, p. 128) also asked several vital questions related to studies of user goals:

- Does a user pursue a single goal in one search session, or is the goal dynamic and changes in the search process?
- Does a user divide the search goal into several search sessions?
- What determines goals and search strategies?

Strategies/Behaviors and Affecting Factors

Information-seeking strategies and behaviors are the center of OPAC interaction studies because they represent how interactions take place. In this section, the author reviewed the research focusing on identification of types of strategies and patterns of behaviors, and the factors affecting these strategies and behaviors.

First, the different types of information-seeking strategies are related to task dimensions. One dimension of tasks is type of task. Considering OPAC searching a special kind of communication between humans and computers, Slone (2000) explored and identified information-seeking strategies and behaviors based on three types of searches: unknown-item searches, area searches, and known-item searches. The results showed that term generation is the driving force for unknown-item searches, where the basic strategy is to formulate a query, evaluate the results, and reformulate the query if necessary. Speed and convenience are essential to area searches; therefore, users quickly look for a few records from OPAC and complete their searches by browsing the shelves. Query-matching is appropriate for known-item searches because accuracy and simplicity is most important for this type of search. This study indicates that strategies and behaviors are determined by the dimensions of tasks.

Second, information-seeking strategies and behaviors are related to affective responses. It is a complicated process for users to interact with OPACs. Their behaviors, attitudes, and feelings need to be identified in order to understand their interactions with systems. By applying factor analysis, Dalrymple and Zweizig (1992) demonstrated that benefits and frustration are the two dimensions of users' affective responses to OPAC systems, and that both benefits and frustration affect information-searching behavior, especially reformulation behavior. Affective feelings were also investigated with the three types of searches conducted by Slone (2000), discussed above. The unknown-item searchers experienced the most frustration and doubt; the known-item searchers experienced the most disappointment; and the area searchers experienced the most confidence and contentment. In that sense, user tasks, strategies, and affective feelings are interrelated.

Third, types of information-seeking strategies are related to types of users. OPACs are designed for a variety user groups. Some of them are designed for children, so it is important to understand children's information-seeking strategies. By observing, questioning, collecting think-aloud protocols, and analyzing documents, Soloman (1993) explored children's information-retrieval behavior in using an OPAC in an elementary school library. A variety of factors were considered for children's information retrieval success and breakdown in the study, such as user character-istics, the school setting, interface usability, and information access features. Most important, he identified two classes of strategies, planned strategies and reactive strategies. Planned strategies, in which users make decisions prior to and including the first move, consist of author, title, multiple concepts, external support, system features, and index function. Reactive strategies, in which users make decisions to follow up one move with another, include focus shifts, search term relations, error recovery, and external supports.

Borgman and her associates have studied children's information-retrieval behaviors in multiple design iterations of a science library catalog. The objective of these studies is to understand children's information-seeking behaviors and further incorporate search mechanisms facilitating their searching (Borgman, Hirsh, & Hiller, 1996). Borgman, Hirsh, Walter, & Gallagher (1995) proposed an alternative information retrieval model for children that was built on the capabilities and knowledge of children at their respective ages. Children can recognize information, browse for information, use hierarchies, and provide a context for information. Multiple meth-ods, including interview, online monitoring, and focus groups, were applied to four experiments on four versions of the catalog. The studies shed light on how children searched for information in both a hierarchical, browsing, recognition-based system and a keyword and Boolean system. The authors concluded that the ideal system for children may combine the browsing and keyword features that do not require children to use content spelling, or use Boolean logic.

These studies characterize the patterns of information-seeking strategies or behaviors displayed by different types of users. They also identify the task, affective, and age factors that affect information-seeking strategies and behaviors. However, further research needs to examine more in-depth the dimensions of these factors and other factors that might influence users' strategies and behaviors. In addition, researchers also need to look into whether users exhibit different types of strategies or behaviors in interacting with different types of online IR systems.

Effect of Knowledge Structure on Search Success

In order to successfully interact with OPAC systems, users need to possess different types of knowledge because the existing OPAC systems do not provide assistance to enhance their knowledge structure.

First, they need to have domain knowledge for understanding the topic of their searches. Employing interviews, online monitoring techniques, observations, and card-sorting tasks, Hirsh (1997) focused her research on how children found information through different types of searches, and found that task complexity and the children's domain knowledge affected their success in finding information in the online catalog. More IR tools that are designed specifically for children are essential to help children seek information in digital environments. Knowledge about the searching topic is important for subject searching, and knowledge about the items that users look for is essential for known-item searching.

Second, users need to have specific knowledge about the retrieved items, particularly for known-item searching. This specific knowledge can be an extension of the domain knowledge. After analyzing interviewing protocols, Wildemuth and O'Neill (1995) examined what information users had for known-item searches and how that affected their success in known-item searching. They found that searchers normally knew the title, publication date, page numbers, or the author of a known-item based on bibliographies, search results, published references, hand-written notes, or recalled memory, and the information was accurate for finding the known items. The results of this study suggested that OPACs can be enhanced to reduce users' efforts to describe a known item in OPAC searching.

Third, users need to have system knowledge to understand how the system works. Ease-of-use of OPACs is not necessarily good for users' effective information retrieval. By applying questionnaires and transaction logs to collect data, Hildreth (1997) studied whether users understood how the system processed keyword and Boolean searching while searching an OPAC. He discovered that although users conducted more keyword searches than other types of searches, they failed more and they did not understand the process behind keyword searching. He called for the need to improve the design of OPACs based on interactive models of information-seeking behavior.

Fourth, and most import, users need to integrate and apply the above knowledge to their interactions with OPAC systems. Connell (1995) found that metaknowledge is used in the subject searching process by experienced searchers in online catalogs. Metaknowledge is an integration of factual, process, and experiential knowledge about the search and the search context. This finding was based on data collected from think-aloud protocols, transaction logs, and structured interviews. The study recommended the construction of aids about metaknowledge to assist users, mainly novice users, in searching online catalogs.

It is no doubt that users need different types of knowledge for successful interactions with OPACs. The problem is that users probably won't be able to have all the needed knowledge. Researchers have not explored how IR systems can enhance users' knowledge structure in the interaction process. Another question is how knowledge structure affects users' search strategies and behaviors in addition to search performance.

Evaluation Studies and Usability Testing

Relevance is a fundamental concept for the evaluation of IR systems. O'Brien (1994) pointed out that it is essential to understand what relevance in the context of OPAC searching is, because developments in OPACs are based on more interactive approaches with relevance feedback capabilities. However, not all users liked relevance feedback mechanisms. Applying questionnaire and transaction logs, Hancock-Beaulieu, Fieldhouse, and Do (1995) evaluated an interactive query expansion mechanism based on relevance feedback in an OPAC system. They found the use of the interactive query expansion option was lower and the retrieval performance less effective because this option gave users too much control. There is a need to further investigate the relationship between interactive interface environments and their impact on searching behavior.

Most of the evaluation studies have been usability studies that concentrate on the evaluation of the interfaces and features of OPAC systems. These usability tests are conducted by comparing an OPAC with another OPAC or other types of IR systems. A browsable graphical interface, Public Access Catalogue Extension (PACE) is an alternative interface designed to enhance online catalogs. It simulates the images of books and library shelves to facilitate users' browsing of the online catalog. The interface was evaluated and tested against a text-based OPAC. The results showed that a majority of the users preferred a visual interface to a command-driven, text-based OPAC because it required a smaller cognitive load. The familiar metaphor of the bookshelves was more intuitive (Beheshti, Large, & Bialek, 1996). Drabenstott and Weller (1996) conducted an experiment to compare two catalogs: search tree controlled the selection of subject searching in one, and the subject-searching approach was randomly selected in another. Although the results showed that there were mixed results in terms of whether search tree improved subject searches, the results did show that users preferred the OPAC system that controlled the subject search. The same system was also selected for its ease-of-use and efficiency.

In evaluating the usability of OPACs, researchers also examined the problems of subject searching. After comparing the usage of an OPAC and the card catalogue of a library, Sridhar (2004) looked into the problems of subject searching. Users are required to have technical skills and conceptual and semantic knowledge in order to articulate the query for a subject search. In order to facilitate subject searching, Sridhar (2004) called for the need to enhance interactive searching features, such as drag and drop text from hits, "more like this" features, online thesauri with classification links, and so forth.

Do all users prefer the same features of an OPAC? In order to understand the relationships between user characteristics and OPAC features, Kim, Chung, Hong, Moon, and Park (1999) tested the correlations between user characteristics—such as age, gender, educational status, computer skills, and OPAC experience— and the preferred usability features of Web OPACs, such as interaction styles, character and image on screen, browsing and navigating style, screen layout, and ease of learning. Although this study was based on a small-scale sample, the result discovered significant correlation between user characteristics and the preferred features of a Web OPAC. It further identified that age was the most significant variable, followed by gender, subjects' computer skills, and OPAC experience. To sum up, OPAC system design needs to consider user demographics.

The existing evaluation studies on OPACs mainly concentrate on usability studies. In addition, they have not identified the criteria for the evaluation of interactive IR systems. Researchers also need to pay more attention to how to take users' characteristics into account for the evaluation of interactive IR systems or features.

Intermediary Studies and their Implications

Intermediary studies are one of the important approaches for interaction studies. The objectives of intermediary studies are two-fold: first, to understand how users interact with information professionals; second, to offer design principles enabling users to interact with OPACs as they normally interact with information professionals. Nordlie (1996) examined the patterns of interactions between librarians and public library users, in particular how users formulated their problems, how librarians elicited information from the users, what information users provided to librarians, and how these factors affected the outcomes of the interactions. He found that users' ambiguities and information needs were cleared up by not only interacting with librarians but also interacting with the materials on the shelf. He further discussed the implications of the results in order to incorporate these interactions into OPAC design.

The ultimate objective for intermediary studies is to design interactive IR systems. Based on actual user-librarian negotiations, the Book House was built to assist library users to find work of fictions. Pejtersen (1979, 1980, 1989) identified three strategies that were used in user-librarian negotiations in the book retrieval process: analytical search, search by analog, and browsing. She incorporated these strategies and a flexible search dialog into the user-system interaction. Icons and metaphors were used for easy navigation. The Book House was evaluated and received positive responses regarding subject indexing and the user interface. All three strategies were used by different types of users (Pejtersen, 1989).

Human help for OPAC use is another type of intermediary study. Users need more human help than printed or online Help when they search OPACs. Mendelsohn (1994) investigated human Help at OPAC terminals. Two groups of users participated in the study: one group was approached by librarians who offered help, another group was not. The interactions between a user and a librarian were observed, and the two groups of users also filled out a questionnaire. When offering help, the librarians provided instruction as well as information to users. The most frequent type of help was offering procedural help related to the search process. Help was mostly given under two conditions: search failure or to reduce the number of hits. The procedural help needed indicated that OPAC systems did not fully support self-service. The results of this study can be further applied to design a better Help mechanism for OPAC systems. One limitation of these intermediary studies is that they have not uncovered the similarities and differences between human-human interactions and human-system interactions.

Research Methods for Interaction Studies

OPAC searching is an interactive and iterative process. In order to investigate the complexity of user-OPAC interactions, multiple research methods that can capture the interaction process are needed. Online monitoring, or transaction log analysis, is one of the most effective approaches for studying users' interactions with OPACs. According to Borgman, Hirsh, and Hiller (1996), by applying an online monitoring method, researchers can identify cycles of search actions and patterns of search behavior, predict users' search actions and usage of system features, analyze errors, and so forth. They discussed the variables of OPAC searching studies by drawing examples from their 7-year study of children's searching behavior with an experimental OPAC system. Transaction log analysis helps designers identify users' problems when they interact with OPACs. Blecic et al. (1998) reported an OPAC transaction log analysis study for a 6-month period. Analysis of the transaction logs revealed that many users experienced problems with basic search techniques that led to a redesign of the introductory screen. The simplification and clarification of wording on introductory screens, avoidance of jargon, and rearrangement of the order of search options appeared to be the changes responsible for improving information retrieval. On the one hand, monitoring data provides detailed information about what a searcher is doing. On the other, researchers cannot tell why the searcher is doing what he or she is doing.

In order to collect data to understand users' interactions with OPAC systems, it is not enough just to apply one method. After conducting three experiment studies, Hancock-Beaulieu, Robertson, and Neilson (1991) found that transaction logs can only be effective if they are combined with other data collection methods. They suggested three ways to enhance transaction logs: replay logs to solicit users' perceptions of their searching process, use online pre- and post-search questionnaires to gather users' overall objectives for a search task, and employ online interactive questionnaires to connect types of interactions to the information-seeking behavior.

Verbal protocol technique is another effective method for studying interactions between users and systems. Verbal protocol technique can also be termed as "think aloud" or "current verbalization." It can solicit information about the cognitive processes of a user's internal states. It can also provide insightful information about human problem-solving processes (Yang, 2003). Sullivan and Seiden (1985) designed a protocol study to investigate users' OPAC use. Verbal protocols techniques proved to be an effective method for providing information about how users defined their problems, what search strategies users employed, and how users reacted to their errors. This study revealed that users had difficulty in interpreting the nature of the question and focusing on key points. The search strategy problems were derived from users not knowing available options, misunderstanding options, and having too many options, as well as their prior experience. In order to recover from errors, users tried to shift search strategies, modify search terms, or change the search path or queries. Verbal protocols were also employed to examine how users interacted with an OPAC and navigated within the system, and their overall perception of their OPAC interactions (Guha & Saraf, 2005).

Verbal protocol techniques also have their tradeoffs. After using a verbal protocol to identify common problems in using an online catalogue, Morrison (1999) identified the advantages of this method. First, data collected from this method is more detailed than answers to interview questions, because after a while, people cannot remember details of a complicated problem. Second, it can help determine the impact of problems on a search. At the same time, she pointed out that this method might also affect subjects' usual search strategies, which needs to be further investigated.

The methods employed to study interactions between users and OPAC systems focus on either what they do or how they think. None of the methods is prefect. Each of the methods has its advantages and disadvantages. It is important to apply multiple methods to capture detailed information about different aspects of the interaction between users and OPAC systems.

Summary

Just as Borgman (1996) pointed out, the reason that online catalogs are still hard to use is that online catalogs still require users to specify a query even though queries may not be easy to input. Users need assistance in translating the information they need into queries. In other words, users need to interact with OPACs to clarify their information needs and find relevant documents to solve their problems. Table 2.1 presents a summary of OPAC interaction studies.

The studies of user goals and their impact have helped researchers understand the driving force behind interactions between users and OPACs. They also have left unresolved questions about whether user goals change in a search process because different studies produced different results. Other related questions include whether users apply one or multiple goals in one search session or whether users apply one goal in multiple search sessions. In addition, further research on how to define user goals and subgoals might provide clues for clarification of relationships among goals, tasks, problems, and problematic situations.

The studies of strategies and behaviors and affecting factors present how types of searches, affective modes, and types of users influence users' information-seeking strategies. However, most of the research has explored children's information seeking-strategies. More studies are needed to investigate other types of users' information-seeking strategies to further examine whether different types of users exhibit different types of strategies/behavior. In addition, other factors that have impact on information-seeking strategies need to be identified. Further research also needs to investigate whether users apply the same search strategies in interacting with different types of online IR systems.

The studies of the effects of knowledge structure on search process reveal that users need to have domain knowledge, system knowledge, and metaknowledge to successfully retrieve relevant information from OPACs. If a user's knowledge structure determines the success or failure of OPAC searching, more studies need to test how knowledge structure affects a user's information-seeking strategies in addition to search success. More research needs to focus on the design of OPACs to offer users different types of knowledge when needed.

Evaluation studies and usability testing enable researchers to test and identify the types of systems, interfaces, or features that facilitate interactions between users and OPACs. However, there are no standard criteria for the evaluation of OPACs

Table 2.1. Summary of interaction studies in OPAC environments

Types	Research Focus	Problems/Questions	Implications
User goals and their impact	User goals and how they affect search strategies and search behaviors.	Do users apply one or multiple goals in one search session? Do users apply one goal in multiple search sessions? Do users change their goals in a search session? What are the relationships among user goals, tasks, and problems?	Understand the driving force for interaction; Incorporate user goals and patterns between user goals and search strategies into system design.
Strategy/Behavior and affecting factors	Dimension of tasks affecting search strategies; Affective factors affecting search strategies; Types of users affecting search strategies.	Do different types of users exhibit different types of behaviors/strategies? What are the other factors affect information-seeking strategies? Do users apply the same types of search strategies in interacting with different types of online systems?	Understand how users interact with OPACs and what factors affect their interactions; Design OPAC systems to facilitate and guide users in applying their seeking strategies
Effects of knowledge structure on search success	Types of knowledge needed for interaction with OPAC systems: domain knowledge, system knowledge, and metaknowledge	How does knowledge structure affect users' information-seeking strategies? When and under what circumstances do users need different types of knowledge?	Understand the knowledge structure required to effectively interact with OPACs; Offer aids in OPAC systems to enhance user knowledge structure.
Evaluation studies and usability testing	Evaluation of interactive OPACs; Usability testing on different interfaces/ features of systems; Exploring the relationships between user characteristics and system features.	What are the criteria for evaluating OPACs and other interactive IR systems? How to take users' characteristics and their preferences into account in the design and evaluation of interactive features of IR systems?	Find what types of systems, interfaces, or features facilitate interactions between users and OPACs; Design more intuitive, easy-to-use systems that facilitate interactive searching; the design needs to take into account user characteristics.

continued on following page

Table 2.1. continued

Intermediary studies and their implications	The interactions between an intermediary and a user in searching OPACs. The interactions between a librarian and a user in using libraries.	What are the similarities and differences between human-human interactions and human-system interactions?	Understand how users interact with information professionals; Incorporate a dialogue module between intermediaries and users into the design of OPACs.
Research methods for interaction studies	Transaction logs and verbal protocols are the effective methods for collecting and analyzing data. The importance of applying multiple methods for interaction studies.	Each research method has its disadvantages; How to avoid research methods' influence on user behaviors?	Identify the appropriate methods for the investigation of user-system interactions.

and other types of interactive IR systems. In addition, more studies need to consider how to account for users' characteristics and their preferences for the design and evaluation of the interactive features and interfaces of OPACs so that interactive OPAC systems can be designed to satisfy different types of user needs.

Intermediary studies make it possible for researchers to understand the interactions between users and information professionals, and further incorporate these communication patterns into system design. However, there is a lack of research on the comparison of the similarities and differences between human-human interactions and human-system interactions.

It is a challenge for researchers to find appropriate research methods to explore the interactions between users and OPACs. Transaction logs and verbal protocols are the two most effective methods for investigating the interaction process. However, the complexity nature of the interaction process and the limitations of each research method require researchers to apply multiple methods to collect and analyze data. More important, researchers also need to look into how to avoid the influence of some of the research methods on users' strategies and behaviors.

References

Beheshti, J., Large, V., & Bialek, M. (1996). PACE: A browsable graphical interface. *Information Technology and Libraries, 15*(4), 231-240.

Belkin, N. J., Chang, S., Downs, T., Saracevic, T., & Zhao, S. (1990). Taking account of user tasks, goals and behavior for the design of online public access catalogs. In D. Henderson (Ed.), *Proceedings of the 53rd ASIS Annual Meeting,* (Vol. 27, pp. 69-79). Medford, NJ: Learned Information.

Blecic, D. D., Bangalore, N. S., Dorsch, J. L., Henderson, C. L., Koenig, M. H., & Weller, A. C. (1998). Using transaction log analysis to improve OPAC retrieval results. *College and Research Libraries, 59*(1), 39-50.

Borgman, C. L. (1996). Why are online catalogs still hard to use? *Journal of the American Society for Information Science, 47*(7), 493-503.

Borgman, C. L., Hirsh, S. G., & Hiller, J. (1996). Rethinking online monitoring methods for information retrieval systems: From search product to search process. *Journal of the American Society for Information Science, 47*(7), 568-583.

Borgman, C. L., Hirsh, S. G., Walter, V. A., & Gallagher, A. L. (1995). Children's searching behavior on browsing and keyword online catalogs: The Science Library Catalog Project. *Journal of the American Society for Information Science, 46*(9), 663-684.

Chang, S. (1995). *Toward a multidimensional framework for understanding browsing.* Unpublished doctoral dissertation, Rutgers University, New Brunswick, New Jersey.

Connell, T. H. (1995). Subject searching in online catalogs: Metaknowledge used by experienced searchers. *Journal of the American Society for Information Science, 46*(7), 506-518.

Dalrymple, P., & Zweizig, D. L. (1992). Users' experience of information retrieval systems: An exploration of the relationship between search experience and affective measure. *Library and Information Science Research, 14*(2), 167-181.

Daniels, P. (1986). *Developing the user modeling function of an intelligent interface for document retrieval systems.* Unpublished doctoral dissertation, The City University, London, England.

Drabenstott, K. M., & Weller, M. S. (1996). Failure analysis of subject searches in a test of a new design for subject access to online catalogs. *Journal of the American Society for Information Science, 47*(7), 519-537.

Embrey, T. A. R. (2002). Today's PDAs can put an OPAC in the palm of your hand. *Computers in Libraries, 22*(3), 14-22.

Fayen, E. G. (1983). *The online catalog: Improving public access to library materials.* London: Knowledge Industry.

Guha, T. K., & Saraf, V. (2005). OPAC usability: Assessment through verbal protocol. *The Electronic Library, 23*(4), 463-473.

Hancock-Beaulieu, M., Fieldhouse, M., & Do, T. (1995). An evaluation of interactive query expansion in an online library catalog with a graphical user interface. *Journal of Documentation, 51*(3), 225-243.

Hancock-Beaulieu, M., Robertson, S., & Neilson, C. (1991). Evaluation of online catalogues: Eliciting information from the user. *Information Processing and Management, 27*(5), 523-532.

Hayes, P. J., Ball, J. E., & Reddy, R. (1981). Breaking the man-machine communication barrier. *Computer, 14*(3), 19-30.

Hert, C. A. (1996). User goals on an Online Public Access Catalog. *Journal of the American Society for Information Science, 47*(7), 504-518.

Hert, C. A. (1997). *Understanding information retrieval interaction: Theoretical and practical implications.* Greenwich, CO: Ablex.

Hildreth, C. R. (1982). *Online public access catalogs: The user interface.* Dublin, OH: OCLC.

Hildreth, C. R. (1985). Online public access catalogs. *Annual Review of Information Science and Technology, 20*, 223-285.

Hildreth, C. R. (1991). Advancing toward the E3OPAC: The imperative and the path. In N. V. Pulis (Ed.), *Think Tank on the Present and Future of the Online Catalog: Proceedings of American Library Association Midwinter Meeting,* (pp. 17-38). Chicago: Reference and Adult Services Division, American Library Association.

Hildreth, C. R. (1997). The use and understanding of keyword searching in a university online catalog. *Information Technology and Libraries, 16*(2), 52-62.

Hirsh, S. G. (1997). How do children find information of different types of tasks? Children's use of the science library catalog. *Library Trends, 45*(4), 725-745.

Kim, H., Chung, H., Hong, G., Moon, B., & Park, C. H. (1999). Correlations between users' characteristics and preferred features of Web-based OPAC evaluation. *ETRI Journal, 21*(4), 83-93.

Kochtanek, T. R., & Matthews, J. R. (2002). *Library information systems: From library automation to distributed information access solutions.* Westport, CO: Libraries Unlimited.

Large, A., & Beheshti, J. (1997). OPACs: A research review. *LISR, 19*(2), 111-133.

Larson, R. R., McDonough, J., O'Leary, P., Kuntz, L., & Moon, R. (1996). Cheshire II: Designing a next-generation online catalog. *Journal of the American Society for Information Science, 47*(7), 555-567.

Lewis, D. W. (1987). Research on the use of online catalogs and its implications for library practice. *Journal of Academic Librarianship, 13*(3), 152-157.

Mathias, E. C. (2003). Using a Web OPAC to deliver digital collections. *Online Information Review, 27*(1), 28-36.

Matthews, J. R. (1985). *Public access to online catalogs.* New York: Neal-Schuman.

Matthews, J. R., Lawrence, G. S., & Ferguson, D. (1983). *Using online catalogs: A nationwide survey.* New York: Neal-Schuman.

McCracken, P. (2003). Beyond title lists: Incorporating e-journals into the OPAC. *The Serials Librarian, 45*(1), 101-108.

Mendelsohn, J. (1994). Human help at OPAC terminals is user friendly: A preliminary study. *RQ, 34*(2), 173-190.

Morrison, H. G. (1999). Online catalogue research and the verbal protocol method. *Library Hi Tech, 17*(2), 197-206.

Nordlie, R. (1996). Unmediated and mediated information searching in the public library. In S. Hardin (Ed.), *Proceedings of the 59th ASIS Annual Meeting,* (Vol. 33, pp. 41-46). Medford, NJ: Learned Information.

Novotny, E. (2004). I don't think I click: A protocol analysis study of use of a library online catalog in the Internet Age. *College and Research Libraries, 65*(6), 525-537.

O'Brien, A. (1994). Online catalogs: Enhancements and developments. *Annual Review of Information Science and Technology, 29,* 219-241.

Pace, A. K. (2005). Technically speaking: My kingdom for an OPAC. *American Libraries, 36*(2), 48-49.

Pejtersen, A. M. (1979). Investigation of search strategies in fiction based on an analysis of 134 user-librarian conversations. In T. Henriksen (Ed.), *Proceedings of the 3rd International Research Forum in Information Research,* (pp. 107-132). Oslo, Norway: Statens Biblioteksskole.

Pejtersen, A. M. (1980). Design of a classification system for fiction based on analysis of actual user-librarian communications, and use of the scheme for control of librarians' search strategies. In O. Harboe & L. Kajberg (Eds.), *Theory and application of information research* (pp. 146-159). London: Mansell.

Pejtersen, A. M. (1989). The "Bookhouse:" An icon based database system for fiction retrieval in public libraries. In H. Clausen (Ed.), *Proceedings of the 7th Nordic Conference for Information and Documentation,* (pp. 1-19). Denmark: Aarhus University.

Peters, T. A. (1991). *The online catalog: A critical examination of public use.* Jefferson, NC: McFarland & Company.

Ramesh Babu, B., & O'Brien, E. A. (2000). Web OPAC interfaces: An overview. *Electronic Library, 18*(5), 316-327.

Rogers, M. (2001). WebFeat offers simultaneous search OPAC/Database. *Library Journal, 126*(6), 27.

Saffady, W. (1999). *Introduction to automation for librarians*. Chicago: ALA.

Seymour, S. (1991). Online public access catalog user studies: A review of research methodologies. *LISR, 13*(2), 89-102.

Slone, D. J. (2000). Encounters with the OPAC: Online searching in public libraries. *Journal of the American Society for Information Science, 51*(8), 757-773.

Slone, D. J. (2002). The influence of mental models and goals on search patterns during Web interaction. *Journal of the American Society for Information Science and Technology, 53*(13), 1152-1169.

Soloman, P. (1993). Children's information retrieval behavior: A case analysis of an OPAC. *Journal of the American Society for Information Science, 44*(5), 245-264.

Sridhar, M. S. (2004). Subject searching in the OPAC of a special library: Problems and issues. *OCLC Systems & Services: International Digital Library Perspectives, 20*(4), 183-191.

Sullivan, P., & Seiden, P. (1985). Educating online catalog users: The protocol assessment of needs. *Library Hi Tech, 3*(10), 11-19.

Theimer, S. (2002). When a 21st century user meets a 20th century OPAC: How word choice impacts search success. *Pacific Northwest Library Association Quarterly, 66*(3), 11-12, 23-24.

Wildemuth, B. M., & O'Neill, A. L. (1995). The "known" in known-item searches: Empirical support for user-centered design. *College and Research Libraries, 56*(3), 265-281.

Xie, H. (2000). Shifts of interactive intentions and information-seeking strategies in interactive information retrieval. *Journal of the American Society for Information Science and Technology, 51*(9), 841-857.

Xie, H. (2002). Patterns between interactive intentions and information-seeking strategies. *Information Processing and Management, 38*(1), 55-77.

Yang, S. C. (2003). Reconceptualizing think-aloud methodology: Refining the encoding and categorizing techniques via contextualized perspectives. *Computers in Human Behavior, 19*(1), 95-115.

Yee, M. M. (1991). System design and cataloguing meet the user: User interfaces to online public access catalogs. *Journal of the American Society for Information Science, 42*(2), 78-98.

Yee, M., & Layne, S. S. A. (1998). *Improving online public access catalogs.* Chicago: American Library Association.

Yu, H., & Young, M. (2004). The impact of Web search engine on subject searching in OPAC. *Information Technology and Libraries, 23*(4), 168-180.

Chapter III

Interactive IR in Online Database Environments

Overveiw of Online Database Environments

History and Background

The Internet has introduced the concept and capability of information retrieval to millions of users. There is an increasing growth in databases, producers, vendors, records, and searches. Williams (2006) has monitored the growth of the online industry for about 30 years. From 1975 to 2005, databases increased considerably, from 301 to 17539, database records from 52 million to 21.02 billion, and database entries from 301 to 16532. The number of producers has not grown as fast as databases because one producer might publish multiple databases. The number of publishers increased from 200 to 3208 from 1975 to 2005. In 2005, the average producer produced 5.13 databases. Because each vendor might provide services from multiple databases, the number of vendors grew at a slower pace from 105 to 2811.

According to Walker and Janes (1999), the development of online databases started in the 1960s. The US National Library of Medicine provided the off-line on-demand batch searching of their MEDLARS systems to Medical professionals in 1964. After that, Lockheed Missiles Corporation (Dialog), Systems Development Corporation (SDC), and Chemical Abstracts Service (CAS) developed their versions of search services. In 1968, Medline was the first to offer online dial-up service. Right after that, in 1972, Dialog and ORBIT (SDC) started commercial online services. Williams (2006) identified the major vendors of abstracting and indexing databases: OCLC (FirstSearch), Questel Orbit, STN International, Thomson Dialog (Dialog and DataStar), and the US National Library of Medicine. Vendors of numeric databases are Genios, Reuters, CSA, FIZ technik, and STN International. LexisNexis and Westlaw are popular vendors for law databases.

Definition of Online Databases and Major Elements of the Online Industry

An online database is a database of either full-text documents or citations and abstracts accessible via telephone or Internet connection. The online industry is responsible for the development, design, dissemination, and use of online databases and services. It consists of three basic elements: database producers, online vendors, and information searchers. Walker and Janes (1999) illustrated the three elements of the online industry:

- Database producers collect and index documents, and transfer the records into machine-readable form. Database producers consist of government agencies (e.g., National Library of Medicine), professional/academic organizations (e.g., American Psychological Association), and commercial organizations (e.g., Institute for Scientific Information).

- Online vendors create a common interface and common language for users to search for a variety of databases online. Some of the major vendors are discussed in the previous section.

- Information searchers are the users that search for online databases. Information professionals are the major searchers for online databases at the early stage of online database development, and they are the intermediaries between general users and online systems. In recent years, end users have become the searchers of online databases, because of the emergence of Internet and Web search engines as well as the simplified interfaces of online databases.

Traditionally online searching is conducted by information professionals including librarians. In their review of end user searching, Mischo and Lee (1987) concluded that because the availability of online searching, at that time, it was primarily trained intermediaries who had direct interaction with online databases. End users mainly interact with intermediaries about the search formulation and reformulation. This has been attributed to the high cost of online searching, the complexity of command language, and the variations in command language. Quint (1991a, 1991b) identified the seven stages of online searching by information professionals:

- Reference interview
- Tactical review
- Database selection
- Search strategy formulation
- The online search
- Feedback or reviewing results
- Presenting final search results

After the emergence of the Internet, some Windows-based online system providers transferred their services to the Web in the 1990s. According to Notess (1998), in 1998, increased consolidation of Web-based search systems and greater sophistication on the part of database vendors in their delivery of database information via the Web has emerged. Within this environment, some Windows-based online system providers moved their services to the Web environment. For example, in 1996, Dow Jones Interactive built a Web interface with all the functionality of the latest Windows software. The Dow Jones News/Retrieval software version 5.0 marks the transition for the entire service to a full Web interface (Feldman, 1996). In 1998, Lexis/Nexis developed eight information channels for Internet Explorer, including legal, insurance, and finance channels (Poynder, 1998).

End users gradually become searchers of online systems as more systems become available online. Marchionini (1995) defined a sequence of tasks for end users' information-seeking in an electronic environment:

- Selection of information source
- Query formulation
- Search execution
- Result examination
- Information extraction

- Information search reflection
- Iteration
- Completion

Xie and Cool (2000) specifically identified six subtasks that users have to go through in searching online databases:

- Database selection
- Query formulation
- Query reformulation
- Help mechanisms access
- Results organization and display
- Results delivery

Current Developments

The most significant development in online databases is the availability of Web versions of online database services. In general, Web interfaces are more intuitive and flexible to use. Koehler and Mincey (1996) compared the dial-up access and Web access method, and concluded that FirstSearch Web was a major improvement. Sabin-Kildiss, Cool, and Xie (2001) compared and evaluated eight Web versions of online systems—DialogWeb, Feactiva's Dow Jones Interactive (DJI) Publications Library, OCLC's FirstSearch Service, LexisNexis, ProQuestWeb, WilsonWeb, Ovid, and SilverPlatter—based on five evaluation criteria. They identified the following features in each of the criteria that a majority of the selected online systems had:

- **Database selection:** Database identification aids and simultaneous database searching.
- **Formulation/reformulation of searches:** Browsing indexes, vocabulary mapping, hotlinked subject terms/author names, varied search experience interface levels, command field searching capability, and search history.
- **Help mechanisms:** Easily located, well organized, field information provided, and some contextual help available.
- **Results presentation and organization:** Search statement included in view, number of viewable records can be defined, search terms highlighted, ability to select/deselect all records, sort record chronologically, sort by relevance, limit by publication type, and limit by date range.

- **Record management:** Clean format available, different file-save formats available, ability to e-mail records, and ability to include search history in e-mail.

Two fundamental characteristics of Web-based searching are that it is inherently interactive and that it facilitates a variety of ways for users to interact with both information and systems. Some of the significant characteristics of these new interactive access mechanisms are that they:

- Guide user access to a variety of databases
- Facilitate multiple interactive search strategies, such as browsing, searching, and so forth
- Assist mapping to thesaurus terms
- Offer a variety of help features
- Afford multiple manipulations of output
- Provide iterative movement by links

Researchers have worked to design expert systems to provide advices for novice users in online searching. For example, Zahir and Chang (1992) developed a prototype expert system to facilitate users in selecting databases by incorporating knowledge from human exerts and printed documents. Sutcliffe, Bennett, Doubleday, and Ryan (1995) designed the prototype of the Intelligent Strategy Planner (ISP) within the INTUTIVE system to offer intelligent help for novice users to formulate and reformulate their queries.

New developments in online databases focus on easy access. Online databases are no longer the exclusive province of information professionals. The era of inter-mediated searching contributed to the emergence of the current universal online databases with high quality (Quint, 2005). End users can access online databases at home and in the office via proxy servers of their institutions and libraries. For example, several states provide free online database services to their residents and have received positive feedback about these services (Xie & Wolfram, 2002). Rynkiewicz (2006) reported the Atlantic City Free Public Library delivered the services of online databases and a subject page of links of various topics on its Web site. The easy-to-use Web interfaces of online databases has contributed to these changes. In addition, the prices of online services are more affordable than before. Dialog is now offering its Dialog Choice pricing plan, featuring unlimited access to key research databases at fixed annual rates, to academic institutions worldwide (Sabroski, 2006). New technology also extends online services to users on the run. Chemical Abstracts Service (CAS) announced the emergence of CAS Mobile, which allows users to search CAS' chemical information database from hand-held devices (Anonymous, 2006a).

New developments in online databases also emphasize offering high-quality materials, as well as extending their collections backward to earlier times. Information Today (2006), H.W. Wilson has introduced color page images on its Wilson Web full-text periodicals databases. These images bring researchers the complete text consisting of accompanying charts, illustrations, diagrams, and other graphics (Anonymous, 2006b). ProQuest Information and Learning announced that it would digitize nearly six million pages of British periodicals from the 17th, 18th, 19th, and early 20th centuries (Rynkiewicz, 2006). The American Psychological Association (APA) will add the 1894 to 1984 archive from 24 APA journals to PsycARTICLES, to create the world's largest full-text database in psychology (Sabroski, 2005b).

Customization is another new development for the online industry. As part of the DialogLink 5 software package, Dialog offers users the ability to search for and edit graphical chemical structures for over 10 million chemical compounds, including drug pipeline databases and patent files (Sabroski, 2005a). H.W. Wilson announced the launch of WilsonWeb 2.5 for its online reference database. Users can automatically format their citations, export records to bibliographic software, use interlibrary loan services, and so forth (Anonymous, 2005).

In the near future, online databases will no longer be offered only by vendors. The general public can provide its own content for public access. Peek (2006) described the opening of Google Base, which organizes information in the world, and makes it universally available. People can submit their own items.

Challenges for Users

Almost every online database system has its Web version, and Web-based online systems have opened a new avenue for end users to retrieve information. However, the inherent interactive nature of Web-based online systems is double-sided. On the one hand, they are intuitive and easy to use; on the other, they are less efficient to control. Users prefer the ease-of-use of a variety of functions of Web interfaces, but they are also concerned that they might lose control in this new environment (Xie & Cool, 2000). On the other hand, not all functions of Web interfaces are easy to use. One of the most important characteristics of the Web-based interfaces is, as noted above, that they are interactive, and as such they provide a wider range of possibilities for searchers, which might bring greater complexity and require increased effort. Searchers want both greater user control and greater ease-of-use. They do not want one without the other. However, the existing online systems do not support both ease of use and user control. The emergence of Web-based IR systems calls for the need to support ease-of-use as well as user control (Xie, 2003).

One related issue is the diversity of user needs and preferences, in particular the differences between the skill levels of novice users and experienced users. Not everyone agrees that the Web interfaces are better than the non-Web interfaces of online databases. In studied comparisons of non-Web interfaces and Web interfaces of online databases, one issue emerges: it seems that experienced users do not benefit as much as novice users from the Web interfaces. For example, in a study of Web-searching behavior, van Brakel (1997) found that experienced online searchers seemed skeptical that Web interfaces could provide the same search sophistication level as traditional dial-up searching does. Bates (1997) compared Web-based packages—Dialog Web and DataStar Web—with the Classic, ASCII, dial-up version of Dialog that most experienced online searchers learned to search with. She acknowledged the benefits of the Web-based product, but also considered the Web-based product to be less efficient and responsive for the experienced searcher than the ASCII product. In a comparison of DataStar Web and DataStar command language searching, Barker (1998) concluded that although both interfaces offer access to the same information, there are significant differences. Many of these differences might affect retrieval effectiveness among both novice and experienced searchers alike.

Each online system has its own design, and in online systems, users can only rely on Help to help them. A well-designed Help mechanism facilitates the use of a system. In contrast, a poorly- designed Help mechanism hinders the use of a system. However, most Help mechanisms cannot satisfy user needs. After surveying 16 interactive information retrieval systems, Trenner (1989) found that online Help in interactive IR systems is inadequate, especially the commercial online systems. System designers need to explain to users how to access Help, how to find particular information, and how to exit Help. In addition, Help needs to be comprehensive and friendly; more important, Help needs to accommodate heterogeneous user groups. Xie and Cool (2000) compared Web interface and non-Web interface of the Help mechanisms of eight online systems. The results showed the overwhelming advantage of the Help mechanisms of Web interfaces over non-Web interfaces, except for Dow Jones' Interactive. The percentage of subjects that rated the system "somewhat more" or "a great deal" helpful for Web interfaces are Ovid Web (78.5%), WilsonWeb (57.2%), ProQuest Web (53.6%), FirstSearch Web (50%), and Dialog Web (46.4%) compared to non-Web interface such as Dialog (28.6%) and LexisNexis (25%). Many searchers in this study stressed the need for a system to offer help specific to their problems in the search process, and most of the Web interfaces did not provide the context-sensitive help that searchers needed. Often it was very difficult for users to figure out not only how to solve their problems but also how to characterize or name their problems.

Another problem derives from the conversion from printed materials to electronic formats. Mi and Nesta (2005) pointed out that content and context may be lost in online databases because full-text databases do not allow for the complexity of the interaction of the human eye and brain that printed materials do. A reader can easily comprehend the analytical materials on a printed page based on data elements, but the computer screen may not be able to provide supporting data because charts or tables may not be indexed. They presented several examples to show the loss of contexts in online databases; they further suggested that database producers and Web content designers to adopt new metatags to preserve context.

Research Overview

A series of review articles have been published about online databases and their uses. Based on the literature review of her doctoral dissertation, Bellardo (1985) surveyed the literature about online searchers. She focused on the personal traits of the best online searchers, especially expert intermediaries. This review also identified and discussed the factors that affect searching performance, such as searchers' institutional affiliation, training, experience, aptitudes, personality, creative orientation, as well as searching errors and searching style. After reviewing the historical development of online database searching by intermediaries, Mischo and Lee (1987) examined end user searching activities. They found that end users are keen to use inexpensive and user-friendly IR systems. However, they cannot perform as effective searches as trained intermediaries can.

Focusing on online database development and production, O'Neill and Vizine-Goetz (1988) reviewed diverse topics associated with online database quality, mainly error detection and the impact of errors. There are a variety of ways to detect and correct errors, including spelling correction, automated authority control, and duplicate detection. Vickery and Vickery (1993) reviewed different aspects of the design of online search interfaces, especially different online search aids offered to inexperienced searchers for effective retrieval. They further discussed the knowledge that should be incorporated into an interface design for providing search aids. They also pointed out that although design issues have become clear; little has been done to evaluate different aspects of design.

There are also large-scale studies about online searching worth noting. Saracevic and Kantor (1988a, 1988b, 1988c) conducted a large-scale study to investigate information-seeking and retrieval in online databases focusing on users, questions, effectiveness measures, searchers, searches, and overlap studies. Forty users submitted their search questions and evaluated the search results derived from Dialog searching performed by information professionals. This study provided insightful information about the context of user questions, questions' structure and classification, searchers' cognitive traits and decision-making, and different searches for the same questions in terms of overlapping in search terms and items retrieved. They further discussed implications for information searching and interface design. A joint research project conducted by the University of North Texas and the University of Sheffield, U.K., focused on the investigation of the mediated information retrieval process in the online database environment. The study tried to characterize different aspects of the information-seeking process, covering information seekers' situational contexts, information problems, uncertainty reduction, successive searching, cognitive styles, as well as cognitive and affective states. This project is guided by the theoretical framework of interactive information retrieval and human information behavior (Ellis et al., 2002; Ford, Wilson, Foster, Ellis, & Spink, 2002; Spink et al., 2002a, 2002b; Wilson, Ford, Ellis, Foster, & Spink, 2002).

Interaction Studies

Interaction studies on interactive IR in online database environments can be summarized into the following types: (1) tasks and their impact, (2) levels of search strategies, (3) shifts in search strategies, seeking stages, and foci, (4) users' knowledge structure, (5) searcher characteristics/cognitive styles/search styles, (6) ease of use vs. user control, and (7) evaluation criteria for interactive IR systems.

Tasks and their Impact

According to Kuhlthau's (1996) information-seeking process model, phases in task performance affect the types of information searched and different ways of searching. Based on Kuhlthau's model (1996), Vakkari and his associates (Pennanen & Vakkari, 2003; Vakkari, 2000a, 2000b, 2001; Vakkari & Hakala, 2000; Vakkari, Pennanen, & Serola, 2003) investigated how the task performance process is related to information retrieval by examining students' information-seeking process when writing a research proposal for a master's thesis. Students were asked to search in the LISA database three times in the process to collect data at the prefocus, focus formation, and postfocus phases. This longitudinal study demonstrated that stages of tasks affected the search tactics, terms selected, information sought, relevance judgments, and types of documents obtained. Varkkari (2000a) and Vakkari, Pennanen, and Serola (2003) also investigated how changes in users' problem stages were associated with changes in search tactics and term choices. The more focused users' understanding of their tasks, the more specified search terms, more operators, and more tactics were used. Varkkari (2000b) and Pennanen and Vakkari (2003) focused on the research of relationship between the changes in users' problem stages and types of information sought. They found in the prefocus stages, users were searching for background information and for theories and models for the research proposal. In the focus phase, they still sought what they were looking for in the first stage, but also acquired methods and focused information. In the final stage, users looked for specific information, and methods and empirical research results were also useful to them. Vakkari and Hakala (2000) explored how changes in problem stages affected changes in relevance criteria during the task performance process. There was a relationship between a changing understanding of task and how the relevance of documents was judged. The study showed that the more knowledge the user had of the problem, the fewer the number of relevant items generated. That is contradictory to Spink, Greisdorf, and Bateman's (1998) findings that higher knowledge of a problem led to a higher number of relevant documents and a lower number of partially relevant references. In Spink et al.'s study, the measurement of level of knowledge—not the stage in task performance—was attributed to the inconsistency. The results of these studies support Kuhlthau's model of the information search process. Simultaneously, Vakkari's theory is more specific in the area of information retrieval in terms of contributing information types, degree of relevance, relevance criteria, search terms, operators, and search tactics. Based on the findings of these studies, Vakkari (2001) further developed a theory of the task-based IR process.

Not only the task stages but also the levels of task complexity have impact on users' searching behavior. Applying pre- and post-search questionnaires, transaction logs, and postsession interviews, Shiri and Revie (2003) investigated the effects of topic complexity and familiarity on the cognitive and physical moves in online searching. The results showed that complex topics led to more cognitive and physical moves, which is comparable to the findings of Marchionini et al. (1991). This can also be explained by Byström and Järvelin's (1995) research that the increase in task complexity leads to the increase in the complexity of information need, the increase in the needs for domain information and problem-solving information, and the increase in the number of sources. The complexity of tasks can also be caused by the description of the tasks if these tasks are assigned. After investigating end user information-searching of the MEDLINE database, Sutcliffe, Ennis, and Watkinson (2000) found that the ambiguous statement of search tasks might contribute to the poor performance of these tasks.

While these studies determine that tasks have their impact on the information-seeking process and on search behavior, the issue is how to characterize tasks. There are still several questions to be answered:

- What are the relationships between tasks and goals?
- How can the complexity of tasks be defined?
- What are the other dimensions of tasks in addition to complexity?

Levels of Search Strategies

Search strategies are one of the major research areas in interactive IR in online database environments. When users conduct information searches, they must have some search strategies that are combinations of the choice of search terms, operators, and tactics (Vakkari, 2003). Researchers have examined search strategies from two levels. Tactics and moves represent search choices and actions in the search processes, while search strategies highlight the most frequently employed approaches in the search process.

Adapted from her own experience, the relevant literature, and comments from her colleagues and students, Bates (1979a) specified and grouped a set of 29 **information tactics** into the following four categories: monitoring tactics, file structure tactics, search formulation tactics, and term tactics. Monitoring tactics are tactics to track the search. File structure tactics are tactics to explore the file structure to find desired information, source, or file. Search formulation tactics are tactics to assist in the formulation and reformulation of searches. Term tactics are tactics to help select and revise terms in search formulation. According to Bates, "A search strategy is a plan for the whole search, while a tactic is a move made to further a search" (p. 207). Bates (1979b) further presented 17 idea tactics that help to create new ideas and provide resolutions to problems in information searching, such as think, brainstorm, mediate, consult, and so forth.

After analyzing an expert human intermediary's interactions with 17 information seekers in performing online searching, Shute and Smith (1993) discovered 13 knowledge-based search tactics in relation to broadening, narrowing, and changing topic scope. By observing and analyzing experienced searchers' online searches, Fidel (1985) identified a list of **moves** that modify query formulations. A move is defined as any change in formulating a query. Among them, 18 operational moves keep the meaning of query components unchanged, and 12 conceptual moves change the meaning of query components. Searchers made moves to reduce the size of a retrieved set, enlarge the size of a retrieved set, or improve both precision and recall. Shiri and Revie (2003) presented two categories of moves focusing on cognitive and physical aspects of user interaction with online IR systems. Cognitive moves refer to moves that users conceptually analyze terms or documents, while physical moves refer to moves that users use system features.

A number of studies have also examined search moves and tactics in various online searching databases, such as INQUIRER (Wildemuth, 2004), PsychINFO (Vakkari, Pennanen, & Serola, 2003), and MEDLINE (Sutcliffe, Ennis, & Watkinson, 2000). Despite numerous studies on search tactics and moves, Wildemuth (2004) pointed out that it is difficult to draw general conclusions because each study uses a different set of search move definitions. Bates (1990) further expanded tactics and moves into "**stratagem,**" which is a complex of number of moves or tactics that involve both information domains and modes of seeking. Studies of tactics and moves characterize users' search process at the microlevel, but these studies only concentrate on the tactics and moves themselves.

Focusing more on online search, Markey and Atherton (1978) analyzed users' **online search strategies**, identifying five basic types: building block, pearl-growing, successive-fractions, most-specific-facet-first, and lowest-postings-facet-first. Hawkins and Wagers (1982) labeled a frequently used **strategy** as "interactive scanning" that requires more user interaction with the system and information based on online bibliographic study. This strategy can make the best use of the interactive qualities of online systems. This approach is especially useful when a user is not familiar with the topic and needs high recall. Drabenstott (2003) identified that nondomain experts' information-seeking strategies are different from strategies applied by domain experts. Perseverance, trial-and-error, serendipity, and a combination of all three were employed in their information-seeking process.

After investigating the cognitive processes of users in online document-based information retrieval, Chen and Dhar (1991) found five types of **strategies** employed by users: the known-item instantiation strategy; the search-option heuristic strategy, which consists of a set of heuristics for applying each search option: heuristics for controlled subject search, for keyword subject search, title search, and keyword title search; the thesaurus-browsing strategy; the screen-browsing strategy; and the trial-and-error strategy. Some of the search strategies identified by different researchers in different names are actually the same. For example, Chen and Dhar's known-item instantiation strategy is similar to Markey and Atherton's pearl-growing. Chen and Dhar (1991) further discussed a cognitive-process-based design retrieval systems based on the findings of the studies. These search strategies are incorporated into the system as knowledge sources to assist users' online searching. Marchionini (1995) classified **search strategies** into two high levels of categories: analytical and browsing strategies. Analytic strategies are more goal-oriented and systematic, while browsing strategies are more informal and interactive.

Another issue highly related to search strategy is feedback. Feedback is referred to as interactive feedback in the context of interactive IR. Based on models of interactive IR, Spink (1997) and Spink and Saracevic (1998) identified five types of interactive feedback: content relevance feedback, term relevance feedback, magnitude feedback, tactical review feedback, and term review feedback. They extended Saracevic, Mokros and Su's (1990) two types of interactive feedback from relevance and magnitude to strategy judgments. Interactive relevance, magnitude, and strategy feedback are part of the online search process. The identification and incorporation of five types of interactive feedback enhanced the model of interactive IR.

Studies of levels of search strategies illustrate the information-seeking process and emphasize levels of search approaches that users take, but researchers fail to answer how appropriate search tactics/strategies are employed under different situations. In other words, what leads to the selection of different search tactics or strategies in the process of user-system interactions?

Shifts in Search Strategies/Stages/Foci

The nature of interactive information retrieval determines the dynamic process of information retrieval, which, in turn, also leads users to shift their strategies in the retrieval process. Research has been conducted in online environments about these shifts. Shenouda (1990) investigated 20 users' searching of Dialog in terms of how they modified their search strategies. The modifications focused on two types of actions: actions related to search strategy reformulation, for example, term addition, term deletion, facet addition, facet deletion, and so forth, and actions related to search strategy implementation, for example, following initial search strategy, reuse of search strategy, changing of databases, correcting error, and limitation of search results. These strategy modifications are actually search tactics modifications based on Bates' (1979a) definition of search tactics and search strategies.

Shifts in search stages are also the products of the interactive IR process. Analyzing the randomly selected data from the joint project conducted by the University of North Texas and the University of Sheffield, U.K., Olah (2005) identified 12 search stages, from search intentions to exit system/end task. She further illustrated the transition patterns between search stages. Either a user or an intermediary can initiate shifts. Shifting occurred in two patterns: a linear pattern and a reiterating pattern. The interaction process is composed of patterns of shifts, extent of shifts, and critical points of multiple shifts (e.g., database selection, review results, and delivery of results) in the interaction. The major contribution of her work is that she not only identified the shifts but also predicted the predictability of the shifting of search stages. Specifically, the research demonstrated that 63% of typical transitions occur outside the query formulation/result set loop. She further developed the model of shifting patterns. Shifts in information-seeking stages also occur in successive searching. In the mediated searching study of successive searching, Spink et al. (2002b) found that users shifted their information-seeking stages during and between successive searches. Different users experienced different levels of change at different times, for example, in the work stage of their topics, familiarity with their problems, completeness of the retrieval, satisfaction with results, and so forth.

Shifts in foci are another approach for studying interactions between users and intermediaries, further enabling researchers to understand users' shifts in behavior. Robins (1997, 2000) examined the interactions between users and intermediaries during the interactive IR process. The analysis of the discourses between the two parties in the retrieval process revealed that on average, users and intermediaries change topics every seven utterances. The majority of time in interaction was spent after the participants went online. Robins identified six focus areas: documents, evaluation of search results, search strategies, IR system, topic of the search, and information about the user. Among them, strategy and evaluation are the main foci of the interactions. This study also found that it was difficult to find a pattern of IR interaction because the interactions among user, search intermediary, and IR system bring more issues along the way. This study offers suggestions of strategy assistant and learning modules related to the evaluation of documents for IR system design.

As to what leads to shifts in search strategies/stages/foci, Shenouda's (1990) study demonstrated that the most frequent cause for modifications is the relevance of examined documents. Many users were not satisfied with the retrieved documents that forced them to modify their search tactics. In addition, information derived from interactions with documents and systems, domain knowledge, initiating searching, number of postings, and error discovery were also the driving force behind users' shifts in search tactics. Spink and Wilson (1999) and Spink (2002) explained that information seekers changed their behaviors during their information-seeking and problem-solving processes; this results from their interactions with IR systems and subsequent changes in their information problems. Robins (1997, 2000) pointed out that there are two reasons for the changes: situated aspects and the uncertainty of information problems. According to him, the majority of time in interaction was spent after the participants went online, which demonstrated that information retrieval is a dynamic process and is affected by situated aspects, as suggested by previous studies (Xie, 1998, 2000). At the same time, a majority of utterances were about participants' cognitive state and problem space, suggesting that they moved between certainty and uncertainty related to the information problem. Information searchers are not just passively shifting their search stages—they also have their plans and try hard to pursue them. Olah (2005) noted that the shifting between search stages outside of query formulation and results reviewing loop demonstrated that users not only react to the system response but also actively pursue their cognitive and operational strategies in their dynamic interaction with the IR systems. Hider (2007) discovered that the design of the IR system, such as the availability of abstract and hyperlinking descriptors, affects search goal redefinition. More in-depth studies need to be conducted to identify the factors that lead to shifts in strategies/stages/foci and the patterns between types of factors and types of shifts.

Users' Knowledge Structure

In the process of interaction with online databases, users' knowledge structure affects their online searching. Domain knowledge has an impact on users' search strategy and tactics. Shute and Smith (1993) examined domain knowledge's impact on on-line searching. An expert intermediary made extensive use of domain knowledge to generate suggestions for refining a topic; the intermediary also frequently applied knowledge-based search tactics in each search. In the expert's knowledge-based suggestions, 80.3% were generated spontaneously, which is more than another nonexpert intermediary's 47.8% suggestions. The results of the study help researchers to model cognitive processes of searchers, and further offer implications for computerized intermediary systems that suggest topic refinement for information seekers. Shiri and Revie's (2003) findings are partly consistent with Shute and Smith's (1993) results that topics identified as moderately or very familiar were connected with more cognitive and physical moves than topics identified as unfamiliar.

Domain knowledge has different effects on users with different levels of information retrieval knowledge. Hsieh-Yee (1993) further investigated the effects of subject knowledge on search tactics of novice as well as experienced users. After analyzing data collected by protocols, transaction logs, and observation, she found that subject knowledge affected experienced searchers' search tactics but not novice users' search tactics. In other words, subject knowledge does not have an effect on searching until only after users become experienced users. At the same time, searchers' experience affected their search tactics differently depending on whether they searched questions in their subject area or not. She suggested a new interface facilitating novice searchers' search style and promoting system features, for example, prompting features to guide novice users using system features. She also posed a question about system design: "Should an interface be designed to such a way that little adjustment would be required of its users? Or should it be designed to change their behavior as painlessly as possible?" (p. 170). However, not every study showed the effects of domain knowledge on online searching. For example, Wildemuth, de Blieck, Friedman, and File (1995) found that personal domain knowledge has little relationship to search proficiency, such as search results, term selection, efficiency, and so forth.

Information retrieval knowledge is also essential in online searching. The experience of online searchers also determines their behaviors and performance. Howard (1982) found that the most experienced group performed the most cost-effective searches and achieved the highest precision ratio. Siegfried, Bates, and Wilde (1993) discovered that scholars had a high level of competence in searching Dialog after one day of training. Sutcliffe, Ennis and Watkinson (2000) discovered the marked differences between novices' and experts' search behavior, especially in query construction. After monitoring a group of law students searching QUICKLAW, Yuan (1997) found that searching experience affected end user behavior, such as the increase in participants' set of commands and features used, increase in search speeds, change of learning approaches, and so forth. It is an effective approach for enhancing online IR systems by incorporating expert knowledge into systems. Fidel (1991) explored the process of search-key selection based on actual searches performed by professional online searchers. She developed the selection routine, which is a decision tree that searchers intuitively use when they select search keys. The selection routine was determined by two criteria: 1) whether a term is a common term or a single-meaning term, and 2) whether a term can be mapped to a descriptor. She suggested the incorporation of the selection routine into the knowledge base of intermediary expert systems.

One type of knowledge is not enough for users to effectively interact with online databases. Both domain knowledge and information retrieval knowledge are needed for online searching. Marchionini, Dwiggins, Katz, and Lin (1993) analyzed the roles of domain and search expertise in online information-seeking. A series of studies was conducted in searching hypertext or full-text CD-ROM and involving professional search intermediaries and domain exerts from computer science, business/economics and law. These studies demonstrated that information-seeking is a problem-solving process. It requires both domain and search knowledge. While domain knowledge helps experts quickly understand the problem and have clear expectation about possible answers, search knowledge helps professional searchers develop a high level of expertise both conceptually and procedurally, enabling them to effectively retrieve information. The major contribution of these studies is that the findings unveil different roles domain knowledge and search knowledge play in users' information retrieval process. More research needs to explore when and how users need different types of knowledge and the interplay among different types of knowledge.

Searcher Characteristics/Cognitive Styles/Search Styles

There is no agreement as to whether user characteristics affect their behavior and search performance. Harter (1984) pointed out there were wide differences in terms of online searchers' attitudes as well as behaviors. In early research, mathematical ability was found to be correlated with the ability to search interactively or with better search performance (Davis, 1977; Vigil, 1983). The reason might be that at that time, the design of online databases was more for expert intermediaries instead of end users. Bellardo (1985) investigated attributes of online searchers and their relationships to search outcome. The results indicated that verbal and quantitative GRE scores are predictors of searching skill, but only to a small extent. She raised doubts about whether searching performance can be predicted or determined by users' cognitive or personality traits.

Among all the personal characteristics, cognitive styles and search styles were the characteristics that had most impact on searching. Cognitive styles affect users' interactions with IR systems; to be more specific, information-seeking behavior and search performance. Cognitive styles are defined as "tendencies displayed by individuals consistently to adopt a particular type of information processing strategy" (Ford et al., 2002, p. 728). After correlating cognitive style measures with 111 postdoctoral researchers' perceptions of their problem-solving and information-seeking behavior and with those of the search intermediary who performed searches for them, Ford et al. (2002) found that field-independent users took a more analytic and active approach in retrieving information than field-dependent ones. Simultaneously, holists exhibited more exploratory and serendipitous behavior than serialists, who might prefer a step-by-step approach in seeking information. The results of the study help the development of models of interactive IR and design of interactive IR systems to facilitate users with different types of cognitive styles.

The findings of this study are consistent with a previous study of searching CD ROM databases, in which Ford, Wood, and Walsh (1994) also found that cognitive styles (global/analytic) were highly related to search behavior; specifically, global users employed more broad search strategies than analytic users. Cognitive styles influence search behavior as well as perceived search performance. For example, in a study of undergraduate students' online searches of CD ROM databases, users' cognitive styles (global/analytic) were found to be associated with levels of satisfaction with search results and perceived search success (Wood, Ford, Miller, Sobczyk, & Duffin, 1996).

According to Bellardo (1985), "interactive" and "fast batch" are the two types of searching styles that are the subject of investigation in early research. Many of the searchers were fast batch searchers who made little use of the interactive capabilities of online systems. They did not reformulate queries, nor did they browse titles of retrieved documents for relevancy (Fenichel, 1981; Oldroyd & Citroen, 1977). These studies explored the search styles of users, but they did not further analyze characteristics of search styles. After analyzing 47 professionals performing job-related searches, Fidel (1991) found that search styles, especially three characteristics of searching styles, have impact on searching behavior: the level of interaction during a search; the preference for types of moves, operational or conceptual; and the preference of type of search key, textwords, or descriptors. In particular, interactive searchers make more moves than less interactive searchers, but the level of interaction does not represent quality. Compared to conceptualist searchers, operationalist searchers use textwords more frequently, consult a thesaurus less, and make fewer recall moves. Textwords searchers are operationalist searchers, and do not use a thesaurus.

Cognitive styles and search styles are interrelated. Cognitive styles influence users' search styles. The existing research has explored cognitive styles and search styles and their impact on search behavior and search performance. Few researchers have investigated the relationships between cognitive styles and search styles. In addition, each style has its value and problems. Thus, the question is whether the design of online IR systems should guide users to different styles or introduce different styles to users so that they can integrate them together.

Ease of Use vs. User Control

Lancaster (1979) pointed out that ease-of-use is an important criterion for the selection of an information retrieval system. Krichmar (1981) compared Dialog's and ORBIT's command language in terms of their ease of use from users' attitudes and perceptions. His study is based on the following factors that define ease of use: the difficulty of recalling a command, the effort and frustration involved in entering a given command, the need to remember the sequence of argument values following a command, not completely understand the meaning of a command. The results showed that frustration with one or more important features of a system could have a negative impact on the perception of an entire system. Researchers have proposed measurable elements for ease of use, such as learnability, speed of user task performance, user error rates, and subjective user satisfaction (Hix & Hartson, 1993; Shneiderman & Plaisant, 2004). However, research on the standard measures for ease-of-use is ongoing. Furthermore, ease-of-use is a complicated concept involving different tradeoffs (Thimbleby, 1990).

Not every user prefers ease-of -use. Different users have different requirements for what they need IR systems to do for them. Ease-of -use vs. user control becomes an issue more for online databases because these IR systems were traditionally designed for information professionals and only recently started being designed for end users. These systems have to take into account needs of both novice and expert users. Bates (1990), in her influential article, asked a reflective question about online systems: "What capabilities should we design for the system, and what capabilities should we enable the searcher to exercise?" (p. 576).

Influenced by this idea, Xie (2003) studied users' evaluation of features of a variety of online databases in terms of ease-of-use and user control based on questionnaires, diaries, logs, and open-ended reports. The results showed that users considered both ease-of-use and user control as important for effective information retrieval. Users' requirements for ease-of-use and user control did change in the course of their interactions with the system and in the course of learning different systems. They needed more control after they had more understanding of IR systems and acquired more retrieval skills. The results also indicated that experienced users preferred more user control over novice users. While ease-of-use can mostly be achieved by system design, user control can only be accomplished by the collaboration between system design and user involvement. According to Vickery and Vickery (1993), user involvement is the decision that has to be made for interface design. Some interfaces only ask users for information statements, while others require users to be actively involved in the process of formulating search queries by providing guidance for users. More research is needed to define ease-of-use and user control from users' perspectives, in particular from different types of user groups to examine whether users have same perceptions of ease-of-use and user control.

Evaluation Criteria for Interactive Online IR Systems

Relevance is a traditional measurement for IR system evaluation, and it is also a crucial measurement for interactive IR systems. However there are issues that need to be dealt with for relevance judgment during user-system interactions. First, it is difficult to control the situational dynamism of user-centered relevance estimation during the interaction between users and systems. In studying subjects' engaging the LISA ondisc, Bruce (1994) identified a method to allow users to articulate the cognitive schema for estimating relevance at each phase of the IR interaction: problem state, system interaction, and document interaction. This methodology provides a mechanism for monitoring the impact of the IR interaction on user-centered relevance judgment. Second, it is difficult for users to have dichotomous choices for relevance judgment for interactive online systems. Researchers have defined the middle range of relevance to cover partially relevant and partially not relevant in addition to relevant and not relevant based mainly on what is missing and what is present by users (Greisdorf & Spink, 2001; Spink & Greisdorf, 2001; Spink, Greisdorf, & Bateman, 1998). After analyzing 32 users' searching and evaluating results derived from Dialog, Greisdor (2003) suggested that the relevance judgment process is a problem-solving and decision-making exercise involving cognitive activities. According to Greisdor (2003), users went through a multiple-stage process of relevance evaluation during IR system interaction, and considered the topicality, pertinence, and then utility of a retrieved item in relevance judgment. Not on topic, not pertinent, not useful, and useful can be associated to not relevant, partially not relevant, partially relevant, and relevant, respectively.

IR system evaluation is a crucial component of IR research. The key question is what the unique criteria for evaluating interactive IR systems are. Su (1992, 1994) conducted a study to identify appropriate measures for evaluating interactive information retrieval. After analyzing the data from 40 users' interactions with six professional intermediaries searching large online systems, she tried to identify the best evaluation measures for interactive IR performance. The results revealed that value of search results is the best single measure for IR performance. Users' satisfaction with search results and users' satisfaction with precision of the search were strongly correlated with value of search results. However, precision is not significantly correlated with success. To users, recall is more important than precision. There are several reasons for this: first, high precision does not mean high quality, and users' satisfaction with precision is a better indicator of IR performance. Second, users' tasks that lead them to look for information also affect whether recall is more important to them. The high percentage of users in this study that require complete information to accomplish their tasks (e.g., dissertation/thesis, grant application, etc.) also influences the result. Users' satisfaction with the completeness of the search results, users' confidence in the completeness of the search results, and users' satisfaction with the precision of the search may serve as good measures of interactive search performance. Both interaction and effectiveness factors are important in IR evaluation, and interaction factors are more important than effectiveness factors. In addition, time is a significant factor of success.

Su's findings demonstrate that relevance is not the only measurement for IR system evaluation. Her identified measurements were partly verified by other studies. Hersh, Pentecost, and Hickam (1996) compared two commercial MEDLINE systems by applying a task-oriented approach to IR system evaluation, including measuring success at answering questions, user certainty in answering questions, time to answer questions, ability to find relevant articles, and satisfaction with the user interface. They concluded that the task-oriented approach was an effective evaluation method for assessing IR systems in terms of whether these systems can be used to solve real information problems. In their large-scale study, Saracevic and Kantor (1988b, 1988c) discussed the five utility measures (worth scale, user's time, dollar value assigned, problem resolution scale, and satisfaction scale) as effectiveness measures for IR systems in addition to precision and recall, especially their relationships with relevance odds. They found that when relevance and precision odds increased, users considered the results to be worth more time, to have high dollar values, to make a high contribution to the problem solution, and to provide a high level of satisfaction. One utility measure is related to recall odds. When recall odds increased, less time was taken for users to evaluate results. The major contribution of this study is the identification of the utility measures and their relationship to relevance odds. Although researchers used different terms to name evaluation criteria, they identified similar key evaluation criteria. However, the identified evaluation criteria mainly focused on the search performance of online systems, they failed to assess the user-system interaction process in online searching.

Summary

One unique phenomenon in online database environments is that intermediary studies have accounted for a large portion of the interactive studies mainly because professional intermediaries were the main searchers of online databases before the emergence of the Web. The cost and complexity of command language have contributed to the problem. At the same time, intermediary studies can shed some lights on how users interact with searchers, online systems, and documents. In online environments, intermediary studies have contributed to the research on domain knowledge's impact on online searching by Shute and Smith (1993); types of interactive feedback by Spink (1997) and Spink and Saracevic (1998); cognitive styles affecting information seeking behavior by Ford et al. (2002); shifts in search problems/stages/focus by Robins (1997, 2000), Spink and Wilson (1999) and Olah (2005); intermediaries' elicitation styles by Wu and Liu (2003); and evaluation criteria for interactive IR systems by Su (1992, 1994). Many of these studies also suggest how to incorporate their findings into system design, specifically to implement the role of the intermediary into the design of online IR systems. Table 3.1 presents a summary of interaction studies in online database environments.

Task studies enable researchers to understand the impetus for information retrieval and to further develop theories of task-based IR process. The remaining question is: What is the relationship between tasks and user goals? User goals are also considered the driving force of information retrieval, as discussed in chapter 2. Are tasks a part of user goals? How can tasks and user goals be defined? In addition, how can the complexity of tasks be defined? Are levels of task complexity different for different users, or is there a standard way to define them? What are the other dimensions of tasks that influence online searching? These questions need to be investigated further.

Levels of search strategies are the center of attention in interaction studies of online databases. Compared with OPAC studies, researchers have conducted more in-depth studies on search strategies, and have identified different types of micro- and macro-levels of strategies. However, the strategy studies are still on the level of the identification of the types of search strategies; they do not go further to explore what lead to the users' application of different search strategies. In addition, researchers need to further examine the relationships among tactics, moves, and strategies. Are tactics and moves a part of strategies, and if so, how are strategies constituted by them? Identification of shifts in search strategies, stages, and foci is just the first step in understanding users' information-seeking behavior during their interactions with intermediaries, IR systems, and information. In order to design IR systems to facilitate those shifts, we need to further identify the patterns between the shifts and the factors that lead to the shifts.

In general, researchers agree that domain knowledge and information retrieval knowledge affect users' information-seeking behavior and search performance. Expert users can make better use of domain knowledge than novice users. While providing term selection is a popular tool for assisting domain knowledge, offering different interfaces for expert users as well as novice users is a suggestion for offering retrieval knowledge help. However, research on knowledge structure has not been incorporated into the design of Help systems for online databases. That is why online Help is inadequate in existing online systems (Trenner, 1989; Xie & Cool, 2000). Further research needs to look into when and how users need different types of knowledge, and the interactions among different types of knowledge and their impact.

Although there is a disagreement about whether searcher characteristics affect search performance, researchers do agree that searcher characteristics, especially their cognitive styles/search styles, do influence searchers' behavior. Interactive IR systems need to be designed to help users with different cognitive styles/search

Table 3.1. Summary of interaction studies in online database environments

Types	Research Focus	Problems/Questions	Implications
Tasks and their impact	Impact of stages of tasks on search behavior and search performance; Impact of complexity of tasks on search behavior and search performance.	What are the relationships between tasks and user goals? How can levels of task complexity be defined? What are the other dimensions of tasks that influence online searching?	Develop theory of task-based IR process; Understand the driving force for information retrieval; Incorporate the stages of tasks and corresponding information seeking behavior into system design.
Levels of search strategies	Types of search tactics, moves, and search strategies.	What are the relationships among search tactics, moves, and search strategies? What factors affect different levels and types of search strategies?	Understand patterns of search behavior; Design IR systems to facilitate users applying different levels and different types of search strategies.
Shifts in search strategies, seeking stages, and foci	Shifts in search strategies, seeking stages, foci; Factors leading to shifts in strategies, stages, and foci.	What are the patterns among factors that lead to the shifts and shifts in strategies/stages/ foci?	Understand the nature of interactions between users and intermediaries, IR systems, and information; Design IR systems to facilitate/guide the shifts.
Users' knowledge structure	Domain knowledge and information retrieval knowledge affect search behavior and search performance	When and how users do need different types of knowledge? What are the interplays among different types of knowledge and their impact on online searching?	Provide term selection to assist users with domain knowledge; Offer multiple interfaces to novice users and expert users.
Searcher characteristics/ Cognitive Styles/Search Styles	Attitudes, mathematic ability, cognitive styles, and search styles and their impact on search behavior and search outcome.	What are the relationships between cognitive styles and search styles? What role should systems play: try to help users with different styles or introduce all the styles to users so they can integrate different styles?	Understand the impact of users' characteristics on their search behavior and search performance; Design IR systems to facilitate users with different cognitive/search styles.

continued on following page

Table 3.1. continued

Ease-of-use vs. user control	Ease-of use vs. user control; System role and user involvement.	Do users from diverse user groups have the same perceptions of ease-of-use and user control?	Understand what users desire for ease-of-use and user control; Design IR systems to balance system role and user involvement.
Evaluation of interactive IR systems	System performance criteria; Utility criteria.	How can interactive IR systems be defined? What are the criteria needed to evaluate the interaction process between users and online IR systems?	Determine the appropriate criteria for evaluating interactive IR systems; Improve the interactivity of existing IR systems based on evaluation results.

styles. While the cognitive styles of users affect their search styles, the relationships between cognitive styles and search styles need to be further explored. Each style has its benefits and problems. The problem is whether system design should just try to help users with different styles or it should guide users to integrate different styles.

In order to design effective interactive IR systems, it is important to understand what users desire for ease-of-use and user control. IR system design needs to consider system role as well as user involvement. The key point is that we need more research to understand users' perceptions of ease-of-use and user control from diverse groups, such as novice users vs. expert users, female users vs. male users, younger users vs. older users, and so forth.

In order to design effective interactive IR systems, it is also important to identify the criteria for evaluating those systems. Research on the evaluation of online IR systems focuses on the identification of the appropriate criteria for improving the interactivity of existing IR systems. However, in these studies, there is no clear definition of interactive IR systems. Moreover, the evaluation criteria are limited to system performance and utility; they need to be extended to assess the interaction process between users and systems.

References

Anonymous. (2005). H. W. Wilson unveils WilsonWeb 2.5. *Information Today, 22*(8), 51-52.

Anonymous. (2006). Scientific online searching via handhelds. *Information Today, 23*(1), 36.

Anonymous. (2006b). H.W. Wilson periodicals databases offer color pages. *Information Today*, 23(2), 35.

Barker, A. L. (1998). DataStar Web: A comparison with "Classic" DataStar command language searching. *Online and CD-ROM Review, 22*(3), 155-167.

Bates, M. J. (1979a). Information search tactics. *Journal of the American Society for Information Science, 30*(4), 205-214.

Bates, M. J. (1979b). Idea tactics. *Journal of the American Society for Information Science, 30*(5), 280-289.

Bates, M. J. (1990). Where should the person stop and the information search interface start? *Information Processing and Management, 26*(5), 575-591.

Bates, M. E. (1997). Knight-Ridder on the Web: A brave new world for searchers? *Searcher, 5*(6), 28-37.

Bellardo, T. (1985). What do we really know about online searchers? *Online Review, 9*(3), 223-239.

Bruce, H. W. (1994). A cognitive view of the situational dynamism of user-centered relevance estimation. *Journal of the American Society for Information Science, 45*(3), 142-148.

Byström, K., & Järvelin, K. (1995). Task complexity affects information seeking and use. *Information Processing and Management, 31*(2), 191-213.

Chen, H., & Dhar, V. (1991). Cognitive processes as a basis for intelligent retrieval system design. *Information Processing and Management, 27*(5), 405-432.

Davis, C. H. (1977). Computer programming for librarians. *Journal of Education for Librarianship, 18*(1), 41-52.

Drabenstott, K. M. (2003). Do nondomain experts enlist the strategies of domain experts? *Journal of the American Society for Information Science and Technology, 54*(9), 836-854.

Ellis, D., Wilson, T. D., Ford, N., Foster, A., Lam, H. M., Burton, R., et al. (2002). Information seeking and mediated searching: Part 5. User-intermediary interaction. *Journal of the American Society for Information Science and Technology, 53*(11), 883-893.

Feldman, S. E. (1996). Dow Jones Interactive News/Retrieval's new software: Something for everyone. *Searcher, 4*(6), 42-48.

Fenichel, C. H. (1981). Online searching: Measures that discriminate among users with different types of experience. *Journal of the American Society for Information Science, 32*(1), 23-32.

Fidel, R. (1985). Moves in online searching. *Online Review, 9*(1), 61-74.

Fidel, R. (1991). Searchers' selection of search keys: I. The selection routine: II. Controlled vocabulary or free-text searching: III. Searching styles. *Journal of the American Society for Information Science, 42*(7), 490-527.

Ford, N., Wilson, T. D., Foster, A., Ellis, D., & Spink, A. (2002). Information seeking and mediated searching: Part 4. Cognitive styles in information seeking. *Journal of the American Society for Information Science and Technology, 53*(9), 728-735.

Ford, N., Wood, F., & Walsh, C. (1994). Cognitive styles and searching. *Online and CD-ROM Review, 18*(2), 79-86.

Greisdorf, H. (2003). Relevance thresholds: A multi-stage predictive model of how users evaluate information. *Information Processing and Management, 39*(3), 403-423.

Greisdorf, H., & Spink, A. (2001). Median measure: An approach to IR system evaluation. *Information Processing and Management, 37*(6), 843-857.

Harter, S. P. (1984). Online searching styles: An exploratory study. *College and Research Libraries, 45*(4), 249-258.

Hawkins, D.T., & Wagers, R. (1982). Online bibliographic search strategy development. *Online, 6*(3), 12-19.

Hersh, W., Pentecost, J., & Hickam, D. (1996). A task-oriented approach to information retrieval evaluation. *Journal of the American Society for Information Science, 47*(1), 50-56.

Hider, P. M. (2007). Search goal redefinition through user-system interaction. *Journal of Documentation, 63*(2), 188-203.

Hix, D., & Hartson, H. R. (1993). *Developing user interfaces: Ensuring usability through product and process*. New York: John Wiley & Sons.

Howard, H. (1982). Measures that discriminate among online users with different training and experience. *Online Review, 6*(4), 315-326.

Hsieh-Yee, I. (1993). Effects of search experience and subject knowledge on the search tactics of novice and experienced searchers. *Journal of the American Society for Information Science, 44*(3), 161-174.

Koehler, W. C., & Mincey, D. (1996). FirstSearch and NetFirst-Web and dial-up access: Plus ca change, plus c'est la meme chose? *Searcher, 4*(6), 24-28.

Krichmar, A. (1981). Command language ease-of-use: A comparison of DIALOG and ORBIT. *Online Review, 5*(3), 227-240.

Kuhlthau, C. C. (1996). The concept of a zone of intervention for identifying the role of intermediaries in the information search process. In S. Hardin (Ed.), *Proceedings of the 59th ASIS Annual Meeting* (Vol. 33, pp. 91-94). Medford, NJ: Information Today.

Lancaster, F. W. (1979). *Information retrieval systems: Characteristics, testing, and evaluation.* New York: John Wiley & Sons.

Marchionini, G. (1995). *Information-seeking in electronic environments.* Cambridge, MA: Cambridge University Press.

Marchionini, G., Dwiggins, S., Katz, A., & Lin, X. (1993). Information seeking in full-text end-user-oriented search-systems: The roles of domain and search expertise. *Library and Information Science Research, 15*(1), 35-69.

Marchionini, G., Meadow, C. T., Dwiggins, S., Lin, X., Wang, J., & Yuan, W. (1991). A study of user interaction with information retrieval interfaces: Progress report. *The Canadian Journal of Information Science, 16*(4), 42-59.

Markey, K., & Atherton, P. (1978). *ONTAP. Online training and practice manual for ERIC database searchers.* Syracuse, NY: ERIC Clearinghouse on Information Resources.

Mi, J., & Nesta, F. (2005). The missing link: Context loss in online databases. *Journal of Academic Librarianship, 31*(6), 578-585.

Mischo, W. H., & Lee, J. (1987). End-user searching of bibliographic databases. *Annual Review of Information Science and Technology, 22*, 227-263.

Notess, G. R. (1998). The year databases moved to the Web. *Database, 21*(6), 56-58.

O'Neill, E. T., & Vizine-Goetz, D. (1988). Quality-control in online databases. *Annual Review of Information Science and Technology, 23*, 125-156.

Olah, J. (2005). Shifts between search stages during task-performance in mediated information seeking interaction. In A. Grove (Ed.), *Proceedings of the 68th ASIST Annual meeting,* (Vol. 42, No. 1). Retrieved January 2, 2008, from http://eprints.rclis.org/archive/00005262/01/Olah_Shifts.pdf

Oldroyd, B. K., & Citroen, C. L. (1977). Study of strategies used in online searching. *Online Review, 1*(4), 293-310.

Peek, R. (2006). Google Base mayhem. *Information Today, 23*(1), 17-18.

Pennanen, M., & Vakkari, P. (2003). Students' conceptual structure, search process and outcome while preparing a research proposal. *Journal of the American Society for Information Science, 54*(8), 759-770.

Poydner, R. (1998). Lexis-LEXIS-NEXIS: Past and future. *Online and CD-ROM Review, 22*(2), 73-80.

Quint, B. (1991a). Inside a searcher's mind: The seven stages of an online search-Part 1. *Online, 15*(3), 13-18.

Quint, B. (1991b). Inside a searcher's mind: The seven stages of an online search-Part 2. *Online, 15*(4), 28-35.

Quint, B. (2005). The elusive un-client. *Searcher, 13*(7), 4-5.

Robins, D. (1997). Shifts of focus in information retrieval interaction. In C. Schwartz & M. Rorvig (Eds.), *Proceedings of the 60th ASIS Annual Meeting,* (Vol. 34, pp. 123-134). Medford, NJ: Information Today.

Robins, D. (2000). Interactive information retrieval: Context and basis notions. *Informing Science, 3*(2), 57-61.

Rynkiewicz, R. P. (2006). Delivering services to patrons' doorsteps. *Computers in Libraries, 26*(2), 55-56.

Sabin-Kildiss, B., Cool, C., & Xie, H. (2001). Assessing the functionality of Web-based versions of traditional search engines. *Online, 25*(2), 18-26.

Sabroski, S. (2005a). Dialog. *Online, 29*(4), 8.

Sabroski, S. (2005b). Social science and humanities. *Online, 29*(5), 6.

Sabroski, S. (2006). Online services. *Online, 30*(1), 11.

Saracevic, T., & Kantor, P. (1988a). A study of information seeking and retrieving: I. Background and methodology. *Journal of the American Society for Information Science, 39*(3), 161-176.

Saracevic, T., & Kantor, P. (1988b). A study of information seeking and retrieving: II. Users, questions, and effectiveness. *Journal of the American Society for Information Science, 39*(3), 177-196.

Saracevic, T., & Kantor, P. (1988c). A study of information seeking and retrieving: III. Searchers, searches, and overlap. *Journal of the American Society for Information Science, 39*(3), 197-216.

Saracevic, T., Mokros, H., & Su, L. (1990). Nature of the interaction between users and intermediaries in online searching: A qualitative analysis. In D. Henderson (Ed.), *Proceedings of the 53rd ASIS Annual Meeting,* (Vol. 27, pp. 47-54). Medford, NJ: Learned Information.

Shenouda, W. A. (1990). *Online bibliographic searching: How end users modify their search strategies in the light of new information presented during their interaction with an information retrieval system.* Unpublished doctoral dissertation, Rutgers University, New Brunswick, New Jersey.

Shiri, A. A., & Revie, C. (2003). The effects of topic complexity and familiarity on cognitive and physical moves in a thesaurus-enhanced search environment. *Journal of Information Science, 29*(6), 517-526.

Shneiderman, B., & Plaisant, C. (2004). *Designing the user interface: Strategies for effective human-computer interaction reading* (4th ed.). Reading, MA: Addison-Wesley.

Shute, S. J., & Smith, P. J. (1993). Knowledge-based search tactics. *Information Processing and Management, 29*(1), 29-45.

Siegfried, S., Bates, M. J., & Wilde, D. N. (1993). A profile of end-user searching behavior by humanities scholars: The Getty online searching project (Rep. No. 2). *Journal of the American Society for Information Science, 44*(5), 273-291.

Spink, A. (1997). Study of interactive feedback during mediated information retrieval. *Journal of the American Society for Information Science, 48*(5), 382-394.

Spink, A. (2002). A user-centered approach to evaluating human interaction with Web search engines: An exploratory study. *Information Processing and Management, 38*(3), 401-426.

Spink, A., & Greisdorf, H. (2001). Regions and levels: Measuring and mapping users' relevance judgments. *Journal of the American Society for Information Science and Technology, 52*(2), 161-173.

Spink, A., Greisdorf, H., & Bateman, J. (1998). From highly relevant to not relevant: Examining different regions of relevance. *Information Processing and Management, 34*(5), 599-622.

Spink, A., & Saracevic, T. (1998). Human-computer interaction in information retrieval: Nature and manifestation of feedback. *Interacting with Computers, 10*(3), 249-267.

Spink, A., & Wilson, T. D. (1999). Toward a theoretical framework for information retrieval (IR) evaluation in an information seeking context. In *Proceedings of MIRA 99: Evaluation Framework for Multimedia Information Retrieval Applications,* (pp. 75-92). Scotland: Department of Computing Sciences, University of Glasgow.

Spink, A., Wilson, T. D., Ford, N., Foster, A., & Ellis, D. (2002a). Information-seeking and mediated searching: Part 1. Theoretical framework and research design. *Journal of the American Society for Information Science and Technology, 53*(9), 695-703.

Spink, A., Wilson, T. D., Ford, N., Foster, A., & Ellis, D. (2002b). Information seeking and mediated searching study: Part 3. Successive searching. *Journal of the American Society for Information Science and Technology, 53*(9), 716-727.

Su, L. T. (1992). Evaluation measures for interactive information retrieval. *Information Processing and Management, 28*(4), 503-516.

Su, L. T. (1994). The relevance of recall and precision in user evaluation. *Journal of the American Society for Information Science, 45*(3), 207-217.

Sutcliffe, A. G., Bennett, I., Doubleday, A., & Ryan, M. (1995). Designing query support for multiple databases. In K. Nordby, P. H. Helmersen, D. J. Gilmour, & S. A. Arnesen (Eds.), *Proceedings of INTERACT-95,* (pp. 207-212). London: Chapman and Hall.

Sutcliffe, A. G., Ennis, M., & Watkinson, S. J. (2000). Empirical studies of end-user information searching. *Journal of the American Society for Information Science, 51*(13), 1211-1231.

Thimbleby, H. (1990). *User interface design.* New York: Addison-Wesley.

Trenner, L. (1989). A comparative survey of the friendliness of online "help" in interactive information retrieval systems. *Information Processing & Management, 25*(2), 119-136.

Vakkari, P. (2000a). Cognition and changes of search terms and tactics during task performance: A longitudinal study. In *Proceedings of the RIAL 2000 Conference,* (pp. 894-907). Paris: C.I.D.

Vakkari, P. (2000b). Relevance and contributory information types of searched documents in task performance. In *Proceedings of the 23rd Annual International ACM SIGIR Conference on Research and Development in Information Retrieval,* (pp. 2-9). New York: ACM Press.

Vakkari, P. (2001). A theory of the task-based information retrieval process. *Journal of Documentation, 57*(1), 44-60.

Vakkari, P. (2003). Task-based information searching. *Annual Review of Information Science and Technology, 37*, 413-464.

Vakkari, P., & Hakala, N. (2000). Changes in relevance criteria and problem stages in task performance. *Journal of Documentation, 56*(5), 540-562.

Vakkari, P., Pennanen, M., & Serola, S. (2003). Changes of search terms and tactics while writing a research proposal. *Information Processing and Management, 39*(3), 445-463.

van Brakel, P. A. (1997). Online database vendors: Will they transform to pull technology? *South African Journal of Library and Information Science, 65*(4), 234-242.

Vickery, B., & Vickery, A. (1993). Online search interface design. *Journal of Documentation, 49*(2), 103-187.

Vigil, P. J. (1983). The psychology of online searching. *Journal of the American Society for Information Science, 34*(4), 281-287.

Walker, G., & Janes, J. (1999). *Online retrieval: A dialogue of theory and practice* (2nd ed.). Englewood, CO: Libraries Unlimited.

Wildemuth, B. M. (2004). The effect of domain knowledge on search tactic formulation. *Journal of the American Society for Information Science and Technology, 55*(3), 246-258.

Wildemuth, B.M, de Blieck, R., Friedman, C., & File, D. (1995). Medical students' personal knowledge, searching proficiency, and database use in problem solving. *Journal of the American Society for Information Science, 46*(8), 590-607.

Williams, M. (2006). The state of databases today. In *2006 gale girectory of databases 2006*. Detroit, MI: Gale Research.

Wilson, T.D., Ford, N., Ellis, D., Foster, A., & Spink, A. (2002). Information seeking and mediated searching: Part 2. Uncertainty and its correlates. *Journal of the American Society for Information Science and Technology, 53*(9), 704-715.

Wood, F., Ford, N., Miller, D., Sobczyk, G., & Duffin, R. (1996). Information skills, searching behavior and cognitive styles for student centered learning: A computer assisted learning approach. *Journal of Information Science, 22*(2), 79-92.

Wu, M. M., & Liu, Y. H. (2003). Intermediary's information seeking, inquiring minds, and elicitation styles. *Journal of the American Society for Information Science and Technology, 54*(12), 1117-1133.

Xie, H. (1998). Access to online database: An exploration of users' experiences with Web interfaces. In M. E. Williams (Ed.), *Proceedings of the 19th National Online Meeting*, (pp. 481-494). Medford, NJ: Information Today.

Xie, H. (2000). Shifts of interactive intentions and information-seeking strategies in interactive information retrieval. *Journal of the American Society for Information Science, 51*(9), 841-857.

Xie, H. (2003). Supporting ease-of-use and user control: Desired features and structure of Web-based online IR systems. *Information Processing and Management, 39*(6), 899-922.

Xie, H., & Cool, C. (2000). Ease-of-use vs. user control: An evaluation of Web and nonWeb interfaces of online databases. *Online Information Review, 24*(2), 102-115.

Xie, H., & Wolfram, D. (2002). State digital library usability: Contributing organizational factors. *Journal of the American Society for Information Science and Technology, 53*(13), 1085-1097.

Yuan, W. (1997). End-user searching behavior in information retrieval: A longitudinal study. *Journal of the American Society for Information Science, 48*(3), 218-234.

Zahir, S., & Chang, C. L. (1992). Online-expert: An expert system for online database selection. *Journal of the American Society for Information Science, 43*(5), 340-357.

Chapter IV

Interactive IR in Web Search Engine Environments

Overview of Web Search Engine Environments

History and Background

Tim Berners-Lee wrote the initial proposal for the World Wide Web in 1989, and developed it online in 1991 by using a hypertext model (Berners-Lee, 1989, 1996). The World Wide Web was developed to allow people to collaborate on projects; it began at CERN, the European Particle Physics Laboratory in Geneva, Switzerland, and expanded across nations and disciplines. Berners-Lee (1996) defined the components of the Web: the boundless information world, the address system (URI), a network protocol (HTTP), a markup language (HTML), a body of data, and the client-server architecture of the Web. The creation in 1993 of Mosaic, a graphic Web interface that was the precursor of Netscape, enabled millions of people to easily access the Web. Since then, the increase in Web resources has been phenomenal, and Web search engines are the essential tools for navigating those Web resources.

The emergence of the Web signifies the era of end users. In IR history, this is the first time that millions of users have been able to search for online information themselves without help from intermediaries. Nielsen//NetRatings (Sullivan, 2006), a global leader in Internet media and market research, reported that the volume of Internet search queries grew to more than 5.1 billion by October 2005; the top five search engines are Google, Yahoo!, MSN, AOL, and Ask Jeeves.

Montgomery and Faloutsos (2001) analyzed data collected from Internet users from 1997 to 1999 and found that Internet usage had grown dramatically. However, the way users interact with the Web remains same, and their viewing habits have not changed despite changes in Web size and content. Hills and Argyle (2003) surveyed 220 adults to assess the frequency and location of their use of Internet services. The results showed that getting information in general is the second most popular service used by participants. One hundred seventy of the participants searched the Web, and the mean frequency of use was 3.27 (between sometimes to frequently). According to Fox (2002), 85% of American Internet users have used search engines to find information. For a typical day, men (33%) and college students (39%) are more likely to use a search engine than women (25%) and high school graduates (20%). Search engines are the most popular tools for finding health, government, and religious information. Based on the 2004 digital future report (USC Annenberg School, Center for the Digital Future, 2004), Web surfing, or browsing (ranked 2nd), finding hobby information (ranked 4th), finding entertainment information (ranked 5th), finding medical information (ranked 7th), and finding travel information (ranked 8th). About 77.2% of users used the Internet for Web surfing and browsing. The results of this study are comparable to the previous data.

Definitions and Types of Web Search Engines

Search engines include crawler-based engines, human-powered directories, and hybrid search engines. Search engines in general can be classified into four types:

1.   Web directories are hierarchically organized indexes that guide users in browsing through lists of Web sites by category or subject, such as Yahoo! Directory (http://www.dir.yahoo.com).

2.   Search engines create a database of sites using robots or spiders, and they assist users in searching for information, such as Google (http://www.google.com).

3.   Meta-search engines query multiple search engines simultaneously and return a complete set of hits, such as MetaCrawler (http://www.metacrawler.com).

4.   Specialized search engines create a database of sites on a specific topic using robots or spiders, such as Diseases, Disorders, and related topics (www.mic. ki.se/Diseases/index.html).

Sullivan (2004) provided a guide for users to choose major Web search engines based on their reputation and usage. The top choices are: Google for its comprehensive coverage and great relevancy, Yahoo for its excellent search results and oldest directory, and AskJeeves for its smart search. Those strongly considered are: AllTheWeb. com for its customizability, AOL search for AOL users, Hotbot for easy access to three major crawler-based search engines, and Teoma for its relevancy and "Refine" feature. Although there have been changes in top choices of search engines over time, the criteria for ranking Web search engines are still relevant.

A search engine represents one type of IR system and has a mechanism similar to that of an IR system. Liddy (2001) summarized four essential modules of a search engine: a document processor, a query processor, a search and matching function, and a ranking capability. The ranking capability is based on term frequency, location of terms, link analysis, popularity, date of population, length, proximity of query terms, and proper nouns. Popularity yields good relevant retrieved results. For example, Google's PageRanking technology determines relevance based on how frequently a site is linked to other sites. Arasu, Cho, Garcia-Molina, Paepcke, and Raghavan (2001) identified the following modules for a search engine: crawlers, crawler control, indexer module, collection analysis module, utility index, query engine, and ranking. Compared with Liddy's modules, Arasu et al. added a crawler module that extracts URLs in the retrieved pages and sends this information to the crawler control module. This module determines which links to visit next time. Crawlers visit the Web until the local resources are exhausted.

Current Developments

Web search engines have been experiencing new advancements in recent years. First, there is a trend of developing personalized searching tools on Web. Notess (2006) noted that search engines have recently begun exploring personalized searching. These personalized search engines offered such features as saving URLs, archiving pages, organizing saved results into folders, blocking specific sites, and recording a search history. After search history had been offered in online databases for decades, a search history feature was first introduced by A9, the Amazon-owned search engine, in April 2004. The search history feature is also available at Ask Jeeves, Google, Yahoo!, and several other search engines. In order to use this feature, a searcher usually needs to establish a free account and log in. It is a useful tool for searchers to track their own searches and understand their search patterns. However, that also raises the issue of privacy. Question answering (QA) systems are developed to satisfy users who want the answers directly instead of browsing the documents in which the answers to their queries are embedded (Bar-Ilan, 2004).

Second, visual media account for a large portion of Web content, but very few search engines allow users to search effectively for images. According to Lew (2000), Web search engines such as Webseek, PictoSeek, and ImageRover apply the query-by-similar images paradigm. By applying the query-by-icons paradigm, Lew and his colleagues developed a prototype system named ImageScape to search visual media on the Web. The main difference between the query-by-similar images paradigm and the query-by-icons paradigm is that the latter allows users to state their queries in their own language and specify the importance of local pictorial features. The system enables users to search for image via keywords, semantic icons, and user-drawn sketches. O'Leary (2006) introduced blinkx.tv, a search engine that has the ability to search Web audio and video (AV) content. Blinkx.tv automatically reads AV content and creates text metadata that can be searched and browsed. For each item, the blinkx technology generates a text record consisting of a title, short description, date, source, and short video or thumbnail image for most videos. For the time being, it only indexes AV content on 41 news, entertainment, and informational Web sites.

Third, researchers have worked on the best practice and design for new Web search engines and interfaces to facilitate users' interactions with search engines. The one-size-fits-all approach of Web search engines cannot satisfy diverse user needs. Rose (2006) suggested the design of different interfaces or different forms of interactions to match different search goals. The interface needs to facilitate the selection of contexts for the search as well as support iterative task process. Users interact with the Internet via searching, browsing, and monitoring. Based on the nature of interactions, Beale (2006) designed and implemented a system called Mitsukeru to support browsing behaviors. It employs an agent-based system to model the user's behavior and determines interaction context. The system consists of three parts: determining the current browsing context, determining the relevance of future pages, and communicating to users. Jones, Buchanan, Cheng, and Jain (2006) explored a relaxed Web searching style that asynchronously combined an off-line handheld computer and an online desktop personal computer. Users can enter search terms on the off-line handheld computer. All the queries captured are sent to a search engine when the handheld computer is connected to the PC. The search results can be distributed in different ways depending on the device.

Fourth, the technology development focuses on results presentation. Contradictory to the general search engine's list of retrieved results, Grokker sorts search results into subject categories (O'Leary, 2005). Grokker offers users an opportunity to explore the different aspects of a complex topic and examine all of the Web sites related to a particular aspect of a subject. Grokker is an interface to Yahoo! recently created by Groxis and Yahoo!. It provides a visual representation of categories and subcategories of retrieved results, and further enables easy browsing among them.

Fifth, another new development in Web search engines is the emergence of a new breed of "community" search engines, sites where users share among themselves the search results, such as Clipmarks. According to Broida (2005), communities of knowledgeable, interested people can identify relevant sites with greater accuracy than a search engine. Moreover, users can save time and effort by building their own work on other users' work.

Sixth, Web search engines offer services beyond searching Web sites. Many of the Web search engines extend their services from Web search to desktop search application. Google, AskJeeves, HotBot Desktop, Yahoo, and AOL all offer their versions of desktop applications either as a stand-alone system or an Internet Explorer add-on (Pace, 2005). Rupley (2005) reported that Google offered the following new services: 1) allow users to search within the text of books (http://print.google.com), and 2) enable scientists and academic researchers to search across peer-reviewed papers, books, abstracts, and more (Google Scholar, http://scholar.google.com). Google Scholar has the potential to become the world's most exhaustive academic library.

Challenges for Users

The Web is associated with "cognitive overload" and "disorientation" (Bilal, 2000, 2002). Web search engines are one type of IR system, and they use IR algorithms and techniques. However, IR algorithms were developed for relatively small and coherent collections. Web materials are massive, less coherent, and change rapidly (Arasu et al., 2001). Sullivan (2005) reported how search engines have increased their sizes over time. Altavista indexed the largest number of documents in December 1995 when it first became available. At the end of 1997, AltaVista and Northern Light hit the 150 million document mark. At the same time, AllTheWeb reached the 200 million record. Google's 500 million pages in June 2000 set a new record. After several years of competition with AllTheWeb and MSN, in November 2004, Google increased its index to 8 billion pages to compete with MSN's 5 billion increase. That leads to one of the most cited problems, that users are not able to find information effectively (Kobayashi & Takeda, 2000). The huge size of search engines does not guarantee equal accessibility of information. Lawrence and Giles (1999) discussed the problem of accessibility of information on the Web. People cannot access all the information on the Web because no search engine indexes more than 16% of it, and it takes months before search engines index new pages. To make things worse, search engines only index a bias sample of sites based on links and popularity.

The emergence of the Internet has brought millions of users to search for information on the Web. Web users bring their mental models in searching Web search engines to other types of information retrieval systems, such as OPAC and online systems, because of the simplicity of search engines' interfaces. At the same time, users bring their mental models of one search engine to another even though each search engine has its own interface and search functions. Based on their study results, Wang, Hawk, and Tenopir (2000) concluded that there was little evidence that users changed their mental models from one search engine to another. Moreover, users did not change their search strategies. If a particular strategy did not work, they instead moved from one search engine to another.

Another challenge that users face is that they engage in low levels of interaction with search engines. Studies of commercial search engines show that users enter short queries, and they do not apply complicated search strategies, nor do they use Boolean operators and advanced search features. Moreover, they only view very few retrieval results. They expect Web search engines to act as humans, and the way they communicate with systems is the same as they communicate with humans. Moukdad and Large (2001) investigated users' perceptions of the Web based on an analysis of the transaction logs of WebCrawler. They found the extensive use of either single keywords or complete sentences, and the linguistic structure of their queries was similar to that of the human-human communication model; this cannot produce useful results in a human-computer communication environment. Their findings indicated that the Web search engine was approached as a human expert. It is crucial to design more intelligent and interactive Web search engines.

Further, users cannot effectively interact with Web search engines to find relevant information, and they cannot effectively evaluate the retrieved information. They normally spend only a little time reviewing retrieved documents. More importantly, in the Web, there is no quality control mechanism. It is a challenge for users to make judgments about information quality and authority on the Web. Henzinger, Motwani, and Silverstein (2002) discussed the challenges in Web search engines, one of the major problems being content quality on the Web. The Web consists of low-quality, unreliable, and sometimes contradictory information. Henzinger et al. called for the need for Web search engines to offer quality Web pages for all search requests. After reviewing a series of Web studies and conducting her own study, Rieh (2002) concluded that the Web environment, with its heterogeneous objects and diverse approaches of information organization, made this problem worse. Not all user groups challenged the quality and authority of the retrieved information. Children in particular blindly trusted information they retrieved on the Web. They need to be taught to challenge and question what they found there (Schacter, Chung, & Dorr, 1998).

Research Overview

Although research on Web search engines and their uses started in the 1990s, there have been quite a few review articles providing overviews of various aspects of Web search engine researches. Bar-Ilan (2004) comprehensively reviewed the literature about the use of Web search engines in information science research. This review concentrated on the following aspects of Web search engine research: 1) social perspectives (the ways users interact with Web search engines and the social effects of Web searching), 2) theoretical perspectives (the structure and dynamic nature of the Web, link analysis, Web impact factors, other bibliometric applications for the Web, and characterizing information on the Web), and 3) applications-centered perspectives (evaluation of search engines, improvements of existing tools, and new directions). Yang (2005) presented an overview of information retrieval on the Web emphasizing Web retrieval strategies. In addition, the review also includes studies on characteristics of the Web search environment, essential approaches in Web IR research, and the classification of Web documents. In his review, Large (2005) focused on the Web use of children and teenagers, ranging from a national survey of access to and use of the Web; information-seeking behavior; designed criteria; Web applications of education, leisure, and social interaction; Web content and personal safety in the Web environment; and future research agendas. He pointed out that more research on children and teenagers' information-seeking behavior on the Web is needed despite the increasing number of studies on them, especially the comparison of their behavior and adults' behavior.

Some of the reviews concentrate on patterns of Web searching. For example, Jansen and Pooch (2001) reviewed Web-searching studies on query analysis mainly based on log analysis. They further compared traditional IR, OPAC, and Web search studies in terms of document collection size, number of queries in the data set, session length, query length, use of Boolean operators, failure rate, use of modifiers, and number of relevant documents viewed in a session. Spink (2003) provided an overview of research on Web searching from 1997 to 2002 focusing on large-scale Web data from commercial Web search engines. The overview covers the search topics, query usage patterns, and types of searches for different types of information. According to the review, while users still entered short queries across time, they did shift their searches from entertainment to e-commerce. She also noted the emergence of successive and multitasking searches in the Web environment.

Technology and techniques for Web search engine retrieval is another important aspect for review. Rasmussen (2003) summarized current research on indexing and ranking of Web search engines focusing on automated techniques for indexing and retrieval. Kobayashi and Takeda (2000) reviewed studies of the Internet and technology that are useful for information retrieval on the Web. The review focused on three sessions. The first session discussed the three major components on the Internet: search engine ratings and features, information covered on the Internet, and the growth of users. The second session covered the tools for Web retrieval, which consisted of both traditional retrieval tools and new generation tools. The third session pointed out the future directions of Web retrieval. According to Kobayashi and Takeda, intelligent and adaptive Web services are the future direction.

Evaluation of Web search engines is the essential component of research on search engines. Oppenheim, Morris, McKnight, and Lowley (2000) reviewed the literature of the evaluation of Web search engines, mainly emphasizing methodologies for evaluation and the actual evaluation criteria. The problem for evaluation is there are no standard tools developed for the evaluation of Web search engines. Su (2003a) reviewed relevant literature from 1995-2000 for the development of a model of user evaluation of Web search engines. The proposed model focuses on performance measures associated with both users and systems and nonperformance characteristics related to users. She found there was a lack of evaluation from the end-user perspective.

Interaction Studies

Interaction studies in Web search engine environments can be classified into the following categories: (1) levels of user goals/tasks, (2) usage pattern: patterns of query formulation and reformulation, (3) patterns of multimedia IR, (4) information search behaviors/strategies of different user groups, (5) the impact of knowledge structure, (6) criteria for the evaluation of Web search engines, and (7) comparison with other online IR systems.

Levels of User Goals/Tasks

User goals and tasks have been determined as a driving force for information retrieval in OPAC and online database interaction studies. They are also essential in the context of Web search engine research. Furthermore, users try to accomplish more diverse goals in this environment. After analyzing AltaVista user surveys and search logs, Broder (2002) classified Web searches into three categories: informational searches, transactional searches, and navigational searches. While informational queries accounted for about 50% of searches, transactional and navigational queries took about 30% and 20%, respectively. The findings of this study showed that users were not always searching for information; they also had to make transactions, such as downloading and navigating, to find the specific URL of a site. Rose and Levinson (2004) extended Broder's work, further creating a hierarchy of goals instead of simple classifications. In the hierarchy, informational searches were refined to have a series of subgoals: directed, undirected, to get advice, to locate information, and to obtain a list. Transactional searches were renamed "resource searches," as the underlying user goal is to obtain a resource, such as to download a file. The richness of user goals in retrieving information requires Web search engines to have corresponding interfaces. However, these studies limited user goals only to the current search goal level.

Users not only have diverse goals for their current searches, but they also hold levels of goals in the Web environment. In her Web searching at-home study, Rieh (2004) validated Xie's (2000) four levels of user goals in the Web environment: long-term goals (e.g., gain knowledge, professional achievement, etc.), leading search goals (prepare for an event, prepare for an online class, plan for a vacation, etc.), current search goals (look for papers, products, hotels, etc.), and interactive intentions (locate, find, read, etc.). The levels of user goals also impose a goal structure in that higher levels of user goals have an impact on lower levels of user goals. Furthermore, the findings of this study indicated that people in a Web-searching environment engaged in all four levels of goals, and they had more diverse tasks in the Web-searching environment than in the work places identified by Algon (1997) and goals in the libraries discussed by Xie (2000). In this environment, users sometimes looked for information just for curiosity or for entertainment purposes.

Researchers have also examined the impact of levels of goals and other factors on Web searching. Based on observation and interviews with 31 participants' Internet and Web online catalogue searching, Slone (2003) examined how three levels of goals—broad or situational, specific, and format—plus age differences influenced search approaches. Broad goals represent the situations that lead users to search, such as educational, recreational, personal, and so forth, and they have an impact on other goals. Specific goals are related to what users search for, such as a specific subject, known organization, and so forth. Format goals are associated with the types of information users want, such as full-text articles, images, e-mail, and so forth. The findings showed that children and adults older than 45 presented similar search approaches. One possible reason is that recreational goals were identified more by children while personal goals were highly related to older adults, and both of these goals were found less motivating than educational or job-related goals. Another significant finding is that the homogeneity of user goals is affected by age group. Children (recreational goals) and adults older than 45 (personal goals) have homogeneous user goals, but the age groups of 18 to 25 years, 26 to 35 years, and 36 to 45 years all have multiple goals within a group.

Task, another term related to user goals, is an important variable that affects users' behaviors and outcomes. Bilal (2002) compared children's behavior and success on three tasks: assigned fact-finding tasks, assigned research-oriented tasks, and self-generated tasks. Fifty percent of the children succeeded on the fact-finding tasks, 69% partially succeeded on the research-oriented tasks, and 73% succeeded on the fully self-generated tasks. The results indicated that children were more successful on the fully self-generated tasks than the other two types of tasks. Their success on the fully self-generated tasks was attributed to the simplicity of the topics, their ability to modify the topics as they needed to, and their motivation in pursuing topics of interest. Children also exhibited different behaviors for different types of tasks. They performed the highest analytic searches on fact-based and self-generated tasks and the lowest analytic searches on research-based tasks. They used more natural language queries on fact-based tasks, less on research-based tasks, and none on the fully self-generated tasks. They browsed more and made more moves on the fully self-generated tasks than other two tasks. They looped and backtracked more searches on the fact-based tasks than other tasks. To sum up, tasks influence users' search behaviors and performance.

Schacter, Chung, and Dorr (1998) found a similar difference in their study between ill-defined tasks and well-defined tasks, which are comparable to research-based tasks and fact-based tasks. Children performed better on ill-defined tasks than well-defined tasks, because ill-defined tasks require fewer analytical strategies. Children employed more analytic behaviors in achieving the well-defined tasks than in fulfilling the ill-defined tasks. The only difference is that Schacter et al. discovered that children overwhelmingly used browsing strategies regardless of their tasks. Ford, Miller, and Moss (2002) examined the relationships between tasks and system performance. Even though the selected two tasks all fell into the category of fact-based tasks, they represented tasks with different levels of difficulty. The results showed that simpler tasks correlated significantly with higher relevance scores. The findings of this study echoes the results of Bilal and Schacter et al.'s studies that retrieval performance is affected by task differences.

Not only tasks but also the interactions between tasks and other variables have impact on Web search activities. Kim and Allen (2002) explored the cognitive and task influences on Web search activities and outcomes based on two experiments. The results showed that tasks had a significant effect on search outcomes as well as search activities. Relatively high precision and recall were related to known-item tasks, which is comparable to the results of previous studies. The interactions among task effects, cognitive abilities and problem-solving styles influenced the number of searches completed, sites viewed, keywords searched, and bookmarks made. The interaction effect indicated that compared with other IR system environments, the Web is more flexible for users to choose different search tools for different tasks. Navarro-Prieto, Scaife, and Rogers (1999) associated tasks, search conditions, and levels of experience with users' search strategies. They found that users' cognitive strategies were affected by types of task (fact-finding and exploratory), search conditions (whether the information they looked for was in Web-dispersed structure or category structure), and levels of users' search experience. The type of task had a strong influence on the experienced users' search strategies. For example, in the Web-dispersed structure, experienced users took a bottom-up strategy or chose a mixed strategy at the beginning, and selected a bottom-up strategy later for the specific fact-finding task. Simultaneously, they chose a top-down strategy for the exploratory task. The interactions among multiple variables make it difficult for researchers to uncover the relationships between tasks and searching behaviors. Further research is needed to reveal direct relationships between tasks and search behaviors/strategies.

Usage Pattern: Patterns of Query Formulation and Reformulation

Unlike studies on online databases, little research has investigated tactics or strategies in Web searching. Most studies of users' interactions with search engines focus on patterns of query formulation and reformulation based on analysis of transaction logs submitted to search engines or Web sites. AltaVista and Excite data are the most examined by researchers. Silverstein, Henzinger, Marais, and Moricz (1999) analyzed nearly one billion queries representing 285 million user sessions captured by the Altavista search engine over a period of 6 weeks. They found some patterns of usage: (1) short sessions (average 2.02 queries per sessions), (2) short queries (average 2.35 terms per query), (3) minimum use of operators (average 0.41 operators per query with 80% of queries without any operators), (4) minimum viewing results (average 1.39 screens per query), and (5) search topics mainly related to sex.

In addition, researchers have analyzed Excite data for a long period (Jansen, Spink, & Saracevic, 2000; Spink & Jansen, 2004; Spink, Wolfram, Jansen, & Saracevic, 2001), and they tend to analyze logs quantitatively. They discovered the following usage patterns in Excite search queries, with results apparently consistent with those of AltaVista queries: (1) Users do not frequently reformulate their queries (average 2.5 queries per session in 1997 and 2.3 queries in 2001); (2) users formulate short queries (average 2.4 terms per query in 1997 and 2.6 terms in 2001); (3) users do not view all the results (average 1.7 pages per query); (4) users increasingly submit Boolean queries over the years (5% of queries in 1997 and 10% in 2001); and 5) users' search topics range from entertainment, recreation, and sex to e-commerce. Spink, Bateman, and Jansen's (1999) Excite user survey results echo the results from log analysis. Users do not use many search terms or complex search strategies. They do not access many search features, either. The results of these studies indicated that users have a low level of interactions with search engines.

After analyzing the transaction logs of 2000 queries derived from WebCrawler, Moukdad and Large (2001) reported similar Boolean operators' usage by users (7.8%) and higher multiterm queries submitted by users (average 3.4 terms per query). Although 28.7% of the queries had search modifiers, only 55.5% of them were correctly used. This study also reported high usage of complete sentences (20.4%). It is difficult to know whether the higher average terms per query is because users were more sophisticated and able to specify the information needed or they used more complete sentences. Many users seemed to form a model that considered human-Web communication as human-human communication. Wang, Berry, and Yang (2003) analyzed longitudinal user queries submitted to an academic Web site during a 4-year period. They found that the patterns of user queries between the academic Web site and search engines such as Excite and AltaVista were compatible, for example, most of the queries are unique, short queries. The longitudinal data present similar patterns across time, especially the problem of null output. Thirty percent of queries consistently resulted in zero hits over the years. Lack of basic IR knowledge and misspelling contributed to a high number of zero hits.

Most of these studies focus on the identification of patterns of general query formulation; significantly fewer focus on patterns of query reformulation. Silverstein et al. (1999) reported that users did not modify their queries much (average 2.02 queries per session). Adding terms (7.1%), deleting terms (3.1%), and modifying operators only (1.4%) consisted of 12% of the query reformulations, while complete modifications of queries comprised of 35.2% of the query reformulations. That indicated that users had to refine or change their information need based on the results of their previous queries. Spink, Jansen, and Ozmultu (2001) examined the patterns of query reformulation by Excite users based on the data set of 1,369 queries from 191 user sessions. Users had limited use of query reformulations. They found that only one of the five users reformulated queries, and an average of 6.67 queries were entered for users who modified their queries. Users did not add or delete much in their reformulations. Changing a term is the most common query reformulation, because about 35% of queries that were modified had the same number of terms as the preceding query. About an equal number of reformulations either increased (52%) or decreased (48%) the terms. Spink et al.'s analysis also showed less subject change, as 73% of user sessions included one topic and 27% consisted of two topics. These studies of query reformulations demonstrated limited query reformulations in the searching process, but they concentrated more on adding terms, deleting terms, and modifying operators.

Bruza and Dennis (1997) analyzed the logs of a prototype search engine, manually categorizing 1040 Web queries into 11 query transformation types. They found that users frequently repeated a query that they had already submitted. Other main categories of reformulation were term substitutions, additions, and deletions, in order of frequency. The results also revealed that users did not often split compound terms; make changes to spelling, punctuation, or grammatical case; or use derivative forms of words and abbreviations. Based on these findings, Bruza and Dennis developed a *hyperindex* to aid users in query term additions and deletions by presenting more specific terms that often contain contextual information. Lau and Horvitz (1999) analyzed a data set of 4,960 queries on the Excite search engine. They hand-tagged the data and partitioned queries into classes representing different search actions while focusing on a refinement strategy for query sequences. Seven refinement classes were derived from the data: new, generalization, specialization, interruption, requests for additional results, duplicate queries, and blank queries. Their analysis revealed that most actions are either new queries or requests for additional information. Relatively few users refined their searches by specialization, generalization, or reformulation.

Rieh and Xie (2001, 2006) examined query reformulation from a semantic level based on log data derived from Excite. They characterized the facets of query reformulation in Web searching and identified the patterns of multiple query reformulations in sequences. The data consist of 313 search sessions from two data sets randomly sampled over two time periods. Three facets of query reformulation as well as nine subfacets were derived from the data. Most query reformulations involve changes of content, which account for 80.3% of query reformulations. About 14.4% of the query reformulations are related to format alone, and only 2.8% of the modifications are associated with resource reformulation. More important, the analysis of modification sequences generated eight distinct patterns: specified, generalized, parallel, building-block, dynamic, multitasking, recurrent, and format reformulation. Some of the identified reformulation patterns—for example, specified reformulation, parallel reformulation, generalized reformulation, recurrent, and building-block reformulation—are not necessarily new findings, as they have already been identified in previous studies (e.g., Bruza & Dennis, 1997; Lau & Horvitz, 1999). However, this study examined these patterns of query reformulation based on analysis of sequences of multiple queries rather than of just one query movement.

In addition, this study also identified new patterns reformulations, such as dynamic, multitasking, and so forth. Saracevic's (1996, 1997) stratified model, especially his insightful comments about the fact that there is a direct interplay between the surface and deeper levels of interaction, was adapted as a theoretical framework for the study. The deeper-level cognitive, affective, and situational aspects are employed on the surface level to specify and modify queries. Query formulation and reformulation demonstrate the existence of the interplay. The deeper-level aspects of interactions can change frequently, which can lead to interactions on surface level, for example, changes in queries or tactics. Rieh and Xie (2006) further developed a model of Web query reformulation and suggested interactive query reformulation tools.

Studies of patterns of query formulation and query reformulation demonstrated that users take the least effort approach in Web searching. Simultaneously, their query reformulation process is dynamic in a variety of situations. It is imperative that the design of Web search engines support users' query formulation and reformulation process. Yang (2005) calls for the need to design support features that can shift the cognitive burden from users to systems. One major problem of the above log analysis is that researchers only examined the log data that provide an overview of usage pattern. Log analysis can only account for what users have done, but it cannot answer what directs user actions, and why.

Patterns of Multimedia IR

Multimedia retrieval is much more complicated compared to text retrieval because of the multimodal context. Because multimedia searching is a complicated interaction, it is important to understand how users interact with IR systems to obtain nontextual information. Goodrum, Spink, and their associates conducted a series of studies exploring image searching and related behaviors and strategies and concluded that image searching is different from textual information searching. When Goodrum and Spink (2001) examined image queries of a major Internet search service, they found that users input few queries (average 3.36 image queries per user) with few terms (average 3.74 per query) for their image searching. Unique terms represented a large number of the image queries. However, their query analysis cannot account for the reasons behind the data. Similar results were also found by the study conducted by Spink and Jansen (2006) on multimedia searching. They also identified the differences among search patterns for different types of collections. Users only entered one to two terms per image and audio query when submitting their queries to a metasearch engine. Audio searches had longer sessions with few queries per session. While the majority of users did not seek system Help, more users who looked for images and videos tried to find system Help.

Not only did users exhibit different behaviors in searching for information in different media, but users in different regions also showed different behaviors in multimedia Web searching. Ozmutlu, Spink, and Ozmutlu (2002) compared multimedia Web searching by one US (Excite) and another European (FAST) search engine. They found while users of Excite submitted longer and more complicated queries than FAST users, FAST users spent more time on queries and sessions—except audio queries—than Excite users. Goodrum, Bejune, and Siochi (2003) further identified image search patterns based on state transition analysis. Within the 198 patterns identified, there were two main characteristics of patterns of transitions. First, long strings with lengthier search times happened when users searched for images via text-only search tools that generated Web site surrogates instead of image surrogates. Second, users inspected more image surrogates than Web site surrogates because relevance feedback needs to be judged based on the images themselves. The results of this study indicated that users did employ different types of tactics and search strategies in their image retrieval process.

It seems that research in multimedia retrieval, in particular how users interact with IR systems and multimedia information in their searching process, is still in the exploratory stage. More research is needed to solicit information about not only how but also why. In other words, further research needs to extend query analysis of user queries to diary analysis or think-aloud protocol analysis of the search process.

Information Search Behaviors/Strategies of Different User Groups

Different user groups exhibit different searching behaviors. College students are one of the most studied groups, because they frequently use Web search engines and they are normally the convenience sample for researchers. For example, researchers (Hawk & Wang, 1999; Wang, Hawk, & Tenopir, 2000) examined 24 graduate students' cognitive, affective, and physical behaviors during user-Web interactions. Based on analysis of participants' verbalizations during searches, they identified 10 problem-solving strategies: surveying, double-checking, exploring, link following, back and forward going, shortcut seeking, engine using, loyal engine using, engine seeking, and metasearching ranging. Furthermore, they associated the problem strategies with the physical, situational, cognitive, and affective factors related to user-Web interactions. Cognitive factors influence users in question analysis and in the selection of search and problem-solving strategies. Cognitive styles affect the search process; to be more specific, field-dependent users have more difficulty in searching the Web. Simultaneously, affective and physical factors can support or undermine an interaction. The identification of problems and problem-solving strategies helps researchers understand user-Web interactions. However, in order to design IR systems to facilitate these interactions, further research needs to connect types of problems/situations with types of corresponding strategies.

Fidel et al. (1999) investigated eight high school students' (grades 11 and 12) Web-searching behavior for homework assignments based on data collected from observation and interviews. They characterized students' searching behavior as performing focused searching in general, conducting swift and flexible searching in the process, using landmarks, making the assumption of always starting a new search, and asking for help. They called for the need to train students and design Web search engines considering users' behavior, for example, providing easy access to knowledge tools, navigational tools, correction tools, filtering tools, and visual tools. Large, Beheshti, and Rahman (2000) held four focus groups of users ranging from 10 to 13 years old to explore design criteria for Web portals. Although the purpose of the study was not to identify information-seeking strategies, they did observe the steps taken by each group to find answers to four questions. They found that young users' information-seeking strategies were affected by the design of the search engines, especially their interfaces, and the search statement. Word and phrase searches were applied the most in their searching for the four questions in four search engines, mainly because it is relatively easy to extract keywords from two of the questions. Users preferred general searching to directory, and they explored directory in one search engine because the search box was not placed in an obvious location.

Cothey (2002) conducted a longitudinal study of the information-searching behavior of high school students based on log analysis. Contradictory to the general notion that users are more systematic in their information-seeking behavior, she found that high school students adopted a more passive or browsing approach to Web searching after they gain experience in Web searching. To be more specific, students accessed the Web less and used link-click as opposed to active searching as they became more experienced. In addition, they also became more diverse in selecting Web hosts when their experience increased.

Bilal (2000, 2001) reported on children's (seventh grade students) cognitive, physical, and affective behavior in using the Yahooligans! Search engine on fact-based tasks and research tasks. For fact-based tasks, more children adopted the keyword searching approach (64%) than the browsing approach (36%). The children who took the keyword approach were nonconforming and certain about the keywords, while the children who applied the browsing approach were systematic and orderly. For research tasks, children browsed more than they searched by keyword. Only one child used natural language queries. The results indicated that the children browsed and searched by keyword more in fact-based tasks than in research tasks. Simultaneously, they made more moves and took more time to accomplish fact-based tasks than research tasks. The findings of this study uncovered the problems of the design of Yahooligans! Bilal further suggested that a search engine for children should support children's learning requirements and cognitive demands.

After analyzing computer trace data of 32 elementary school students' (fourth and fifth grade) search process, Schacter, Chung, and Dorr (1998) found that children were interactive searchers, and they did not plan for their search tasks. They preferred browsing strategies, and they did not systematically plan or use sophisticated analytical search techniques. This finding echoes Bilal's results. As was reported in Bilal's (2000, 2001) study, children exhibited more analytical behavior for well-defined tasks than for ill-defined tasks. Boys browsed more than girls because they either browsed documents faster or they did not read as much as the girls did. Children also liked to use full sentence requests as their queries. This study indicated that ill-defined tasks are better suited for children because they offer more potential answers and require less analytical techniques.

The above-cited studies revealed different searching patterns for college students, high school students, and children. College students can master more complicated search strategies or problem-solving strategies than younger group users, and their strategies are affected by cognitive factors, especially cognitive styles. Compared with high school students, children's searching processes were less focused; they switched back and forth between keyword searching, browsing and visiting sites, and they frequently looped searches. The limited recall knowledge of children often led to frequent looping. Children's learning and cognitive abilities might also influence their behavior. Large (2005) summarized patterns of young people's information-seeking behavior on the Web: difficult to select search terms in searching, less time spent in viewing information, difficult to make relevance judgments, and difficult to express their information needs in the form of query formulations and strategies shifts. However, existing research needs to be enhanced to have a more representative sample of users to uncover the information-seeking strategies applied during user-Web interactions.

The Impact of Knowledge Structure

As reported in studies of OPAC and online databases, domain knowledge and information retrieval knowledge are the main types of knowledge that users need for effective information retrieval. This statement also applies in Web retrieval. Experienced users are the more effective searchers in Web-searching environments. Based on examining 25 students' search processes, Lazonder, Biemans, and Wopereis (2000) investigated the differences between novice and experienced users in searching Web information in two steps: locating the appropriate Web sites and finding the relevant information. Their findings showed that expert users were faster, produced more correct responses to the tasks, and took less action in locating Web sites, while there was no difference between expert and novice users in terms of finding information. Expert users were better at searching than novice users but not at browsing, because the log data indicated that users searched instead of browsing to locate sites, and they had to browse to locate information. Experienced users were more plan-oriented than novice users.

Echoing Lazonder, Biemans, and Wopereis' (2000) results, Navarro-Prieto, Scaife, and Rogers (1999) found that experienced users started with a plan for their searches while novice users did not start with a plan; novice users were highly influenced by external representations; and different types of tasks had a stronger influence on the experienced users than novice users in terms of search strategies. The results also indicated that users needed Web searching knowledge before they could identify the differences among tasks. Pollock and Hockley (1997) explored 32 Internet-naïve users' searching for information on the Web in their everyday lives. The results suggested that novice users do not have a concept of searching. They further explored the reason that users had difficulty in formulating queries, because they were used to interacting with humans or browsing through items. These studies demonstrated that retrieval knowledge is essential for novice users to effectively retrieve information from Web search engines. However, not all the experienced user groups exhibited same pattern of information searching behavior. For example, contradictory to results of the above studies, Cothey (2002) discovered that high school students adopted a more passive, or browsing, approach to Web searching after they gained experience in Web searching.

Retrieval knowledge as well as its interaction with domain knowledge has an impact on Web search performance. In Pollack and Hockley's (1997) study, many of the novice users could not find relevant information because they did not have the domain knowledge that was related to their searches. Hölscher and Strube (2000) presented the combined effects of Web experience and domain knowledge for successful search performance based on two experimental studies. Users who relied on both types of expertise were more successful in their searching on the Web. Users lacking one type of expertise exhibited compensatory behavior. For example, domain-experts/Web-novices avoided query formulation and reformulation. These results suggest that Internet skill training is needed for novice users.

The results of these studies emphasize the value of retrieval knowledge as well domain knowledge for the successful retrieval of information. However, existing search engines do not provide the tools to enhance users' domain and retrieval knowledge. Researchers have begun to design new tools to help users, especially novice users. Bhavnani et al. (2006) identified three reasons for the need for procedural search knowledge, especially for novice users who intend to search comprehensive information in unfamiliar domain: information scatter, information density, and information specialization. They designed a domain portal called a Strategy Hub, which consists of two characteristics: 1) selection categories were offered to enable users to learn more precisely how information in the domain is organized and to select interested topics, and 2) explicit search procedures were provided consisting of ordered subgoals plus reliable links to find comprehensive information about a selected topic for each subgoal. The Strategy Hub was further compared to conventional tools. The results of the evaluation demonstrated, in general, that Strategy Hub significantly improved the quality of answers to a search question in comparison to other search tools within the time constraint.

The interaction between retrieval knowledge and personal characteristics also affects Web search performance. Palmquist and Kim (2000) investigated the effect of cognitive styles and online database search experience on Web search performance. Their findings indicated that cognitive styles have little impact on experienced users while cognitive styles do have an impact on novice users. Field-dependent novice users need to spend more time and visit more nodes than field-independent novice users. Field-dependent novice users navigated the Web in a more passive linear mode than the field-independent novice users. Designers of Web interfaces need to consider users' cognitive styles and search experiences, especially the needs of field-dependent novice users. The interaction effects make it difficult to detect the impact of users' knowledge on their search behaviors and search performances. Further research needs to explore the influence of users' knowledge structure as well as its interaction with other personal characteristics on users' behaviors and search performances.

Criteria for the Evaluation of Web Search Engines

In order to improve or design better Web search engines, researchers need to evaluate them. However, there is no standard evaluation criteria and approach available for researchers to evaluate Web search engines. Chen, Fan, Chau, and Zeng (2001) stressed the need to have both quantitative and qualitative data in evaluating Web search engines. Retrieval effectiveness, measured by precision and recall, and efficiency, represented by time and effort spent, are the most commonly used quantitative criteria. Qualitative data are collected by encouraging subjects to express their likes and dislikes concerning the system as well as to give reasons behind their preferences.

Among all the criteria, retrieval performance and the usability of features are no doubt the key criteria. Retrieval performance is mainly measured by relevance (precision and recall) and effectiveness (time and effort), while usability is largely measured by ease-of-use, learnability, errors, satisfaction, and so forth. Chu and Rosenthal (1996) evaluated three Web search engines in terms of their search capabilities and retrieval performance. Search capabilities consist of Boolean logic, truncation, field search, word and phrase search, and retrieval performance include precision and response time. Ding and Marchionini (1996) compared three popular free Web search services based on their features (databases, indexing quality, functionality, and usability) and search performance (precision, salience, and relevance concentration). Clarke and Wilett (1997) created a method for evaluating the recall of the Web search engines in order to consider both recall and precision when evaluating the effectiveness of search engines. Spink (2002) developed a user-centered approach including effectiveness and usability to evaluate a Web metasearch tool.

Dennis, Bruza, and McArthur (2002) conducted an experiment to compare Web search effectiveness among three interactive search paradigms by using a query-based search engine, a directory-based search engine, and a phrase-based, query-reformulation-assisted search engine. Time, relevance of documents, and cognitive load are the measurements. The results revealed that directory-based search took longer and did not provide increased relevance over query-based search. Query formulation could improve the relevance, but users had to spend more time and work harder. The main advantage of query formulation is to offer discriminating terms instead of increasing query length. There is not sufficient evidence to conclude there are any significant variations of cognitive load across the states during the search process.

Precision and recall are the classical measures for IR system performance, but the Web search engine environment poses a challenge for how to assess precision and recall. Recall cannot be calculated because of the large and ever-changing data in each of the Web search engines. Su (2003a) found that precision is the traditional information retrieval evaluation measurement, and it was also the most frequently applied measurement for the evaluation of Web search engines. In evaluating Web search engines, precision measurement is calculated based on either the first 20 documents or the first 10 documents evaluated by users. Leighton and Srivastava (1999) evaluated five search engines by comparing precision on the first 20 hits, ranking effectiveness, lack of redundancy, and the active links retrieved. The study identified three top services: AltaVista, Excite, and Infoseek. Precision was calculated based on the relevance judgments for the first 20 matches in Ding and Marchionini's (1996) study and the first 10 matches in Chu and Rosenthal's (1996) study.

Traditionally, relevance judgment is the major evaluation criteria for IR systems. The Web-interactive environment assigns relevance judgment a new meaning. Rieh (2002) considered the importance of judgment of information quality and authority on the Web. She observed 15 scholars' searching behaviors in the Web, and examined their judgment of information quality and cognitive authority. The findings showed that quality and authority are the important relevance criteria for users in their interaction with information in the uncontrolled environment. To be more specific, information quality consisted of five facets: goodness, accuracy, currency, usefulness, and importance; cognitive authority was characterized as six facets: trustworthiness, reliability, scholarliness, credibility, officialness, and authoritativeness. The results of the study also revealed that quality and authority judgment was affected by the characteristics of information objects, the characteristics of sources, knowledge, situation, ranking in search output, and general assumption. This study extends the research of relevance judgment from relevancy to quality and authority. The study also raised new challenges for Web search engine design to facilitate users' information quality and cognitive authority judgment.

It is important for researchers to come up a set of standard criteria for the evaluation of Web search engines, especially the evaluation of the interactions between users and systems. Oppenheim, Morris, McKnight, and Lowley (2000) identified a number of criteria for the evaluation of Web search engines employed by researchers: number of Web pages covered and coverage, freshness/broken links, relevance, search syntax, subject areas/choice of query, the changing nature of the Web, response time, different system features, search options, human factors and interface issues, and quality of abstracts. They found that there is inconsistency in method and approach in evaluating Web search engines, and they recommended development of a standard tool for the evaluation of Web search engines.

After reviewing research on the evaluation of Web search engines, Su (2003a) provided a more comprehensive and organized evaluation criteria list. She identified 16 performance measures of five evaluation criteria: relevance (precision ratio of relevant and partially relevant hits based on the first 20 hits, precision ratio of relevant hits based on the first 20 hits, user's relevance vs. system's relevant ranking), efficiency (search time, number of search queries submitted), utility (value of search results), user satisfaction (user satisfaction with response time, search interface, online document, output display, interaction, precision, time saving, and user's judgment of overall success), and connectivity (valid links). In addition, she added three categories of nonperformance characteristics consisting of user back grounds, user experiences, and user information needs. The main difference between Oppenheim, Morris, McKnight, and Lowley's (2000) and Su's (2003a) evaluation criteria list is that the latter considers more user perceptions while the former is comprised of more coverage/quality of presented content information. In addition, the latter also stresses the criterion that other researchers have neglected: users' satisfaction with their interactions with search engines.

The above evaluation criteria were derived from researchers' perspectives. What are the users' perspectives in terms of evaluation criteria of search engines? Based on 36 subjects' interaction with four major search engines to find information for their own problems, Su (2003b) examined user evaluation of the four search engines. Sixteen performance measures of five evaluation criteria were applied to the study. The study found significant differences among the four search engines and disciplines, especially in precision, relative recall, user satisfaction with output display, time saving, value of search results, and overall performance. None of the four search engines ranked high in all the criteria. The analysis of the verbal data yielded 14 user criteria for satisfaction with system features: time, search effectiveness-precision, effectiveness-relevance, output-format, interaction-affect, search effectiveness-coverage, search effectiveness-expectancy, efficiency-effort, interface-ease, interface-options, search effectiveness-relevance ranking, connectivity-hyperlinks, online documentation-help, and user-prior experience. She pointed out that the similarities between this study and her previous study of user criteria indicated that some user criteria remain same across time as technology moves forward. The difference may be attributed to users' professional status and their purpose for the search. Interestingly, users' perspectives are comparable to researchers' perspectives except that users also care about their feelings and emotions toward their interaction with search engines.

Researchers have compiled a comprehensive list of evaluation criteria for the assessment of Web search engines from both researchers and users' perspectives. These criteria also consider the unique environment of Web search engines. However, the measurements for the evaluation of users' interaction with Web search engines, especially the interaction process, are not discussed, tested, and validated even though interaction was identified as one of the evaluation criteria.

Comparison with Other Online IR Systems

Online database systems and Web search engines are interrelated. On the one hand, online database systems, such as Dialog and Lexis-Nexis, are called "original" or "ultimate" search engines, and certainly current search engines are in debt to these online databases (Garman, 1999). In addition, Web search engines are entering a new era. They are not limited to search old ordinary Web sites. According to Hock (2002), Web search engines offer more than Web pages now. Therefore, information professionals should apply the same evaluation techniques to a Web search engine as they do to traditional online databases. At the same time, these original search engines are moving toward the Web. According to Xie (2003), almost every online database system has its Web version. For example, in 2000, Dialog announced three new Web-oriented products: Dialog Portals, Dialog Power Portal, and WebTop, a Web search engine (O'Leary, 2000).

Researchers have compared users' searching in OPACs, online databases, and Web search engines. Jansen and Pooch (2001) compared searching studies of traditional IR, OPAC, and Web studies, finding both similarities and differences among the three types of IR systems. While the use of advanced features and number of documents viewed is similar across the three types of IR systems, the use of traditional IR systems produces higher failure rates, longer session lengths, longer query lengths, and greater use of Boolean operators. Web users show different search patterns compared to users searching traditional IR systems such as online databases (Silverstein et al., 1999; Spink et al., 2001). For example, Jansen and Pooch (2001) discovered the differences in sessions and query length between traditional IR systems and Web search engines. The average Web search has a session of about two queries, with each query consisting of two terms, while traditional IR systems have 7 to 16 queries in session length, and the query length is from six to nine terms.

Researchers not only compared previous studies on the usage of different types of online IR systems but also conducted studies to compare the impact of one type of system use on another. Slone (2005) observed 31 participants' searching the Web or a Web online catalog. The results showed that participants applied their knowledge and experience in one system to another one. Their mental models of one system affected their interaction with another system. Users who had traditional online catalogue experience were more comfortable conducting Web searching than those who did not have experience. Users with Web experience expected online catalogues to be searched just like the Web was searched. Simultaneously, Slone (2005) also noted that the application of the mental model of one system to another sometimes caused difficulty and confusion when there were differences in the two systems/environments. Feldman (1998) compared the effectiveness of online databases (DIALOG and Dow Jones Interactive) to that of Web search engines, concluding that professional searchers preferred Web search engines for use and online databases for relevant results.

In most of the previous comparison studies, the evaluation criteria are predetermined, not derived from users. Xie (2004) evaluated the advantages and disadvantages of online IR systems, in particular Web search engines (directory, search engine, metasearch engine, and specialized search engines) vs. online databases (Dialog and Factiva) from the users' perspectives. The results show that interface design, system performance, and collection coverage are essential to users in the evaluation of online IR systems. While users preferred the ease of use and intuitive interfaces of Web search engines, they also liked the credible and useful information offered by online databases. It is difficult to conclude which type of IR systems had higher precision. Comparatively speaking, online databases have more sophisticated interfaces than Web search engines. Most participants liked the simple and self-explanatory interfaces of Google, and complained about the complicated rules and codes in using online databases. Simultaneously, some participants loved the control and efficiency they had in using the Dialog command model. To the participants, Web search engines were designed for novice users while online databases were developed for experienced users. Furthermore, participants liked the unique and in-depth information provided by online databases that is not available from search engines, but they also liked the nonscholarly documents from the Web sites.

To sum up, users have to access different types of online IR systems to achieve their personal and working tasks. Different types of online IR systems have their unique collection coverage and interface design. Users of one type of IR system bring their mental models of that type of IR system into the new type of IR system that they access. Plus, users also bring their knowledge structure and personal characteristics into their interaction with online IR systems. However, little research has investigated how these factors affect users' interaction with online IR systems, and moreover, which factors play the key roles influencing the interaction.

Summary

Table 4.1 presents the summary of interaction studies in Web search engine environments. Research on tasks/user goals and their influence on search behavior and search performance comes to two conclusions: 1) users engage in more diverse user goals in searching Web search engines, and 2) user tasks and goals have an impact on their search behavior and search performance. These studies have contributed to theoretical Web model creation and Web search engine design for facilitating users to accomplish different types of user goals/tasks. However, researchers have not examined the relationships between tasks and user goals. Although evidence from previous research has demonstrated that tasks/goals have an impact on search behavior, no patterns between the two have been identified. Moreover, the interactions between tasks and other variables pose a challenge for researchers in unveiling how these interactions influence search behavior and performance and which variable plays a more important role in determining different search behaviors and search performance.

Patterns of query formulation and reformulation account for a large portion of the studies on Web search engine usage. One problem in Web search engine studies is related to the limitation of applying log analysis. On the one hand, transaction log analysis allows researchers to unobtrusively collect and analyze a large amount of data; on the other hand, this type of data only reveals how—not why—users interact with Web search engines. Wang, Berry, and Yang (2003) pointed out that the results of log analysis are limited because users' information needs cannot be fully understood. Therefore, researchers should interpret results with caution. Further research needs to explore why users only engage in low-level interactions with search engines and what leads to patterns of query formulation and reformulation in their searching Web search engines. Only by answering these questions can researchers unveil the nature of query formulation and reformulation, and further design search engines or tools to facilitate users' effective interaction with search engines.

Compared with patterns of text retrieval, patterns of multimedia retrieval have their own unique characteristics. Not only are they different from textual retrieval, but also they are differences among audio retrieval, video retrieval, image retrieval, and so forth. In addition, users in different regions display different multimedia searching behaviors. The question is what leads to the differences, the media themselves, the users, or the systems? Another question is what are the unique tactics and strategies applied by users in their searching for different types of multimedia information? Moreover, what are the factors that affect the formation or selection of different types of tactics and strategies?

Research has demonstrated that different user groups interact with Web search engines in different ways. The majority of the studies have focused on one group of users per study; few researchers have compared the searching behavior of different user groups. It is difficult to relate the findings of these studies because so many factors affect their results. Even though researchers did identify some of the factors that influence the searching behavior of a specific group, it is still not clear what leads to different user groups' unique searching behaviors. In other words, what are the key factors that determine different user groups' searching behaviors? Furthermore, how does the interaction of different factors affect the searching behavior of different user groups? For example, tasks/goals have been shown to be one of the important factors that affect users' search behavior. If users from two different groups work on the same tasks, will that lead to same or different searching behavior?

Compared with studies of OPAC and online databases, studies of Web search engines reveal one unique finding: not only do retrieval knowledge and domain knowledge have an impact on search behavior and performance, but the interaction of different knowledge structures and other personal characteristics influence search behavior and performance. That raises the question of which types of knowledge are more important in affecting search behavior and search performance. Simultaneously, researchers still need to explore when and how users need different types of knowledge during their interaction with Web search engines.

There are several challenges for the evaluation of Web search engines. First, there are no standard criteria or measurements for evaluation, and each study takes its own criteria/measurements and approach. Further research needs to identify a set of core criteria with appropriate measures for the evaluation of Web search engines.

Table 4.1. Summary of interaction studies in Web search engine environments

Types	Research Focus	Problems/questions	Implications
Levels of user goals/tasks	Types of goals users intend to accomplish in Web environments; Impact of types of user goals/tasks on search behaviors and search performance; Impact of tasks and other variables on search behaviors and search performance.	What is the relationship between user tasks and user goals? What is the pattern between types of tasks/goals and search behaviors? How do the interaction between tasks and other variables affect search behavior and search performance?	Create Web search model; Understand the driving force for information retrieval in Web environments; Incorporate tasks and corresponding information-seeking behaviors into system design.
Usage pattern: patterns of query formulation and reformulation	Quantitative analysis of patterns of query formulations and reformulations; Qualitative analysis of patterns of query formulations and reformulations.	Why do users engage in low-level interactions with search engines? What leads to patterns of query formulation and reformulations?	Understand the nature of query formulations and reformulations; Design tools to facilitate users to formulate and reformulate their queries.
Patterns of multimedia IR	Identification of search patterns for different types of multimedia; Identification of search patterns for different types of users.	What leads to search patterns for different types of multimedia? What are the unique tactics and strategies applied by users in their searching for different types of multimedia information? What are the factors that affect the formation or selection of different types of tactics and strategies?	Understand the nature of multimedia IR; Design Web search engines to facilitate users' effective multimedia IR.
Information search behaviors/strategies of different user groups	Patterns of information searching behaviors/ strategies of college students, high school students, and children.	What are the similarities and differences among search behaviors/strategies for different user groups? What leads to/ determines the different search behaviors/strategies in different user groups?	Understand information search behaviors of different user groups; Design Web search engines to facilitate different users to effectively retrieve information.

continued on following page

Table 4.1. continued

The impact of knowledge structure	Retrieval knowledge and its impact on search behavior and performance; Impact of interaction between retrieval and domain knowledge on search performance; Impact of interaction between retrieval knowledge and personal characteristics on search performance.	Which types of knowledge are more important in affecting search behavior and search performance? When and how do users need different types of knowledge?	Understand how knowledge structure influences search behavior and performance; Design tools to enhance users' knowledge in retrieval skills and search topics; Offer different forms of interactions for different levels of users.
Criteria for the evaluation of Web search engines	Evaluation criteria from researchers; Measurements for precision and recall for search engines; New quality and authority criteria for the evaluation of Web materials; Evaluation of interactions between users and systems; Evaluation criteria from users.	What are the standard criteria for evaluating search engines? What are the criteria needed to evaluate the interaction process between users and IR systems? How do search engines help users evaluate the quality and authority of retrieved documents?	Determine the appropriate criteria for evaluating Web search engines, especially users' interaction with systems; Compare and evaluate a variety of Web search engines; Design new tools to assist users to make quality and authority judgments.
Comparison with other online IR systems	Comparison of search patterns of OPACs, online databases, and Web search engines; Comparison of advantages and disadvantages of online databases and Web search engines based on users' perspectives.	What leads to the different search patterns among OPACs, online databases, and Web search engines?	Understand the similarities and differences among the usage of OPACs, online databases, and Web search engines; Improve the design of IR systems by considering the advantages of different types of IR systems.

Second, although both researchers and users have realized the importance of measuring the interaction, there is not enough research on what criteria are essential for evaluating the interactions between users and Web search engines. Third, users are concerned with the quality and authority of the Web material, but Web search engines have done little to facilitate their assessment. Further research needs to design new tools to be incorporated into Web search engines to ease users' concern for the quality of the materials.

Researchers have identified the similarities and differences in users' searching OPAC, online databases, and Web search engines. These comparison studies help researchers understand how users interact with different types of online IR systems. The question is what leads to the different search patterns among OPACs, online databases, and Web search engines. Based on the previous research on OPACs, online databases, and Web search engines, the design of different IR systems, in particular their interfaces (simplicity of the interfaces vs. command-driven interfaces, ranked retrieval results vs. retrieved results organized by date, etc.), types of users (users with different knowledge structures, users in different age groups, end-users vs. intermediaries), and the content covered in different systems (bibliographies of books and other items, bibliographies and full-text of scholarly articles, and general unfiltered information sites) all have an impact on the search patterns of different IR systems. Further research needs to investigate the key factors that lead to different search patterns and in what ways these factors influence these patterns.

References

Algon, J. (1997). Classification of tasks, steps, and information-related behaviors of individuals on project teams. In P. Vakkri, R. Savolainen, & B. Dervin (Eds.), *Information seeking in context: Proceedings of an International Conference on Research in Information Needs, Seeking and Use in Different Contexts,* (pp. 205-221). London: Taylor Graham.

Arasu, A., Cho, J., Garcia-Molina, H., Paepcke, A., & Raghavan, S. (2001). Searching the Web. *ACM Transactions on Internet Technology, 1*(1), 2-43.

Bar-Ilan, J. (2002). Methods for measuring search engine performance over time. *Journal of the American Society for Information Science and Technology, 53*(4), 308-319.

Bar-Ilan, J. (2004). The use of Web search engines in information science research. *Annual Review of Information Science and Technology, 38,* 231-288.

Beale, R. (2006). Improving Internet interaction: From theory to practice. *Journal of the American Society for Information Science and Technology, 57*(6), 829-833.

Berners-Lee, T. (1989). *Information management: A proposal.* Retrieved January 3, 2008, from http://www.nic.funet.fi/index/FUNET/history/internet/w3c/proposal.html

Berners-Lee, T. (1996). *The World Wide Web: Past, present and future.* Retrieved

January 3, 2008, from http://www.w3.org/People/Berners-Lee/1996/ppf. html

Bhavnani, S. K., Bichakjian, C. K., Johnson, T. M., Little, R. J., Peck, F. A., Schwartz, J. L., et al. (2006). Strategy hubs: Domain portals to help find comprehensive information. *Journal of the American Society for Information Science and Technology, 57*(1), 4-24.

Bilal, D. (2000). Children's use of the Yahooligans! Web search engine: I. Cognitive, physical, and affective behaviors on fact-based search tasks. *Journal of the American Society of Information Science, 51*(7), 646-665.

Bilal, D. (2001). Children's use of the Yahooligans! Web search engine: II. Cognitive and physical behaviors on research tasks. *Journal of the American Society for Information Science, 52*(2), 118-136.

Bilal, D. (2002). Perspectives on children's navigation of the World Wide Web: Does the type of search task make a difference? *Online Information Review, 26*(2), 108-177.

Broder, A. (2002). Taxonomy of Web search. *ACM SIGIR Forum, 36*(2), 3-10.

Broida, R. (2005). Never search alone. *PC Magazine, 24*(21), 28-30.

Bruza, P.D., & Dennis, S. (1997, June). *Query-reformulation on the Internet: Empirical data and the hyperindex search engine.* Paper presented at the RIAO Conference: Intelligent Text and Image Handling, Montreal, Canada.

Chen, H., Fan, H., Chau, M., & Zeng, D. (2001). MetaSpider: Meta-searching and categorization on the Web. *Journal of the American Society for Information Science and Technology, 52*(13), 1134-1147.

Chu, H., & Rosenthal, M. (1996). Search engines for the World Wide Web: A comparative study and evaluation methodology. In S. Hardin (Ed.), *Proceedings of the 59th ASIS Annual Meeting,* (Vol. 33, pp. 127-135). Medford, NJ: Information Today.

Clarke, S. J., & Willett, P. (1997). Estimating the recall performance of Web search engines. *ASLIB Proceedings, 49*(7), 184-189.

Cothey, V. (2002). A longitudinal study of World Wide Web users' information searching behavior. *Journal of the American Society for Information Science and Technology, 53*(2), 67-78.

Dennis, S., Bruza, P., & McArthur, R. (2002). Web searching: A process-oriented experimental study of three interactive search paradigms. *Journal of the American Society for Information Science and Technology, 53*(2), 120-133.

Ding, W., & Marchionini, G. (1996). A comparative study of Web search service performance. In S. Hardin (Ed.), *Proceedings of the 59ᵗʰ ASIS Annual Meeting,* (Vol. 33, pp. 136-142). Medford, NJ: Information Today.

Feldman, S. (1998). The Internet search-off. *Searcher, 6*(2), 28-35.

Fidel, R., Davies, R. K., Douglass, M. H., Holder, J. K., Hopkins, C. J., Kushner, E. J., et al. (1999). A visit to the information mall: Web searching behavior of high school students. *Journal of the American Society for Information Science, 50*(1), 24-37.

Ford, N., Miller, D., & Moss, N. (2002). Web search strategies and retrieval effectiveness: An empirical study. *Journal of Documentation, 58*(1), 30-48.

Fox, S. (2002). Search Engines: A pew Internet project data memo. *The Pew Internet & American Life Project.* Retrieved January 3, 2008, from http://www. pewinternet.org/reports/toc.asp

Garman, N. (1999). The ultimate, original search engine. *Online, 23*(3), 6.

Goodrum, A., Bejune, M., & Siochi, A. (2003). A state transition analysis of image search patterns on the Web. *Lecture Notes in Computer Science, 2728,* 281-290.

Goodrum, A., & Spink, A. (2001). Image searching on the World Wide Web: Analysis of visual information retrieval queries. *Information Processing and Management. 37*(2), 295-311.

Hawk, W. B., & Wang, P. (1999). Users' interaction with the World Wide Web: Problems and problem solving. In M. M. K. Hlava & L. Woods (Eds.), *Proceedings of the 62nd ASIS Annual Meeting,* (Vol. 36, pp. 256-270). Medford, NJ: Information Today.

Henzinger, M. R., Motwani, R., & Silverstein, C. (2002). Challenge in Web search engines. *ACM SIGIR Forum, 36*(2), 11-22.

Hills, P., & Argyle, M. (2003). Uses of the Internet and their relationships with individual differences in personality. *Computers and Human Behavior, 19*(1), 59-70.

Hock, R. (2002). A new era of search engines: Not just Web pages anymore. *Online, 36*(5), 20-27.

Hölscher, C., & Strube, G. (2000). Web search behavior of Internet experts and newbies. In *Proceedings of the 9th International World Wide Web Conference on Computer Networks: The International Journal of Computer and Telecommunications Networking,* (pp. 337-346). Amsterdam, The Netherlands: North-Holland Publishing.

Jansen, B. J., & Pooch, U. (2001). Web user studies: A review and framework for future work. *Journal of the American Society for Information Science and Technology, 52*(3), 235-246.

Jansen, B. J., Spink, A., & Saracevic, T. (2000). Real life, real users, and real needs: A study and analysis of user queries on the Web. *Information Processing and Management, 36*(2), 207-227.

Jones, M., Buchanan, G., Cheng, T. C., & Jain, P. (2006). Changing the pace of search: Supporting "background" information seeking. *Journal of the American Society for Information Science and Technology, 57*(6), 838-842.

Kim, K.S., & Allen, B. (2002). Cognitive and task influences on Web searching behavior. *Journal of the American Society for Information Science and Technology, 53*(2), 109-119.

Kobayashi, M., & Takeda, K. (2000). Information retrieval on the Web. *ACM Computing Surveys, 32*(2), 144-173.

Large, A. (2005). Children, teenagers, and the Web. *Annual Review of Information Science and Technology, 39*, 347-392.

Large, A., Beheshti, J., & Rahman, T. (2000). Design criteria for children's Web portals: The users speak out. *Journal of the American Society for Information Science, 53*(2), 79-94.

Lau, T., & Horvitz, E. (1999). Patterns of search: Analyzing and modeling Web query refinement. In J. Kay (Ed.), *Proceedings of the 7th International Conference on User Modeling,* (pp. 119-128). New York: Springer Wien.

Lawrence, S., & Giles, C. L. (1999). Accessibility and distribution of information on the Web. *Nature, 400*(6740), 107-109.

Lazonder, A. W., Biemans, H. J. A., & Wopereis, I. G. J. H. (2000). Differences between novice and experienced users in searching information on the World Wide Web. *Journal of the American Society for Information Science, 51*(6), 576-581.

Leighton, H. V., & Srivastava, J. (1999). First 20 precision among World Wide Web search services (search engines). *Journal of the American Society for Information Science, 50*(10), 870-881.

Lew, M. S. (2000). Next Generation Web searches for visual content. *IEEE Computer, 33*(11), 46-53.

Liddy, E. (2001). How a search engine works. *Searcher, 9*(5), 38-45.

Montgomery, A., & Faloutsos, C. (2001). Identifying Web browsing trends and patterns. *IEEE Computer, 34*(7), 94-95.

Moukdad, H., & Large, A. (2001). Users' perceptions of the Web as revealed by transaction log analysis. *Online Information Review, 25*(6), 349-359.

Navarro-Prieto, R., Scaife, M., & Rogers, Y. (1999). *Cognitive strategies in Web searching.* Paper presented at the 5th Conference on Human Factors and the Web. Retrieved January 3, 2008, from http://zing.ncsl.nist.gov/hfweb/proceedings/navarro-prieto/index.html

Notess, G. R. (2006). Tracking your search history. *Online, 30*(2), 41-43.

O'Leary, M. (2000). Dialog's new tools for Web-age knowledge workers. *Online, 24*(3), 91-92.

O'Leary, M. (2005). Grokker's new "look" on Web searching. *Information Today, 22*(9), 41-42.

O'Leary, M. (2006). blinkx.tv Reads sight and sound. *Information Today, 23*(2), 33-34.

Oppenheim, C., Morris, A., McKnight, C., & Lowley, S. (2000). The evaluation of WWW search engines. *Journal of Documentation, 56*(2), 190-211.

Ozmutlu, S., Spink, A., & Ozmutlu, H. C. (2002). Multimedia Web searching trends. In E. M. Rasmussen, & E. Toms (Eds.), *Proceedings of the 65th ASIST Annual Meeting* (pp. 403-408). Medford, NJ: Information Today.

Pace, A. K. (2005). Technically speaking: It's probably right in front of you. *American Libraries, 36*(5), 61-62.

Palmquist, R. A., & Kim, K.-S. (2000). Cognitive style and online search experience on Web search performance. *Journal of the American Society for Information Science, 51*(6), 558-567.

Pollock, A., & Hockley, A. (1997). What's wrong with Internet searching? *D-Lib Magazine, 3*. Retrieved January 3, 2008, from http://www.dlib.org/dlib/march97/bt/03pollock.html

Rasmussen, E. (2003). Indexing and retrieval from the Web. *Annual Review of Information Science and Technology, 37*, 91-124.

Rieh, S. Y. (2002). Judgment of information quality and cognitive authority in the Web. *Journal of the American Society for Information Science and Technology, 53*(2), 145-161.

Rieh, S. Y. (2004). On the Web at home: Information seeking and Web searching in the home environment. *Journal of the American Society for Information Science and Technology, 55*(8), 743-753.

Rieh, S. Y., & Xie, H. (2001). Patterns and sequences of multiple query reformulations in Web searching: A preliminary study. In D. H. Kraft (Ed.), *Proceedings of the 64th ASIST Annual Meeting,* (Vol. 38, pp. 246-255). Medford, NJ: Information Today.

Rieh, S. Y., & Xie, H. (2006). Analysis of multiple query reformulations on the Web: The interactive information retrieval context. *Information Processing and Management, 42*(3), 751-768.

Rose, D. E. (2006). Reconciling information-seeking behavior with search user interfaces for the Web. *Journal of the American Society for Information Science and Technology, 57*(6), 797-799.

Rose, D. E., & Levinson, D. (2004). Understanding user goals in Web search. In *Proceedings of the 13th Annual World Wide Web Conference,* (pp. 13-19). New York: ACM Press.

Rupley, S. (2005). Search tool for eggheads (Brief article). *PC Magazine, 24*(1), 25.

Saracevic, T. (1996). Modeling interaction in information retrieval (IR): A review and proposal. In S. Hardin (Ed.), *Proceedings of the 59th ASIS Annual Meeting,* (Vol. 33, pp. 3-9). Medford, NJ: Information Today.

Saracevic, T. (1997a). The stratified model of information retrieval interaction: Extension and applications. In C. Schwartz & M. Rorvig (Eds.), *Proceedings of the 60ᵗʰ ASIS Annual Meeting,* (Vol. 34, pp. 313-327). Medford, NJ: Information Today.

Saracevic, T. (1997b). The stratified model of information retrieval interaction: Extension and applications. In C. Schwartz & M. Rorvig (Eds.), *Proceedings of the 60ᵗʰ ASIS Annual Meeting,* (Vol. 34, pp. 313-327). Medford, NJ: Information Today.

Schacter, J., Chung, G. K. W. K., & Dorr, A. (1998). Children's Internet searching on complex problems: Performance and process analyses. *Journal of the American Society for Information Science, 49*(9), 840-849.

Silverstein, C., Henzinger, M., Marais, H., & Moricz, M. (1999). Analysis of a very large Web search engine query log. *SIGIR Forum, 33*(1), 6-12.

Slone, D. J. (2003). Internet search approaches: The influence of age, search goals and experience. *Library and Information Science Research, 25*(4), 403-418.

Slone, D. J. (2005). A bird's eye view of cross-platform Web interaction. *Journal of Documentation, 61*(5), 657-669.

Spink, A. (2002). A user-centered approach to evaluating human interaction with Web search engines: An exploratory study. *Information Processing and Management, 38*(3), 401-426.

Spink, A. (2003). Web search: emerging patterns. *Library trends, 52*(2), 299-306.

Spink, A., Bateman, J., & Jansen, B. J. (1999). Searching the Web: Survey of EXCITE users. *Internet Research: Electronic Networking Applications and Policy, 9*(2), 117-128.

Spink, A., & Jansen, B. J. (2004). *Web search: Public searching of the Web.* Boston: Kluwer Academic Publishers.

Spink, A., & Jansen, B. J. (2006). Searching multimedia federated content Web collections. *Online Information Review, 30*(5), 485-495.

Spink, A., Jansen, B. J., & Ozmultu, C. (2001). Use of query reformulation and relevance feedback by EXCITE users. *Internet Research, 10*(4), 317-328.

Spink, A., Wolfram, D., Jansen, B. J., & Saracevic, T. (2001). Searching the Web: The public and their queries. *Journal of the American Society for Information Science, 52*(3), 226-234.

Su, L. T. (2003a). A comprehensive and systematic model of user evaluation of Web search engines: I. Theory and background. *Journal of the American Society for Information Science and Technology, 54*(13), 1175-1192.

Su, L. T. (2003b). A comprehensive and systematic Model of user evaluation of Web search engines. II. An evaluation by undergraduates. *Journal of the American Society for Information Science and Technology, 54*(13), 1193-1223.

Sullivan, D. (2004). Major search engines and directories. Retrieved January 3, 2008, from http://searchenginewatch.com/links/article.php/2156221

Sullivan, D. (2005). Search engine sizes. *Search Engine Watch*. Retrieved January 3, 2008, from http://searchenginewatch.com/reports/article.php/2156481

Sullivan, D. (2006). Nielsen/NetRatings search engine ratings. *Search Engine Watch*. Retrieved January 3, 2008, from http://searchenginewatch.com/showPage.html?page=sew_print&id=2156451

USC Annenberg School, Center for the Digital Future (2004). *The digital future report: Surveying the digital future*. Retrieved January 3, 2008, from http://www.digitalcenter.org/downloads/DigitalFutureReport-Year4-2004.pdf

Wang, P., Berry, M., & Yang, Y. (2003). Mining longitudinal Web queries: Trends and patterns. *Journal of the American Society for Information Science and Technology, 54*(8), 743-758.

Wang, P., Hawk, W. B., & Tenopir, C. (2000). Users' interaction with World Wide Web resources: An exploratory study using a holistic approach. *Information Processing and Management, 36*(2), 229-251.

Xie, H. (2000). Shifts of interactive intentions and information-seeking strategies in interactive information retrieval. *Journal of the American Society for Information Science, 51*(9), 841-857.

Xie, H. (2003). Supporting ease-of-use and user control: Desired features and structure of Web-based online IR systems. *Information Processing & Management, 39*(6), 899-922.

Xie, H. (2004). Online IR system evaluation: Online databases vs. Web search engines. *Online Information Review, 28*(3), 211-219.

Yang, K. (2005). Information retrieval on the Web. *Annual Review of Information Science and Technology, 39*, 33-80.

Chapter V

Interactive IR in Digital Library Environments

Overview of Digital Library Environments

History and Background

For centuries, people have been used to printed materials. The emergence of the Internet brings dramatic changes to millions of people in terms of how they collect, organize, disseminate, access, and use information. Researchers (Chowdhury & Chowdhury, 2003; Lesk, 2005; Witten & Bainbridge, 2003) have identified the following factors that contributed to the birth of digital libraries:

1. Vannevar Bush's pioneering concept and idea of Memex. Vannevar Bush (1945) wrote a classic article, "As We May Think," which has had a major impact on the emergence of digital libraries. In the article, he described his Memex device, which was able to organize books, journals, and notes in different

places by linked association. This associative linking was similar to what is known today as hypertext.

2. The advancement in computer and communication/network technology. The computer was first used to manage information. In the 1960s, the emergence of remote online information search services changed the way people access and search information. By the 1980s, people could remotely and locally access library catalogues via Online Public Access Catalogues (OPACs). The invention of the CD-ROM made it easy and cheap for users to access electronic information. Most importantly, Web technology started in 1990, and the occurrence of Web browsers afterwards have enabled users to access digital information anywhere as long as there is an Internet connection. Web search engines offer an opportunity for millions of people to search full-text documents on the Web.

3. The development of libraries and library access. Since the creation of Alexandrian library around 300 B.C., the size and number of libraries have grown phenomenally. A library catalogue goes from a card catalogue to three generations of online public access catalogues started in the 1980s. Library materials include mainly printed resources to multimedia collections, such as images, videos, sound files, and so forth. Simultaneously, the information explosion in the digital age makes it impossible for libraries to collect all of the available materials.

Several pre-Web digital library efforts began at the end of the 1980s and beginning of the 1990s. These include Project Mercury (1989-1992), the TULIp Project (1993-1995), the Chemistry Online Retrieval Experiment (CORE), and the Envision Project (Fox & Urs, 2002). The Digital Library Initiative 1 (DLI1), a $24 million program from 1994-1998 funded by National Science Foundation (NSF), Defense Advanced Research Projects Agency (DARPA), National Aeronautics and Space Administration (NASA), and other agencies, was a major US research development initiative. DLI 1 focused on technical issues, mainly to advance the technology to collect, store, and organize information in digital forms. Digital Library Initiative 2 (DLI2), which offered $44 million in funding, is sponsored by the NSF, DARPA, National Library of Medicine (NLM), Library of Congress (LC), National Endowment for the Humanities (NEH), NASA, and Federal Bureau of Investigation (FBI) in partnership with the Institute of Museum and Library Services (IMLS), Smithsonian Institution (SI), and National Archives and Records Administration (NARA). DLI2 (1999-2004) expanded the scope of inquiry to include the social, behavioral, and economic aspects of digital libraries (Fox, 1999; Fox & Urs, 2002; Chowdhury & Chowdhury, 2003).

Definitions and Types of Digital Libraries

It is difficult to define what a digital library is. Digital libraries incorporate information retrieval systems, although they are not equivalent insofar as digital libraries provide additional services such as preservation, community building, and learning centers. At the same time, digital libraries permit timely access to electronic information in the same way that physical libraries have traditionally provided access to print-based and other tangible information resources. Conceptions of digital libraries vary, and many definitions for digital libraries have been proposed. The concept of a digital library means different things to different people. Khalil and Jayatilleke (2000) surveyed end users' understanding of digital libraries through a variety of listservs all over the world; they found that digital libraries were defined in more than 35 different ways. Fox, Akscyn, Furuta, and Leggett (1995) summarized different perceptions of digital libraries by the key players in digital libraries: librarians, computer scientists, and users. To librarians, digital libraries carry out the functions of libraries in a new way; to computer scientists, a digital library is a distributed text-based information system; a collection of distributed information services, a distributed space of interlinked information, or a networked multimedia information system; to end users, digital libraries are regarded as similar to the World Wide Web (WWW) with improvements in performance, organization, functionality, and usability.

Borgman (1999) identified two competing visions of digital libraries. The research community considers digital libraries as content driven, while librarians share the perception that digital libraries are institution- or service-oriented. Researchers are more concerned with how to design systems for effective access; librarians are more concerned with providing different services for users. The Association of Research Libraries (1995) identified the common elements of digital library definitions:

- The digital library is not a single entity;
- The digital library requires technology to link the resources of many;
- The linkages between the many digital libraries and information services are transparent to the end users;
- Universal access to digital libraries and information services is a goal; and
- Digital library collections are not limited to document surrogates: they extend to digital artifacts that cannot be represented or distributed in printed formats (http://www.arl.org/sunsite/definition.html).

Digital libraries have also been broadly defined "as a collection of electronic resources and services for the delivery of materials in a variety of formats. Digital libraries include personal, distributed, and centralized collections such as online public access catalogs and bibliographic databases, distributed document databases, scholarly and professional discussion lists and electronic journals, other online databases, forums, and bulletin boards" (Covi & Kling, 1996, p. 672). The most comprehensive digital library definition arose from the Social Aspects of Digital Library research workshop (Borgman et al., 1996):

1.   Digital libraries are a set of electronic resources and associated technical capabilities for creating, searching, and using information. In this sense they are an extension and enhancement of information storage and retrieval systems that manipulate digital data in any medium (text, images, sounds; static or dynamic images) and exist in distributed networks. The content of digital libraries includes data, metadata that describe various aspects of the data (e.g., representation, creator, owner, reproduction rights), and metadata that consist of links or relationships to other data or metadata, whether internal or external to the digital library.

2.   Digital libraries are constructed—collected and organized—by a community of users, and their functional capabilities support the information needs and uses of that community. They are a component of communities in which individuals and groups interact with each other, using data, information, and knowledge resources and systems. In this sense they are an extension, enhancement, and integration of a variety of information institutions as physical places where resources are selected, collected, organized, preserved, and accessed in support of a user community. These information institutions include, among others, libraries, museums, archives, and schools, but digital libraries also extend and serve other community settings, including classrooms, offices, laboratories, homes, and public spaces (p. 4-5).

At the beginning of the development of digital libraries, most digital libraries have focused on specialized subject content for specific audiences. Examples include FedStats, a digital library that focuses on government statistical data (Dippo, 1998), and the American Memory collection of historical materials at the Library of Congress (Patitucci, 1999). In response to general public and library interest in increased access to a wider array of informative, quality electronic resources, aided largely by the wider availability of the Internet, general audience digital libraries are now emerging, for example, the New Zealand Digital Library (Witten, Nevill-Manning, McNab, & Cunningham, 1998).

Digital libraries are hosted or sponsored by a variety of organizations or institutions. Here are some examples:

1.   National libraries, for example, Library of Congress American Memory Project (http://memory.loc.gov/)

2.   State libraries, for example, Washington State Digital Library Resource (http://digitalwa.statelib.wa.gov/)

3.   Associations, for example, Association for Computing Machinery (ACM) Digital Library (http://www.acm.org/dl/)

4.   Foundations, for example, International Children's Digital Library (http://www.icdlbooks.org/)

5.   Universities, for example, Electronic Poetry Center at SUNY–Buffalo (http://wings.buffalo.edu/epc/)

6.   Museums, for example, American Museum of Natural History Digital Library Project (http://library.amnh.org/diglib/index.html)

7.   Companies. Many corporate digital libraries are not accessible by general public. They are normally located on company's Intranet.

Current Developments

Interactivity is a new trend in digital library development. Bates (2002) discussed the cascade of interactions in the digital library interface, and illustrated the effective design of digital libraries via interactions among metadata and indexing systems, information system front-ends, user search capabilities, and interface design. Budhu and Coleman (2002) designed interactivities in the components of a digital library, including the resources, objects, collections, interfaces, and metadata. The collections are focused on interactive, multimedia, and educational resources to promote active learning. Each collection offers a hierarchy of learning objects to satisfy user needs. The resources build interactivities by applying graphics and flow of information via storytelling. A glossary and a thesaurus are the two tools developed for contextual interactivities. More important, a concept map, extracted from both the user performance interaction logs and the learning resources, is created as the new interactive resource.

Personalization is an important option for users to effectively interact with digital libraries. Jayawardana, Hewagamage, and Hirakawa (2001) developed a prototype system of two components (DL Browser and Personal Document Editor) to create a personalized information environment for digital libraries. DL Browser, which facilitates navigation in digital libraries, consists of tools for personalized retrieval and personalized filtering. The Personal Document Editor helps users create, open, and maintain their personal documents. Jayawardana et al. plan to further explore other complicated issues of personalization, such as situated personalization.

Visualization is another approach that assists users in effectively interacting with digital libraries, especially with the search results derived from digital libraries. For example, Liu et al. (2000) introduced a search aid for a digital library that helps users analyze as well as display the classification of search query results.

Creating digital libraries for different types of user groups is another trend in digital library development. For example, in partnership with the Internet Archive, the University of Maryland created the International Children's Digital Library featuring over 10,000 digitized children's books in their original languages. A prototype was launched in November 2002 (DiMattia & Ishizuka, 2002; Goldberg, 2003). Applying technological innovations, many libraries and consortia around the nation have been working with Online Computer Library Center (OCLC), OverDrive, Talking Communities, and other partners to develop and test digital collections and services that are accessible to all, including print-impaired patrons. Bell and Peters (2005) reported four representative examples for using digital information technology to improve the accessibility and usability of digital libraries for all users: OPAL: Online Programming for All Libraries, MI-DTB Project (Mid-Illinois Digital Talking Book) Project: Audible E-books, OverDrive: Unabridged Digital Audio Books, and InfoEyes: Virtual Reference infoEyes, interactive training for the visually impaired.

Challenges for Users

The uniqueness of the digital library environment places users in a vital position. Because users are the audiences for digital libraries, understanding user needs and behaviors is essential for the development of digital libraries. Greenstein (2000) emphasized that it is imperative to penetrate and mobilize user communities for three additional reasons: 1) some user communities are the producers of digital content, for example, research data, dissertation, teaching materials, and so forth; 2) some user communities can provide tools for a digital library, for example, GIS, manipulation of sound data, and so forth; 3) potential benefits can be anticipated by engaging with user communities.

The above common elements of the digital library, defined by The Association of Research Libraries (1995), indicate the uniqueness of the digital library environment. It also poses challenges for the development of digital libraries. First, universal access is a goal. People with a variety of background and skills are potential users of digital libraries. Thong, Hong, and Tam (2002) pointed out that while millions of dollars have been spent on building "usable" digital libraries, previous research has suggested users might still not use them. As Borgman (2003) claimed, in a global information infrastructure, digital libraries would serve larger, more diverse, and more geographically distributed audiences than most systems of today. Moreover, individual differences, such as the range of skills, abilities, cognitive styles, and personality characteristics, are found within a given user community. It is a challenge to design digital libraries to satisfy every user's requirement. Furthermore, digital library promotion and education is also essential. According to Oatman (2005), four out of five participating teachers who used the Internet to prepare for class "frequently or always" did not know what a digital library is or where to find one.

Second, digital library collections are digital artifacts that pose technical challenges for systems to store, organize, and distribute information. More importantly, digital library collections pose challenges for users, especially novice users, who need to retrieve multimedia information while they are still struggling for text retrieval. According to Rapp, Taylor, and Crane (2003), digital library construction has resulted in impressive and overwhelming content in the multimedia environment. They called for the need to examine the role of the human processor in digital library experiences. They further discussed how to apply cognitive research on text comprehension, memory, and spatial cognition to the design and functionality of digital libraries.

Third, both digital and physical libraries aim to provide people with the means for effective interaction with information. Guedon (1999) emphasized that librarians should place human interaction at the heart of their operations. However, users of digital libraries do not have the same support as users of physical libraries, especially in the help-seeking process, where users must turn to automated Help assistances, rather than human communication, for solutions to problems they encounter. Because digital libraries are all constructed somewhat differently, this creates a difficult situation for novice users who must learn how to use each unique system. The significance of digital libraries will be diminished if users cannot effectively learn and use them. Research has offered little information about how people respond to new searching environments.

Fourth, transparency of the digital library creation process and digital library services is essential for the successful use of digital libraries. By understanding the digital library process and services, users are able to understand the structure of digital libraries; more important, this system knowledge will allow them to effectively interact with digital libraries. However, the question is how to convey that information to users in digital libraries; in other words, what is the best approach to providing the information to users? It is a challenge for users to interact with digital libraries without knowing the creation process and services of digital libraries.

Fifth, digital libraries need to enhance their community center role in the digital environment. Users are not satisfied that digital libraries are not playing the same role as traditional libraries do. Digital libraries need to support the information needs of that community, and further allow members of the community to communicate with each other. It is a challenge to develop a new form of digital community center.

Research Overview

Digital Library Initiative 1 focuses on the following aspects of digital technologies: (1) geographic information analysis and presentation (e.g., Environmental Planning and Geographic Information Systems by the University of California, Berkeley, The Alexandria Project: Spatially Referenced Map Information by the University of California, Santa Barbara), (2) multimedia technology (e.g., Informedia Digital Video Library by Carnegie Mellon University), (3) full-text process (e.g., Federating Repositories of Scientific Literature by the University of Illinois at Urbana-Champaign), (4) intelligent agents (e.g., Intelligent Agent for Information Location by the University of Michigan), and (5) infrastructure for collaboration (e.g., Interoperation Mechanisms among Heterogeneous Services by Stanford University). Digital Library Initiative 2 extends the research to the following aspects: (1) more research and application of digital libraries (e.g., for special collections, Founding a National Gallery of the Spoken Word by Michigan State University; for reference in digital library, Automatic Reference Librarian for the World Wide Web by University of Washington, etc.), and (2) Undergraduate education (e.g., Columbia Earthscape: a model for a sustainable online educational resource in earth science by Columbia University, etc.). In addition, NSF is also a partner with NSF-JISC (U.S.-UK), NSF-DFG (U.S.-Germany), and NSF-EU (U.S.-European Union), providing funding for international digital library projects.

Fox and Urs (2002) reviewed the diverse dimensions of digital library research and practices including the history and evolution of digital libraries; the content, organization, services, access, and evaluation of digital libraries; and the social, economic, and legal issues of digital libraries. They also identified the challenges of digital library research and practices. For research, an integrated and comprehensive theory for digital library research as well as a methodology for the digital libraries' design, development, and improvement for different user communities are needed. For practice, guidelines for the management of digital libraries are required. Liu (2004) surveyed the best practices, standards, and techniques for digitizing library materials in the US, in particular focusing on the most significant problems or concerns for libraries in digitization and the associated standards and technologies in digitization in US libraries. These reviews of current literature highlighted the best practices, trends, and interests in digitization.

Digital library research is not limited to its technical aspects. Recent research has extended to the social influences, processes, practices, and use of digital libraries. Bishop and Star (1996) presented an overview of the social informatics of digital library use and infrastructure. The review covers the social aspects of digital library design, implementation, and use, with an emphasis on the social informatics of digital library infrastructure and the social informatics of digital library use. They concluded that the technical and social aspects of digital libraries are intermingled and need to be investigated together. Simultaneously, research on the social-technical nature of digital libraries is hampered by technical and social difficulties. In addition, they discussed the research methods that have been applied in studies of digital library social informatics, and proposed questions for further research.

In addition to research overviews, many Web sites also provide comprehensive information about practice and research of digital libraries. Kochtanek, Hein, and Kassim (2001) described the Project DL, which is to provide an integrated resource of diverse topics related to digital libraries' development and research. The project consists of three components: digital library collections, digital library resources, and digital library Web sites.

Interaction Studies

Interaction studies in digital library environments can be summarized into the following aspects: 1) tasks/goals and their impact, 2) usage patterns, 3) online help, 4) usability studies, 5) organizational usability, 6) interactive multimedia information retrieval, and 7) evaluation criteria for digital libraries.

Tasks/Goals and their Impact

Research has demonstrated that tasks have impact on information-seeking behaviors (Algon, 1999; Byström & Järvelin, 1995; Vakkari, 1999). Users' tasks lead them to look for information in digital libraries. In other words, the objective of IR is to accomplish users' tasks. Thus, it is imperative to investigate user tasks, especially to integrate their work process into the investigation. Several studies were carried out in three different settings with different types of users. Employing "think-aloud" scenarios in the laboratory, participant observation in the field, key informant interviews, and focus group sessions, Gorman, Lavelle, Delcambre, and Maier (2002) attempted to understand expert clinicians and their information tasks in hospital settings. Based on their analysis of the data, they revised their approach from assisting familiarization tasks that allow clinicians to become familiar with patients, their condition, and current medications for a management plan to tasks that capture traces of an expert through a collection of documents. They further applied their understanding of user model and task model to the creation of technologies for digital libraries. Sumner and Dawe (2001) compared the stages and associated cognitive activities that faculty members went through in fulfilling two tasks—preparing for a class and preparing for a course—from a digital library resource reuse perspective. The results showed that faculty exhibited different cognitive activities and behaviors when performing the two tasks. Based on their findings, Sumner and Dawe argued that it is critical to design digital libraries to take into account of different types of tasks that users might perform.

Based on Web surveys, a diary method, and open-ended telephone interviews, Xie (2006) investigated human-work interaction in a corporate setting. The first type of interaction activities is task activities. Three dimensions of task activities emerged from the data: (1) whether the nature of task is routine, typical, or new; (2) whether the type of task is to update information or look for specific information, a known item, or items with common characteristics; and (3) whether the timeframe of the task is extremely urgent, urgent, or non-urgent. Higher-level interaction activities affect low-level activities. The three dimensions of task activities greatly affect the other three types of interaction activities: decision, collaboration, and strategy activities. The author further discussed an enhanced model of human-work interaction developed by Pejtersen and Fidel (1998) and its implications for the development of a corporate digital library. The above studies demonstrate that tasks are the driving forces for information retrieval in digital libraries. Moreover, different types of users have their unique types of tasks, which, in turn, influence the way users interact with digital libraries. However, tasks cannot be considered in one dimension only. Instead, multiple dimensions of tasks and their influences need to be further identified and validated.

Tasks lead people to search for information. Therefore, the organization of information in digital libraries should also consider the types of tasks that potential users intend to undertake. Research has taken the approach of organizing information by tasks in digital libraries to facilitate users in fulfilling their tasks. Meyyappan, Foo, and Chowdhury (2004) discussed the design, development, and evaluation of a task-based digital library in which three different information organization approaches (alphabetical, subject category, and task-based) were used to organize heterogeneous resources. By applying several task scenarios, they conducted a user evaluation study to assess the effectiveness and usefulness of the digital library and three information organization approaches. The results indicated that the task-based approach is the most effective in organizing information in the digital library.

In order to develop a problem-based pediatric digital library to meet user needs, D'Alessandro and Kingsley (2002) conducted a literature-based need assessment related to common pediatric problems encountered by pediatric health care providers and families. They identified and categorized common problems, and searched these problems for authoritative Web sites. Based on the results, a pediatric digital library was created with a problem-based interface. Within one year, visitors increased by 57.3% and overall usage increased by 255%. The increase in use demonstrated the usefulness of problem-based interface. The only limitation is that these task/problem categorizations are subject-based, and thus only consist of one dimension of the task. The other dimensions of the tasks, such as the nature of the task and the time frame of the task, as discussed by Xie (2006), are essential in affecting users' information-seeking strategies, and they also need to be incorporated into digital library design.

Usage Patterns

Usage patterns present a picture about how users interact with digital libraries. Based on the data collected from transaction logs, online questionnaires, online comments, interviews, and anecdotes, Entlich et al. (1996) reported that a small number of users are the major users of the digital library. The top 35% of users accounted for 80% of the usage. They further analyzed users' article searching, viewing, reading, and printing habits, and found that users valued the full-text searching capability. The author search was the most popular search, accounting for 32.1% of all searches. The results also revealed that syntax and format errors accounted for 17.6% of searches. Usage data provide not only information about how users interact with digital libraries but also what affects users' interaction with digital libraries. Based on analysis of a 12-month time series of transaction logs derived from the Alexandria Digital Library, Buttenfield and Reitsma (2002) developed a three-dimensional, origin-destination-time flow/transaction matrix to model transactions in terms of their time, origin, and destination components in order to detect the patterns of navigation through an Internet-based digital library. Interactions are represented visually. The findings showed that user training instead of changes in the user interface affected transaction patterns significantly.

Usage patterns have also been analyzed to examine users' interaction with specific features of digital libraries. Lumpe and Butler (2002) investigated how 43 high school science students used the scaffolding features of a digital library in the context of finding science information. The organizational feature scaffolds were the most utilized among the following features: saving and viewing, searching, maintenance, organizational, and collaborative. The use of organizational feature scaffolds was found significantly correlated with student performance. Employing deep log methods of analysis of a million users' request to a digital library, researchers (Nicholas, Huntington, Monopoli, & Watkinson, 2006; Nicholas, Huntington, & Watkinson, 2005) explored users' viewing behaviors, especially what a user is viewing, to understand their degree of penetration of a system. Based on the analysis of the transaction logs of a Korean digital library, Zhang, Lee, and You (2001) concluded that the search function was by far the most frequently used system function.

Usage patterns can also be analyzed to identify research trends and research impact in digital libraries. Bollen, Luce, Vemulapalli, and Xu (2003) analyzed the usage patterns derived from the log analysis of an institution's digital library usage from 1998 to 2001, and compared the usage pattern to Scientific Indexing (ISI) Impact Factor values during the same years to identify the local research trends in the institution. The concept of utility time was brought in to assess the impact of the NASA Astrophysics data system digital library based on usage logs, membership statistics, and gross domestic product (GDP) data (Kurtz et al., 2005). Interestingly,

Kurtz et al. (2005) found that the impact of the digital library in 2002 equaled 736 full-time researchers, or $250 million.

Usage patterns in digital libraries can be characterized and compared to other types of IR environments. Jones, Cunningham, McNab, and Boddie (2000) conducted a transaction log analysis of user interaction with the Computer Science Technical Reports (CSTR) collection of the New Zealand Digital Library, and further compared the similarities and differences between this study and studies of Web search engines and OPACs. Compared with studies of Web search engines, several remarkable similarities were found: 1) short queries (2.21 for Excite and 2.5 for CSTR), 2) short sessions (2.8 queries a session for Excite, and 2.04 queries a session for CSTR), 3) the number of results viewed (61% of Excite users viewed the first 10 results for a query, and CSTR users viewed details of 49.7% of documents within the first 10 results), and 4) the percentage of unique queries (one third of queries for both Excite and CSTR). The main difference between this study and studies of Web search engines is the use of Boolean operators. More queries contain Boolean operators in CSTR data than in Excite data because the users of CSTR are computer scientists who are more knowledgeable about Boolean logic than general search engine users. A comparison with transaction analyses of OPAC studies also yielded similarity in short queries. However, the length of each OPAC search session varies from 7 minutes to 30 minutes. OPAC studies report large proportions of search errors, while the level of search error in CSTR is not unexpected.

Multiple methods have been applied in studying users' usage patterns. The question is what the best method to study digital library use is. Notess (2004) compared three research methods (user satisfaction questionnaires, activity log files, and contextual inquiry) based on analysis of the required expertise, time, and benefits. Each of the methods has its benefits. The integration of the three methods can offer a better understanding of digital library use. One limitation of the study, as stated by Notess (2004), is that the three methods were not applied to study the same digital library use. Banwell et al. (2004) presented the methodology and outcomes of the User Behavior Monitoring and Evaluation Framework for a digital library in its first three annual cycles. They emphasized a multidimensional, across-sector methodology for monitoring user behavior and the factors that impact on behavior. In addition, they compiled a profile of user behavior in the digital library.

Online Help

As noted by Jansen (2005), research and development in the area of online Help has largely proceeded without attention to either the evaluation of automated Help assistants or to the precursors of help-seeking behaviors within the context of IR. In other words, the development of Help functionalities found in virtually all IR systems, including digital libraries, is proceeding without parallel attention to the users for whom these systems are designed. Such a discrepancy is especially important in the area of digital libraries, which are proliferating at a rapid pace and used by novice searchers who are most often in need of assistance to achieve their information goals. At the same time, the design of Help mechanisms also should consider how to assist expert users for their unique Help needs.

For the most part, Help mechanisms have been construed as assistants in the query formulation process rather than as ongoing partners during the information-seeking episode. Furthermore, research within IR has shown that although people frequently report that they believe Help mechanisms to be important components of the overall IR system, they use these Help functions infrequently, even though they might potentially improve search results (Cool & Xie, 2004).

Current research focuses on the evaluation of users' online Help use in digital libraries. Monopoli, Nicholas, Georgiou, and Korfiati (2002) evaluated users' use of a digital library including its online Help. Even though only 34.6% of the 246 respondents used online Help, majority of the respondents (61.2%) who used online Help implied that it was a useful service and easy to use. That is contradictory to Slack's (1991) research examining the effectiveness and use of online Help features in five different OPACs. Using "enhanced" transaction logs, mailed surveys, and focus groups, she found that even though the Help feature was utilized by one-third of the novice users, it did not assist the users in their help-seeking situations. Interestingly, 20% of the respondents of Monopoli, Nicholas, Georgiou, and Korfiati's (2002) study preferred human support, and they agreed with the statement "it is a helpful service, but I prefer asking a person to help me." While half the respondents did not feel the need to use help, about 5.1% of them did not know the availability of online Help. Surprisingly, 22.5% respondents did not understand what online Help was. That echoes Connell's (1995) finding that inexperienced users do not use Help because they do not understand how Help can be helpful to them.

The evaluation studies not only presented the current use of online Help but also provided information about user requirements in designing online Help in digital libraries. Hill et al. (2000) tested user interfaces of the Alexandria Digital Library through a series of studies; they collected feedback about the users' interactions with interfaces of the Alexandria Digital Library, the problems of the interfaces, the requirements of system functionality, and the collection of the digital library, all based on user evaluation studies. Derived from these studies, they found that users require the following Help functions: 1) creation of search examples to assist user query formulation, 2) offering context-sensitive Help, and 3) providing tutorials and FAQ. That is similar to Othman's (2004) findings, derived from users' evaluation of retrieval features of 12 online databases, in which search term Help, search examples, and context-sensitive Help were expected. In addition, users desired the following Help features: relevance feedback, a list of similar terms or synonyms, and assignment of weight values for search terms. Based on the findings of the above studies, it seems that while users require a variety of Help mechanisms in their use of digital libraries, users need more guidance in search refinement and search terms in their use of online databases. More studies are needed to investigate users' use of the Help mechanisms of digital libraries, specifically, the problematic situations that lead users to look for help and types of help desired in the digital library environments.

Research has also been conducted to compare Help mechanisms in digital libraries to other IR systems. Xie and Cool (2006) compared 50 subjects' usage and evaluation of the Help functionalities of the American Memory (AM) Digital Library, hosted by the US Library of Congress, and the image retrieval system at the Hermitage Museum (HM) Web site. Four ways of learning Help mechanisms emerged from the data: (1) using trial and error, (2) using past experience, (3) looking for the Help icon, and (4) using related Help functions. The major problems users encountered when using Help are (1) don't know where to start, (2) need direction, (3) too general, and (4) difficult to understand the content of provided Help. The first two problems are related to the design of online Help; the last two are associated with the content of the Help. The results of the study suggest that people prefer specific help, visual help, and help with demonstration, as presented in HM, instead of general help, text help, and help with description, as shown in AM. Users need help in the information retrieval process. They need assistance in identifying and expressing problems, in locating information regarding a problem, in obtaining relevant information, and in understanding the explanation provided. As to the assistance in overall interaction in the information retrieval process, the Hermitage Museum Help system is more highly rated than the American Memory Help system. The American Digital Library Help system was only rated 2.5 on a 5.0 scale in assisting users' interaction with the digital library. There is a discrepancy between the existing Help mechanisms of IR systems and the Help mechanisms that users need, because the IR Help systems have been designed without paying much attention to users' help-seeking situations and behaviors. We need more knowledge about users' help-seeking situations and behaviors, especially how they interact with Help mechanisms in IR systems, including digital libraries.

In order to design better Help mechanisms, researchers have taken several approaches. The first is to understand how users learn how to use new interfaces and systems. Based on the analysis of videotapes of people using the Illinois Digital Library system and their assumption of the systems as well as transcripts and audiotapes from the sessions, Neumann and Ignacio (1998) examined how users learned to use the interface and the functionality of the system. Their findings revealed that users had a structured exploration of the interface even though it might look like a random trial-and-error use of the interface. The second is to understand the processes of intermediation in digital library research. Library users are used to human help in using physical libraries; now they have to depend on system help in using digital libraries. According to Heckart (1998, p. 251), "Unmediated access is optimized when help is built in as an aspect of user-friendly design and as an explicit option users can invoke when needed." Southwick (2003) reported on an exploratory case study of intermediation in a hospital digital library information service in which a user and an intermediary communicated through an asynchronous, text-based, digital medium. Nine categories of factors perceived as affecting digital intermediation emerged from the data.

The third approach addresses the need to understand how users interact with Help mechanisms. Brajnik and his colleagues (Brajnik, Mizzaro, Tasso, & Venuti, 2002) have developed a conceptual framework of "collaborative coaching" between users and IR systems, stressing the importance of interaction in the design of intelligent Help mechanisms that can provide strategic support to users in help-seeking situations. Their preliminary evaluation of a prototype knowledge-based system showed that participants provided positive assessment of their interaction with strategic Help. Users appreciated the proposed search activities, especially the help provided without users' requests and without interrupting users' activities. Users have the control in interaction with Help mechanisms. Chander, Shinghal, Desai, and Radhakrishnan (1997) suggested an expert system for cataloging and searching digital libraries with an intelligent user interface to provide context-sensitive help to users. The fourth is the need to understand how users organize concepts in digital library Help systems. Faiks and Hyland (2000) employed the card sort technique, in which users impose their own organization on a set of concepts: the goal of this study was to determine how users would organize a set of concepts to be included in an online digital library Help system. The card sort technique proved to be a highly effective and valuable method for gathering user input on organizational groupings prior to total system design.

Usability Studies

Digital library research has received significant attention in recent years. To date, much of the research has emphasized usability issues dealing largely with interface design for specialized collections. The majority of research on usability studies either recommends design principles or improves the existing design. Accepted definitions of usability focus more on users themselves and include multiple usability attributes such as learnability, efficiency, memorability, errors, and satisfaction (Nielsen, 1993). In a workshop on the "usability of digital libraries" at Joint Conference on Digital Libraries (JCDL)'02, usability was broadly extended to cover many aspects, such as performance measures (efficiency of interactions, avoidance of user errors, and the ability of users to achieve their goals), affective aspects, and the search context (Blandford & Buchanan, 2002). After reviewing the research on usability, Jeng (2005a, 2005b) concluded that usability is a multidimensional construct. She further proposed an evaluation model for the evaluation of the usability of digital libraries by examining the effectiveness, efficiency, satisfaction, and learnability of digital libraries. The evaluation model was tested, and the results revealed that effectiveness, efficiency, and satisfaction are interrelated. At the same time, the results also identified users' perceptions of ease of use, organization of information, terminology, attractiveness, and mistake recovery.

The attributes of usability, in particular user needs and user satisfaction, have been investigated in many of the digital library usability studies. In order to understand users' information needs and their perception of existing information systems, Fox et al. (1993) interviewed potential users and experts in the related fields. They designed and conducted usability testing of an interface based on these interviews, which led to the design of a usable prototype of a digital library. Van House, Butler, Ogle, and Schiff (1996) discussed the iterative design process for the University of California Berkeley Electronic Environmental Library Project. After observing and interviewing users about design elements, including query form, fields, instructions, results displays, and formats of images and texts, they enhanced the design of the digital library. Bishop et al. (2000) presented the nature and extent of digital library testbed use, which includes extent of use, use of the digital library compared to other systems, nature of use, viewing behavior, purpose and importance of use, and user satisfaction. Data were collected from potential and actual users through focus groups, interviews, observations, usability testing, user registration and transaction logging, and user surveys.

Bishop et al.'s (2000) usability tests were extended to "situated usability" modeled by Van House and her colleagues (Van House, 1995), in which both the usability and how and why people used the system were investigated. The situated usability studies enable researchers to understand and observe users' context of use for digital libraries as part of the design and evaluation of digital libraries. Adopting an interpretive and situated approach, Yang (2001) evaluated learners' problem-solving in using the Perseus digital library. The findings of the study helped designers develop and refine better intellectual tools to facilitate learners' performance. Kassim and Kochtanek (2003) conducted usability studies of an educational digital library through the use of focus groups, Web log analysis, database usage analysis, satisfaction surveys, remote usability testing, and so forth. These usability studies attempted to understand user needs, find problems, identify desired features, and assess overall user satisfaction.

Although some of these usability studies are part of overall digital library evaluation, they also examine the content and performance of the system in addition to interface usability. Based on data collected from observations, interviews, and document analysis, Marchionini, Plaisant, and Komlodi (1998) applied multifaceted approaches to the evaluation of the Perseus Project. Their evaluation was focused on learning, teaching, system (performance, interface, and electronic publishing), and content (scope, accuracy). Hill et al. (2000) tested user interfaces of the Alexandria Digital Library through a series of studies; they collected feedback about the users' interaction with the interfaces of Alexandria Digital Library, the problems of the interfaces, the requirements of system functionality, and the collection of the digital library based on user evaluation studies. User evaluation generated the following users' requirements for the design of digital library interfaces: unified and simplified search, being able to manage sessions, more options for results display, offering user workspace, holdings visualization, offering more Help functions, allowing easy data distribution, and informing users of the process status.

Indeed, user evaluation provides valuable input for the design and enhancement of digital libraries to satisfy user need. Cherry and Duff (2002) conducted a longitudinal study of a digital library collection of Early Canadiana Materials, focusing on how the digital library was used and the level of user satisfaction with different features of the digital library, including response time, browse capabilities, comprehensiveness of the collection, print function, search capabilities, and display of document pages. These studies provide a basic understanding of how to enable digital libraries to meet, and possibly exceed end user needs and expectations.

Another type of usability study is to compare an experimental group with a control group on different interfaces; in these studies, usefulness and learnability are the main measurements for comparison. Baldonado (2000) conducted two small-scale experiments to evaluate a user-centered interface (SenseMaker) for digital libraries. Her first experiment was to test the value of structure-based actions by comparing the use of an early version of SenseMaker with a baseline system. The results indicated that the majority of the participants understood and used the structure-based searching and filtering mechanisms, and considered the mechanisms useful after training. The second experiment tested the learnability of structure-based actions. The findings showed that the participants exhibited different comprehension of the structure-based actions without training. Two of the three participants understood the structure-based action. The interface needs to be further improved for users to learn the structure. The small sample of these experiments limited the generalizability of the study results.

The comparison of different interfaces also focuses on the effectiveness of the interfaces. In order to support effective user interactions with heterogeneous and distributed information resources, Park (2000) compared users' interaction with multiple databases through a common interface vs. an integrated interface. Her study was based on data collected from transaction logs, thinking-aloud protocols, post-search questionnaires, demographic questionnaires, exit questionnaires, and exit interviews. Most of the 28 subjects preferred the common interface over the integrated interface because of their ability to control database selection. After comparing the recall of two interfaces, the results indicated that users performed better within the common interface over the integrated interface. The search characteristics of two interfaces were also compared, and the findings revealed that users interacted more with the common interface than the integrated interface. This study suggested that in digital libraries, users preferred to interact with databases separately rather than integrally. Besser et al. (2003) conducted usability testing with 4th and 12th graders to compare the effectiveness of an existing finding-aid-based interface with a newly developed prototype interface based on the pretest of the existing finding aid for broad user access in retrieving cultural heritage information from a digital library. The findings of this study indicate that there is a need for research on adaptive and flexible systems for broad user access.

Buttenfield (1999) suggested two evaluation strategies for the usability evaluation of digital libraries: 1) The convergent method paradigm. Evaluation data need to be collected through the system life cycle: system design, development, and deployment, and 2) The double-loop paradigm. Evaluators can identify the value of a particular evaluation method under different situations. In most of the cited studies above, evaluation takes place at different stages of digital library development, which helps the iterative design and evaluation of digital libraries. One concern of the usability studies is that many of the studies have been conducted depending on the prototypes instead of the actual digital libraries, so that the actual use contexts are not taken into consideration. In addition, the small and convenient sample of the usability studies also limits the generalizability of the study results.

Organizational Usability

Usability in digital library design also includes factors beyond the usability of the interface itself (Shackle, 1997). Usability is defined and evaluated differently by the different players involved with digital library development, promotion, and use. According to Crocca and Anderson (1995), digital library systems are codeveloped and coproduced by all the participants, including librarians, library users, engineers, and others. Because of the involvement of different players, researchers have been concerned with the interactions among all the players involved with digital library design and use (Bishop & Star, 1996). In order to design systems for a variety of users, Lamb (1995) claims that usability issues should be extended beyond interface usability to include content usability, organizational usability, and interorganizational usability.

Among the different types of usability, the organizational aspects are considered to be among the most important for the development of digital libraries (Bishop & Star, 1996). Kling and Elliott (1994) introduced organizational usability into digital library research, and they modeled a set of players involved in the design and usage of a digital library in a university setting. The four dimensions of organizational usability were defined by Kling and Elliott as the physical proximity and social restrictions on using the system, the level of compatibility of files in different systems, the possibility of integrating the system into a person or group's work, and the availability of training and help to users. Covi and Kling (1996) examined the organizational dimensions of effective digital library use in university settings, and discussed three dimensions of effective use (connectivity, content, and usability) based on pairing the infrastructural requirements of digital library providers and the competency requirements of users. Elliott and Kling (1997) extended Markus and Robey's (1983) conceptualization of organizational validity into the framework of organizational usability; they presented dimensions of organizational usability at three levels: individual (integrability into work, reliability, and social acceptability), organizational (organization structure, power distribution, institutional norms, and social organization of computing) and environmental (environment structure and home and work/life ecology). These dimensions related to either the interactions among entities associated with digital libraries or the products of these interactions.

Inspired by Kling and Elliott's model, Davies (1997) further developed the model to illustrate different groups of stakeholders in the development of a university electronic library and their influence on the end users. Davies also discussed how organizational factors influence digital library development within a higher education institution. According to Davies (1997), there are many stakeholders who influence academic digital libraries. These include: project/library leaders who are responsible for strategic management, planning and implementation; designers/developers for system specification and design; content providers for document provision; and library staff for user support and training. Guided by Davies' (1997) model, Xie and Wolfram (2002) identified contributing factors for the organizational usability of state digital libraries through corroboratory evidence from the usage statistics of three sources: Internet-based database services available through the digital library, responses to a statewide-administered library survey, and a Web-based survey of end users. They identified three types of interactions among the players of state digital libraries: influenced-based interactions, activities-based interactions and communication-based interactions. As part of influenced-based interactions, different players involved with the digital library influence its coverage, content, and system formats because the players bring different needs, experiences, and expectations to the state digital library. The imbalanced distribution of promotion and training among the users is a major problem for activity-based interactions. For communication-based interactions, the broad range of organizations involved requires multiple avenues for soliciting feedback on service, content, document formats, interface usability, and training; this feedback is solicited from end users, library staff, digital library designer/developers, and content providers. The authors refined and enhanced the organizational usability model of interactions among key players in the unique environment of state digital libraries.

Interactive Multimedia Information Retrieval

One unique characteristic of digital libraries is that they contain multimedia materials from interfaces to collections. The design of digital libraries needs to deal with issues related to interface design and how that affects users interacting with these digital libraries. Based on the data collected from 12 subjects, Butcher, Bhushan, and Sumner (2006) compared users' cognitive processes in their information-seeking process in using a multimedia strand maps interface vs. the textual search interface for a digital library. The results showed that the design of a digital library interface may affect users' cognitive behaviors. To be more specific, while users of the multimedia interface concentrated on interacting with content of the interface and selecting continued search and navigation strategies, users of the textual interface were more likely to interact with surface-level information. Lee and Smeaton (2002) reported how the usability testing of different video browsers with 20 subjects yielded insightful information for the design of the video browser interface for a digital video library. The results suggested that users had different preferences for browsers. It is important to design intelligent interfaces that can offer different options for a specific user with a particular task. In regard to user interaction, a more integrated browser-player was suggested.

A series of studies has been conducted on video browsing under the Open Video Project at the University of North Carolina. One issue researchers focus on is the effect of context and interactivity on users' video browsing. Wildemuth, Russell, Ward, Marchionini, and Oh (2005) analyzed the data collected from 38 subjects who searched a database with video collections in three different systems: a basic system, a system with the context of the sequence of shots, and a system with the context plus interactive features. The results showed that the context plus interactive system was the best in terms of performance with recall measures. Simultaneously, this system was also the most preferred system by users in terms of ease-of-use and usefulness. The results of this study also indicated that for users, context is not as important as interactivity for effectively browsing video results lists. Another issue related to video browsing effectiveness concerns surrogates for digital video. Among the three alternative surrogates for video objects (storyboards with text or audio keywords, slide shows with text or audio keywords, fast forward), fast forward received the most support based on 10 participants' interactions with these surrogates (Wildemuth et al., 2002). Surrogate speed was demonstrated affecting the performance of object recognition, action recognition, linguistic gist comprehension, and visual gist comprehension. At the same time, users also liked to control the fast forward speed depending on the situation and their preferences (Wildemuth et al., 2003). Nine major visual gist attributes were identified related to interacting with fast forward surrogates: object, people, setting/environment, action/activities/events, theme/topic, time/period, geographical location, plot, and visual perception (Yang & Marchionini, 2005).

Compared with other types of IR systems, digital libraries are still in the development stages. Many of the studies are based on the prototypes of digital libraries with a small convenience sample. These studies did involve real users, but subjects of many studies did not work on their real problems. It is essential to understand how users interact with multimedia digital libraries when they work on their own situational problems. In addition, TREC Video Retrieval Evaluation research focuses on problems related to content-based access to digital video, which has implications for the design of interactive digital libraries that facilitates effective interactions between users and systems. These studies are not discussed here because of the space limitation.

Evaluation Criteria for Digital Libraries

Research on the evaluation of digital libraries is still in its infancy. Researchers are still investigating who should evaluate, when to evaluate, what to evaluate, how to evaluate, and why to evaluate. As Saracevic and Covi (2000) argue, the evaluation of digital libraries is a complex undertaking that is conceptually and pragmatically challenging. Borgman, Leazer, Gilliland-Swetland, and Gazan (2001) further suggest that technical complexity, variety of content, uses and users, and the lack of evaluation methods contribute to the problem. Any evaluation is based on the conceptual model of the evaluators, in particular their understanding of the goals of the system and of users' needs and behaviors. Evaluation itself is a form of sense-making, and it is also situated (Van House, Butler, Ogle, & Schiff, 1996).

An evaluation is a judgment of worth. A system is evaluated to ascertain the level of its performance or its value. Digital libraries can be judged by their effectiveness (how well does a system or any of its parts perform the roles or tasks for which it was designed?) and efficiency (at what cost?) (Chowdhury & Chowdhury, 2003; Saracevic & Covi, 2000). Marchionini (2000) further points out that evaluation is a research process that aims to understand the meaning of some phenomenon situated in a context and changes that take place as the phenomenon and the context interact. Evaluation specifies the research process (metrics and procedures), the phenomenon (its mission and salient characteristics), and the context(s) in which the phenomenon occurs. Evaluation of a new phenomenon, such as digital libraries, is affected by the existing criteria for evaluating related institutions or systems. Bertot and McClure (2003) propose a framework for relating the traditional evaluation components and terminology of library services/resource assessment to the networked environment.

Although the amount of research on the evaluation of digital libraries has increased, little discussion pertains to the criteria for evaluation. Currently most of the research on digital library evaluation is based on the existing evaluation criteria for traditional libraries, the performance of information retrieval systems, human-computer interaction, digital technologies, and so forth. Marchionini (2000) suggests that digital libraries are extensions and augmentations of physical libraries.

Researchers might use existing techniques and metrics to evaluate digital libraries, for example, circulation, collection size and growth rate, patron visits, reference questions answered, patron satisfaction, and financial stability. Evaluation criteria for digital technologies can also be useful, such as response time, storage capacity, transfer rate, user satisfaction, cost per operation, and so forth. However, digital libraries provide new services, products, and capabilities, making it more difficult to compare them with physical libraries.

After reviewing evaluation criteria for libraries by Lancaster (1993), for library and information services by Saracevic and Kantor (1997), and for information retrieval systems and human-computer interaction by Su (1992) and Schneiderman (1998), the following list of criteria was presented by Saracevic (2000) and Saracevic and Covi (2000): Traditional library criteria: collection (purpose, scope, authority, coverage, currency, audience, cost, format, treatment, preservation), information (accuracy, appropriateness, links, representation, uniqueness, comparability, presentation), use (accessibility, availability, searchability, usability), standards; Traditional IR criteria: relevance (precision and recall), satisfaction, success; and Traditional human-computer interaction/interface criteria: usability, functionality, efforts; task appropriateness, and failures. As previously noted, most digital library evaluation studies are mainly usability studies. Some of the evaluation studies also assess collection content, system performance, and services. While Marchionini (2000) emphasized applying traditional library evaluation criteria to digital libraries, Saracevic (2000) and Saracevic and Covi (2000) extended the evaluation criteria to include those developed for information retrieval systems and human-computer interaction. Chowdhury and Chowdhury (2003) added that it is also necessary to measure the overall impact of digital libraries on users and society. However, these evaluation criteria were developed by researchers, not users.

As to who should evaluate digital libraries, users of digital libraries should have their voices heard. After all, the ultimate goal of the development of digital libraries is to serve users and to facilitate their effective use of information and services. As Marchionini, Plaisant, and Komlodi (1998) emphasize, all efforts to design, implement, and evaluate digital libraries must be rooted in the information needs, characteristics, and contexts of the people who may use those libraries. Research on digital libraries has moved from the technical aspects of building them to how to design them to satisfy user needs. One way to assess user needs is to investigate digital library evaluation criteria from the user point of view. Drawn from 48 subjects' criteria for the evaluation of digital libraries, Xie (2006) identified users' criteria and applied them to the evaluation of existing digital libraries. A compilation of criteria developed by participants showed that interface usability and collection quality were the most important criteria for evaluating digital libraries. Service quality, system performance efficiency, and user opinion solicitation were also deemed essential criteria.

Xie (2006) further compared digital library evaluation criteria from the perspectives of users, researchers, and previous evaluation studies. Researchers have connected digital library evaluation criteria with previous research that evaluates a variety of IR systems including libraries. Digital library evaluation studies have focused on examining the criteria from selected categories, mostly interface usability. Participants in this study associated their evaluation criteria with their experience in using physical libraries and other types of information retrieval systems. There is a commonality in the overall categories of the evaluation criteria. To be more specific, participants in this study, researchers, and previous studies all have identified the same major categories (e.g., usability, collection quality, service quality, system performance, and user opinion solicitation) of the evaluation criteria. Comparatively speaking, users take a more practical approach in evaluating digital libraries. They care more about whether specific features or options exist rather than how effective these features and options should be. In addition, they consider evaluation criteria from a user and use perspective and not from developers' or administrators' perspectives. That is why they are not concerned with budget, cost, and other related criteria. Simultaneously, they identified some of the criteria that researchers have neglected, such as unique services provided only by digital libraries and different ways to solicit user feedback.

Interactivity is another essential component for digital library evaluation. However, little research has explored the interactivity aspect of digital library evaluation. Budhu and Coleman (2002) identified the key attributes of interactivities: reciprocity, feedback, immediacy, relevancy, synchronicity, choice, immersion, play, flow, multidimensionality, and control. They evaluated interactivities in a digital library with regard to the following aspects: interactivities in resources, resources selection, description of interactivities in metadata, and interactivities in interface. The evaluation of the interactivities in resources focused on how the digital library can enhance learning and retention by comparing the use of the digital library to other systems. The evaluation of the interactivities in resource selection emphasized whether the selected resources were truly interactive. The evaluation of the description of interactivities in metadata measured the usefulness of the new metadata elements for interactivity: type of interactivity, audience, duration, and level of interactivity. The evaluation of interactivities in interface measured universal usability defined by Schneiderman (2000). This study recognizes the importance of the evaluation of interactivities in digital libraries. However, the key emphasis of the evaluation should be placed on the evaluation of the interaction process between users and digital libraries.

Summary

Table 5.1 presents summary of interaction studies in digital library environments.

There is no doubt that tasks and goals are the driving forces for information retrieval. This is also the case in digital library environments. The identification of types of tasks/goals and dimensions of tasks in digital library environments do not yield unique types or dimensions related to digital libraries. Researchers need to ask whether user tasks/goals are same in digital libraries and other types of IR systems, in other words, whether tasks/goals are independent completely of IR systems. Is there a dimension of task associated with IR systems? A related question is whether tasks/goals are independent of user types. Although researchers have begun to incorporate one dimension of task-search problems into digital library interface design, the remaining questions are: What is the best approach for applying dimensions of tasks to system design? Which dimensions need to be incorporated into digital library design?

Unlike usage patterns studies in Web search engine environments, the focus in digital library environments is not limited to query formulation and reformulation. Usage pattern studies in digital library environments extend to feature use and the impact of digital library use. Users perform more complicated searches in digital library environments. Wolfram and Xie (2002) defined the context of digital libraries as representing a hybrid of both "traditional" IR, using primarily bibliographic resources provided by database vendors, and "popular" IR, exemplified by public search systems available on the World Wide Web. In addition, digital libraries have other functions beyond the searching itself. Current usage studies still cannot answer the question of whether there are unique patterns of digital library usage compared to other types of IR systems, and, if so, what the unique patterns of digital library usage are.

Research has indicated that the Help features of digital libraries are not frequently used. Novice users either do not know what online Help is or are unaware of its availability in a digital library. Expert users are not satisfied with Help features' design and content. In a word, Help is not helpful. The question is how to change users' perceptions of Help mechanisms in digital libraries. In order to design Help mechanisms that are helpful, we also need to know under what circumstances users need help and what types of help they desire. Research has shown that users do not like to use the online Help of indifferent IR systems, including digital libraries, instead, they prefer human help when they encounter problems in the information retrieval process. Further research also needs to explore how to incorporate human-human interaction protocols into the design of Help mechanisms in digital libraries.

Usability studies take a major role in digital library research because the design of digital library prototypes and digital libraries themselves began in the 1990s, and no standard design principles have been set up. One advantage of digital library usability studies is that they are conducted in the process of design, evaluation, and implementation. The results of the usability studies yield valuable information for the design and improvement of the interfaces of digital libraries. Moreover, usability studies in digital library research extend from interface usability to organizational usability. However, many of the usability studies cannot provide a complete picture of actual users' reactions to digital libraries because these studies either work on the prototypes of digital libraries or in a simulated environment. Lynch (2003) raised the concern of depending too much on research prototypes because they do not have the same political, economic, governance, and cultural dynamics as real digital libraries have.

Compared to other information systems, the complexity of digital libraries makes it difficult for users to learn how to use them. Simultaneously, that complexity also poses challenges for usability testing. First, what are the usability criteria for testing? More important, current usability studies of digital libraries apply the criteria derived from other types of IR systems. What unique criteria need to be applied in the usability studies of digital libraries? Second, Borgman (2003) pointed out that the design of digital libraries must consider user communities in terms of what, how, and why they use the content. It is understandable that we cannot create a one-type-fits-all digital library. At the same time, how can a digital library be designed to maximally support diverse user groups/communities accommodating individual differences? That leads to the same question for usability studies: how can this factor be taken into account in usability studies?

Interface usability itself cannot guarantee the usability of digital libraries. Users use digital libraries in different organizations and environments. Simultaneously, digital libraries are codeveloped by many players, and it is imperative to promote different levels and different types of interactions among all the players. Organizational usability needs to be considered for the successful development and effective use of digital libraries. However, not all of the players in digital library environments can be easily defined and studied. This is especially true for the players in general audience digital libraries, such as national and state digital libraries, because different organizations and users are involved in the development and use of this type of digital library. Without defining the players and their interactions, digital libraries cannot be designed to be usable for all the potential users. Organizational usability also relates individual users' use of digital libraries. Another critical issue is how to integrate organizational usability and interface usability together to assess the overall usability of digital libraries.

Multimedia collections in digital libraries pose challenges for effective user-digital library interactions. Current research has started to investigate how users interact with multimedia interfaces and objects in digital libraries. However, we need to systematically identify the patterns of users' interaction with different types of multimedia (e.g., audio, video, etc.) and different attributes of multimedia (e.g., context, different facets of multimedia information, etc.). Moreover, we need to

Table 5.1. Summary of interaction studies in digital library environments

Types	Research Focus	Problems/questions	Implications
Tasks/goals and their impact	Identification of types of tasks/goals users have to accomplish in digital libraries; Identification of dimensions of tasks; Impact of types of user goals/tasks on search behavior/ strategies.	Are user tasks/goals the same in searching digital libraries and other types of IR systems? In other words, are user tasks/goals independent of types of IR systems? What is the best approach for applying dimensions of tasks to system design?	Understand the driving force for IR in digital library environments; Design task/ problem-based interfaces for digital libraries; Incorporate tasks and their corresponding information-seeking strategies into system design.
Usage patterns	General patterns of digital library usage; Patterns of digital library feature usage; Impact of usage patterns; Research methods for studying usage patterns; Comparison of usage patterns between digital libraries and other types of IR systems.	Are there any unique patterns of digital library usage? What are the unique patterns of digital library usage?	Understand the nature of digital library usage and the impact of digital libraries; Understand the best methodologies for the study of usage patterns; Design better digital libraries or features to facilitate the use of digital libraries.
Online Help	Users' perception of Help use in digital libraries; Users' use and evaluation of Help features in digital libraries; Users' desired Help features in digital libraries.	How to change users' perception of Help mechanisms in digital libraries? Under what circumstances do users need help and what type of help do they need? How to incorporate human-human interaction protocol into the design of Help mechanisms in digital libraries?	Understand what types of help users need and when they need help; Design/Improve Help mechanisms to be interactive in digital libraries.

continued on following page

Table 5.1. continued

Usability studies	Evaluation of the interface usability of digital libraries, in particular taking into account user needs and user satisfaction; Comparison of experimental and control groups in using different interfaces of digital libraries.	What are the usability criteria for digital libraries, especially the unique criteria? How can usability studies be conducted considering user communities in terms of what, how, and why they use the content? How can usability studies be conducted in real digital library environments, taking into account political, economic, governance and cultural dynamics factors?	Understand users' reaction to the interface usability of digital libraries; Design or improve the interfaces of digital libraries for ease-of-use and ease-of-learning.
Organizational usability	Interactions among players in digital library development and use; Different levels of interaction: individual, organization, and environment.	How to define/identify all the players in the development and use of general audience digital libraries? How to integrate organizational usability and interface usability together in evaluating digital libraries?	Develop models of organizational usability in digital library environments; Design digital libraries to be usable in different organizations and environments.
Interactive multimedia IR	Comparison of different types of interfaces for facilitating user-digital library interactions; Identification of factors affecting effective user-interface/system interactions Users' interaction with multimedia objects of digital libraries.	How to systematically investigate patterns of users' interactions with different attributes of different types of multimedia objects? How to examine/ evaluate users' interactive multimedia IR in digital libraries by involving users with real situational problems? How to design a digital library that enables users to effectively interact with different types of multimedia information?	Design effective and usable interfaces of digital libraries to facilitate effective interactions. Understand how users interact with multimedia materials in digital libraries; Design better digital libraries to assist effective user-digital library interactions.

continued on following page

Table 5.1. continued

Evaluation criteria for digital libraries	Identification of evaluation criteria from researchers;	What are the essential criteria for evaluating digital libraries?	Determine the appropriate criteria for evaluating digital libraries, in particular users' interactions with digital libraries.
	Identification of evaluation criteria from users;	What are the criteria needed to evaluate the interactions between users and digital libraries?	
	Evaluation of interactivities in digital libraries.	What are the similarities and differences between researchers' and users' evaluation criteria for digital libraries, and how can they be integrated?	

incorporate real users with real situational problems into studies, because users' experiences with multimedia might change depending on individual users, their moods, and their circumstances. Finally, it is also crucial to explore how to design digital libraries that facilitate users' interactions with multiple types of media instead of just focusing on one type of media.

The Evaluation of digital libraries is a complicated task because of the nature of their development and usage. Compared to other types of IR system evaluation, digital library evaluation goes beyond usability testing. The evaluation of digital libraries needs to cover their interface, content, services, users, interactions, and impact. Moreover, the evaluation of digital libraries also needs to be conducted in the context of their uses. There is no agreement on what criteria are essential for the evaluation of digital libraries. Furthermore, users have their own perspectives in terms what the most important criteria for the evaluation of digital libraries are. Further research needs to explore the similarities and differences of digital library criteria suggested by researchers and users and how to integrate them. Although the research on digital libraries covers many aspects of those libraries, there are few studies deal with how to evaluate the interactions between users and digital libraries and how these interactions assist users in solving their information problems. Mature of digital library evaluation research depends on the development of actual digital libraries instead of prototypes.

References

Algon, J. (1999). *The effect of task on the information-related behavior of individuals in a work-group environment.* Unpublished doctoral dissertation, Rutgers University, New Brunswick, New Jersey.

Anderson, J. (1995). Have users changed their style? A survey of CD-ROM vs. OPAC product usage. *RQ, 34*(3), 362-368.

Association of Research Libraries. (1995). *Definition and purposes of a digital library.* Retrieved January 3, 2008, from http://www.arl.org/sunsite/definition.html

Baldonado, M. Q. W. (2000). A user-centered interface for information exploration in a heterogeneous digital library. *Journal of the American Society for Information Science, 51*(3), 297-310.

Banwell, L., Ray, K., Coulson, G., Urquhart, C., Lonsdale, R., Armstrong, C., et al. (2004). The JISC user behaviour monitoring and evaluation framework. *Journal of Documentation, 60*(3), 302-320.

Bates, M. M. (2002). The cascade of interactions in the digital library interface. *Information Processing & Management, 38*(3), 381-400.

Bell, L., & Peters, T. (2005). Digital library services for all: Innovative technology opens doors to print-impaired patrons. *American Libraries, 36*(8), 46-49.

Bertot, J. C., & McClure, C. R. (2003). Outcomes assessment in the networked environment: Research questions, issues, considerations, and moving forward. *Library Trends, 51*(4), 590-613.

Besser, H., Afnan-Manns, S., Stieber, D. A., Griest, B., Turnbow, D., & Dorr, A. (2003). Finding aid as interface? Enhancing K-12 access to digitized cultural heritage resources through adaptive systems technology: An exploratory study. In *Proceedings of the 66ᵗʰ ASIST Annual Meeting,* (Vol. 40, No. 1, pp. 511-513).

Bishop, A. P., Neumann, L. J., Star, S. L., Merkel, C., Ignacio, E., & Sandusky, R. J. (2000). Digital libraries: Situating use in changing information infrastructure. *Journal of the American Society for Information Science, 51*(4), 394-413.

Bishop, A. P., & Star, S. L. (1996). Social informatics of digital library use and infrastructure. *Annual Review of Information Science and Technology, 31,* 301-401.

Blandford, A., & Buchanan, G. (2002). Workshop report: Usability of digital libraries at JCDL'02. *SIGIR Forum, 36*(2), 83-89.

Bollen, J., Luce, R., Vemulapalli, S. S., & Xu, W. (2003). Usage analysis for the identification of research trends in digital libraries. *D-Lib Magazine, 9(5).* Retrieved January 3, 2008, from http://www.dlib.org/dlib/may03/bollen/05bollen.html

Borgman, C. L. (1999). What are digital libraries? Competing visions. *Information Processing and Management, 35*(3), 227-243.

Borgman, C. L. (2003). Designing digital libraries for usability. In A. P. Bishop, N. A. V. House, & B. P. Buttenfield (Eds.), *Digital library use: Social practice in design and evaluation* (pp. 85-118). Cambridge, MA: The MIT Press.

Borgman, C. L., Bates, M. J., Cloonan, M. V., Efthimiadis, E. N., Gilliland-Swetland, A. J., Kafai, Y. B., et al. (1996, February). *UCLA-NSF Social aspects of digital libraries workshop: Final report to National Science Foundation.* Retrieved January 3, 2008, from http://is.gseis.ucla.edu/research/dl/UCLA_DL_Report.html#introduction

Borgman, C. L., Leazer, G. H., Gilliland-Swetland, A. J., & Gazan, R. (2001). Iterative design and evaluation of a geographic digital library for university students: A case study of the Alexandria Digital Earth Prototype (ADEPT). In P. Constantopoulos & I. Sølvberg (Eds.), *Proceedings of the 5th European Conference on Research and Advanced Technology for Digital Libraries,* (pp. 390-401). London: Springer-Verlag.

Brajnik, G., Mizzaro, S., Tasso, C., & Venuti, F. (2002). Strategic help in user interfaces for information retrieval. *Journal of the American Society for Information Science, 53*(5), 343-358.

Budhu, M., & Coleman, A. (2002). The design and evaluation of interactivities in a digital library. *D-Lib Magazine, 8*(11). Retrieved January 3, 2008, from http://www.dlib.org/dlib/november02/coleman/11coleman

Bush, V. (1945). As we may think. *Atlantic Monthly, 176*(1), 101-108.

Butcher, K. R., Bhushan, S., & Sumner, T. (2006). Multimedia displays for conceptual discovery: Information seeking with strand maps. *Multimedia Systems, 11*(3), 236-248.

Buttenfield, B. (1999). Usability evaluation of digital libraries. *Science & Technology Libraries, 17*(3/4), 39-50.

Buttenfield, B. P., & Reitsma, R. F. (2002). Loglinear and multidimensional scaling models of digital library navigation. *International Journal of Human-Computer Studies, 57*(2), 101-119.

Byström, K., & Järvelin, K. (1995). Task complexity affects information-seeking and use. *Information Processing and Management, 31*(2), 191-213.

Chander, P. G., Shinghal, R., Desai, B. C., & Radhakrishnan, T. (1997). An expert system to aid cataloging and searching electronic documents on digital libraries. *Expert Systems with Applications, 12*(4), 405-416.

Cherry, J. M., & Duff, W. M. (2002). Studying digital library users over time: A follow-up survey of Early Canadiana Online. *Information Research, 7*(2). Retrieved January 3, 2008, from http://informationr.net/ir/7-2/paper123.html

Chowdhury, G. G., & Chowdhury, S. (2003). *Introduction to digital libraries.* London: Facet.

Connell, T. H. (1995). Subject searching in online catalogs: Metaknowledge used by experienced searchers. *Journal of the American Society for Information Science, 46*(7), 506-518.

Cool, C., & Xie, H. (2004). How can IR help mechanism be more helpful to users? In L. Schamber & C. L. Barry (Eds.), *Proceedings of the 67th ASIST Annual Meeting,* (pp. 249-255). Medford, NJ: Information Today.

Covi, L. M., & Kling, R. (1996). Organizational dimensions of effective digital library use: Closed rational and open natural systems models. *Journal of the American Society for Information Science, 47*(9), 672-689.

Crocca, W.T., & Anderson, W.L. (1995). Delivering technology for digital libraries: Experience as vendors. In F.M. Shipman, R. Furuta, & D.M. Levy (Eds.), *Digital libraries'95* (pp.1-8). Austin, TX: Department of Computer Science, Texas A&M University.

D'Alessandro, D., & Kingsley, P. (2002). Creating a pediatric digital library for pediatric health care providers and families: Using literature and data to define common pediatric problems. *Journal of the American Medical Informatics Association, 9*(2), 161-170.

Davies, C. (1997). Organizational influences on the university electronic library. *Information Processing & Management, 33*(3), 377-392.

DiMattia, S., & Ishizuka, K. (2002). U of MD creates international digital library. *School Library Journal, 48*(10), 27.

Dippo, C. S. (1998). FedStats promotes statistical literacy. *Communications of the ACM, 41*(4), 58-60.

Elliott, M., & Kling, R. (1997). Organizational usability of digital libraries: Case study of legal research in civil and criminal courts. *Journal of the American Society for Information Science, 48*(11), 1023-1035.

Entlich, R., Garson, L., Lesk, M., Normore, L., Olsen, J., & Weibel, S. (1996). Testing a digital library: User response to the CORE project. *Library Hi Tech, 14*(4), 99-118.

Faiks, A., & Hyland, N. (2000). Gaining user insight: A case study illustrating the card sort technique. *College and Research Libraries, 61*(4), 349-357.

Fox, E. A. (1999). Digital Libraries Initiative (DLI) projects 1994-1999. *Bulletin of the American Society for Information Science, 26*(1), 7-11.

Fox, E. A., Akscyn, R. M., Furuta, R. K., & Leggett, J. J. (1995). Digital libraries. *Communications of the ACM, 38*(4), 23-28.

Fox, E. A., Hix, D., Nowell, L. T., Brueni, D. J., Wake, W. C., Health, L. S., et al. (1993). Users, user interfaces, and objects–envision, a digital library. *Journal of the American Society for Information Science, 44*(8), 480-491.

Fox, E. A., & Urs, S. R. (2002). Digital libraries. *Annual Review of Information Science and Technology, 36*, 503-589.

Goldberg, B. (2003). Digital children's library debuts: Media buzz ensues. *American Libraries, 34*(1), 21.

Gorman, P., Lavelle, M., Delcambre, L., & Maier, D. (2002). Following experts at work in their own information spaces: Using observational methods to develop tools for the digital library. *Journal of the American Society for Information Science and Technology, 53*(14), 1245-1250.

Greenstein, D. (2000). Digital libraries and their challenges. *Library Trends, 49*(2), 290-303.

Guedon, J. C. (1999). The digital library: An oxymoron? *Bulletin of the Medical Library Association, 87*(1), 9-19.

Heckart, R. J. (1998). Machine help and human help in the emerging digital library. *College & Research Libraries, 59*(3), 250-259.

Hill, L. L., Carver, L., Larsgaard, M., Dolin, R., Smith, T. R., Frew, J., et al. (2000). Alexandria Digital Library: User evaluation studies and system design. *Journal of the American Society for Information Science, 51*(3), 246-259.

Jansen, B. J. (2005). Seeking and implementing automated assistance during the search process. *Information Processing and Management, 41*(4), 909-928.

Jayawardana, C., Hewagamage, K. P., & Hirakawa, M. (2001). A personalized information environment for digital libraries. *Information Technology and Libraries, 20*(4), 185-197.

Jeng, J. (2005a). Usability assessment of academic digital libraries: Effectiveness, efficiency, satisfaction, and learnability. *LIBRI, 55*(2-3), 96-121.

Jeng, J. (2005b). What is usability in the context of the digital library and how can it be measured? *Information Technology and Libraries, 24*(2), 47-56.

Jones, S., Cunningham, S. J., McNab, R., & Boddie, S. (2000). Human-computer interaction for digital libraries: A transaction log analysis of a digital library. *International Journal on Digital Libraries, 3*(2), 152-169.

Kassim, A. R. C., & Kochtanek, T. R. (2003). Designing, implementing, and evaluating an educational digital library resource. *Online Information Review, 27*(3), 160-168.

Khalil, M. A., & Jayatilleke, R. (2000). Digital libraries: Their usage from the end user point of view. In *Proceedings of the Twenty-First National Online Meeting,* (pp. 179-187).

Kling, R., & Elliott, M. (1994). Digital library design for organizational usability. *SIGOIS Bulletin, 15*(2), 59-70.

Kochtanek, T. R., Hein, K. K., & Kassim, A. R. C. (2001). A digital library resource Web site: Project DL. *Online Information Review, 25*(1), 29-40.

Kurtz, M. J., Eichhorn, G., Accomazzi, A., Grant, C., Demleitner, M., & Murray, S. S. (2005). Worldwide use and impact of the NASA astrophysics data system digital library. *Journal of the American Society for Information Science and Technology, 56*(1), 36-45.

Lamb, R. (1995). Using online information resources: Reaching for the *.*'s. In F. M. Shipman, R. Furuta, & D. M. Levy (Eds.), *Proceedings of Digital Libraries '95: The Second Annual Conference on the Theory and Practice of Digital Libraries,* (pp. 137-146). Austin, TX: Department of Computer Science, Texas A&M University.

Lancaster, F. W. (1993). *If you want to evaluate your library* (2nd ed.). Urbana-Champaign, IL: University of Illinois.

Lee, H., & Smeaton, A. F. (2002). Designing the user-interface for the Físchlár digital video library. *Journal of Digital Information, 2*(4). Retrieved January 3, 2008, from http://journals.tdl.org/jodi/article/view/jodi-53/57

Lesk, M. (2005). *Understanding Digital Libraries* (2nd ed.). San Francisco, CA: Morgan Kaufman.

Liu, Y. Q. (2004). Best practices, standards and techniques for digitizing library materials: A snapshot of library digitization practices in the USA. *Online Information Review, 28*(5), 338-345.

Liu, Y.-H., Dantzig, P., Sachs, M., Corety, J. T., Hinnesbusch, M. T., Damashek, M., et al. (2000). Visualizing document classification: A search aid for the digital library. *Journal of the American Society for Information Science, 51*(3), 216-227.

Lumpe, A. T., & Butler, K. (2002). The information seeking strategies of high school science students. *Research in Science Education, 32*(4), 549-566.

Lynch, C. (2003). Colliding with the real world: Heresies and unexplored questions about audiences, economics, and control of digital libraries. In A. P. Bishop, N. A. V. House, & B. P. Buttenfield (Eds.), *Digital library use: Social practice in design and evaluation* (pp. 191-218). Cambridge, MA: The MIT Press.

Marchionini, G. (2000). Evaluation digital libraries: A longitudinal and multifaceted view. *Library Trends, 49*(2), 304-333.

Marchionini, G., Plaisant, C., & Komlodi, A. (1998). Interfaces and tools for the Library of Congress National Digital Library Program. *Information Processing and Management, 34*(5), 535-555.

Markus, M. L., & Robey, D. (1983). The organization validity of management information systems. *Human Relations, 36*(3), 203-226.

Meyyappan, N., Foo, S., & Chowdhury, G. G. (2004). Design and evaluation of a task-based digital library for the academic community. *Journal of Documentation, 60*(4), 449-475.

Monopoli, M., Nicholas, D., Georgiou, P. & Korfiati, M. (2002). A user-oriented evaluation of digital libraries: Case study: The "electronic journals" service of the library and information service of the University of Patras, Greece. *Aslib Proceedings, 54*(2), 103-117.

Neumann, L. J., & Ignacio, E. N. (1998). Trial and error as a learning strategy in system use. In C. M. Preston (Ed.), *Proceedings of the 61st ASIS Annual Meeting,* (pp. 243-252). Medford, NJ: Information Today.

Nicholas, D., Huntington, P., Monopoli, M., & Watkinson, A. (2006). Engaging with scholarly digital libraries (publisher platforms): The extent to which "added-value" functions are used. *Information Processing and Management, 42*(3), 826-842.

Nicholas, D., Huntington, P., & Watkinson, A. (2005). Scholarly journal usage: The results of deep log analysis. *Journal of Documentation, 61*(2), 248-280.

Nielsen, J. (1993). *Usability engineering.* San Diego, CA: Academic Press.

Notess, M. (2004). Three looks at users: A comparison of methods for studying digital library use. *Information Research-An International Electronic Journal, 9*(3). Retrieved January 3, 2008, from http://InformationR.net/ir/9-3/paper177

Oatman, E. (2005). Listen up, Web developers! *School Library Journal, 51*(7), 16.

Othman, R. (2004). An applied ethnographic method for evaluating retrieval features. *The Electronic Library, 22*(5), 425-432.

Park, S. (2000). Usability, user preferences, effectiveness, and user behaviors when searching individual and integrated full-text databases: Implications for digital libraries. *Journal of the American Society for Information Science, 51*(5), 456-468.

Patitucci, B. (1999). Developing your own digital library. *Multimedia Schools, 6*(4), 56-58.

Pejtersen, A. M., & Fidel, R. M. (1998). *A framework for work-centered evaluation and design: A case study of IR on the Web.* Paper presented at the MIRA Workshop, Grenoble, France.

Rapp, D. N., Taylor, H. A., & Crane, G. R. (2003). The impact of digital libraries on cognitive processes: Psychological issues of hypermedia. *Computers in Human Behavior, 19*(5), 609-628.

Saracevic, T. (2000). Digital library evaluation: Toward an evolution of concepts. *Library Trends, 49*(2), 350-369.

Saracevic, T., & Covi, L. (2000). Challenges for digital library evaluation. In D. Soergel, P. Srivivasan, & B. Kwasnik (Eds.), *Proceedings of the 11th ASIST Annual Meeting,* (Vol. 37, pp. 341-350).

Saracevic, T., & Kantor, P. (1997). Studying the value of library and information services: Part II. Methodology and taxonomy. *Journal of the American Society for Information Science, 48*(6), 543-563.

Schneiderman, B. (1998). *Designing the user interface strategies for effective human-computer interaction* (3rd ed.). Reading, MA: Addison-Wesley.

Schneiderman, B. (2000). Universal usability. *Communications of the ACM, 43*(5), 84-91.

Shackle, B. (1997). Human-computer interaction—whence and whither? *Journal of the American Society for Information Science, 48*(11), 970-986.

Slack, F. E. (1991). *OPACs: Using enhanced transaction logs to achieve more effective online help for subject searching.* Unpublished doctoral dissertation, Manchester Polytechnic, Manchester.

Southwick, S. B. (2003). Digital intermediation: An exploration of user and intermediary perspectives. In *Proceedings of the 66th ASIST Annual Meeting,* (Vol. 40, pp. 40-51). Medford, NJ: Information Today.

Su, L. T. (1992). Evaluation measures for interactive information retrieval. *Information Processing and Management, 28*(4), 503-516.

Sumner, T., & Dawe, M. (2001). Looking at digital library usability from a reuse perspective. In *Proceedings of the 1st ACM/IEEE-CS Joint Conference on Digital Libraries,* (pp. 416-425). New York: ACM Press.

Thong, J. Y. L., Hong, W. Y., & Tam, K. Y. (2002). Understanding user acceptance of digital libraries: What are the roles of interface characteristics, organizational context, and individual differences? *International Journal of Human-Computer Studies, 57*(3), 215-242.

Vakkari, P. (1999). Task complexity, problem structure and information actions—integrating studies on information seeking and retrieval. *Information Processing and Management, 35*(6), 819-837.

Van House, N. A. (1995). User needs assessment and evaluation for the UC Berkeley electronic environmental library project: A preliminary report. In I. F. M. Shipman, R. K. Furuta, & D. M. Levy (Eds.), *Proceedings of Digital Libraries 95: The Second Annual Conference on the Theory and Practice of Digital Libraries,* (pp. 71-76).

Van House, N. A., Butler, M. H., Ogle, V., & Schiff, L. (1996, February). User-centered iterative design for digital libraries: The cypress experience. *D-Lib Magazine, 2*(2). Retrieved January 3, 2008, from http://www.dlib.org/dlib/february96/02vanhouse.html

Wildemuth, B. M., Marchionini, G., Wilkens, T., Yang, M., Geisler, G., Fowler, B., et al. (2002). Alternative surrogates for video objects in a digital library: Users' perspectives on their relative usability. In *Proceedings of the 6th European Conference on Digital Libraries,* (pp. 493-507). London, UK: Springer-Verlag.

Wildemuth, B. M., Marchionini, G., Yang, M., Geisler, G., Wilkens, T., Hughes, A., et al. (2003). How fast is too fast? Evaluating fast forward surrogates for digital video. In *Proceedings of the 3rd ACM/IEEE-CS Joint Conference on Digital Libraries,* (pp. 221-230). New York: ACM Press.

Wildemuth, B. M., Russell, T., Ward, T. J., Marchionini, G., & Oh, S. (2005). *The influence of context and interactivity on video browsing: TREC VID 2005 notebook paper.* (Publication No. TR-2006-01). Chapel Hill: School of Information and Library Science, University of North Carolina.

Witten, I. H., & Bainbridge, D. (2003). *How to build a digital library.* San Francisco, CA: Morgan Kaufmann.

Witten, I. H., Nevill-Manning, C. G., McNab, R., & Cunningham, S. J. (1998). A public library based on full text retrieval. *Communications of the ACM, 41*(4), 71-75.

Wolfram, D., & Xie, H. (2002). Traditional IR for Web users: A context for general audience digital libraries. *Information Processing & Management, 38*(5), 627-648.

Xie, H. (2006). Understanding human-work domain interaction: Implications for the design of a corporate digital library. *Journal of the American Society for Information Science and Technology, 57*(1), 128-143.

Xie, H., & Cool, C. (2006). Toward a better understanding of help seeking behavior: An evaluation of help mechanisms in Two IR systems. In A. Dillon & A. Grove (Eds.), *Proceedings of the 69th ASIST Annual Meeting* (Vol. 43). Retrieved January 3, 2008, from http://eprints.rclis.org/archive/00008279/01/Xie_Toward.pdf

Xie, H., & Wolfram, D. (2002). State digital library usability: Contributing organizational factors. *Journal of the American Society for Information Science and Technology, 53*(13), 1085-1097.

Yang, S. C. (2001). An interpretive and situated approach to an evaluation of Perseus digital libraries. *Journal of the American Society for Information Science and Technology, 52*(14), 1210-1223.

Yang, M., & Marchionini, G. (2005, April). *Deciphering visual gist and its implications for video retrieval and interface design.* Paper presented at the Conference on Human Factors in Computing Systems, Portland, OR.

Zhang, Y., Lee, K., & You, B. J. (2001). Usage patterns of an electronic theses and dissertations system. *Online Information Review, 25*(6), 370-377.

Chapter VI

TREC and Interactive Track Environments

Overview of TREC

History and Background

The Text REtrieval Conference (TREC) is sponsored by three agencies—the U.S. National Institute of Standards and Technology (NIST), the U.S. Department of Defense, Advanced Research Projects Agency (DARPA), and the U.S. intelligence community's Advanced Research and Development Activity (ARDA)—to promote text retrieval research based on large test collections. Overviews of TREC (Harman & Voorhees, 2006; Voorhees & Harman, 2005) and the TREC Web site (trec.nist. gov) have provided a comprehensive review of TREC conferences. This section is compiled based on these resources. TREC started in 1992 with 25 participating groups, including the leading text retrieval groups, to search two gigabytes of text. For each TREC, NIST offers a test collection and questions. Participating teams follow the guidelines, run the data on their own IR systems, and return the results to NIST. NIST evaluates the submitted results and organizes workshops for participants to discuss their experience and present results. By the end of 2005, 14 TREC conferences had been held.

According to the TREC Web site, the objective of TREC is to achieve the following four main goals:

- To encourage research in text retrieval based on large test collections;
- To increase communication among industry, academia, and government by creating an open forum for the exchange of research ideas;
- To speed the transfer of technology from research labs into commercial products by demonstrating substantial improvements in retrieval methodologies on real-world problems; and
- To increase the availability of appropriate evaluation techniques for use by industry and academia, including the development of new evaluation techniques more applicable to current systems (http://trec.nist.gov/overview.html).

Types of Tracks

Table 6.1 (as shown in Voorhees, 2006, p. 7) reviews the number of participants per track and total number of distinct participants in each TREC. Adapting and expanding Voorhees and Harman's classification of tracks (2005, pp. 8-13) as well as examining the TREC home page (http://trec.nist.gov), the author summarizes all the tracks of TREC to 2005 and the types of tasks performed in TREC.

The tasks performed in TREC consist mainly of the following:

- **Static text:** The Ad Hoc Track is a typical document retrieval task on a static collection of text documents. The Robust Retrieval Track reintroduces the traditional ad hoc retrieval tasks, but the evaluation focus is on topic effectiveness instead of average effectiveness.
- **Streaming text:** The Filtering Track and Routing Track deal with retrieving documents from a stream of text. While the purpose of the Routing Track is to formulate a basic task, the Filtering Track occurs afterward to make binary decisions about whether to retrieve a document that should be retrieved. The Spam Track is similar to the Filtering Track but focuses more on general e-mail filtering.
- **Human-oriented:** The Interactive Track investigates users' interaction with IR systems focusing on the process and the results. The Interactive Track, which started in TREC 3, became the interactive part of the Web track in TREC 12.

Table 6.1. Number of participants per track and total number of distinct participants in each TREC. From "Overview of TREC 2005" by E. M. Voorhees. The Fourteenth Text Retrieval Conference (TREC 2005) Proceedings (p. 7). NIST Special Publication 500-266 Gaithersburg, MD: U.S. Department of Commerce, NIST.

Track	92	93	94	95	96	97	98	99	00	01	02	03	04	05
Ad hoc	18	24	26	23	28	31	42	41	—	—	—			
Routing	16	25	25	15	16	21	—	—	—	—	—			
Interactive	—	—	3	11	2	9	8	7	6	6	6			
Spanish	—	—	4	10	7	—	—	—	—	—	—			
Confusion	—	—	—	4	5	—	—	—	—	—	—			
Database merging	—	—	—	3	3	—	—	—	—	—	—			
Filtering	—	—	—	4	7	10	12	14	15	19	21			
Chinese	—	—	—	—	9	12	—	—	—	—	—			
NLP	—	—	—	—	4	2	—	—	—	—	—			
Speech	—	—	—	—	—	13	10	10	3	—	—			
Cross-language	—	—	—	—	—	13	9	13	16	10	9			
High precision	—	—	—	—	—	5	4	—	—	—	—			
Very large corpus	—	—	—	—	—	—	7	6	—	—	—			
Query	—	—	—	—	—	—	2	5	6	—	—			
Question answering	—							—	20	28	36	34	33	33
Web	—	—	—	—	—	—	—	17	23	30	23	27	18	—
Video	—	—	—	—	—	—	—	—	—	12	19	—	—	—
Novelty	—	—	—	—	—	—	—	—	—	—	13	14	14	—
Genome	—	—	—	—	—	—	—	—	—	—	—	29	33	41
HARD	—	—	—	—	—	—	—	—	—	—	—	14	16	16
Robust	—	—	—	—	—	—	—	—	—	—	—	16	14	17
Terabyte													17	19
Enterprise														23
Spam														13
Total participants	25	31	33	36	38	51	56	66	69	87	93	93	103	117

Some groups joined the High Accuracy Retrieval from Documents (HARD) track. The purpose of the HARD track is to support users by providing accurate results to specific users.

- **Multi-language:** The Spanish, Chinese, and Cross-language tracks focus on non-English retrieval. While the Spanish and Chinese Tracks concentrate on issues related to retrieval information in Spanish and Chinese, the Cross-language Track involves research on the information retrieval of documents regardless of their languages.

- **Multimedia formats:** In the digital age, users retrieve information not limited to text, and they also try to find information in multimedia formats. The optical Character Recognition Track and the Speech Recognition Track attempt to explore how to offer original data without errors or with reduced error rates. The Video Track is devoted to research in the content-based retrieval of digital video independent of text.

- **Web and large collection searching:** The Very Large Corpus (VLC) track evaluates the speed with which retrieval results are displayed when searching for a very large collection. The Terabyte Track is another type of very large collection track. Its objective is to study whether traditional IR test-collection-based evaluation can be applied to much larger collections. The Web track specifically examines search tasks on a collection set that represents a snapshot of the World Wide Web.

- **Answers, not documents:** The Question Answering Track works on a higher level of information retrieval. Instead of providing a set of relevant documents, question-answering systems return answers to the questions.

- **Domain-oriented:** The Genomics Track and the Legal Track study information retrieval in a specific domain to improve retrieval effectiveness.

- **Organization-oriented:** The Enterprise Track investigates users' search behaviors in organizational environments.

Overview of Interactive Track

The Interactive Track explores the complexity of interactive retrieval evaluation. Hersh and Over (2001) pointed out that these studies bridged the "user-oriented'" and "system-oriented" IR approaches even though they were limited by small sample sizes, small numbers of queries, laboratory settings, and less-than-ideal document collections. Over (2001) described the focuses of interactive track:

1. The searcher interacting with the IR system
2. The search behavior, search process, and interim results as well as final results
3. The effects of system, topic, and searcher, and their interactions
4. The assessment of the evaluation methodology

In the special issue of *Information Processing and Management* dedicated to the Interactive Track, Over (2001) provided an overview of the history and development of the Interactive Track, as well as annotated bibliography of it, from TRECs 3-8. Dumais and Belkin (2005) highlighted the key developments in each Interactive Track in addition to presenting general information about participants, approaches, tasks, and methods. Moreover, they further illustrated the challenges and new research directions in evaluating interactive information retrieval systems in the context of TREC. Each year's interactive track report (part of the overview of TRECs 3-4 and TRECs 5-12) in the annual proceedings of TRECs outlined detailed information about each Interactive Track's background, design, participants, results, and discussion.

Beginning with TREC3, the Interactive Track began to gain experience with the evaluation of interactive information retrieval systems. Four groups participated in the track to test either the tools needed for the IR systems for the Interactive Track or how users interact with new techniques based on TREC3 routing topics (Harman, 1995). There were no specific protocols and guidelines for participants to follow. The objective of TREC3 was to compare the performance of interactive IR systems to fully automatic routing systems (Over, 2001). In TREC4, 11 teams involved in the Interactive Track employed a subset of the ad hoc topics (Harman, 1996). The participants followed the same guidelines for search topics, tasks, and results recording. This interactive track tested new interfaces and compared the results of interactive ad hoc searches with automatic searching while focusing on the interactive search process, behavior, results, and methodologies (Dumais & Belkin, 2005). In TREC5 and TREC6, comparison of experimental systems to a common system was a theme (Over, 1997, 1998). Two teams did the pilot study in TREC5, and nine groups took part in TREC6. The Interactive Track from TREC6 through TREC8 used the aspectual/instance recall task as a common task. Users had to identify as many aspects (in TREC6) or instances (in TREC7 and 8) as possible for each topic.

While TREC6 represents the first true cross-site comparison in the Interactive Track, in TREC7, cross-site comparison was dropped because it was difficult to have a direct cross-site comparison considering the requirements of the Interactive Track. In TREC7 and TREC8, the searchers needed to save documents containing as many instances as possible within a 15-20-minute timeframe. A small set of ad hoc topics was used for TREC7 and 8, and eight and seven groups, respectively, engaged in these two TRECs (Over, 1999; Hersh & Over, 2000). In order to reduce the overall length of a search session and explore more tasks and collections, six teams participated in TREC 9 working on the fact-finding task. Some teams experimented with different document presentation interfaces. In TREC10 and TREC11, six groups did their individual experiments on Web searching (Hersh & Over, 2002, 2003). The TREC Web-track collection was used as a common collection for the comparability of results in TREC11. The Interactive Track became a subtrack of the Web track in TREC12 (Craswell et al., 2004). At the same time, some teams took part in the HARD track.

Compared with other tracks, the Interactive Track has its own uniqueness in dealing with users' interaction with IR systems. The TREC structure is not appropriate for research on interactive IR. Dumais and Belkin (2005) identified two reasons for the fundamental problem. The first is that TREC protocol is designed for evaluating and comparing batch searching; it is not well suited for the interactive environment. Second, while TREC is designed to compare the performance of IR systems across sites, the performance of interactive IR is affected by searcher characteristics. However, the searchers are limited by the number of topics they can search in each experiment. Interaction effects among searcher, topic, and system further complicate cross-site comparison.

Types of Interactive Studies

Since the Interactive Track became part of a subtrack of the Web track and HARD track beginning with TREC12, the author identified the five main themes that emerged from studies of the Interactive Track from TREC3 to TREC11: (1) the impact of searchers' knowledge vs. the impact of the dimensions of tasks, (2) query formulation and reformulation: relevance feedback and query length, (3) search tactics and strategies, (4) results organization structure and delivery mechanisms, and (5) the comparison of different retrieval models and evaluation methods. This section focuses on the different approaches applied by TREC participants and the associated results of the interactive studies performed in the Interactive Track. In addition, this section also covers research on interactive multilingual/cross-language information retrieval (CLIR), mainly in the interactive track of Cross-Language Evaluation Forum (iCLEF).

The Impact of Searchers' Knowledge vs. the Impact of the Dimensions of Tasks

Research has demonstrated that domain knowledge affects users' information-seeking behavior/strategies in environments of OPACs, online databases, Web search engines, and digital libraries. In TREC10, one finding that emerged from several research groups is that domain expertise influences search behavior/strategies (Dumais & Belkin, 2005). Bhavnani (2002) identified the cognitive components of domain-specific search knowledge and their impact on search behavior in the Interactive Track. Five information retrieval experts performed tasks within and outside their domain of expertise. The results showed that searchers applied more effective declarative and procedural components of domain-specific search knowledge when searching tasks within their domains; they employed less effective general-purpose search methods when searching tasks outside their domains. The declarative components include three types of knowledge: classification knowledge of classes of Web sites, URL knowledge, and content knowledge. Procedural components consist of two types of knowledge: sequencing knowledge, which determines a search plan, and termination knowledge, which determines the exit point in accomplishing a search task. The findings of this study demonstrated that expert users were more effective when they were able to apply domain-specific search knowledge than when they could only employ domain-general knowledge. The results also indicated that general-purpose search engines could not effectively support domain-specific search tasks. The major contribution of this study is the identification of cognitive components of domain-specific search knowledge, but the study is limited by its small sample. More research needs to test the generalizability of the results.

However, in two of the other studies in TREC10, the results demonstrated that the domain of the task, instead of searchers' domain knowledge, affects searchers' perception and behavior. After analyzing 48 nonexpert participants' searching on shopping, medicine, travel, and research topics, Toms, Kopak, Bartlett, and Freund (2002) found that the domain of the task had little effect on search results, but it did have an effect on user perception of their difficulty and satisfaction with results. The shopping tasks were more difficult to accomplish and less satisfying than the other tasks. Hersh, Sacherek, and Olson (2002) observed 24 experienced searchers performing searches on their choices of Web tools. They found that domain of the task affected the searchers' behavior; for example, searchers took the most time and the most page views for shopping tasks among all the tasks. They also reported results to those of Toms et al. (2002): although the differences across different tasks were small, the domain of the task influenced users' perceptions. In both of the studies, shopping tasks affected searchers' perceptions or behaviors, but this type of task was not the one that the searchers were least familiar with. In other words, searchers' domain knowledge on shopping tasks was not the lowest, but they still found shopping tasks the most difficult among all the tasks. The question is whether the domain knowledge of a searcher or the nature of the task itself, or both, influence searchers' perceptions or behaviors.

In addition to domain knowledge, searchers' spatial visualization ability and its impact on the success of searches were also explored. Even though no significant difference was found, the results indicated that searcher differences in spatial visualization ability were predictive of search success (Hersh et al., 2001; Hersh, Moy, Kraemer, Sacherek, & Olson, 2003). The nature of the TREC experiment, with its short cycle for experimentation, especially sample sizes, makes it difficult to achieve needed statistical power.

The dimensions of tasks have been regarded as the essential components for interactive information retrieval, and they are demonstrated to be influential factors for system performance and human behavior in a variety of digital environments. In addition to the domain of the tasks discussed above, the level of complexity of the tasks and the timeframe of the tasks and their relationships with the effectiveness of different interactive features of IR systems and system performance are also investigated in the Interactive Track. In TREC8, Beaulieu, Fowkes, Alemayehu, and Sanderson (2000) found that the impact of query expansion depended on nature of the task. While automatic query expansion improved the results for simple topics, complex questions required interactive query expansion and contributions from both the searcher and the system, because users had to examine the documents more carefully for complicated topics. At the same time, the effectiveness of features facilitating relevance judgments, such as displaying query term information in the retrieval results and highlighting best passages and query terms in documents, was also affected by the level of complexity of the task. These features were more helpful in assisting users in making relevance judgments for simple topics than complicated topics.

In TREC 9, Beaulieu, Fowkes, and Joho (2001) focused on the characteristics of two types of tasks and their impact on searcher and system performance. While the first type of tasks required searchers to find as many different instances as possible, the second type required searchers to choose a single correct answer from two possible choices. Searchers were required to accomplish each search topic within 5 minutes. After comparing their results with the overall results of the Interactive Track, they found that time and type of task were the two interdependent success factors in addition to searcher characteristics and behavior. More searchers indicated that they did not have enough time to accomplish type 1 tasks than type 2 tasks. Unlike in TREC8, the searchers' engagement with the documents was not evident because of the time limitation. It seemed more demanding for searchers to find different instances than to find the single answer within 5 minutes. The short time element was deemed a more important possible success factor than the complexity of the topic. Time is another dimension of task in addition to level of complexity of task and domain of task.

Query Formulation and Reformulation: Relevance Feedback and Query Length

Query formulation and reformulation is a difficult task in the interactive information retrieval process. Relevance feedback is known as one of the effective approaches to support query formulation and reformulation. In the Interactive Track, relevance feedback is a main topic for research. Interactive studies explored different approaches to providing relevance feedback, such as automatic query expansion, term selection, passage feedback, explicit feedback, and implicit feedback.

Relevance Feedback: Automatic Query Expansion

Automatic query expansion is a classical approach for relevance feedback. According to Robertson, Walker, and Beaulieu (2000), Okapi interactive experiments focused on the user search process. The objectives were to (1) support user query expansion, and (2) determine how and when users engage in the search process. Query expansion in an incremental format was used in TRECs 5 and 6 in which the system extracted terms and automatically added to the working query; correspondingly, all the terms were reweighted when a searcher made a positive relevance feedback. Interestingly, the interactive experimental system (Okapi) did not perform better than the controlled system (ZPRISE), mainly because query expansion is more useful for finding items that are the same instead of different from those identified as relevant. At the same time, users were more satisfied with the search outcomes derived from the experimental system than the controlled system partly because users liked the support offered by the experimental system.

In TREC 7, Robertson, Walker, and Beaulieu (1999) conducted a three-way comparison between two versions of Okapi (one with relevance feedback, and another one without relevance feedback) and a control system (ZPRISE). The findings of TREC 7 echoed TREC 6 results. The Okapi with relevance feedback outperformed Okapi without relevance feedback on both precision and recall. However, the control system (ZPRISE) achieved better results than Okapi with relevance feedback. Even though recall was marginally better, the difference was in precision. In TREC 8, the results of comparison of Okapi with and without relevance feedback revealed that Okapi with relevance feedback was marginally better in precision but worse in recall than Okapi without relevance feedback (Beaulieu et al., 2000). Interestingly, Beaulieu et al. (2000) found that the results depended on the complexity of search topics; more specifically, automatic query expansion could improve the results of simple, straightforward topics while interactive query expansion plus both system and user contributions were needed for complicated topics.

Relevance Feedback: Term Selection

Belkin et al. (2001) suggested a new revisionist model of relevance feedback taking account of people's information-seeking behaviors in interactive IR. Important terms in negatively judged documents that do not occur in positively judged documents are considered indicators of the inappropriate topic. While in TREC 5 relevance feedback was accomplished automatically, and the results showed that searchers had no problems understanding the concept of relevance feedback; however, they could not effectively use the relevance feedback function. There were two reasons for the problem: (1) searchers could not identify negatively relevant documents, and (2) they could not control the terms added or not added by relevance feedback. Based on the findings of the TREC 5, several changes have been made for TREC 6. First, both negative and positive relevance feedback were included. Second, users had the control to select and de-select positive and negative terms. Third, relevance feedback was implemented according to the new revisionist model that considered context. TREC 6 revealed some problems of implementing relevance feedback in the system, mainly the confusion of too many windows.

In TREC 7, one editable query window was designed for users to manually enter positive and negative terms. In TREC 8, the problems of system functionality and interface in TREC 7 were tackled. The objective of the TREC 8 study is to compare the usability of two different term suggestion methods for interactive IR: user control over suggested terms, implemented as positive relevance feedback vs. system-controlled term suggestion, implemented as a form of local context analysis. The results indicated that in a relevance feedback system, users spent more effort generating query terms, while in a local context analysis system, users spent less effort generating query terms and selected more terms provided by the system. The qualitative data showed that searchers preferred the local context analysis feature over relevance feedback because they had to spend additional effort to use relevance feedback. However, there was no difference in the effectiveness of the two systems. The experience of the Rutgers team is a typical example of research in the Interactive Track that focuses on one specific issue in a series of studies, and where the latter study is built on the previous one. That helps researchers have a more in-depth understanding of their research problems and results, and further improves interactive IR system design.

Relevance Feedback: Passage Feedback

Unlike the Rutgers team working on allowing searchers to select feedback terms from a system-suggested term list, the North Carolina group (Yang, Maglaughlin, & Newby, 2001) reported its Interactive Track studies on passage feedback. They conducted a series of experiments to compare a user-defined passage feedback system to a document feedback system. In TREC 7, in one of the interactive experiments, Yang, Maglaughlin, Meho, and Summer (1999) compared the effectiveness of a user-defined passage feedback system to a document feedback system. The inconclusive results indicated that a passage feedback system performed better than a document feedback system, and that user intervention positively affected retrieval performance. However, the passage feedback features were not fully used. Users complained about the usability problems in the passage feedback interface.

In TREC 8, Yang, Maglaughlin, and Newby (2001) compared two exact same systems except for how relevance feedback was implemented: the document feedback system with a conventional feedback mechanism and the passage feedback system allowing users to select relevant and nonrelevant parts of a document. The findings yielded results contrary to the previous experiments. The document feedback system performed slightly better than the passage feedback system in terms of mean instance precision and mean instance recall. Further analysis showed that the first passage feedback use performed poorer than the first document feedback use. The transaction logs and questionnaire data indicated that searchers found the passage feedback system difficult to learn, and using the feedback system first might impose additional cognitive burdens to searchers. Searchers spent more time evaluating documents in the passage feedback system than the document feedback system. The design oversight that did not boldface the query terms contained in documents retrieved by the passage feedback system might have contributed to the problem.

In the Interactive Track, some other studies on relevance feedback take the approach of offering short summaries of documents or copying passages from displayed text. In TREC 9, Alexander, Brown, Jose, Ruthven, and Tombros (2001) tested the use of query-biased summaries of documents as evidence for interactive and automatic query expansion. Searchers reported they did not understand the relevant feedback mechanism well, and they would prefer entering new search terms to using the relevance feedback option. In TREC10, Belkin et al. (2002) explored the use of the query modification feature as a "copy-and-paste" facility for moving text from displayed pages directly into the query. However, there was little use of this feature, probably because of the usability problem of the feature, users' unfamiliarity with the feature, the inappropriateness of the tasks, and time constraints. The researchers concluded that searchers did not use explicit feedback as the major approach for query modifications in their retrieval process.

Explicit Feedback vs. Passive/Implicit Feedback

Previous studies demonstrate that it is a challenge for users to use explicit feedback features because that adds a cognitive burden. Researchers started to test some of the implicit feedback approaches. For example, Vogt (2001) traced user actions to implicitly identify relevance by recording queries, documents views, redisplay of query results, and their relative timing. After comparing the user performance and preference of system 1 (the controlled system) and system 2 (the experimental system that was designed to uprank relevant documents directly based on half of the subjects' experience using system 1), he found that system 2 performed slightly better than system 1. User preference data corresponded with the data of performance results. He analyzed the cleanest data (after tossing out data caused by design flaws) provided by the 13 subjects in terms of the time they spent viewing each document and how that corresponded to relevance. The results indicated that viewing time, normalized by document length, was a more accurate indicator of relevance than a "clickthrough" (a user selecting a document for display).

White, Jose, and Ruthven (2002) compared the effectiveness of the explicit and implicit feedback approaches to examine to what extent implicit feedback can substitute for explicit feedback. They took a different approach to implement implicit feedback. While the explicit feedback interface allowed users to explicitly mark relevant documents, the implicit interface considered relevant any document for which a summary was requested. After analysis of the 16 subjects' searching process, the findings showed that the type of interface did not affect the number of results pages viewed or query iterations needed. There is no significant difference between the number of tasks that users accomplished on the "implicit" and the "explicit" systems and the time taken on the two systems. This suggests that implicit feedback can be used as a substitute for explicit feedback. Research on interactive studies indicates that searchers prefer implicit feedback to explicit feedback because less effort is required for the former. Then the next question is: What are the effective approaches for implementing implicit feedback mechanisms that capture searchers' real needs?

Query Length and its Relationship to Interaction

Query length is a hot topic in Web search engine research. Users generally enter short queries in Web search engine environments, and short queries normally lead to unsatisfied results. In the Interactive Track, Belkin et al. (2002) explored the methods for increasing query length and their relationship to task performance and interaction. Thirty-four subjects searched four of the interactive track topics under two conditions, which consisted of a "box" query input mode and a "line" query input mode. They were either asked to enter entire queries as complete sentences/ questions or lists of words/phrases. While there was no significant difference in query length between the two query input modes, query instruction seemed useful for generating longer queries. The results showed that searchers entered longer queries when instructed to enter questions or statements. The results also identified the positive relationships between query length and user satisfaction and query length and search performance.

However, not all studies generate positive relationships between query length and search performance. Influenced by Belkin et al.'s study (2002) on query length, Toms, Freund, and Li (2003) designed two types of interface tools: one with Agency Locator and Acronym Identifier to restrict searches, and another with Keyword Finder to suggest keywords. This study tested whether restricting a search would improve results for a "known-item" search and whether amplifying the query with additional keywords would improve the search results. The results were inconclusive about the effectiveness of the two types of tools. The Keyword Tool did affect query generation because searchers entered significantly longer queries in the Augment condition than those in the Limit condition. However, the tool did not affect the search results. They attributed the problems to the nature of the data collection, the lack of knowledge and experience of the subjects with the type of data, and the ineffectiveness of the tools and the search engine for the experiment.

In TREC 11, Belkin et al. (2003) continued investigating the relationship between query length and search performance. One of the hypotheses was tested: a search interface that instructs users to describe their problems will lead to longer queries than one that instructs users to input words or phrases as queries. Two interfaces were implemented into the study: one with full-text available with information problem elicitation and the other with a list of ranked titles with regular query elicitation. The results showed that the information problem elicitation method led to significantly longer queries than the query elicitation method. Significant correlations were found between satisfaction level and mean query length. In other words, increasing the query length led to users' satisfaction with the search results. However, there was no significant statistical difference between the two methods for other measures of the performance, such as the number of documents saved or the correctness of answers. More studies are needed to test the relationship between query length and search performance and to identify different ways to assist users in generating longer queries.

Search Tactics and Strategies

In order to understand the relationship between browsing and searching, Toms et al. (2002) compared 48 nonexpert searcher strategies in Web retrieval by using: "queries only," "categories only," "queries and then selected categories," or "categories and then selected queries." The key findings were between the two single-tactic strategies and between the single and mixed strategies. Searchers using "categories only" viewed significantly fewer hit lists and spent less time viewing those lists than searchers using "queries only," maybe because the use of categories led searchers to more specific sites. Searchers preferred the "query only" tactic over "category only" when a searcher could not map the task to one of the available categories. Searchers applying single-tactic strategies were more satisfied and more confident about their search results and found the search process easier than searchers applying mixed approaches. Searchers applying single-tactic strategies were also more successful than searchers applying mixed approaches. The results of this study echoed the results derived from relevance feedback studies that nonexpert searchers preferred the simple and straightforward strategy and features. More research is needed on expert searchers in terms of their preferences in strategies and features.

Results Organization Structure and Delivery Mechanism

Organization Structure: Clustering, Ranked List, and Integration of the Two

As tasks normally lead to information retrieval, it is important to know how to design interfaces to be comparable with task structure and what the different approaches are for the design of interfaces that facilitate interactions between users and IR systems. Wu, Fuller, and Wilkinson (2001) conducted a series of experiments investigating whether applying clustering and classification to present information with respect to task structure facilitated interactive retrieval. Experiment I was to examine whether a clustering algorithm could group the retrieved documents and whether users could select relevant clusters. The findings suggested that the cluster algorithm could group topic-relevant documents but could not separate documents with instance relevance. Experiment II concentrated on the comparison of two interfaces implemented: one based on clusters and the other on ranked list. There is no significant difference between two systems on the average instance recall. However, for five topics, the cluster organization is better than the list organization interface. The results also showed that users did prefer structured presentations of a retrieved result set rather than a list-based approach.

Experiment III examined whether clustering assisted users in performing instance retrieval tasks. There was no significant difference in instance recall between two interfaces. At the same time, the results suggested that there were variations in mental maps betweens subjects and assessors. Experiment IV explored simple document classification to replace unguided clustering, for instance retrieval task. Although there was no significant difference between the classification-based interface and the ranked-list interface, searchers did save more instances on average using the classification-based interface. The findings also suggested that the organization of retrieved documents affected searchers' perception of the documents. Searchers were more satisfied with classification-based interface in terms of its presentation form, the retrieved data, its ease-of-use, and the time available for searching.

Taking another approach to enhance the power of the clustering technique, Osdin, Ounis, and White (2003) designed a system (HuddleSearch) that used hierarchical clustering and summarization approaches to help users interact with the system. Users were able to judge a cluster's relevance before viewing its content. The experiment compared the system and a baseline with the classical list-based approach. Even though some of the results were not statically significant, the findings of the study clearly showed that the experimental system performed better than the base system in terms of fewer number of incomplete tasks and less time to accomplish tasks on average. More important, 13 of 16 users preferred HuddleSearch to the baseline, and they were more satisfied with the results provided by the experimental system.

Overall users did prefer clustering to ranked list in presenting retrieved results, although no statistical significant difference was found between the two systems in their performances.

Considering the tradeoff of clustering and ranked list, Allan, Leuski, Swan, and Byrd (2001) combined clustering with the traditional ranked list to overcome the problems of only providing ranked list or clustering and have the benefits of the two techniques. They first evaluated the effectiveness of two versions of the system in the TREC 6 Interactive Track: one with and another one without visualization that combines a ranked list with clustering. There was no significant advantage to using the visualization, although the researchers observed examples where the visualization offered valuable help. According to Allan et al. (2001), the reasons for the results cannot be detected in the Interactive Track environment because the value of visualization might be obscured by other variations in users and systems. A new system was built to incorporate interdocument similarity visualization to the ranked list. Using the TREC collection and relevance judgments, they conducted a noninteractive study evaluating the performance of the ranked list, relevance feedback, and the combination of ranked list and clustering. The results showed that the combination outperformed the ranked list. This approach is as powerful as the relevance feedback approach, but much easier for searchers to understand.

In TREC10, Craswell, Hawking, Wilkinson, and Wu (2002) further investigated the correlation between the three delivery mechanisms (a ranked list interface, a clustering interface, and an integrated interface with ranked list, clustering structure, and expert links) and two searching tasks (search for an individual document and a set of documents). They then conducted experiments with 24 subjects with three groups: Group 1 subjects were informed about the characteristics of each searching mechanism; Group 2 subjects were informed about the advantages of each search mechanism related to the type of tasks; and Group 3 subjects used two interfaces: the ranked list interface and the clustering interface. The researchers found no significant difference among the groups in terms of the number of documents read. Subjects from Group 3 used the least time when using ranked list interface, probably because they concentrated on one interface without distraction. Overall, search tasks did not affect the use of delivery mechanism, and searchers only used one delivery mechanism.

In TREC 11, Craswell, Hawking, Wilkinson, and Wu (2003) continued working on the organization of retrieved documents. Based on 16 subjects' searching on two types of interfaces, they compared the delivery method of traditional ranked list with a new organizational structure that applied level two domain labels and their corresponding organization names to classify the retrieved documents for the collection of U.S. government Web documents. The new organizational structure was developed based on the idea that people try to match their mental model about the organization with their information needs when accessing information from an organization's Web site. The results showed that subjects read more documents with the category interface than with the ranked list interface, which indicated that the category interface promoted more browsing behavior. Category interface also brought relevant documents that scattered in the ranked list to a category. Although there was no significant difference between the two delivery methods during the first 5 and 10 minutes of searching, the results did present a significantly better performance with the category interface at the end of the 15 minutes of searching.

The above studies suggest that organizational structure needs to be designed based on user mental models and tasks. More research on the design of organizational structure needs to not only improve users' perceptions but also their search performances.

Display Methods and their Relationships with Interaction

The organizational structure only offers searchers an overview of the retrieved results; the display method provides an opportunity for searchers to view documents or surrogates of documents. Belkin et al. (2001) compared two interfaces in terms of performance, effort, and user preference to test whether they are better at supporting one of the two types of tasks: comparison-type tasks and list-type tasks. One offered Single Document Display (SDD), presenting the top 10 document titles and the text of the first document; another provided Multiple Document Display (MDD), presenting the title and text of the top six documents that displayed the "best passage" generated by the system. The analysis of 16 subjects' experience with the two systems indicated that the MDD system did not support the comparison-type task better than the SDD system, and the SDD system did not support the list-type task better than the MDD system, based on performance and effort measures. Overall, the MDD system had a minor advantage in supporting the question-answering task over the SDD system.

In TREC 11, Belkin et al. (2003) continued their investigation of the relationship between the amount of interaction and the level of user satisfaction with search results and search performance. Specifically, they tried to test one hypothesis on this topic: a search interface that directly displays the ranked retrieved documents by a search will lead to less user system interaction than the one that displayed only ranked titles. Two interfaces were implemented into the study: one, MDD, with full-text available with information problem elicitation, and the other, SDD, with a list of ranked titles with regular query elicitation. The results reported that MDD resulted in less user interaction, and searchers were more satisfied with the search results and saved significantly more documents when searching with MDD than with SDD, even though the two interfaces did not lead to significant differences in terms of the number of complete and correct answers. The results indicated that reducing interaction for a searcher led to a better user experience. Once again, the results of these studies are common in the Interactive Track that no statistical significance was found in the studies, but the results did identify some interesting findings that warrant further research.

Display Methods for Relevance Judgments

How to assist users to effectively evaluate the relevance of retrieved documents is a critical research topic. Robertson, Walker, and Beaulieu (2000) found that highlighting the best passages of documents enabled searchers to effectively make relevance judgments; this was especially useful for long documents and documents with different topics. In TREC8, Beaulieu et al. (2000) further examined best-passage retrieval and other related features, finding that these features were related to the nature of topics. Highlighting best passages and query terms in documents, as well as displaying query term information in the retrieved list, helped users make relevance judgments for simple topics, but this was less useful for more complicated topics because users had to examine the content of the documents more carefully.

Instead of using the existing passages from a document, Alexander et al. (2001) came up with the idea of applying query-biased summary. In TREC 9, they tested the effectiveness of query-biased summaries for question-answering tasks. The experimental system offered searchers short summaries of documents that consisted of main points of the original documents based on a query expressed by a searcher. The findings showed that subjects performed better using the experimental system. Although subjects found the same number of unique documents that supported the answer for a query in both systems, they spent less effort in discovering these supporting documents. All subjects favored the use of summaries; however, they disliked the long process it took for the summaries to be generated. The process of summary generation needs to be improved. Taking another approach, D'Souza et al. (2001) compared two types of summaries in two experimental systems: one used the title and the first 20 words (First20) of a document; another used the document title and the best three Answer Indicative Sentences (AIS3) extracted from the document. After analyzing 16 subjects' transaction logs and questionnaires, they concluded that the summary with best three Answer Indicative Sentences was significantly better than the summary with first 20 words. The AIS3 system was more effective than the First20 system in terms of the number and the quality of saved answers. Even though there was not much difference in learning effort between the two systems, user perception of the usefulness of the AIS3 system was higher than the First20 system.

Delivery mechanisms are essential for assisting searchers to effectively evaluate the relevance of retrieved documents. Researchers in the TREC Interactive Track tested the effectiveness and usefulness of different approaches to organize and display retrieved results. These studies shed lights on how to design IR systems to support users to efficiently evaluate the retrieved results. The limitation of the

TREC setting, tasks, and sample size calls for the need to enhance these studies to improve their statistical power.

Comparison of Different Retrieval Models and Evaluation Methods

There are different retrieval models employed in a variety of IR systems. Larson (2001) reported UC Berkeley's participation in the TREC 6, 7, and 8 Interactive Tracks based on papers published in the TREC proceedings (Gey, Jiang, Chen, & Larson, 1999; Larson, 2000; Larson & McDonough, 1998). The objective of the interactive studies is to compare the IR system based on the probability ranking principle (Cheshire II) and the IR system with a vector space model (ZRISE). The Cheshire II search engine supports both probabilistic and Boolean searching. It provides a generic interface to Z39.50 servers. In TREC 6 and 7, the interface design was constructed from only brief metadata records, not full-text documents viewed in the search interface. Based on users' comments, a separate full-text display window with some selecting buttons was added. The results showed that the Cheshire system had the highest average instance recall of all systems in TREC6, but the controlled system outperformed the experimental system in both TREC7 and TREC8. One reason could be that searchers required more interactions with the experimental system than the control system that was preferred by most of the searchers. As suggested by other interactive studies, more interactions between a user and a system led to an unsatisfying experience and search performance. Analysis questionnaire responses revealed that users were less familiar with search topics on average when using the experimental system than the control system, and it was difficult for them to start and conduct the search. Further research with a variety of search topics is needed.

Researchers in information retrieval hold two common assumptions: (1) Natural language searching outperforms Boolean searching, and (2) batch-style evaluation results can be generalized to real information retrieval. Hersh et al. (2001) challenged the two assumptions in TREC 7 and 8. In TREC7, they compared the search performance of 24 experienced searchers working with Boolean and natural language interfaces. The findings revealed that experienced searchers highly preferred Boolean interface because they might have more control over the search, but no statistical significant difference was found in searching success between using a Boolean and a natural language interface. Further analysis showed that user attributes were associated with success. The types of libraries that subjects came from influenced the searching success; in particular, special library librarians outperformed public library librarians. Positive relationships were found between success and users' satisfaction with their results, number of documents viewed, and number of search terms used per cycle. Negative relationships were found between success and the number of search cycles used and experience with a point-and-click interface. In TREC8, they compared the search performance of batch-style evaluation to real user evaluation. The results from the two types of evaluation were not comparable. That raised the question of whether batch studies could be a definite assessment of system performance. Further experiments that employed more queries and diverse user tasks were suggested. In TREC9, Hersh et al. (2001) analyzed whether batch and user evaluation could generate comparable results by using a different task-question-answering. The results corresponded with TREC8 results that the improved performance for the better weighting scheme could not be generalized to user evaluation.

Users are the ultimate assessors of the effectiveness of different retrieval models. Therefore, evaluation methods should consider real user evaluation. Limited by the Interactive Track environment, the results of interactive studies are not conclusive. Further research also needs to discuss how to extend interactive studies from the Interactive Track to other real digital environments.

Interactive Multilingual/Cross-Language Information Retrieval (CLIR)

It is the objective of universal text retrieval to enable users to effectively obtain the information they need without considering the language of the texts (Davis & Ogden, 2000). Multilingual/cross-language retrieval becomes an important issue for IR in a variety of digital environments. However, the application of multilingual/cross-language in commercialized systems is rare (Gey, Kando, & Peters, 2005). The majority of research is still in its preliminary stages. In this section, the author discusses relevant works on interactive multilingual/cross-language retrieval research, mainly in the interactive track of Cross-Language Evaluation Forum (iCLEF). In iCLEF, researchers explore how to facilitate users to retrieve information in unknown languages, in particular in European languages. Users are at the center of the information retrieval process, especially when they have to search for information in languages that they are not familiar with. They need help in formulating and reformulating queries as well as identifying relevant documents from the retrieved results (Peters, 2005).

Query formulation and reformulation is one of the main research areas for interactive CLIR. It seems there are multiple approaches for researchers to deal with multilingual/cross-language retrieval issues on query formulation. Assisted translation is a major research area for interactive cross-language retrieval, in particular the query formulation process in which users are involved in the process. One approach is to offer online bilingual resources for improving query modifications. Davis and Ogden (2000) conducted a preliminary experiment on an interactive, cross-language text retrieval system that provides a browser-based interface for entering English queries. A subject with no knowledge of German formed an English query based on TREC topics, and modified the German query by evaluating documents and using online bilingual resources. The results of the study showed that a bilingual dictionary was the main resource for query modifications. In this study, the subject interacted with online bilingual resources for query modifications. However, it was difficult to generate compound terms in German.

Lopez-Ostenero, Gonzalo, and Verdejo (2005) reported their results on using noun phrase for query formulation, translation, and modification based on their iCLEF 2002 experiment. The results revealed that phrase-based summaries performed better in assisting users to formulate and refine their queries than interactive word-by-word-assisted translation. Corroborating the quantitative results, the observation data revealed that users were unwilling to select translations for words that had different choices for the translation from the assisted translation system. While Lopez-Ostenero, Gonzalo, and Verdejo (2005) focused on assisted translation from interacting users to obtain a phrase-based query, Dorr et al. (2004) examined the assisted translation by selecting individual query terms based on three resources: the document-language term, possible synonyms, and example of usage. After comparing users' query reformulations under the automatic and manual conditions, Dorr et al. (2004) found that user-assisted translation selection for query terms was useful because it achieved the same search effectiveness with fewer query iterations compared with the automatic condition. One limitation is it did not have the same effect in query reformulation. This study also identified different search behaviors under automatic and manual conditions. Under the former condition, users' tactics were similar to monolingual tactics. Under the latter, their tactics were varied and complicated.

Similar to Dorr et al.'s (2004) study, Petrelli, Demetriou, Herring, Beaulieu, and Sanderson (2003) examined two different levels of control over the query translation mechanism with four subjects: delegation and supervision. When users input queries, the system translated queries. No user interventions were involved in the delegation condition, but users verify and modify queries in the supervision condition. Even though users found more relevant documents when they had greater control over the translation, the results also found differences among users, topics, and tasks. Petrelli, Levin, Beaulieu and Sanderson (2006) enhanced their previous research with 16 subjects involving four different languages pairs (Finnish to English, English to Finnish, Swedish to English, and English to Swedish) to further explore which interaction model should be used in cross-language retrieval. Interestingly, the performance data and user feedback did not correspond to each other. The results of this study showed that supervised mode performed better than delegated mode in both precision and recall, although the difference was small. At the same time, user feedback revealed that users preferred the delegated mode, but the difference was not big either. That echoed their previous research that users favored the simplest interaction, if they were happy about their retrieved documents with their initial queries (Petrelli et al., 2004; Petrelli, Hansen, Beaulieu, & Sanderson, 2002). Users had different opinions toward the delegated and supervised modes. While some participants favored the delegated mode because it offered speed and less effort, the other participants liked the supervised mode for their ability to check and update the query translation process as well as to get inspiration for query reformulations. To balance users' preferences, the solution is to take the delegated mode as the default, but also provide query translation on top of the result list, enabling users to supervise the translation.

Document selection is another important area for CLIR research. Researchers have conducted a series of experiments to compare different techniques for facilitating interactive relevance judgment. At three sites with about 20 subjects participating in the main experiments, Oard, Gonzalo, Sanderson, Lopez-Ostenero, and Wang (2004) compared three techniques for document selection: full machine translation, rapid term-by-term translation, and focused phrase translation. The results showed that machine translation performed better in supporting relevance judgment tasks than term-by-term translation, while focused phrase translation enhanced recall. The subjects of the study reported that it was easy to accomplish relevance judgment tasks with the machine translation system, and phase translation required more user interpretation for the same task. Lopez-Ostenero, Gonzalo, and Verdejo (2005) compared the standard Systran translations with phrase-based translations in supporting document selections. The quantitative data and user feedback indicated that noun phrase translation summary was a valuable feature in supporting relevance judgments. Moreover, it was cheaper to generate noun phrase translations than the full machine translation. In addition to phrase translation, thumbnails were also used to assist making relevance judgments.

In Davis and Ogden (2000)'s study discussed above, the subject examined the retrieved documents in thumbnails and German equivalents, and then submitted them to be translated into English. The top 10 documents were judged as relevant or not-relevant. The results of the study showed a low percentage of error. Dorr et al. (2004) explored how the two approaches supported users in recognizing relevant documents: one extracts the first 40 translated words in each news story, and another one uses an automated parse-and-trim approach to generate headlines. Overall, it was easier for users to make relevance judgments in using the first 40 words approach than the headline approach, and therefore they were more confident in making relevance judgments. However, the researchers did point out that the headlines generated in this study could not represent the informative summary in general. In addition, the headlines generated in this study were shorter than 40 words.

Tasks play important roles in interactive IR as well as in interactive multilingual IR. Zhang, Plettenberg, Klavans, Oard, and Soergel (2007) explored subjects' task-based interaction with an integrated multilingual and multimedia IR system. Eight participants were involved in different types of search tasks, and multiple methods were applied to collect data. The results of the study demonstrated that tasks did have an impact on the performance of users' multilingual retrieval. In general, users were able to obtain answers for factual questions. However, they had great difficulty in searching for high-level questions related to opinions and reactions because they could not develop search strategies that worked well with the multilingual IR system. This study also yielded some unique characteristics of users' information-searching behavior for multilingual retrieval. For example, users broadened their searches instead of applying specific query terms because of their ineffectiveness in multilingual IR. Working on the same types of tasks, He, Wang, Luo, and Oard (2005) compared two types of summarizations for answering factual questions: Keyword-In-Context (KWIC) summary and passage summary for CLIR. The results showed there was little difference between the two types of summaries for this type of task in an experiment with eight subjects. However, the difficulty of the task did affect CLIR. To be specific, the time spent on the task and the number of query iterations was correlated with question difficulty.

Summary: Impact and Limitation of TREC Interactive Track Studies

The TREC environment provides a platform for researchers to compare results and their experience. The TREC Interactive Track has made significant contributions to research on interactive information retrieval:

1. The major contribution of the TREC Interactive Track is the development of a general framework for the investigation of interactive information retrieval, and for the evaluation and comparison of the performance of interactive IR systems (Dumais & Belkin, 2005). This framework includes the applied methodologies, the experimental designs, and the techniques for reporting the evaluation and comparison results.

2. The interactive track encourages researchers, and, more importantly, offers an opportunity for researchers to share common tasks, topics, document collections, evaluation methods, and their experience in interactive IR research.

3. In this environment, different aspects of an interactive retrieval process can be controlled to a certain degree in order for researchers to understand how user-system interactions affect the retrieval outcome (Yang, Maglaughlin, & Newby, 2001). The controlled environment enables researchers to analyze the key relationships in interactive IR.

4. In the Interactive Track, each team conducted a series of studies along the way. More important, their latter studies are built on their prior results and

experience, especially the problems reported in the previous studies. Therefore, researchers are able to have an in-depth investigation of some of the critical issues in interactive IR.

5. Although the results of many interactive studies are not statistically significant, the findings did shed light on some of the new techniques, new approaches, and new methods for facilitating users' interactions with IR systems. In addition, the findings also reveal user preferences in using different interactive features of IR systems as well the reasons behind their preferences. For example, explicit relevance feedback was not favored because of the extra cognitive load required.

At the same time, the Interactive Track also has its limitations:

1. The limitation of the setting. Interactive studies need to take place in a natural setting. The fixed search task, topics and collection, and judgments from NIST assessors do not represent actual interactive search (Over, 2001). They cannot reflect real interactions between users and IR systems. This also poses questions for conclusiveness and generalizability of the results.

2. The limitation of assigned tasks and convenience sample. Subjects in TREC lacked motivation to search for information assigned to them, and they also did not understand the search topics and search tasks well (Wu, Fuller, & Wilkinson, 2001). In general, subjects could not represent diverse types of searchers (Hersh et al., 2001), because in many of the studies subjects were recruited from populations that were related to the researchers, such as students in a university. Real users with real problems in real settings are needed for interactive IR studies.

3. The limitation of data/collection and the nature of tasks. The limitation of the collection and tasks, such as the aspectual/instance recall task, affect the results of the studies. For example, Interactive Track data lacked enough relevant documents for each topic instance. It is impossible for classification-based interface to outperform ranked-list interface (Wu, Fuller, & Wilkinson, 2001).

4. The limitation of statistical power. The individual differences of searchers and the potential interactions among searchers, topics, and systems pose challenges for the evaluation and comparison of interactive IR systems. Several new interface designs were developed to support interactive query expansion, results presentation, and individual differences in the search process. These experimental systems were compared with the base systems. However, in many cases, no statistical significance was reported. It is difficult to detect whether there are no actual effects or the effects were obscured by other variations.

A reduction in the variability or an increase in the number of searches might help find significant effects. Dumais and Belkin (2005) suggest increasing the number of tasks per searcher or focusing on subtasks for further research.

5. The limitation of TREC assessors. There are differences in making relevance judgments between searchers and TREC assessors. The authoritative relevance judgments made by TREC assessors allowed for the possibility of cross-cite comparison in noninteractive tracks. However, Dumais and Belkin (2005) pointed out that it is difficult to evaluate interactions between the searcher and the system in an interactive setting because precision and recall might be affected by the degree of overlap between the searchers' and the assessors' relevance judgments. Often, the searchers and the assessors do not agree with each other on the relevance of the documents. For example, Beaulieu, Fowkes, and Joho (2001) found that over half of the items deemed relevant by the assessors were rejected by the searchers in their interactive track study in TREC9.

6. The limitation of the short TREC cycle. The short TREC cycle puts pressure on participants to present results without fully analyzing the data. It also easily leads to hardware and software problems and errors (Hersh & Over, 2000). Some of the teams have to give up or modify their original plans because of the short TREC cycle.

In SIGIR Workshop on Interactive Retrieval at TREC and Beyond, researchers proposed the following suggestions to solve some of the interactive track problems (Hersh & Over, 2000):

- Run the track on a 2-year cycle to extend the cycle of TREC for participants to prepare experiments and analyze results.

- Create a real world information searching environment for search tasks, collection, and so forth.

- Define actual Web search tasks for interactive track tasks.

- Allow participants to conduct observational studies as well as studies of metrics-based comparisons of systems.

- Provide more track topics.

Most important, the interactive studies should not be limited to the TREC environment. It is essential to continue interactive research with real users, real problems, and real settings, especially in a variety of digital environments.

Interactive CLIR research, in particular research in iCLEF, shares similar benefits and limitations as Interactive TREC studies because they all conduct exploratory studies in interactive IR areas. Interactive CLIR research has focused on the major issues in relation to how to design interactive CLIR systems to support users in effectively formulating and reformulating queries as well as in selecting relevance documents. The iCLEF offers an environment for researchers to develop methodologies, experimental designs, and techniques for comparing their approaches, results, and ideas. Moreover, each team has conducted a series of studies on the same issue, and latter ones enhance the previous research. At the same time, interactive CLIR system design goes through the iterative process based on system performance and user feedback. In addition, the results of these studies help researchers understand users' information-seeking strategies/behaviors in the CLIR process. They further uncover the factors affecting user-CLIR system interactions, such as tasks, contexts, user knowledge structures, and so forth.

Just as with TREC studies, the interactive CLIR research, in particular research in iCLEF, has its limitations. The small sample size and convenience sample determine that the generalizability of the results of these studies is an issue. That also limits the statistical power for these studies because very few studies reported statistical significance. Furthermore, the selected collections and assigned tasks make it difficult to understand users' actual information-seeking strategies/behaviors in real situations. Of course, the short cycle restricts the ability of researchers to fully design their studies and analyze their data. More emphasis on real users' multilingual search tasks awaits iCLEF 2006. According to the iCLEF Web site, "This year we want to explore user behaviour in a collection where the cross-language search necessity arises more naturally for average users. We have chosen Flickr, a large-scale, Web-based image database based on a large social network of WWW users, with the potential for offering both challenging and realistic multilingual search tasks for interactive experiments" (http://terral.lsi.uned.es/iCLEF/index.htm).

References

Alexander, N., Brown, C., Jose, J., Ruthven, I., & Tombros, A. (2001). Question answering, relevance feedback, and summarization: TREC-9 interactive track report. In E. M. Voorhees & D. K. Harman (Eds.), *The Ninth Text REtrieval Conference (TREC-9)*, (pp. 523-532). Gaithersburg, MD: U.S. Department of Commerce, NIST.

Allan, J., Leuski, A., Swan, R., & Byrd, D. (2001). Evaluating combinations of ranked lists and visualizations of inter-document similarity. *Information Processing and Management, 37*(3), 435-458.

Beaulieu, M., Fowkes, H., Alemayehu, N., & Sanderson, M. (2000). Interactive Okapi at Sheffield-TREC-8. In E. M. Voorhees & D. K. Harman (Eds.), *The*

Eighth Text REtrieval Conference (TREC-8), (pp. 689-698). Gaithersburg, MD: U.S. Department of Commerce, NIST.

Beaulieu, M., Fowkes, H., & Joho, H. (2001). Sheffield interactive experiment at TREC-9. In E. M. Voorhees & D. K. Harman (Eds.), *The Ninth Text REtrieval Conference (TREC-9),* (pp. 645-654). Gaithersburg, MD: U.S. Department of Commerce, NIST.

Belkin, N. J., Cool, C., Jeng, J., Keller, A., Kelly, D., Kim, J., et al. (2002). Rutgers' TREC 2001 interactive track experience. In E. M. Voorhees & D. K. Harman (Eds.), *The Tenth Text REtrieval Conference (TREC 2001),* (pp. 465-472). Gaithersburg, MD: U.S. Department of Commerce, NIST.

Belkin, N. J., Cool, C., Kelly, D., Lin, S. J., Park, S. Y., Perez-Carballo, J., et al. (2001). Iterative exploration, design and evaluation of support for query reformulation in interactive information retrieval. *Information Processing and Management, 37*(3), 403-434.

Belkin, N. J., Keller, A., Kelly, D., Perez-Carballo, J., Sikora, C., & Sun, Y. (2001). Support for question-answering in interactive information retrieval: Rutgers TREC-9 interactive track experience. In E. M. Voorhees & D. K. Harman (Eds.), *The Ninth Text REtrieval Conference (TREC-9),* (pp. 463-474). Gaithersburg, MD: U.S. Department of Commerce, NIST.

Belkin, N. J., Kelly, D., Kim, G., Kim, J.-Y., Lee, H.-J., Muresan, G., et al. (2003). Rutgers interactive track at TREC 2002. In E. M. Voorhees & L. P. Buckland (Eds.), *The Eleventh Text REtrieval Conference (TREC 2002),* (pp. 539-548). Gaithersburg, MD: U.S. Department of Commerce, NIST.

Bhavnani, S. K. (2002). Important cognitive components of domain-specific search knowledge. In E. M. Voorhees & D. K. Harman (Eds.), *The Tenth Text REtrieval Conference (TREC 2001),* (pp. 571-578). Gaithersburg, MD: U.S. Department of Commerce, NIST.

Craswell, N., Hawking, D., Upstill, T., McLean, A., Wilkinson, R., & Wu, M. (2004). TREC-12 Web and interactive tracks at CSIRO. In E. Voorhees & L. P. Buckland (Eds.), *The Twelfth Text REtrieval Conference (TREC 2003),* (pp. 193-204). Gaithersburg, MD: U.S. Department of Commerce, NIST.

Craswell, N., Hawking, D., Wilkinson, R., & Wu, M. (2002). TREC-10 Web and interactive tracks at CSIRO. In E. M. Voorhees & D. K. Harman (Eds.), *The Tenth Text REtrieval Conference (TREC 2001),* (pp. 151-158). Gaithersburg, MD: U.S. Department of Commerce, NIST.

Craswell, N., Hawking, D., Wilkinson, R., & Wu, M. (2003). TREC-11 Web and interactive tracks at CSIRO. In E. Voorhees & L. P. Buckland (Eds.), *The Eleventh Text REtrieval Conference (TREC 2002),* (pp. 197-206). Gaithersburg, MD: U.S. Department of Commerce, NIST.

Davis, M. W., & Ogden, W. C. (2000). Towards universal text retrieval: Tipster text retrieval research at New Mexico State University. *Information Retrieval, 3*(4), 339-356.

Dorr, B. J., He, D., Luo, J., Oard, D. W., Schwartz, R., Wang, J., et al. (2004). iCLEF 2003 at Maryland: Translation selection and document selection. *Lecture Notes in Computer Science, 3237,* 435-449.

D'Souza, D., Fuller, M., Thorn, J., Vines, P., Zobel, J., & de Krester, O. (2001). Melbourne TREC-9 experiments. In E. M. Voorhees & D. K. Harman (Eds.), *The Ninth Text REtrieval Conference (TREC-9),* (pp. 437-452). Gaithersburg, MD: U.S. Department of Commerce, NIST.

Dumais, S. T., & Belkin, N. J. (2005). The TREC interactive tracks: Putting the user into search. In E. M. Voorhees & D. K. Harman (Eds.), *TREC: Experiment and evaluation in information retrieval* (pp. 123-152). Cambridge, MA: The MIT Press.

Gey, F. C., Jiang, H., Chen, A., & Larson, R. R. (1999). Manual queries and machine translation in cross-language retrieval and interactive retrieval with Cheshire II at TREC-7. In E. M. Voorhees & D. K. Harman (Eds.), *The Seventh Text REtrieval Conference (TREC-7),* (pp. 527-540). Gaithersburg, MD: U.S. Department of Commerce, NIST.

Gey, F.C., Kando, N., & Peters, C. (2005). Cross-language information retrieval: The way ahead. *Information Processing and Management, 41*(3), 415-431.

Harman, D. (1995). Overview of the Third Text REtrieval Conference (TREC-3). In D. Harman (Ed.), *Overview of the Third Text REtrieval Conference (TREC-3),* (pp. 1-19). Gaithersburg, MD: U.S. Department of Commerce, NIST.

Harman, D. K. (1996). Overview of the Fourth Text REtrieval Conference. In D. Harman (Ed.), *The Fourth Text REtrieval Conference (TREC-4),* (pp. 1-24). Gaithersburg, MD: U.S. Department of Commerce, NIST.

Harman, D. K., & Voorhees, E. M. (2006). TREC: An overview. *Annual Review of Information Science and Technology, 40,* 113-155.

He, D., Wang, J., Luo, J., & Oard, D. W. (2005). Summarization design for interactive cross-language question answering. *Lecture Notes in Computer Science, 3491,* 348-362.

Hersh, W., Moy, S., Kraemer, D., Sacherek, L., & Olson, D. (2003). More statistical power needed: The OHSU TREC 2002 interactive track experiments. In E. Voorhees & L. P. Buckland (Eds.), *The Eleventh Text REtrieval Conference (TREC 2002),* (pp. 505-511). Gaithersburg, MD: U.S. Department of Commerce, NIST.

Hersh, W., & Over, P. (2000). SIGIR workshop on interactive retrieval at TREC and beyond. *SIGIR Forum, 34*(1), 24-27.

Hersh, W., & Over, P. (2001). Interactivity at the Text Retrieval Conference (TREC). *Information Processing and Management, 37*(3), 365-367.

Hersh, W., & Over, P. (2002). The TREC 2001 interactive track report. In E. M. Voorhees & D. K. Harman (Eds.), *The Tenth Text REtrieval Conference (TREC 2001),* (pp. 38-41). Gaithersburg, MD: U.S. Department of Commerce, NIST.

Hersh, W., & Over, P. (2003). TREC 2002 interactive track report. In E. Voorhees & L. P. Buckland (Eds.), *The Eleventh Text REtrieval Conference (TREC 2002),* (pp. 40-45). Gaithersburg, MD: U.S. Department of Commerce, NIST.

Hersh, W., Sacherek, L., & Olson, D. (2002). Observations of searchers: OHSU TREC 2001 interactive track. In E. M. Voorhees & D. K. Harman (Eds.), *The Tenth Text REtrieval Conference (TREC 2001),* (pp. 434-441). Gaithersburg, MD: U.S. Department of Commerce, NIST.

Hersh, W., Turpin, A., Price, S., Kraemer, D., Olson, D., Chan, B., et al. (2001). Challenging conventional assumptions of automated information retrieval with real users: Boolean searching and batch retrieval evaluations. *Information Processing and Management, 37*(3), 383-402.

Hersh, W., Turpin, A., Sacherek, L., Olson, D., Price, S., Chan, B., et al. (2001). Further analysis of whether batch and user evaluations give the same results with a question-answering task. In E. M. Voorhees & D. K. Harman (Eds.), *The Ninth Text REtrieval Conference (TREC-9),* (pp. 407-416). Gaithersburg, MD: U.S. Department of Commerce, NIST.

Larson, R. R. (2000). Berkeley's TREC-8 interactive track entry: Cheshire and ZPRISE. In E. M. Voorhees & D. K. Harman (Eds.), *The Eighth Text REtrieval Conference (TREC-8),* (pp. 613-622). Gaithersburg, MD: U.S. Department of Commerce, NIST.

Larson, R. R. (2001). TREC interactive with Cheshire II. *Information Processing and Management, 37*(3), 485-505.

Larson, R. R., & McDonough, J. (1998). Cheshire II at TREC-6: Interactive probabilistic retrieval. In E. M. Voorhees & D. K. Harman (Eds.), *The Sixth Text REtrieval Conference (TREC-6),* (pp. 649-659). Gaithersburg, MD: U.S. Department of Commerce, NIST.

Lopez-Ostenero, F., Gonzalo, J., & Verdejo, F. (2005). Noun phrases as building blocks for cross-language search assistance. *Information Processing and Management, 41*(3), 549-568.

Oard, D., Gonzalo, J., Sanderson, M., Lopez-Ostenero, F., & Wang, J. (2004). Interactive cross-language document selection. *Information Retrieval, 7,* 205-228.

Osdin, R., Ounis, I., & White, R. W. (2003). Using hierarchical clustering and summarization approaches for Web retrieval: Glasgow at the TREC 2002 interactive track. In E. M. Voorhees & L. P. Buckland (Eds.), *The Eleventh*

Text REtrieval Conference (TREC 2002), (pp. 640-644). Gaithersburg, MD: U.S. Department of Commerce, NIST.

Over, P. (1997). TREC-5 interactive track report. In E. M. Voorhees & D. K. Harman (Eds.), *The Fifth Text REtrieval Conference (TREC-5),* (pp. 29-56). Gaithersburg, MD: U.S. Department of Commerce, NIST.

Over, P. (1998). TREC-6 interactive track report. In E. M. Voorhees & D. K. Harman (Eds.), *The Sixth Text REtrieval Conference (TREC-6),* (pp. 73-82). Gaithersburg, MD: U.S. Department of Commerce, NIST.

Over, P. (1999). TREC-7 interactive track report. In E. M. Voorhees & D. K. Harman (Eds.), *The Seventh Text REtrieval Conference (TREC-7),* (pp. 65-72). Gaithersburg, MD: U.S. Department of Commerce, NIST.

Over, P. (2001). The TREC Interactive track: An annotated bibliography. *Information Processing and Management, 37*(3), 369-381.

Peters, C. (2005). Comparative evaluation of cross-language information retrieval systems. *Lecture Notes in Computer Science, 3379,* 152-161.

Petrelli, D., Demetriou, G., Herring, P., Beaulieu, M., & Sanderson, M. (2003). Exploring the effect of query translation when searching cross-language. In C. Peters (Ed.), *Advances in Cross-language Information Retrieval: Third workshop of the Cross-Language Evaluation Forum, CLEF 2002: revised papers* (pp. 430-445). Berlin: Springer.

Petrelli, D., Hansen, P., Beaulieu, M., & Sanderson, M. (2002). User requirement elicitation for cross-language information retrieval. *The New Review of Information Behaviour Research, 3,* 17-35.

Petrelli, D., Hansen, P., Beaulieu, M., Sanderson, M., Demetriou, G., & Herring, P. (2004). Observing users-designing clarity: A case study on the user-centered design of a cross-language retrieval system. *Journal of the American Society for Information Science and Technology, 55*(10), 923-934.

Petrelli, D., Levin, S., Beaulieu, M., & Sanderson, M. (2006). Which user interaction for cross-language information retrieval? Design issues and reflections. *Journal of the American Society for Information Science and Technology, 57*(5), 709-722.

Robertson, S. E., Walker, S., & Beaulieu, M. (1999). Okapi at TREC-7: Automatic ad hoc, filtering, VLC, and interactive track. In E. M. Voorhees & D. K. Harman (Eds.), *The Seventh Text REtrieval Conference (TREC-7),* (pp. 253-264). Gaithersburg, MD: U.S. Department of Commerce, NIST.

Robertson, S. E., Walker, S., & Beaulieu, M. (2000). Experimentation as a way of life: Okapi at TREC. *Information Processing and Management, 36*(1), 95-108.

Toms, E. G., Freund, L., & Li, C. (2003). Augmenting and limiting search queries. In E. M. Voorhees & L. P. Buckland (Eds.), *The Eleventh Text REtrieval Con-*

ference (TREC 2002), (pp. 813-822). Gaithersburg, MD: U.S. Department of Commerce, NIST.

Toms, E. G., Kopak, R. W., Bartlett, J., & Freund, L. (2002). Selecting vs. describing: A preliminary analysis of the efficacy of categories in exploring the Web. In E. M. Voorhees & D. K. Harman (Eds.), *The Tenth Text REtrieval Conference (TREC 2001),* (pp. 653-662). Gaithersburg, MD: U.S. Department of Commerce, NIST.

Vogt, C. (2001). Passive feedback collection-An attempt to debunk the myth of click-throughs. In E. M. Voorhees & D. K. Harman (Eds.), *The Ninth Text REtrieval Conference (TREC-9),* (pp. 141-150). Gaithersburg, MD: U.S. Department of Commerce, NIST.

Voorhees, E. M. (2006). Overview of TREC 2005. In E. M. Voorhees & L. P. Buckland (Eds.), *The Fourteenth Text REtrieval Conference (TREC 2005) Proceedings,* (pp. 1-15). Gaithersburg, MD: U.S. Department of Commerce, NIST.

Voorhees, E. M., & Harman, D. K. (2005). The Text REtrieval Conference. In E. M. Voorhees & D. K. Harman (Eds.), *TREC: Experiment and evaluation in information retrieval* (pp. 3-19). Cambridge, MA: The MIT Press.

White, R. W., Jose, J. M., & Ruthven, I. (2002). Comparing explicit and implicit feedback techniques for Web retrieval: TREC-10 interactive track report. In E. M. Voorhees & D. K. Harman (Eds.), *The Tenth Text REtrieval Conference, TREC 2001,* (pp. 534-538). Gaithersburg, MD: U.S. Department of Commerce, NIST.

Wu, M. F., Fuller, M., & Wilkinson, R. (2001). Using clustering and classification approaches in interactive retrieval. *Information Processing and Management, 37*(3), 459-484.

Yang, K., Maglaughlin, K. L., Meho, L., & Summer Jr., R. G. (1999). IRIS at TREC-7. In E. M. Voorhees & D. K. Harman (Eds.), *The Seventh Text REtrieval Conference (TREC-7),* (pp. 555-566). Gaithersburg, MD: U.S. Department of Commerce, NIST.

Yang, K., Maglaughlin, K. L., & Newby, G. B. (2001). Passage feedback with IRIS. *Information Processing and Management, 37*(3), 521-541.

Zhang, P., Plettenberg, L., Klavans, J. L., Oard, D. W., & Soergel, D. (2007). Task-based interaction with an integrated multilingual, multimedia information system: A formative evaluation. In *Proceedings of the 2007 Conference on Digital Libraries,* (pp. 117-126). New York: ACM Press.

Chapter VII

Interactive IR Models

Three Major IR Models

The nature of information retrieval (IR) is interaction. However, the traditional IR model only focuses on the comparison between user input and system output. It does not illustrate the changeable interaction process (Saracevic, 1997). The human involvement of IR makes the process complicated and dynamic. Belkin (1993) further identified the two underlying assumptions of the traditional IR view: (1) The information need is static, and can be specified; and (2) there is only one form of information-seeking behavior. The limitations of the traditional IR model are becoming more evident. In the 1990s researchers started to develop interactive IR models. Among them, Ingwersen's cognitive model (1992, 1996), Belkin's episode model of interaction with texts (1996), and Saracevic's stratified model (1996a, 1997) are the most cited ones.

Ingwersen's Cognitive Model and Applications

The Basis of the Integrated IS&R Research Framework

The information-seeking and retrieval research framework has been developed for over a decade by Ingwersen (1992, 1996, 1999) and Ingwersen and Järvelin (2005). Ingwersen (1992, 1996) developed and enhanced the cognitive model of IR interaction, which set up the foundation for the integrated IS&R research framework proposed by Ingwersen and Järvelin (2005). The five components (an individual user's cognitive space, a user's social-organizational environment, the interface/intermediary, the information objects, and the IR system setting), the cognitive transformation and influence from one component to another, and the interactive communication of cognitive structures via an interface or intermediary constitute the cognitive model of interaction. In this model, "cognitive structures are manifestations of human cognition, reflection or ideas. In IR they take the form of transformation generated by a variety of human actors" (Ingwersen, 1996, p. 8).

Ingwersen and Järvelin (2005) proposed an integrated IS&R research framework based on the holistic cognitive viewpoint and relevant theoretical and empirical research in information-seeking and retrieval. The shift to the holistic cognitive view started in the 1990s. Situational relevance (Schamber, Eisenberg, & Nilan, 1990), the proposal for relevant, cognitive, and the interactive revolution (Robertson & Hancock-Beaulieu, 1992), and De May's (1980, 1982) view of cognition in contextual social interaction and the four evolutionary stages of information processing are the theoretical basis for Ingwersen's 1992 and 1996 IR model from an interactive perspective. Theoretical and empirical research in information-seeking and retrieval come from three areas: (1) The development of information-seeking research from 1960 to 2000, especially information-seeking models represented by Dervin's sense-making approach (Dervin, 1983; Dervin & Nilan, 1986), Ellis' information-seeking features (Ellis, 1989; Ellis, Cox, & Hall, 1993), Kuhlthau's process model (1991), Wilson's model on information behavior (Wilson 1997, 1999), and a model on task-based information-seeking (Byström & Järvelin, 1995; Vakkari, 1998; Vakkari & Kuokkanen, 1997), and so forth; (2) the development of system-oriented information retrieval research from 1960 to the present including the development of several major mathematical retrieval models and the discussion of major issues and findings in systems-oriented research, such as document, request, and relevance; interaction and query modification; and so forth; and (3) the development of cognitive and user-oriented IR research exemplified by models of cognitive IR, such as the conceptual models by Ingwersen (1992, 1996) and Saracevic (1996a), and so forth; cognitive information-seeking and retrieval theory-building represented by Taylor's information need formation (Taylor, 1968); the ASK hypothesis (Belkin, Oddy, & Brooks, 1982a, 1982b), and so forth; and research on searchers' behavior, cognitive models and styles, online IR interaction, Web IR interaction, relevance issues, and so forth.

The Integrated IS&R Research Framework

Originating from Ingwersen's (1992) description of the processes of IR interaction, Ingwersen and Järvelin (2005, p. 261) proposed an integrated IS&R research framework with the model of interactive information-seeking, retrieval and behavioral processes. While the former model positions the searcher— influenced by his/her social or organizational environment—at the center of the interaction, the latter one is a generalized model that considers cognitive actor(s) or teams derived from their organizational, cultural, and social context as the central component of the model. A revised model (Figure 7.1) is developed by Ingwersen per correspondence in 2007. In this model, the cognitive actor(s) or teams can represent different groups or roles of human actors; accordingly, the contextual elements also change.

As a central component of the model, cognitive actor(s) or teams can be represented by the following human groups in the information creation, organization, dissemination, and use process:

Figure 7.1. Modified version of Ingwersen and Järvelin's model of interactive information-seeking, retrieval and behavioral processes. From The Turn: Integration of Information Seeking and Retrieval in Context (p. 261) by P. Ingwersen and K. Järvelin, 2005. Heidelberg: Springer. Copyright 2007 by P. Ingwersen. Used with copyright permission.

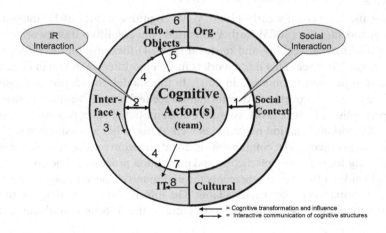

- Creators of information objects;

- Indexers analyzing and generating representations of information objects to facilitate retrieval of information objects;

- Designers of interface and software to facilitate users' interaction with systems;

- Designers of retrieval engines, structures, and algorithms to facilitate users' effective retrieval of relevant information;

- Gatekeepers determining the availability of information objects into a collection or a carrier;

- Information-seekers or searchers looking for information to solve their problems; and

- Communities representing different groups from different organizational, social, and cultural contexts.

Four numbers (1-4) on the model (Figure 7.1) illustrate the processes of interaction; another four numbers (5-8) represent types of generation and transformation of cognition or cognitive influence. Again, cognitive actor(s) are the key players in the model. On the one hand, they make social interactions within organizational, social, and cultural contexts. On the other hand, they interact with system design and system collection via interfaces. In other words, cognitive actors are affected mainly by their interaction with different levels of contexts, the texts in an information system, and the design of an information system. The information system is mainly represented by interactions between information technology and information objects. At the same time, cognitive transformation and influence may take place at the request of cognitive actor(s) and of organizational, social, and cultural contexts toward information objects and information technology. Collaborative IR is one form of cognitive transformation and influence.

Extending the Ingwersen's early (1996, p. 9) cognitive model of IR interaction, Ingwersen and Järvelin (2005) further illustrated the cognitive framework of longitudinal information-seeking and retrieval (p. 274) focusing on the information seeker's cognitive space. This framework is further modified as shown in Figure 7.2 by Ingwersen per correspondence in 2007. In this model, interaction and perception are the essential processes. An information seeker's cognitive space consists of his/her perception of: work tasks, cognitive and emotional state, problem situation, search tasks, and information behavior as well as his or her assessment and use of the information objects. The components in an information seeker's cognitive space are the driving force for the interaction and perception processes. The environment on the right side of the model represents the community's norms and behaviors, to which an information seeker easily adapts. The information technology on the left side of the model represents the main structure of the information object and the central cognitive structure of information technology. The interface with functions is the bridge between information technology and information space. In this framework, "models" is same in each of the five components. It reflects the perception or interpretation of its own context by any given actor or component of the framework at a certain situation.

Implications and Limitations of the Model

As the most comprehensive model for information-seeking and retrieval from the cognitive view, the contributions of Ingwersen and Järvelin's (2005) integrated IS&R research framework can be summarized into the following aspects: 1) This IS&R framework is a general framework, the cognitive actors are varied and not limited to information-seekers, and this framework can account for all types of actors and their related interactions within different organizational, social, and cultural contexts and information technologies. This research framework demonstrates its flexibility and dynamic nature, corresponding to the complexity of information-seeking and

Figure 7.2. Modified version of Ingwersen and Järvelin's complex cognitive framework of longitudinal interactive IS&R. From The Turn: Integration of Information Seeking and Retrieval in Context (p. 274) by P. Ingwersen and K. Järvelin, 2005. Heidelberg: Springer. Copyright 2007 by P. Ingwersen. Used with copyright permission.

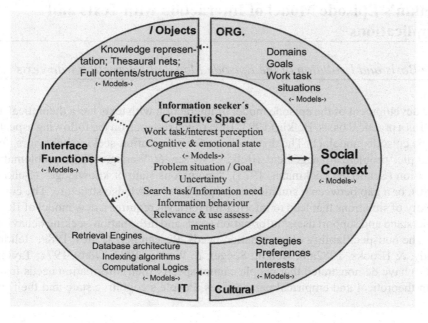

retrieval. 2) Although this framework focuses on the cognitive viewpoint of interactive IR, it integrates the socio-organizational context into the cognitive framework. It is a media-independent framework. 3) This framework not only provides a framework for understanding the cognitive activities involved in information-seeking and retrieval, but it also offers detailed guidance for multidimensional research designs for nine information-seeking and retrieval research variables. The model further proposes research methods and data collection methods to investigate interactive information-seeking and retrieval in a variety of contexts.

The integrated IS&R research framework contributes significantly to the research on interactive IR. However, it also has its limitations. One of those is that the framework has not been tested or validated in a large-scale-of-study event, although some empirical studies have been conducted to test part of the model. Another critical issue for the framework is that it does not suggest design principles for the design of interactive IR systems to support users in interacting with information technology in different social-organizational contexts. Without offering design principles, this framework can only understand users' information-seeking and retrieval activities but cannot assist them effectively to accomplish the information-seeking and retrieval process. Finally, this framework can only illustrate the macrolevel of cognitive actor(s) interactions; it cannot present and predict microlevel information-seeking or retrieval behavior, the factors leading to different information-seeking and retrieval behavior, or shifts in information-seeking and retrieval behaviors. The macrolevel of the model might also limit its implications for IR system design.

Belkin's Episode Model of Interaction with Texts and Applications

The Basis and Evolution of the Episode Model of Interaction with Texts

The development of the episode model of interaction with texts has a theoretical as well as a practical basis. Belkin (1993, 1996) cited research on the following aspects of the episode model: (1) The driving force for information-seeking behaviors, for example, problem management (Belkin, Seeger, & Wersig, 1983), problematic situation (Schutz & Luckmann, 1973), "anomalous state of knowledge" (Belkin, 1980), or a gap between a situation and a person's knowledge structure. The complexity of situations that lead to information retrieval requires a new model of IR to understand and support users' information needs and information-seeking behavior. (2) The nonspecifiability of information needs. Researchers (Bates, 1989; Belkin, Oddy, & Brooks, 1982a,b; Belkin, Seeger, & Wersig, 1983; Oddy, 1977; Taylor, 1968) have demonstrated that people cannot specify their information needs from both theoretical and empirical perspectives. People's cognitive state and their interaction with texts both influence the information-seeking process. (3) Multiple information-seeking behaviors or strategies identified from user studies. In addition to citing Ellis (1989) and Hancock-Beaulieu's (1990) work regarding the multiple information-seeking behaviors exhibited by users, Belkin and his associates (Belkin, Marchetti, & Cool, 1993; Belkin, Cool, Stein, & Thiel, 1995) identified four facets of information-seeking strategies from a variety of settings: goal of the interaction, method of interaction, mode of retrieval, and type of resource interacted with. They further associated each region of the information-seeking strategies with a typical interaction or dialogue structure. They proposed the BRAQUE system that is based on real cases of interactions to support both users' multiple information-seeking strategies and changes from one information-seeking strategy to another. (4) New approaches to designing IR systems. Oddy's (1977) THOMAS system, Croft and Thompson's (1987) I³R system, and Frisse's (1988) hypertext system allow users to retrieve information without query specification.

The development of the episode model of interaction has evolved over 10 years. Belkin and his associates (Belkin, 1984; Belkin, et al., 1983; Ingwersen, 1992; Ingwersen & Wormell, 1986) started with a general model of the IR system that includes the users within the IR system. The user is an inherent component of the IR system. Three major components are constituted in the IR system: the user, the knowledge resource that users interact with, and the intermediaries (persons or devices) that mediate users' interaction with texts. The IR system consists of five processes: (1) representation of users' information problem and texts in the system, (2) comparison of representations of the information problem and texts, (3) interaction between users and intermediaries, (4) judgment of relevance of retrieved texts to the information problem, and (5) modification of representation of the information problem. Belkin (1993) suggested that IR should be a form of interaction with texts.

The Episode Model of Interaction with Texts

In 1993, Belkin suggested that IR is interaction with texts; in 1996, he extended the view and formally proposed the model (Belkin, 1996, p. 29) as shown in Figure 7.3. The model was based on the following assumptions that contradict to the traditional view of IR:

- People cannot specify their information needs because of their cognitive state and the dynamic nature of the problem situation.
- People engage in multiple seeking behaviors, and change their interactions with texts according to differential goals, knowledge, intentions, and so forth.
- Therefore, the nature of IR is interaction, and people's interaction with texts is the central process.

- Supporting multiple information-seeking behaviors is the objective of an IR system.

The key part of the model—users' interaction with texts—is the central process of IR. Based on observation of users' information-seeking behaviors or strategies (ISS), these behaviors or strategies can be classified. Furthermore, the design of IR systems can support different types of interactions for different kinds of ISS. Belkin and his colleagues (Belkin, et al., 1993, 1995) designed a dialogue-based IR system supporting different types of ISS and shifting from one ISS to another one. IR systems need to effectively support users' interaction with information. For that purpose, these are the questions need to be answered:

- What types of interactions do people engage in?
- What are the sequences of ISS occurring in an information-seeking episode?
- What are the patterns between situations or goals and specific types of interactions? What leads to shifts from one ISS to another one?
- How is the nature of the interaction affected by the nature of the information objects that users interact with?
- How can different types of interactions be supported?

Users interact with some type of information in an information-seeking episode depending on user goals, tasks, knowledge, problems, or uses. A variety of processes, such as representation, comparison, presentation, navigation, and visualization, support users' interaction with texts. Within an information-seeking episode, users engage in sequential interactions according to their plans, driven by their goals and their tasks, as well as their interaction with texts at any given time. From that perspective, users' interaction with texts is not static; instead, it is dynamic.

Implications and Limitations of the Model

As one of the pioneers in developing the interactive IR model, Belkin considers users' interaction with texts as a central process of information retrieval. In the episode model of interaction with texts, users are no longer outside of an IR system; instead, they are an inherent part of the IR system, and all the IR processes are designed to support users' interaction with texts. This model not only provides a theoretical framework for understanding and supporting multiple information-seeking strategies, but also offers guidance for IR system design to support multiple information-seeking strategies and, more important, shifts from one information-seeking strategy to another by connecting dimensions of information-seeking strategies to different interaction structures. By incorporating different interaction structures of ISS and sequences of ISS into system design, an intelligent IR system can effectively support users' interaction with information.

As this model is a pioneering work, it also has limitations. Users' interaction with texts is a central process. However, this model limits users' interaction only to the IR system without considering other entities that users might also interact with, such as the social-organizational context. The model lays out a high-level foundation for understanding interactive information retrieval; however, it does not offer information regarding the interaction process. For example, multiple information-seeking strategies and shifts in information-seeking strategies are the basis of the development of the model, but they are not incorporated directly into the model. Shifts in information-seeking strategies are the representation of the dynamic nature of interactive IR, but the model does not show how and when the shifts in information-seeking strategies take place. These make it difficult to validate and test the model in practical settings.

Figure 7.3. Belkin's episode model of interaction with texts. From "Intelligent information retrieval: Whose intelligence?" by N. J. Belkin, 1996. ISI '96: Proceedings of the 5th International Symposium for Information Science (p. 29). Konstanz: Universtaetsverlag Konstanz. Copyright 1996 by Universtaetsverlag Konstanz.

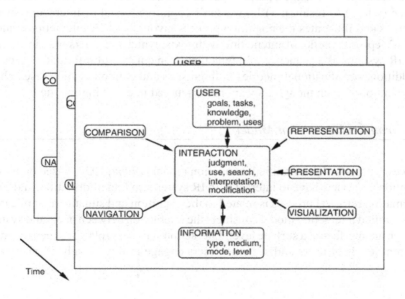

Saracevic's Stratified Interaction Model and Applications

The Evolution and Theoretical Basis of the Stratified Interaction Model

Saracevic formally proposed the stratified interaction in 1996, and further enhanced the model in 1997. In his 1996 paper, he summarized some of the previous works about nature of interaction in IR (Saracevic, Kantor, Chamis, & Trivison, 1988; Saracevic, Mokros, & Su, 1990), IR interaction from a communication perspective (Mokros, Mullins, & Saracevic, 1995), and some of the doctoral dissertations (Wu, 1992; Spink, 1993). In his 1997 paper, he synthesized five of his own articles and the articles he collaborated on with his associates. These papers include his original review of interaction models and a proposal for his stratified interaction model (Saracevic, 1996a), relevance (Saracevic, 1996b), users and their interaction with intermediaries (Saracevic, Spink, & Wu, 1997), search terms effectiveness during mediated searching (Spink & Saracevic, 1997), and the nature of feedback (Spink & Saracevic, 1998).

Saracevic (1996a, 1997) proposed and enhanced the stratified interaction model based on the following theoretical models and frameworks: 1) The traditional IR model that represents IR as comparison, or matching user request to document representation; 2) human-computer interaction (HCI) as a general framework that encompasses IR interaction. The definition of HCI applies to IR interactions. The essential elements of HCI are same for IR interaction: participants (users and systems), exchange (communication between users and systems or intermediaries), interface (the platform for exchange), purpose (intentions associated with participants), and change (related to results); 3) Ingwersen's cognitive model of interaction, which identifies and illustrates the cognition process involving in IR interactions; and 4) Belkin's episode model of interaction with texts, which considers user interaction with IR systems as a sequence of interaction in an episode of information seeking. In addition, stratificational theories in linguistics and communication research are also mentioned even though they are not discussed in detail in the articles.

The Stratified Interaction Model

Saracevic proposed the stratified interaction model (1996a, 1997) based on two assumptions: 1) Users have to interact with IR systems to find information; and 2) the information retrieval process is related to the cognition and situational application. The stratified interaction model considers the interaction between users and systems through an interface at a surface level. Interaction is the interplay between or among different levels of users and systems. Users engage in three levels of interaction:

cognitive, affective, and situational. The system side also includes three levels of involvement: engineering, processing, and content. Saracevic (1997 as shown in Figure 7.4, p. 316) presents the stratified interaction model.

Users are involved in three levels of interaction:

- On the cognitive level, users have to make relevance judgments about the retrieved texts, and their state of knowledge might change because of their interaction with texts and their representations. The interaction is between the cognitive structure of users and texts.

- On the affective level, intentions and related affective factors are what users interact with, mainly users' intentions, beliefs, and motivations.

- On the situational level, the situation and problem that lead users to look for information are what users interact with. Tasks and problems are the foci of the investigation.

Figure 7.4. Saracevic's stratified model of IR interaction. From "The stratified model of information retrieval interaction: Extension and applications." By T. Saracevic, 1997. Proceedings of the ASIS Annual Meeting (p. 316) Medford, NJ: Information Today. Copyright 1997 by Information Today. Used with copyright permission

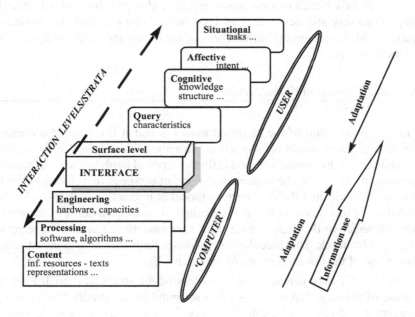

Three levels of system involvement are suggested:

- On the engineering level, the hardware and its operational and design attributes are the center of the analysis.

- On the processing level, the software, especially the algorithms, lies beneath the essential processes that are associated with the interplay between user and system levels.

- On the content level, information resources, the texts, and their representations are the concentration of the analysis. The analysis focuses on the accuracy, credibility, validity, reliability, and quality of the content.

The interface offers a platform for users to interact with systems on the surface level. Users interact with IR systems by searching, browsing, navigating, organizing and viewing search results, providing feedback, and so forth. The systems interact with users by requesting user information, providing responses to users, and so forth. However, the interaction is complicated and dynamic. On the user side, users cannot always clearly specify their information needs, and their information problems could be ill-defined. Their state of knowledge, cognition, and intentionality also affect the way they interact with IR systems. During the interaction, their problem/task might be redefined or refocused. Interaction involves interplays between the deeper and surface levels, and that might lead to the changes on the surface level, such as new terms, new tactics or strategies selected or changed, and so forth. A series of adaptations may also occur at every level on both the user and system sides in the form of shifts or changes. Shifts represent the important events analysis of the interaction process.

Impact and Limitation of the Model

The major contribution of the stratified model is that it illustrates the elements involved in different levels of interaction. Moreover, it integrates different types of interactions on the human side and different types of hardware and software attributes and processes on the system side. For that perspective, it incorporates the traditional IR model and Belkin's episode model of interaction with texts. Another contribution of this model is that it is extended to encompass some of the critical issues of interactive IR, such as relevance, user modeling, search term selection, and types of feedback. This model offers guidance for researchers to investigate or explain some of the essential issues of interactive IR.

Saracevic (1997) acknowledged the weakness of the stratified model. First, the limitation of the stratified model is same as found in the stratificational models in linguistics and communication. It is very difficult to specify and decompose interplays between different levels. Second, the stratified model does not provide enough details for testing in larger interaction studies. The practical applications need to be further explored.

Applications and Implications of the Three IR Models

These three models are well cited and applied in providing a theoretical framework for research on information-seeking and retrieval. Many of the theoretical models on information-seeking and retrieval are based on one or more the interactive models discussed above. Considering the multiple levels or layers of the structure for IR interactions and the multidimensional information-seeking strategies suggested by the interactive IR models, Cool (1997) proposed a model of the information-seeking situation that regards IR as a process of social interaction between the authors of texts and the users of IR systems. The central cognitive aspect of the model is situation assessment. Citing the three interactive IR models as the main theoretical basis, Xie (2000, 2002) created a model of interactive IR focusing on shifts in the microlevel of user goals, "interactive intention," and information-seeking strategies that users engage in within an information seeking episode. Influenced by components presented in interactive IR models, Pharo (2004) presented a model of information behavior emphasizing the search situation and transition with five main elements: the work task, the searcher, the social/organizational environment, the search task, and the search process. The search process shifts between the search situation and transition. Detlor (2003) created a model of Internet-based information use in organizations, borrowing theoretical insights from major information behavioral models including the interactive IR models.

The implications of these interactive IR models are not limited to general information-seeking and retrieval; they also extend to specific issues in the information-seeking and retrieval process. Influenced by the cognitive viewpoint introduced by Ingwersen, Wang and Soergel (1998) developed a cognitive model of document selection that depicts how users apply their personal knowledge and decision strategies in the document selection process. Adapting Saracevic's stratified model (1996a, 1997), Rieh and Xie (2006) developed a model of Web query reformulation based on qualitative analysis of the Excite data. It is the surface level on which users interact with a system interface to express their needs in the form of query formulation and reformulation. Query reformulation is the product of users' involvement in the interaction at the cognitive, affective, and situation levels. Moreover, some of the interactive IR models and approaches discussed below are also influenced by the three models, such as Vakkari's (2001) theory of the task-based IR process, Hert's (1997) IR interaction relation to the information-seeking process, Spink's (1997) feedback framework in the interactive information-seeking and retrieval process, and Wang, Hawk, and Tenopir's (2000) multidimensional model of user-Web interaction.

Not only are these interactive IR models applied to theoretical research, they also guide in empirical research in related areas. Mostly they serve as a context and theoretical framework for practical research. Researchers applied the interactive IR models into a series of studies of information-seeking and mediated searching (Ellis et al., 2002; Spink, Wilson, Ford, Foster, & Ellis, 2002) and shifts in focus during mediated interactive IR (Robins, 2000). The cognitive paradigm provides the background for Bilal (2005) to study children's information-seeking in the affective paradigm. Belkin's and Saracevic's models provide a context of interactive IR for Rieh (2002) to examine users' judgment of information quality and cognitive authority in the Web environment. These interactive IR models were perceived as the cognitive approach and theoretical basis for Cole and Mandelblatt (2000) in modeling information retrieval systems to decode and encode IR system messages. Taking into account the interactive IR process depicted by the interactive models, Crudge and Johnson (2004) designed the repertory grid technique and investigated the appropriateness of the technique for the evaluation of interactive search engines. This method can elicit a set of constructs from information seekers without bias. Yang, Maglaughlin, and Newby (2001) explored the common theme underlying interactive IR models to answer the question of how various types of interaction in IR processes affect the retrieval outcome. In their interactive track studies, they concluded that a passage feedback system instead of a conventional document feedback system is an effective mechanism for interactive IR.

Limitations of the Three Models

There are no large-scale empirical studies that have tested or validated these models. A related issue is how these interactive IR models account for key specific issues in interactive IR. While these models identify the factors that might affect the interactive information-seeking and retrieval process, they do not associate these factors with information-seeking strategies or behaviors. For example, Foster and Ford (2003) pointed out that current models of information-seeking and behavior, including Ingwersen's and Saracevic's models, had not offered a clear understanding of serendipity in information-seeking. Spink, Griesdorf, and Bateman (1999) revealed that major interactive IR models had not been tested nor were they able to represent successive searches. Although IR systems offering automated assistance could facilitate user and system interactions, Jansen (2005) argued that automatic searching assistance as a concept is not clearly expressed in interactive IR models and other information searching models. All the specific models introduced in the following section also indicate that many of the key issues in interactive IR cannot be accounted for by these three models. Another problem with these models is related to user characteristics. General interactive IR models need to be enhanced to include different types of user groups, different types of task dimensions, different information-seeking and retrieval processes, different interactive activities, different IR systems or environments, and so forth.

At the same time, while these models emphasize the theoretical implications for research on information-seeking and research, their impact on practical implications, especially the design of interactive IR systems, is not as significant as their theoretical implications. The models do not provide constructive suggestions in terms of how to design interactive IR systems to represent and support interactions illustrated in these models. This is a critical weakness for these models because there is a gap between user-oriented IR research and actual IR system design.

Microlevel of Interactive IR Models and Approaches

In addition to the three major interactive IR models, researchers have also developed different interactive IR models or approaches to illustrate or highlight one aspect of information-seeking and retrieval interaction. While Ellis' model of information-seeking behavior (Ellis, 1989; Ellis & Haugan, 1997) and Bates' (1989) berrypicking approach highlight the dynamic interactive IR process, Vakkari (2001) focuses on a theory of the task-based IR process, and Spink (1997) extended the interactive model by incorporating five types of interactive feedback. Hert (1997) further differentiated and associated the microlevel of IR interaction with the macrolevel of the information-seeking process. Differing with other interactive IR model and approaches, Wang, Hawk, and Tenopir (2000) chose to depict a model of IR interaction in a specific environment, the Web space. These microlevel interactive IR models illustrate the specific aspect of interactive IR that the macrolevel models cannot account for. In addition, Pharo (2002) developed the search situational and transition method schema to analyze the information search process, which can be applied to other information seeking and retrieving process.

Ellis' Model of Information-Seeking Behavior

Ellis (Ellis, 1987, 1989) developed the model of information-seeking behavior based on empirical studies of social scientists for the design of information retrieval systems. The behavior approach rather than cognitive approach is the underlying principle of the model. The essential part of the model is the six types of information-seeking characteristics:

- Starting refers to the initial work or search for information on a new topic or area.

- Chaining refers to following citation connections between materials. Backward chaining and forward chaining are the two frequently occurring chaining types.

- Browsing refers to glancing through an area with potential interest; it is one form of semidirected or structured searching.

- Differentiating refers to identifying differences among sources, such as the substantive topic of study; the approach or perspective adopted; the quality, level, or type of treatment; and so forth, to filter the materials examined.

- Monitoring refers to keeping up with the developments of a field of study by checking specific information sources.

- Extracting refers to identifying relevant material from a particular source.

Ellis and his associates further applied and extended the model to other types of users and other important issues in information-seeking and retrieval. For example, Ellis and Haugan (1997) modeled the information-seeking patterns of engineers and research scientists in an industrial environment. This group of users showed consistent patterns of information-seeking behavior with surveying, chaining, monitoring, browsing, distinguishing, extracting, filtering, and ending. Applying the model and other theoretical frameworks, Ellis and his associates (Ellis et al., 2002; Ford et al., 2002; Spink et al., 2002; Wilson et al., 2002) investigated uncertainty, successive searching, cognitive styles, and user-intermediary interaction. The information-seeking patterns of different groups of users demonstrate that users do employ multiple information-seeking strategies in the retrieval process. This unique behavioral approach opens a different avenue for researchers to explore information-seeking behavior. Even though Ellis' model does not connect patterns of information-seeking with factors that lead to these patterns, the identification of patterns of information-seeking behavior of different user groups contributes significantly to the user-oriented IR research. The model has been widely cited in information-seeking and retrieval research, especially in the early models of IR interaction.

Bates' Berrypicking Approach

Bates' (1989) berrypicking approach is one of the most cited approaches in interactive IR research. It is also the basis for several interactive IR models. The berrypicking approach (Bates, 1989) is a simulation of searchers' information-seeking behavior. This article is one of the pioneering works that identify the problems and limitations of the traditional IR model; it further suggests that the berrypicking model can better characterize users' real information-seeking behavior. The berrypicking approach can be summarized as:

- Searchers' search queries evolve in the information-seeking process.
- Searchers seek information piece by piece rather than in one retrieved set.
- Searchers apply multiple search techniques in the search process.
- Searchers access different sources in addition to bibliographic databases.

Based on Ellis' (1989) and Stoan's (1984) findings, Bates (1989) identified six typical information-seeking strategies: (1) footnote chasing or backward chaining, (2) citation searching or forward chaining, (3) journal run, (4) area scanning, (5) subject searches in bibliographies and abstracting and indexing, and (6) author searching. She analyzed searching behavior corresponding to the six techniques focusing on browsing behaviors. This approach offers a real picture of searchers' information-seeking processes, contrary to the traditional IR model. Moreover, she discussed how to apply the berrypicking approach into the implementation of database and interface design online to facilitate searchers' information-seeking processes.

Vakkari's Theory of the Task-Based IR Process

Vakkari and his associates (Pennanen & Vakkari, 2003; Vakkari, 2000a, 2000b, 2001; Vakkari & Hakala, 2000) conducted a series of studies on how the task performance process is related to information retrieval by examining students' information-seeking processes in writing a research proposal for a master's thesis. Kuhlthau's (1993) model of the information search process, especially how the stages of task performance influence the information-searching tactics and types of information searched for, is the framework of these studies. The hypothesis is that the stages of task performance are associated with the types of information searched for, the shifts in search tactics and terms, and relevance judgments.

Vakkari (2001) compared the findings of the studies conducted by Kuhlthau and Vakkari. In both studies, the stages of the task performance are same, and the mental model of the subjects is considered as a dominant factor between the stages of the task performance and information-seeking and retrieval behavior. Vakkari (2001) did refine and enhance the major concepts in Kuhlthau's model such as search tactics, search terms, relevance feedback, and so forth. Based on the hypotheses and findings in these studies, Vakkari (2001, p. 58) presented a theory of the task-based IR process (as shown in Figure 7.5). This model summarizes the results of a series of studies and concludes that the stage of the task performance process and the mental

Figure 7.5. Vakkari's theory of the task-based IR process. From "A theory of the Task-based Information Retrieval Process" by P. Vakkari, 2001. Journal of Documentation, 57, p. 58. Copyright 2001 by Emerald Group Publishing Limited. Used with copyright permission.

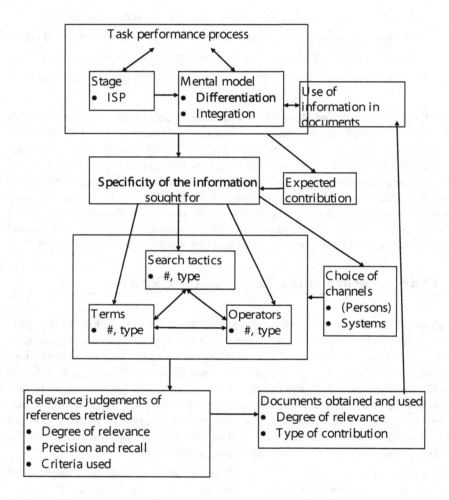

model of the searcher determine the information sought, search tactics applied, term choices selected, relevance judgments assessed, and type and degree of documents obtained and used. To summarize, users' information retrieval process is driven by the task performance process.

Spink's Model of Interactive Feedback

Spink (1997) found one of the limitations of existing interactive IR models was that they could not account for the role of feedback in IR interaction. She conducted a study to examine the types of interactive feedback that occurred during mediated IR. Based on the analysis of a total of 885 feedback occurrences, she extended the interactive IR model to consist of five types of interactive feedback:

- Content relevance feedback refers to user query based on user relevance assessment of previously retrieved items.

- Term relevance feedback refers to user query based on user selection of a new search term(s) from previously retrieved items.

- Magnitude feedback refers to user query based on user judgment of the size of the output of a previous query.

- Tactical review feedback refers to user input based on the strategy of displaying and reviewing past search history.

- Term review feedback refers to user input based on the strategy of displaying and reviewing terms in the inverted file.

According to Spink (1997, p. 391), a series of search strategies with one or more cycles constitutes an interactive search process (as shown in Figure 7.6). Each cycle may consist of interactive feedback loops that include search tactics or moves and user judgments of system output. Interactive feedback is the result of situational factors and the cognitive status of users, and it further enhances the interaction between users and IR systems. After comparing the traditional and interactive IR models, she came to the conclusion that users took more active roles in the interactive IR models. User and cognitive process replaced IR system and automatic process in the query reformulation process. In addition, five types of feedback, instead of just the relevance feedback, occurred in the interactive IR process.

Hert's IR Interaction in Relation to the Information-Seeking Process

Hert (1997) reported a large-scale inductive and qualitative study by investigating users' interactions with the OPAC in a university setting. Two major findings of this study are (1) Situational elements that are embedded in the goal, and stopping elements defined the goal and stopping criteria, and (2) user goal was not modified in the IR interaction. These two major findings lead to the model of IR interaction in relation to the larger information-seeking process (Hert, 1997, p. 109).

Figure 7.6. Spink's elements of the interactive search process. From "Study of interactive feedback during mediated information retrieval" by A. Spink, 1997. Journal of the American Society for Information Science, 48, p. 391. Copyright 1997 by John Wiley & Sons, Inc. Used with copyright permission.

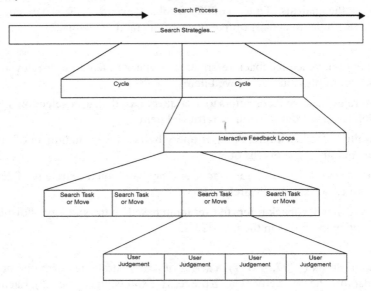

The model (as shown in Figure 7.7) portrays two time-scales: the macro-time-scale of information-seeking-and-use and the micro-time-scale of IR interaction. People in general have to move in the microlevel of IR interaction as well as the macrolevel of information-seeking process. This problematic situation leads users to search for information in an IR system. When a user is searching in an IR system, he/she is moving in IR interaction, but not in the larger information problem. When he/she finishes the search, the results of interaction can be used to move the larger information seeking-and-use process. Situational elements define goal and stopping criteria rather than changing goals because they are embedded in a larger information-seeking process. The searching behaviors are dynamic, because they are situated in IR interaction.

Wang, Hawk, and Tenopir's Multidimensional Model of User-Web Interaction

Wang, Hawk, and Tenopir (2000) proposed a multidimensional model of user-Web interaction in IR. The user, the interface, and the Web space are the three components of the model. In IR interaction in the Web environment, the user, the most important component, interacts with the Web space via the interface that facilitates the interactions between the two.

The following dimensional factors influence the user dimension:

- Situational factors, such as the task, the information need, and so forth.
- Cognitive behaviors, such as personal thoughts, search strategies, problem-solving decisions, metal models, and so forth.
- Affective state, such as satisfied, frustrated, and so forth.
- Physical skills, such as hand-eye coordination, control of input, and so forth.

The interface consists of the following five types of elements:

- Access methods, such as default home page, bookmarks, and so forth.
- Navigation tools, such as back button, history, and so forth.
- Access results/objects, such as a single page, a list of URLs, and so forth.
- Messages/clues referring to the messages that users get when their access fails
- Input/output devices, such as keyboard, mouse, and so forth.

The Web includes the following elements:

- Objects refer to the basic unit of the Web, and can be in any digital format.
- Activated objects refer to sections of the Web that have been activated in the interaction.
- Web spaces refer to spaces on the Web that contain collections of networked objects accessible by certain methods.
- Organization schemes refer to how the Web and each Web space are organized.
- Metadata refer to the description information about an object.

They further tested the model by conducting an exploratory study of 24 graduate students' interaction with a university Web site. The results of the study validated the model, because the findings showed that all the factors specified in the model played roles in the user-Web interaction. To be more specific, cognitive factors influenced the users in analysis of questions, in constructing searching, and in developing problem-solving strategies. Affective factors, such as negative feelings, have an impact on users' decisions about strategy adoption and use. Physical factors can lead to efficient or incompetent interactions. Based on the model, the researchers associated user behavior with problems in the design of Web interfaces, and they further made suggestions to Web designers and content providers.

Pharo's Search Situation and Transition Method

Integrating the perspectives from information retrieval and information seeking, Pharo and his associate (Pharo, 2002, 2004; Pharo & Järvelin, 2004) developed the search situation transition method schema to analyze the Web information search process and related information-seeking behaviors. The method was presented via its domain, method, and justification. The conceptual framework of the method domain consists of five categories: the work tasks, the searcher, the social/organizational environment, the search task, and the search process. The framework emphasizes the search process with a series of transitions and situations and their relationships. The attributes of transitions and situations include actions, accumulated results, accumulated effort, information space, time, relevance judgment, relevance level, remaining needs, resource type, and technical problems. The following data collection methods were suggested to portray the Web search process: video and observation for search process; interview and output data for work tasks; interview, observation, and video logs for search tasks; interviews and questionnaires for searchers; and interviews as well as annual reports and written documents for social/organizational environments. This method serves as a useful tool for interactive IR studies.

Summary: Major Components of and Limitations of Existing Macro- and Microlevel of Interactive IR Models

The limitation of the traditional IR model that compares and matches the representation of text and the representation of user need is evident. While commonly recognized system-oriented models can be classified as the Boolean logic model, vector space model, probabilistic model, and so forth, it is more difficult to categorize interactive

IR models because they focus on different components or structures of interactive IR. Figure 7.7 presents the classification of interactive IR models discussed in this chapter. The emergence of interactive IR models considers the nature of IR as the process of users' interaction with IR systems. Researchers have put forward interactive IR models in which three models take the leading role in interactive IR research: Ingwersen and Järvelin's (2005) integrated IS&R research framework extending from Ingwersen's cognitive model of IR interaction, Belkin's episode model of interaction with text, and Saracevic's stratified model. All these interactive IR models deal with how users interact with IR systems, but they have different foci. Cognitive structures of different types of human actors and their transformation are the key elements of Ingwersen and Järvelin's framework, interaction with text is the center of Belkin's episode model, and participants in the interaction process at different levels are the focus of Saracevic's stratified model. While Ingwersen and Järvelin's cognitive framework integrates information-seeking and retrieval, Belkin's episode model identifies the dimensions of information-seeking strategies. In Saracevic's stratified model, understanding the interplays between levels of strata is essential in understanding IR interaction. Just as summarized by Beaulieu (2000), theses interactive IR models offer a complementary perspective on the complicated and dynamic interactive IR process.

These interactive IR models are not just the product of research from library and information science; instead, they take into account perspectives from multiple disciplines. Moreover, they represent many years of work from researchers in

Figure 7.7. Classification of interactive IR models

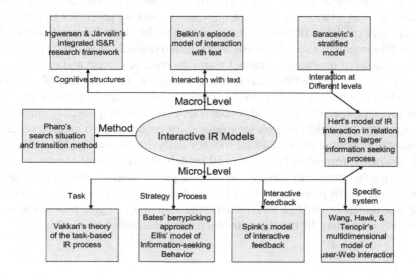

related fields. These models go beyond the debates between system-oriented and user-oriented research. These interactive IR models indicate that the nature of information-seeking and retrieval is interaction, and the nature of the interaction and factors affecting the interaction should be the key part of the investigation.

The macrolevel of interactive IR models is a double blessing. On the one hand, they provide an IR interaction context and offer guidance for researchers to develop a microlevel of theoretical models as well as to conduct empirical studies. They illustrate the interactive IR process and highlight the major components involved in the interactive IR process. They further identify the factors that influence IR interaction and how the interaction might take place. On the other hand, the macrolevel models also determine their limitations. First, they cannot account for all the specific processes or issues that might occur in the interactive IR process, such as serendipity in information-seeking, interactive relevance feedback, users' characteristics, and so forth. Second, they cannot be used to predict information-seeking strategies or behaviors. Third, they cannot associate factors affecting IR interactions with specific information-seeking strategies or behaviors. In other words, they cannot answer the question: Under what circumstances might users select different types of information-seeking strategies or behaviors? Finally, they need to be tested and validated in a variety of interactive IR settings involving different types of users.

The microlevel of interactive IR models complements the macrolevel of interactive IR models to further explore specific processes or issues in the interactive IR process. These models highlight the most essential processes or issues in IR interaction. These include: the nature of the task's impact on information-seeking and retrieval behavior (Vakkari's theory of the task-based IR process); dynamic information-seeking processes and shifts in information-seeking strategies (Ellis' model of information-seeking behavior and Bates' berrypicking approach); the effects of situational elements and the relationship between information-seeking processes and IR interaction (Hert's model of IR interaction in relation to the larger information seeking process); the interactive search process with interactive feedback playing a major role (Spink's model of interactive feedback); and the specific system and environment users are interacting with (Wang, Hawk, and Tenopir's multidimensional model of user-Web interaction). Strictly speaking, Hert's model covers both the macro- and micro-levels of interactive IR, as it connects IR interaction emphasizing situational elements to the larger information-seeking-and-use process. Pharo's search situation and transition method offers a useful tool for analyzing interactive IR at different levels. Just as do macrolevel interactive IR models, the microlevel of interactive IR models have their own limitations. While they depict the specific processes or issues in the interactive IR process, many of the models cannot be generalized into other processes, issues, or settings. Researchers still need to investigate how to integrate microlevel interactive IR models with macrolevel interactive IR models.

Based on the macro- and micro-level of interactive models, the following components of interactive IR can be summarized:

- Organizational and social context,
- User goals or tasks,
- User cognitive status/knowledge structure,
- Information-seeking strategies,
- The interface/intermediary of an IR system,
- Information objects/texts,
- System hardware and software, and
- The type of IR system or environment.

There are no standard criteria for the evaluation of interactive IR models. Saracevic (1996a) proposed several ideal characteristics for the evaluation and scientific testing of interactive IR models. These characteristics include: distinguishing different types of interaction processes, identifying major variables or constructs in the IR interaction, associating the models with human-computer interaction, and so forth. Ingwersen and Järvelin (2005) cited Engelbart's (1962) specifications of conceptual models that require the following: key components of the studied system, the relationships of the components, the changes of the components, how the changes affect the system, what lead to these changes, and the objectives and methods of research. The existing interactive IR models have done excellent work in identifying the major components or constructs and their relationships. However, they are weak in offering specific information about how changes in the major components occur or under what circumstances the changes occur, and the impact of these changes. Moreover, further research is needed to scientifically test interactive IR models. Before that, we need to come up with evaluation criteria specifically for the interactive IR models within the context of interactive IR, The following research questions need to be addressed:

- What are the criteria for the evaluation of interactive IR models?
- How can interactive IR models be tested and validated?
- How can macrolevel and microlevel of interactive IR models be balanced?
- How can the patterns between information-seeking strategies and the factors affecting the strategies be identified?

References

Bates, M. J. (1989). The design of browsing and berrypicking techniques for the online search interface. *Online Review, 13*, 407-424.

Beaulieu, M. (2000). Interaction in information searching and retrieval. *Journal of Documentation, 56*(4), 431-439.

Belkin, N. J. (1980). Anomalous states of knowledge as a basis for information retrieval. *Canadian Journal of Information Science, 5*, 133-143.

Belkin, N. J. (1984). Cognitive models and information transfer. *Social Science Information Studies, 4*(2-3), 111-129.

Belkin, N. J. (1993). Interaction with texts: Information retrieval as information seeking behavior. In G. Knorz, J. Krause, & C. Womser-Hacker (Eds.), *Information retrieval '93: Von der Modellierung zur Anwendung* (pp. 55-66). Konstanz: Universitaetsverlag Konstanz.

Belkin, N.J. (1996). Intelligent information retrieval: whose intelligence? In J. Krause, M. Herfurth, and J. Marx (Eds). Harausforderungen an die Informationswirtschaft. Informationsverdichtung, Informationsbewertung und Datenvisualisierung, *Proceedings of the 5th International Symposium for Information Science (ISI '96)*, (pp. 25-31). Konstanz: Universitätsverlag Konstanz.

Belkin, N. J., Cool, C., Stein, A., & Thiel, U. (1995). Cases, scripts and information seeking strategies: On the design of interactive information retrieval systems. *Expert Systems with Applications, 9*(3), 379-395.

Belkin, N. J., Marchetti, P. G., & Cool C. (1993). BRAQUE: Design of an interface to support user interaction in information retrieval. *Information Processing and Management, 29*(3), 325-344.

Belkin, N. J., Oddy, R. N., & Brooks, H. M. (1982a). ASK for information retrieval: Part 1. *Journal of Documentation, 38*(2), 61-71.

Belkin, N. J., Oddy, R. N., & Brooks, H. M. (1982b). ASK for information retrieval: Part 2. *Journal of Documentation, 38*(3), 145-164.

Belkin, N. J., Seeger, T. H., & Wersig, G. (1983). Distributed expert problem treatment as a means for information system analysis and design. *Journal of Information Science, 5*, 153-167.

Bilal, D. (2005). Children's information seeking and the design of digital interfaces in the affective paradigm. *Library Trends, 54*(2), 197-208.

Byström, K., & Järvelin, K. (1995). Task complexity affects information-seeking and use. *Information Processing & Management, 31*(2), 191-213.

Cole, C., & Mandelblatt, B. (2000). Using Kintsch's discourse comprehension theory to model the user's coding of an informative message from an enabling information retrieval system. *Journal of the American Society for Information Science, 51*(11), 1033-1046.

Cool, C. (1997). The nature of situation assessment in new information retrieval environments. In *Proceedings of the ASIS Annual Meeting,* (Vol. 34, pp.135-146).

Croft, W. B., & Thompson, R. H. (1987). I³R: A new approach to the design of document retrieval systems. *Journal of the American Society for Information Science, 38*(6), 389-404.

Crudge, S. E., & Johnson, F. C. (2004). Using the information seeker to elicit construct models for search engine evaluation. *Journal of the American Society for Information Science and Technology, 55*(9), 794-806.

De Mey, M. (1980). *The relevance of the cognitive paradigm for information science.* In O. Harbo & L. Kajberg (Eds.). [IRFIS 2] (pp. 48-61).

De Mey, M. (1982). *The Cognitive Paradigm: An integrated understanding of scientific development.* Dordrecht, Holland: Reidel.

Dervin, B. (1983, May). *An overview of sense-making: Concepts, methods and results to date.* Paper presented at the International Communication Association Annual Meeting, Dallas, TX.

Dervin, B., & Nilan, M. (1986). Information needs and uses. *Annual Review of Information Science and Technology, 21,* 3-33.

Detlor, B. (2003). Internet-based information systems use in organizations: An information studies perspective. *Information Systems Journal, 13*(2), 113-132.

Ellis, D. (1987). *The derivation of a behavioral model for information system design.* Unpublished doctoral dissertation, University of Sheffield, England.

Ellis, D. (1989). A behavioural approach to information retrieval system design. *Journal of Documentation, 45*(3), 171-212.

Ellis, D., Cox, D., & Hall, K. (1993). A comparison of the information seeking patterns of researchers in the physical and social sciences. *Journal of Documentation, 49*(4), 356-369.

Ellis, D., & Haugan, M. (1997). Modeling the information seeking patterns of engineers and research scientists in an industrial environment. *Journal of Documentation, 53*(4), 384-403.

Ellis, D., Wilson, T. D., Ford, N., Foster, A., Lam, H. M., Burton, R., et al. (2002). Information seeking and mediated searching: Part 5. User-intermediary interaction. *Journal of the American Society for Information Science and Technology, 53*(11), 883-893.

Engelbart, D. (1962). *Augmenting human intellect: A conceptual framework.* Menlo Park, CA: Stanford Research Institute.

Ford, N., Wilson, T. D., Foster, A., Ellis, D., & Spink, A. (2002). Information seeking and mediated searching: Part 4. Cognitive styles in information seeking. *Journal of the American Society for Information Science and Technology, 53*(9), 728-735.

Foster, A., & Ford, N. (2003). Serendipity and information seeking: An empirical study. *Journal of Documentation, 59*(3), 321-340.

Frisse, M. (1988). Searching for information in a hypertext medical handbook. *Communications of the ACM, 31*(7), 880-886.

Hancock-Beaulieu, M. (1990). Evaluating the impact of an online library catalogue in subject searching behavior at the catalogue and at the shelves. *Journal of Documentation, 46*(4), 318-338.

Hert, C. A. (1997). *Understanding information retrieval interaction: Theoretical and practical implications.* Greenwich, CO: Ablex.

Ingwersen, P. (1992). *Information retrieval interaction.* London: Taylor Graham.

Ingwersen, P. (1996). Cognitive perspectives of information retrieval interaction: Elements of a cognitive IR theory. *Journal of Documentation, 52*(1), 3-50.

Ingwersen, P. (1999). Cognitive information retrieval. *Annual Review of Information Science and Technology, 34,* 3-52.

Ingwersen, P., & Järvelin, K. (2005). *The turn: Integration of information seeking and retrieval in context.* Heidelberg: Springer.

Ingwersen, P., & Wormell, I. (1986). Improved subject access, browsing and scanning mechanisms in modern online IR. In. F. Rabitti (Ed.), *Proceedings of the ACM SIGIR Conference on Research and Development in Information Retrieval,* (pp. 68-76). Pisa: ACM.

Jansen, B. J. (2005). Seeking and implementing automated assistance during the search process. *Information Processing & Management, 41*(4), 909-928.

Kuhlthau, C. C. (1991). Inside the search process: Information seeking from the user's perspective. *Journal of the American Society for Information Science, 42*(5), 361-371.

Kuhlthau, C. C. (1993). *Seeking meaning: A process approach to library and information services.* Norwood, NJ: Ablex.

Mokros, H. B., Mullins, L. S., & Saracevic, T. (1995). Practice and personhood in professional interaction: Social identities and information needs. *Library and Information Science Research, 17*(3), 237-257.

Oddy, R. N. (1977). Information retrieval through man-machine dialogue. *Journal of Documentation, 33*(1), 1-14.

Pennanen, M. & Vakkari, P. (2003). Students' conceptual structure, search process and outcome while preparing a research proposal. *Journal of the American Society for Information Science, 54*, 759-770.

Pharo, N. (2002). *The Search Situation and Transition method schema: A tool for analysing Web information search processes.* Tampere, Finland: Tampere University Press (Doctoral dissertation. Acta Universitatis Tamperensis, 871). Retrieved January 4, 2008, from http://acta.uta.fi/pdf/951-44-5355-7.pdf

Pharo, N. (2004). A new model of information behaviour based on the Search Situation Transition schema. *Information Research-An International Electronic Journal, 10*(1), 203. Retrieved January 4, 2008, from http://informationr.net/ir/10-1/paper203.html

Pharo, N., & Järvelin, K. (2004). The Search Situation and Transition method: A tool for analysing Web information search processes. *Information Processing and Management, 40*(4), 633-654.

Rieh, S. Y. (2002). Judgment of information quality and cognitive authority in the Web. *Journal of the American Society for Information Science and Technology, 53*(2), 145-161.

Rieh, S. Y., & Xie, H. (2006). Analysis of multiple query reformulations on the Web: The interactive information retrieval context. *Information Processing & Management, 42*(3), 751-768.

Robertson, S. J., & Hancock-Beaulieu, M. (1992). On the evaluation of IR systems. *Information Processing and Management, 28*(4), 457-466.

Robins, D. (2000). Shifts of focus on various aspects of user information problems during interactive information retrieval. *Journal of the American Society for Information Science, 51*(10), 913-928.

Saracevic, T. (1996a). Modeling interaction in information retrieval (IR): A review and proposal. In *Proceedings of the American Society for Information Science,* (Vol. 33, pp. 3-9).

Saracevic, T. (1996b). Relevance reconsidered. In P. Ingewersen, & N. O. Pors, (Eds.), *Information science: Integration in perspectives* (pp. 201-218). Copenhagen: The Royal School of Librarianship.

Saracevic, T. (1997). The stratified model of information retrieval interaction: Extension and applications. In *Proceedings of the ASIS Annual Meeting,* (Vol. 34, pp. 313-327).

Saracevic, T., Kantor. P., Chamis, A. Y., & Trivison, D. (1988). A study of information seeking and retrieving: I. Background and methodology: II. Users, questions and effectiveness: III. Searchers, searches and overlap. *Journal of the American Society for Information Science, 39*(3), 161-176, 177-196, 197-216.

Saracevic, T., Mokros, H., & Su, L. (1990). Nature of interaction between users and intermediaries in online searching: A qualitative analysis. In *Proceedings of the American Society for Information Science*, (Vol. 27, pp. 47-54).

Saracevic, T., Spink, A., & Wu, M.-M. (1997). Users and intermediaries in information retrieval: What are they talking about? In A. Jameson, C. Paris, & C. Tasso (Eds.), *Proceedings of the Sixth International User Modeling Conference*, (pp. 43-54). New York: Springer.

Schamber, L., Eisenberg, M., & Nilan, M. S. (1990). A re-examination of relevance: Toward a dynamic, situational definition. *Information Processing and Management, 26*(6), 755-776.

Schutz, A., & Luckmann, T. (1973). *The structures of the life world*. Evanston, IL: Northwestern University Press.

Spink, A. (1993). The effect of user characteristics on search outcome in mediated online searching. *Online & CD-ROM Review, 17*(5), 275-278.

Spink, A. (1997). Study of interactive feedback during mediated information retrieval. *Journal of the American Society for Information Science, 48*(5), 382-394.

Spink, A., Griesdorf, H., & Bateman, J. (1999). A study of mediated successive searching during information seeking. *Journal of Information Science, 25*(6), 477-487.

Spink, A., & Saracevic, T. (1997). Interaction in information retrieval: Selection and effectiveness of search terms. *Journal of the American Society for Information Science, 48*(8), 741-761.

Spink, A., & Saracevic, T. (1998). Human-computer interaction in information retrieval: Nature and manifestations of feedback. *Interacting with Computers–the Interdisciplinary Journal of Human-Computer Interaction, 10*(3), 241-267.

Spink, A., Wilson, T. D., Ford, N., Foster, A., & Ellis, D. (2002). Information-seeking and mediated searching: Part 1. Theoretical framework and research design. *Journal of the American Society for Information Science and Technology, 53*(9), 695-703.

Stoan, S. K. (1984). Research and library skills: An analysis and interpretation. *College & Research Libraries, 45*(2), 99-109.

Taylor, R. S. (1968). Question negotiation and information seeking in libraries. *College and Research Libraries, 29*, 178-194.

Vakkari, P. (1998). Growth of theories on information seeking. An analysis of growth of a theoretical research program on relation between task complexity and information seeking. *Information Processing & Management, 34*(3/4), 361-382.

Vakkari, P. (2000a). E-cognition and changes of search terms and tactics during task performance: A longitudinal case study. In *Proceedings of the RIAO-2000 Conference,* (pp. 894-907). Paris, France: C.I.D. Retrieved January 4, 2008, from http://www.info.uta.fi/vakkari/Vakkari_Tactics_RIAO2000.html

Vakkari, P. (2000b). Relevance and contributory information types of searched documents in task performance. In *Proceedings of the 23rd Annual International ACM SIGIR Conference on Research and Development in Information Retrieval,* (pp. 2-9). New York: ACM Press.

Vakkari, P. (2001). A theory of the task-based information retrieval process. *Journal of Documentation, 57*(1), 44-60.

Vakkari, P., & Hakala, N. (2000). Changes in relevance criteria and problem stages in task performance. *Journal of Documentation, 56,* 540-562.

Vakkari, P., & Kuokkanen, M. (1997). Theory growth in information science: Applications of the theory of science to a theory of information seeking. *Journal of Documentation, 53*(5), 497-519.

Wang, P., Hawk, W. B., & Tenopir, C. (2000). Users' interaction with World Wide Web resources: An exploratory study using a holistic approach. *Information Processing & Management, 36*(2), 229-251.

Wang, P., & Soergel, D. (1998). A cognitive model of document use during a research project: Study I. Document selection. *Journal of the American Society for Information Science, 49*(2), 115-133.

Wilson, T. D. (1997). Information behaviour: An interdisciplinary perspective. *Information Processing & Management, 33*(4), 551-572.

Wilson, T. D. (1999). Models in information behaviour research. *Journal of Documentation, 55*(3), 249-270.

Wilson, T. D., Ford, N. J., Ellis, D., Foster, A., & Spink, A. (2002). Information seeking and mediated searching: Part 2. Uncertainty and its correlates. *Journal of the American Society for Information Science and Technology, 53*(9), 704-715.

Wu, M. (1992). *Information interaction dialogue: A study of patron elicitation in the IR interaction.* Unpublished doctoral dissertation, Rutgers University, New Brunswick, New Jersey.

Xie, H. (2000). Shifts of interactive intentions and information-seeking strategies in interactive information retrieval. *Journal of the American Society for Information Science, 51*(9), 841-857.

Xie, H. (2002). Patterns between interactive intentions and information-seeking strategies. *Information Processing & Management, 38*(1), 55-77.

Yang, K., Maglaughlin, K. L., & Newby, G. B. (2001). Passage feedback with IRIS. *Information Processing & Management, 37*(3), 521-541.

Chapter VIII

Interactive IR Framework

Nature of IR and Interactive IR in Digital Environments

Representation and comparison are usually considered the two core processes in traditional IR. Comparison is between two representations: representation of text and representation of user need. Much of the research in IR had concentrated on indexing techniques for representing the contents of documents and retrieval techniques that compare documents to queries (Salton & McGill, 1983; van Rijsbergen, 1979). Two underlying assumptions of the traditional IR view are: (1) the information need is static and can be specified; (2) there is only one form of information-seeking behavior (Belkin, 1993).

The nature of IR is interaction. Uncertainty and interactiveness are the two major characteristics of information retrieval. Although the new digital environment is inherently interactive, most traditional IR systems only support one type of information-seeking strategy: specifying queries by using terms to select documents from some databases. The new electronic IR systems, including some of the online databases, Web search engines, and digital libraries, start to offer people opportunities to browse information in addition to searching. However, these IR systems in a variety of new digital environments still cannot satisfy user need.

The empirical studies and theoretical research discussed in previous chapters demonstrate that digital environments require people engaging in multiple information-seeking strategies within an information seeking episode in order to achieve their tasks. These studies and research are supported by everyday information retrieval experience, such as browsing to find information/items that cannot be specified, learning collection/database description to identify relevant collections/databases to search, finding items on a specific topic, evaluating the usefulness of an item, acquiring and disseminating an item(s), and so forth.

Although researchers have created interactive IR models from different perspectives or levels and have conducted studies investigating different components and relationships of interactive IR, there are still unanswered questions in interactive IR research. Following are the major issues need to be further explored:

- What are the major components of interactive IR in digital environments?
- What are the patterns of interactive IR?
- What leads to patterns of interactive IR?
- How can macrolevel and microlevel of interactive IR models be integrated?

Planned-Situational Interactive IR Model

Overview of the Planned-Situational IR Model

The objective of the development of the planned-situational interactive IR model is to integrate macro- and micro-levels of the interactive IR model. The model focuses on the in-depth illustration of the microlevel of user goals (interactive intentions and associated retrieval tactics and their shifts, which are the products of plans and situations). Simultaneously, the social-organizational context and user-system interaction are also depicted in the model as part of the general interactive IR environment.

Figure 8.1. Planned-situational interactive IR model

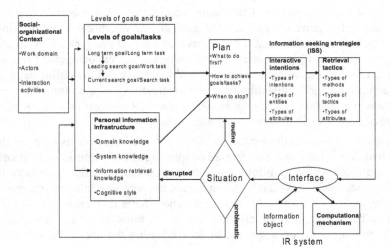

The planned-situational interactive IR model is established on the following theoretical and empirical basis: (1) the macro- and micro-level of interactive IR models discussed in Chapter VII, (2) the user-oriented IR approaches illustrated in Chapter I, (3) the planned model from cognitive science and situated action derived from social science discussed in this chapter, (4) the level of user goal/task and the relationships between levels of user goals and levels of tasks discussed in this chapter, (5) the empirical interactive IR studies in different digital environments introduced in Chapters II to VI, and (6) the author's own research in interactive IR.

The model (Figure 8.1) attempts to present: (1) levels of user goals/tasks and their representation, (2) relationships between levels of user goals and tasks, (3) dimensions of work and search tasks, (4) user personal information infrastructure, (5) social and organizational context, (6) IR systems, (7) dimensions of information-seeking strategies, (8) information-seeking strategies (products of plans and situations), (9) shifts in information-seeking strategies, and (10) factors affecting shifts in current search goals/search tasks and information-seeking strategies.

Levels of User Goals and Tasks and their Representation

User goal and task is the driving force for people to look for information. In order to identify the relationships between user goals and information-seeking strategies, we have to first define user goals and their relationships. According to Heckhausen and Kuhl (1985) from a psychological perspective, goals rest on three levels of end-states with an ascending hierarchical order. The first-order level, the second-order level, and the third-order level refer to an action, the outcome of an action, and the consequences of the outcome, respectively. Each of the goal levels has its own focus as well as its own types of valence. The three levels of endstates are interrelated. In the case of a higher-level goal, the actor focuses on a lower-level endstate, and includes the valence of the higher-level goal. In the case of a lower-level of inclusion, lower-level goals usually borrow their valences from the higher-level goals. Daniels (1986) related user goals to users' current information problems and to their personal background as well as more long-term plans and objectives. She identified four types of user goals: 1) current search goal, which refers to goals that users are currently working on; 2) goal leading to search, which refers to goals that make users aware that a search needs to be carried out; 3) specific intention, which refers to a higher level goal of the current search goal and the goal leading to search; and 4) general goal, which refers to long-term goals.

Adapted from Daniels' (1986) classification of goals, the author reconstructed user goals into four levels of hierarchical structure:

1. Long-term goal
2. Leading search goal

3. Current search goal

4. Interactive intention

Table 8.1 presents level of user goals, definitions, and examples of user goals.

The differences between this structure and Daniel's classification are: (1) This structure not only covers different levels of user goals but also imposes the goal structure of these levels; that is, higher-level goals have effects on lower-level goals. (2) This structure comes up with new microlevel user goals, "interactive intentions," which are the subgoals that a user has to achieve in order to accomplish his or her current search goals. They are the products of levels of user goals and the outcomes of user-system interactions. Interactive intention changes during the information-seeking and -retrieving process and also leads to a change in corresponding retrieval tactics. (3) This structure connects user goals to related levels of tasks. It offers clarifications of the relationships between user goals and tasks.

Relationships Between Levels of User Goals and Tasks

This structure clearly connects user goals to the related task, and imposes the goal structure of these levels; that is, higher levels of goals have effects on lower-level goals. Task and goal are inseparable in the information-seeking and -retrieving process. In HCI literature, task is defined as "what someone does to achieve a goal" (Hackos & Redish, 1998, p. 56). The defining of the task and subtasks depends on the circumstances. Vakkari (2003) pointed out that it is impossible to define tasks in all situations. In his study of students working on master theses, research questions of a study determine the task and associated subtasks.

In the example of this structure, a leading search goal (e.g., writing a thesis) could be a subtask for someone to achieve his/her long term goal (e.g., achieve a master's degree); at the same time, it also could be a task for someone to work on his/her current search goal (e.g., find relevant literature about interactive IR model). In order to avoid

Table 8.1. Levels of user goals

Level	Type of User Goals	Definition	Examples
1	long-term goal	a user's personal goal that he or she will pursue for quite a long time.	professional achievement, personal interest, etc.
2	leading search goal	a user's current task-related goal that leads to a search.	writing a paper, design a Web page, etc.
3	current search goal	what specific search results a user intends to obtain.	look for a model, look for a syntax, etc.
4	interactive intention	subgoals that a user has to achieve in the process of accomplishing his or her current search goal.	identify, learn, explore, find, access, evaluate, keep records, obtain, etc.

the confusion between tasks and search tasks, the concept of work task is borrowed to represent a task that leads to the information searching (Borlund & Ingwersen, 1997; Ingwersen, 1996; Ingwersen & Järvelin, 2005; Vakkari, 2003). Work task analysis, which focuses on specific tasks that people have to accomplish, what the constraints are, and what types of information sources are needed, is also a major component of cognitive work analysis (Fidel & Pejtersen, 2004; Pejtersen & Fidel, 1998). Considering the situation of information seeking and retrieving, leading searching goals are comparable as work tasks while current search goals can be regarded as search tasks that are subtasks in the task performance. Correspondingly, interactive intentions are another level of subtasks. Users' search tasks/current search goals are influenced by work tasks/leading search goals. Simultaneously, long-term goals affect the work tasks/leading search goals in terms of what work tasks users might take on and how they might accomplish these work tasks. At the same time, search tasks/current search goals are influenced by work tasks/leading search goals, and they control both the kind of search results a user tries to obtain, and the means to obtain them. Table 8.2 presents relationships among levels of user goals and levels of tasks.

Both user goals and tasks have been considered as one of the important components in interactive IR in a variety of digital environments. Researchers have used user goal, intention, task, work task, and search task interchangeably. The author uses this goal/task structure to represent different uses of goal and task. In many of the studies, interactive intentions were labeled as goal or subgoals. For example, Belkin, Chang, Downs, Saracevic, and Zhao (1990) and Chang (1995) refer to goal as one dimension of information-seeking strategies, and in their studies, "goal" was actually referred as intention. In the Web environment, Broder (2002) and Rose and Levinson (2004) explored a series of subgoals, such as informational searches, transactional searches, and navigational searches, directed, undirected, to get advice, to locate information, to obtain a list, and so forth. These subgoals are comparable to interactive intentions. In empirical studies, most researchers concentrate on the current search goals and their relationships to information-seeking behavior or strategies. For example, Hert's (1996, 1997) user goal definition—what a user attempts during the interaction—is more comparable to current search goal. In Slone's (2002) investigation of the influence of goals to search patterns in Web interaction, people who sought broad or situational goals, such as job-related, educational purposes, recreational, or personal use information, are related to leading search goals; specific current search

Table 8.2. Relationships among levels of user goals and levels of tasks

Level	Type of User Goals	Levels of Tasks	Examples
1	long-term goal	goal for a work task	professional achievement, personal interest, etc.
2	leading search goal	work task	write a paper, design a Web page, etc.
3	current search goal	search task (subtask of work task)	look for a model, look for a syntax, etc.
4	interactive intention	Subtasks	identify, learn, explore, find, access, evaluate, keep records, obtain, etc.

goals consist of searching for historical or background information, known persons or organizations, current information, and so forth. As part of current search goals, users also set format goals for the needed information, such as detailed text, brief text, nontextual data, and e-mail.

As to studies on tasks, work task is the main focus. In the following studies, work tasks are labelled as tasks. Derived from empirical studies, Kuhlthau's (1991) information-seeking model associated phases in task performance with the feelings, thoughts, and behaviors involved. Vakkari and his associates (Pennanen & Vakkari, 2003; Vakkari, 2000a, 2000b, 2001; Vakkari & Hakala, 2000; Vakkari, Pennanen, & Serola, 2003) conducted a series of studies to examine the task performance of writing a research proposal for a master's thesis. Byström and Järvelin (1995) explored the complexity of work tasks and its impact on information-seeking and use. Applying cognitive analysis, in the Fidel, Pejtersen, Cleal, and Bruce (2004) study of collaborative information retrieval, a work task such as the design of navigation functionality is analyzed. Kim and Allen (2002) probed the effect of two work tasks (writing a term paper vs. writing an article for the student newspaper) on participants' search behavior. Meyyappan, Foo, and Chowdhury's (2004) task-based organizational approach for a digital library is more effective than alphabetical and subject organization approaches. Concurrently, search tasks are the frequently studied variables, such as Shiri and Revie's (2003) topic complexity, Sutcliffe, Ennis and Watkinson's (2000) ambiguous statement of search tasks, Kim and Allen's (2002) known-item and subject search tasks, and D'Alessandro and Kingsley's (2002) common pediatric problems. Within in search tasks studies, assigned tasks are commonly examined in experimental settings. For example, Bilal (2002) compared children's behavior and success on three types of tasks: assigned fact-finding tasks, assigned research-oriented tasks, and self-generated tasks. In TREC-10, researchers found that the types of assigned tasks on shopping, medicine, travel, and research topics affect searchers' perception and behavior (Toms, Kopak, Bartlett, & Freund, 2002; Hersh, Sacherek, & Olson, 2002).

Dimensions of Work Tasks and Search Tasks

It is very difficult to characterize work tasks and search tasks, as many aspects of the tasks influence information seeking and retrieving. It is important to identify dimensions of work tasks and search tasks in order to clearly depict the impact of tasks on information-seeking strategies.

Dimensions of work tasks can be characterized as stages of the task, timeframe of the task, and nature of the task.

- Stages of the task

Users have to go through different stages in order to achieve their work tasks. Kuhlthau's (1991) information search process model indicates that the phases in task performance determine how and what people search for information. Vakkari and his colleagues (Pennanen & Vakkari, 2003; Vakkari, 2000a, 2000b, 2001; Vakkari & Hakala, 2000; Vakkari, Pennanen, & Serola, 2003) identified three stages in task performance: prefocus, formulation, and postfocus. While the prefocus stage corresponds to Kuhlthau's initiation and selection, the postfocus stage associates with collection and presentation. They further investigated the relationships   between problem stages of students' writing their research proposals for their master's theses and the types of information sought, changes in search tactics and term selections, and patterns of relevance judgments.

- Timeframe of the task

Timeframe is an important dimension in defining tasks. In studying corporate employees' information-seeking, Xie (2006) identified whether the timeframe of the task is extremely urgent, urgent, or nonurgent as one dimension of task. In her study of the corporate context, extremely urgent, urgent, and nonurgent refer to those tasks that have to be accomplished within half an hour, 24 hours, and more than 24 hours, respectively. The timeframe of the task greatly affects users' decisions and strategy activities. In order to complete the task within extremely urgent and urgent timeframes, people have to have alternative plans, and change information-seeking strategies. However, in different settings, extremely urgent, urgent, and nonurgent might be defined differently.

- Nature of the task

Nature of the task can be defined by structuredness of the task, familiarity of the task, and situations of the task. Based on *a priori determinability or structuredness of task*, Byström & Järvelin (1995) classified tasks into the following categories: automatic information-processing tasks, normal information-processing tasks, normal decision tasks, known tasks, and genuine decision tasks. They concluded that task complexity had systematical relationships with the types of information, information channels, and sources needed. In Xie's (2006) study of corporate employees' information-seeking, routine, typical or new emerged as the nature of the task based on *people's familiarity with the task*; this was also identified by MacMullin and Taylor (1984) as one of the problem dimensions. Routine tasks refer to those same tasks that people have to perform again and again. Typical tasks refer to the types of tasks that users are used to performing, but they haven't performed the exact same task before. New tasks refer to those tasks that people encounter for the first time. In corporate settings, people normally work on similar tasks, and they develop certain information-seeking strategies for each type of the typical tasks. Moreover, these information-seeking strategies become part of their plans in decision activities. For routine tasks, people normally do not have to plan for that; they just apply the same information strategies. New tasks take more planning and need more user involvement in collaboration with human resources. *Based on the situations of the tasks*, Slone (2002)'s broad or situational goals, such as educational, recreational, job-related, and personal-use goals, are similar to work tasks that reflect different types of situations. Focusing on more specific situations, Allen and Kim (2000) found that tasks of different natures affect the search performance. To be more specific, higher recall was achieved for subjects completing a newspaper-article-writing task than in a term-paper writing task. Kim and Allen (2002) revealed that task has significant effect on precision. The term paper task showed higher precision than the newspaper task. Interacting with search engine and cognitive abilities, the type of task was also found to influence how users searched the Web. To sum up, tasks of a different nature require different strategies, and the search performances might also be different.

The dimensions of search tasks can be characterized as origination of the task, type of the task, and domain of the task.

- Origination of the task

Assigned and self-generated tasks represent search tasks that lead users to search for information. In most IR experiments, users are required to search for assigned tasks although real tasks, real users, and real settings are essential to understand users' information needs and behaviors. Very little research compares users' behavior on assigned tasks vs. users' own tasks in digital environments. After comparing children's behavior and success on self-generated tasks with fact-finding and research-oriented tasks, Bilal (2002) discovered that children browsed more and made more moves on the self-generated tasks than the other two types of tasks, and they were more successful on the self-generated tasks. Their motivation to pursue their topics of interest and their ability to modify topics contributed to the success for the self-generated tasks. Simultaneously, the simplicity of the self-generated task is also a main reason for the success on the self-generated tasks. The effects of assigned vs. self-generated tasks, especially real tasks that real users have to work on for a goal, need to be further tested on search behaviors and performances.

- Type of the task

Fact-based searching, known-item searching, and subject- or research-based searching are the common search tasks that researchers have examined. Schacter, Chung, and Dorr (1998) discovered that children were better at performing ill-defined tasks than well-defined tasks that are similar to research-based and fact-based tasks. The children had to apply more analytical strategies in order to complete well-defined/fact-finding tasks. Bilal (2002) and Ford, Miller, and Moss (2002) reaffirmed Schacter et al.'s (1998) findings. Kim and Allen (2002) reported the significant effects of types of tasks (subject search vs. known-item search) on precision and recall, search time, the number of pages viewed, the number of embedded links used, and jump tools used as well as the number of keyword searches completed. Xie (2006) also identified a more comprehensive list of types of task as one dimension of search task. Types of task refers to whether the type of task is to update information (e.g., keep track of information about new agricultural equipments), look for specific information (e.g., look for a syntax), look for a known item (e.g., look for an item when a user knows the title), or look for items with common characteristics (e.g., look for items on the same subject). Looking for specific information and looking for items with common characteristics are the most popularly engaged search tasks. These tasks require different levels of planning and different types of information-seeking strategies.

- Domain of the task

Domain of the task refers to the field of the content of the task. The most popularly searched domain tasks for Web search are shopping, medicine, travel, and research topics, and that is why they were selected as the search tasks for TREC-10. While Hersh et al. (2002) found that the domain of the tasks affects the searchers' behavior and efficiency, Toms et al. (2002) discovered that the perception of search task difficulty and satisfaction with results is associated with the domain of the task. Even though searchers' domain knowledge on the shopping task is not the lowest, searchers took the most time and viewed the most pages for the task, and thus this task was considered as the most difficult one. More research needs to explore the theoretical basis for this phenomenon.

Personal Information Infrastructure

Information seeking and retrieving requires users to apply their knowledge and skills, what might be called "personal information infrastructures," such as their general cognitive abilities, their knowledge skills in relation to the problem/task domain, their knowledge and skills in general, their knowledge and skills specific to a system, and their knowledge and skills regarding information-seeking (Marchionini, 1995). In order to effectively interact with IR systems, users need to have knowledge about the task that drives them to interact with IR systems, knowledge of the IR system that users interact with, and knowledge about how to interact. In addition, the cognitive styles of users determine how they might interact with IR systems. The empirical interactive IR studies in different digital environments from Chapter II to Chapter VI have demonstrated that the following knowledge and style affect IR performance or behavior: (1) domain knowledge related to the task, (2) system knowledge related to the IR system, (3) information retrieval knowledge related to IR skills, and (4) cognitive styles and search styles related to personal traits. Personal information infrastructure is confirmed as an essential component for IR interaction in digital environments.

Among the different types of knowledge, domain knowledge is related to the task domain of IR interaction. Domain expertise was proved to affect search behaviors and strategies in TREC-10 (Dumais & Belkin, 2005). According to Bhavnani (2002), expert searchers are more effective when applying specific domain knowledge than general domain knowledge. At the same time, other researchers in TREC-10 (Hersh et al., 2002; Toms et al., 2002) argued that the types of tasks rather than searchers' domain knowledge shape searchers' behaviors. Both domain knowledge and tasks are demonstrated as having an impact on search performances and behaviors. For example, Hirsh (1997) found that domain knowledge with task complexity affects children's success in interacting with an OPAC. Knowledge of a retrieval item in known item searching is also needed (Wildemuth & O'Neill, 1995). In order to effectively interact with IR systems, users need to understand how a system works and how to use the system. Lacking system knowledge, especially users' not understanding the process behind keyword searching, is linked to the failure of keyword searching (Hildreth, 1997). The success of IR interaction also depends on users' IR knowledge. Experienced users or users with training perform better than novice users in online searching (Howard, 1982; Lazonder, Biemans, & Woperneis, 2000; Sutcliffe, Ennis, & Watkinson, 2000; Yuan, 1997). Interestingly, gaining experience in Web searching also affects users' searching behaviors (Cothey, 2002). For that reason, expert knowledge is incorporated into online IR system design (Fidel, 1991).

Just one type of knowledge is not enough for the complexity of information retrieval tasks, however. Both domain knowledge and information retrieval knowledge are required in the IR process. Marchionini, Dwiggins, Katz, and Lin (1993) explained well the problem-solving IR process: domain knowledge facilitates users to understand the problems and have expectations of the possible answers, and information retrieval knowledge assists users to develop conceptual and procedural strategies. Users who relied on expertise in both domain and retrieval knowledge were the most successful in their Web-searching process (Hölscher & Strube, 2000). At the same time, different types of knowledge are interrelated to each other. For example, domain knowledge was found to affect experienced users' search tactics but not novice users' tactics (Hsieh-Yee, 1993). Shute and Smith (1993) discovered that an expert intermediary made more suggestions based on domain knowledge than a nonexpert intermediary. Bhavnani et al. (2006) developed a domain portal integrating both domain and information retrieval knowledge into the tool. They found it offered better results to search questions.

Of all the personal traits, cognitive styles and searching styles are identified as the main personal traits that influence how users interact with IR systems. Ford et al. (2002) concluded that field-independent users were more active and analytical than field-dependent ones in interacting with online databases. While holists prefer provisional and serendipitous behavior, serialists like to go step-by-step in retrieving information. Cognitive styles influence search behavior as well as search performance. Wood, Ford, Miller, Sobczyk, and Duffin (1996) learned that users' global and analytic cognitive styles were linked with users' levels of satisfaction with search results and perceived search success. Research has also demonstrated that "interactive" and "fast batch" are the two types of searching styles that lead to different searching behaviors (Bellardo, 1985; Fenichel, 1981; Harter, 1983; Oldroyd & Citroen, 1977). Fidel (1991) further explored characteristics of searching styles and their effects on searching behavior: the level of interaction, the preference for types of moves, and the preference of types of search keys. In addition, cognitive styles influence users differently depending on their knowledge level during their interactions with IR systems. search performance and search behavior. For example, Palmquist and Kim (2000) found that cognitive styles have more impact on experienced users than on novice users in their interaction with Web search engines.

Social-Organizational Context

The social-organizational context defines the environment in which users interact with IR systems. In the planned-situational model, context is mostly delineated by the work domain that users interact with as suggested by cognitive work analysis (CWA) (Rasmussen, Pejtersen, & Goodstein, 1994; Vicente, 1999). Cognitive work analysis views human-information interaction in the context of human work activities. The results of cognitive work analysis are context-specific instead of general. The following components and their properties are the essential parts of cognitive work analysis (Fidel & Pejtersen, 2004): (1) work domain, (2) actors, and (3) interaction activities. The reason that CWA focuses on understanding the interaction between people and information within their work context is because personal, social, technological, and organizational facets play a role interdependently and simultaneously (Fidel, Pejtersen, Cleal, & Bruce, 2004).

Work domain analysis focuses on the identification of the goals and constraints, priorities, general functions, work processes, and physical objects for a work domain. For example, in Xie's (2006) study of human-work interaction in a corporate setting, she found that dimensions of work domain, such as priority of the company, company philosophy, and business cycles, all have impact on users' choices of information-seeking strategies. The merger of the two companies posed many problems for users to locate needed information, and also affected the way they looked for information. The uniqueness of the work domain determines people's selection of information-seeking strategies. In Fidel and Pejtersen's (2004) study of the information behavior of teachers in a public elementary school, the environment in which the school operates is the focus of the work domain analysis. The issues need to be explored include the federal, state, and school district regulations under which the school operates; the state policy and standards for the school's curriculum; the population from which the school can recruit students, and so forth. These provide the recommendation for the design of information systems for teachers.

The dimensions of actor analysis concentrate on knowledge about the work domain, cue-action rules, object and symbol manipulation skills and resources, and values. In addition to personality traits, people's knowledge of the domain, system and information-seeking skills play a critical role in determining their choices of interactive intentions and information-seeking strategies. Actors' knowledge enables them to interact with work domain (the social-organizational context and the IR system). Actors' knowledge is comparable to the personal information infrastructure discussed above.

Interaction activities examine interactions between the social-organizational context and the actors. The context is not static; instead, it consists of dynamic interaction activities. Task activities, decision activities, and strategy activities are the main products. Task activities are related to the dimensions of tasks, especially work tasks. Decision activities offer individual decisions about how the actors plan for the information retrieval and how they would deal with different problematic situations. Strategy activities determine what strategies are appropriate for each task and respective decision. In the context of information retrieval, these activities go beyond the interactions between social-organizational context and the actors. They are the products of actor-social-organizational context interactions as well as actor-IR system interactions.

Other social and cultural factors might also influence the ways that users interact with IR systems. For example, although users from different cultures may have the same anticipation of interaction outcomes, their perception of interactions may be different. As to what specific dimensions affect user-interface interaction, it is difficult to generalize, because cultural dimensions are part of the culture, which varies in different studies (Callahan, 2005). However, this model focuses on the actor-work domain interactions because they highly associate with levels of user goals/tasks, and they play a vital role in interactive IR.

IR Systems

In interactive IR, users and IR systems are the two partners. Users interact with IR systems via interfaces of these systems. The interfaces provide a platform for users to enter input and systems to offer output. The interfaces consist of the following essential elements:

- Access methods direct users easily to log on to the system
- Navigational tools direct users to different system features and different collections/databases
- Searching/browsing tools allow users to search or browse items in the collection/database
- Organizing and viewing tools facilitate users to organize their search results and evaluate the usefulness of the items
- Messages inform users about the status of their inputs or possible problems of their actions
- Input/output devices allow users and systems to communicate with each other

Each IR system has its own unique access methods, navigational tools, search/browsing tools, organizing and viewing tools, input/output devices, and messages. Even though the emergence of Web search engines brings easy-to-access interfaces of IR systems, they are not created in the same format and standard. There is no one-fits-all interface for all the IR systems, so it is still a challenge for users to learn different types of IR systems. Moreover, there are different types of interfaces even within one type of IR system.

By interacting with the interfaces of IR systems, users actually interact with the information objects stored in these systems as well as with the computational mechanisms of the software and hardware of the systems. Information resources and their representations are the center of the interaction. Saracevic (1997) proposed three levels of system involvement: the hardware and its operational design on the engineering level, the algorithms behind the processing level, and the information resources and their representations on the content level. When users interact with IR systems, they interact with different levels of IR systems consisting of computational and information capabilities. As suggested by Ingwersen and Järvelin (2005), the information objects represent the cognitive structure of authors for all kinds of information objects, human indexers for selected information objects, and selectors for the availability and inclusion of objects into collections. Concurrently, the information objects represent the cognitive structure of the designers of software and hardware, such as database structure, search engines, and indexing algorithms, in terms of how to help users find information objects needed. In addition, the information objects also represent the cognitive structure of designers of retrieval interface in terms of how to present the information objects to users. In that sense, when users interact with IR systems, they actually interact with the cognitive structures of different players involved in the interface, system and content-building processes.

The design of interfaces of IR systems as well as the information objects stored in these systems affect users' information-seeking strategies in the following ways: 1) the design of the overall user interface could direct users to more or fewer applications of certain strategies; 2) the availability or unavailability of certain features controls whether users could engage in certain strategies; 3) the information objects stored in IR systems that users interact with might influence the outcome of the current strategy, which, in turn, might affect their choices of next strategy. In addition to affecting strategies, the design of IR systems could also lead users to redefine their goals (Hider, 2007).

On the one hand, OPACs, online databases, Web search engines, and digital libraries have commonalities because they are all electronic IR systems. On the other hand, they have their uniqueness because they have different interfaces, different database structures, different algorithms, and different collections. More importantly, these systems are designed and developed by different people with different cognitive structures. There are several challenges for users:

- Users have become used to Web searching since the emergence of the Internet, and they normally bring their own mental models and expectations of the popular Web to a variety of other information retrieval systems. For example, Yu and Young (2004) discussed the influence of users' mental models and behaviors when 21st century users meet a 20th century OPAC. Users also bring their mental models of one Web search engine to another one. Wang, Hawk, and Tenopir (2000) noticed that users did not change their mental models from one search engine to another.

- The collections of IR systems also pose challenges for users. It is a challenge for users to evaluate relevance of the retrieved items. To make things worse, the lack of quality control on the Web makes it more difficult for users to evaluate the quality and authority of the retrieved information (Henzinger, Motwani, and Silverstein, 2002; Rieh, 2002). In addition, the giant size of search engines does not guarantee equal access. Users can only access a small part of the information depending on indexing capabilities of search engines.

- Each IR system normally only has one interface. It is a challenge for one interface to satisfy diverse user needs, especially for both novice and expert users. While one group cares for ease of use, another group prefers user control (Xie, 2003; Xie & Cool, 2000). Another challenge related to interface is Help in online systems. Inadequate Help mechanisms and noninteractive Help mechanisms prevent users to effectively use Help when they encounter problems.

- Electronic IR systems, especially digital libraries and Web search engines, contain multimedia materials. That poses challenges for IR systems to store, organize, and distribute information and for users to effectively retrieve relevant information from different access points.

Dimensions of Information-Seeking Strategies

Previous Studies on Information-Seeking Strategies and their Limitations

Researchers have examined information-seeking strategies from different levels. Tactics and moves represent information-seeking choices and actions in the information-seeking subprocesses, while information-seeking strategies highlight the plans for the information-seeking process. Information-seeking models and patterns attempt to connect information-seeking strategies to the stages of the information-seeking process.

In her classic work, Bates (1979a, 1979b) identified 29 information **tactics** and 17 idea tactics that occurred in the information-seeking process. The former is related to monitoring, file structure, search formulation, and term; the latter is about new ideas and problem solutions. Thirteen knowledge-based search tactics specified by Shute and Smith (1993) are associated with search topics, including broadening topic scope, narrowing topic scope, and changing topic scope. Focusing on query formulation, Fidel (1985) identified 18 operational moves keeping the meaning of the query component unchanged and 12 conceptual **moves** changing the meaning of query components. Shiri and Revie (2003)'s cognitive and physical moves are similar to Fidel's conceptual and physical moves. Studies of tactics and moves characterize users' search process in the microlevel, but they only concentrate on one dimension of that level. Bates (1990) further expanded tactics and moves into "stratagem," which is a complex of number of moves or tactics that involve both information domains and the modes of seeking.

Search strategies are applied in a high-level of information retrieval process involving multiple dimensions of information retrieval in order to accomplish the search tasks. Compared with tactics and moves, search strategies might consist of a series of actions. Search strategies can be **concept-oriented**, which means these strategies intend to manipulate the concepts of the search topic. For example, Markey and Atherton's (1978) four of the five basic types of users' online search strategies are concept-oriented: Building block, pearl-growing, successive-fractions, most-specific-facet-first, and lowest-postings-facet-first are the most cited search strategies for online database searching. Information-seeking strategies reflect not only the choices of approaches that users take to retrieve information but also the IR system's characteristics. Unlike Markey and Atherton's concept-oriented strategies, Chen and Dhar's (1991) five types of search strategies are more related to system feature or user knowledge: the known-item instantiation strategy, the search-option heuristic strategy, the thesaurus-browsing strategy, the screen-browsing strategy, and the trial-and-error-strategy. Chen and Dhar's system-oriented strategies are more related to online databases. The 10 problem-solving strategies identified by Hawk and Wang (1999) and Wang et al. (2000) are closely associated with Web searching. The problem-solving strategies were identified as: surveying, double-checking, exploring, link following, back and forward going, shortcut seeking, engine using, loyal engine using, engine seeking, and metasearching. These strategies indicate the unique design and features of Web and Web searching.

The interaction engagement is another way to classify information-seeking strategies. Hawkins and Wagers' (1982) "interactive scanning" involves more user interaction with the system and information. Marchionini (1995) identified two types of strategies in which browsing strategies require more interactions than the goal-oriented analytic strategies. Cothey (2002) echoed Marchionini's classification of two search strategies, and further discovered that high school students adopted browsing approaches instead of active searching after they gained more experience. Studies of information search strategies illustrate the information-seeking process and emphasize the high level of information-seeking approaches that users take, but they fail to answer how different types of information-seeking strategies are selected under different situations. **Plan vs. situation** is another approach for strategies of information retrieval. Soloman (1993) identified two classes of strategies derived from children's interactions with OPACs. By applying plan strategies, users make decisions about how to search for information before the first move, such as author, title, concepts, external support, system features, and so forth. By applying reactive strategies, users make decisions by following one move after another, such as focus shifts, search term relationships, error recovery, and so forth. Users with different level of knowledge apply different types of information-seeking strategies. Drabenstoot (2003) investigated information-seeking strategies of nondomain experts and found that rarely do nondomain experts enlist strategies from domain experts.

Nondomain experts applied perseverance, trial-and-error, serendipity, or a combination of the all three strategies in their information-seeking process.

Ellis (1989) developed a behavioral model of the **information-seeking patterns** of academic social scientists. He suggested that "if researchers' information-seeking behaviors are broken down into their basic behavioral characteristics—and the retrieval system is provided with facilities that reflect those characteristics—then users should be able to recreate their own information-seeking patterns while interacting with the system" (p. 172). The six types of information seeking characteristics are starting, chaining, browsing, differencing, monitoring, and extractions. Ellis and Haugan (1997) also identified the information-seeking patterns of engineers and research scientists in relation to their research activities in different phases and types of project. They further related the stage of the research process to certain information-seeking patterns. Kuhlthau (1991) developed a **model** of the information search process based on a series of studies of users in information-seeking situations. Six stages of information **search process** were identified with associated **actions** common to each stage. Studies of patterns and models of information seeking begin to explore what determines information-seeking behavior, but are limited to the identifications of the relationships between stages of the research or search process and their corresponding information-seeking strategies.

The above studies identify tactics, moves, stratagem, search strategies, and patterns, and they also develop models. These studies have contributed greatly to the understanding of information-seeking strategies. Current research builds upon these earlier findings. However, these studies also have inherited limitations because of the existing IR system design and its effect on users' behavior. First, most of the studies focus on strategies corresponding to query formulation and reformulations, because query formulation and reformulation are the center of the IR system design, especially in early versions of online IR systems. However, people engage in multiple information-seeking strategies in the IR process. In addition to searching, they have to identify information to get started, they have to learn how to use an IR system, they have to evaluate the retrieved information, and so forth.

Second, most of the studies on information-seeking strategies focus on what strategies users apply in the information-seeking process, and thus are limited to the exploration of one dimension of information-seeking strategies. They only answer the first part of the question: what kinds of information-seeking strategies are employed by users. In order to understand the nature of IR and further design IR systems to facilitate the applications of multiple information-seeking strategies, we also need to investigate under what circumstances these search strategies are applied, and to characterize information-seeking strategies in multiple dimensions. In a word, we need to identify the relations between information-seeking behaviors and the goals or subgoals of users. To be more specific, interactive intentions should be part of the information-seeking strategies so that patterns of information-seeking strategies can be identified.

Third, these studies cannot account for the dynamic shifts in information-seeking strategies in the interactive IR process. Generally speaking, because these strategies are highly interactive, it is difficult to identify relations among actions in the information-seeking process. Therefore, it is difficult to predict the sequence of users' information-seeking strategy use. Hoppe and Schiele (1992) pointed out that highly interactive, flexible, and underdetermined strategies only impose weak constraints on the relation between the actions in sequences; therefore, it is difficult to generate help and advice from them. However, if we can reveal the relationships between plans/situations and their impact on information-seeking strategies, it will be easier for an IR system to predict and suggest appropriate strategies for users to solve their information problems.

Dimensions of Interactive Intentions

Interactive intentions refer to subgoals that a user has to achieve in the process of accomplishing his or her current search goal/search task. Even though users have different leading search goals and current search goals, they share similar interactive intentions in the information retrieval process. Belkin et al. (1990) developed a set of intentions for people to find information in a variety of library environments. The author (Xie, 2000, 2002) expanded the intentions and named them "interactive intentions" because they are the products of human-system interactions. Types of interactive intentions derived from the author's original work are further enhanced by incorporating empirical studies in digital environments such as OPAC, online databases, Web search engines, and digital libraries discussed in the previous chapters. Twelve types of interactive intentions can be characterized. Table 8.3 presents types of interactive intentions with definitions and examples.

The modifications of types of interactive intentions can be summarized into the following aspects: (1) Modifications of interactive intentions are made considering interactive intentions derived from users' interaction with different types of online IR systems. The following interactive intentions are added to the list: exploring, creating, modifying, monitoring, and disseminating. Simultaneously, locating is deleted because it is more for locating items in the library. Users are able to access and locate items in electronic systems altogether. "Finding" is replaced by "creating search statement" and "modifying search statement," because finding is a high level goal (a current search goal instead of an interactive intention). (2) Interactive intentions are further defined by entities and their attributes. In this model, the author introduces

Table 8.3. Types of interactive intentions with definitions and examples

Types of Interactive Intentions	Definition	Examples of Interactive Intentions
Identify Identify a system/database(s)/ collection(s) to get started (A). Identify information/concept/ term/ item/site to get started (B). Identify information/concept/term/ item/site to continue searching (C).	Discover information as search leads at the beginning or in the middle of information-seeking process.	Identify an appropriate system or collections to get started (A). Identify an author to start with (B). Identify a reference to get started (B). Identify concepts/terms from the search results (C).
Learn Learn system features (A). Learn system structure (B). Learn domain knowledge (C). Learn information retrieval skills (D). Learn database/collection content (E).	Gain knowledge of system features, system structure, domain knowledge and database content.	Learn how to use advanced search (A). Figure out the browsing structure (B). Learn synonyms of a specific term (C). Learn how to find items like an specific item (D) Learn about the coverage of a database/ collection (E).
Explore Explore a specific item/site (A). Explore items with common characteristics (B). Explore items without predefined criteria (C).	Survey information/items.	Look at a site or a journal (A). Look at a collection on a specific topic (B). Survey something that might hold one's interest (C).
Create Create a search statement.	Come up with a search statement.	Formulate a query.
Modify Modify a search statement.	Change a search statement.	Reformulate a query.
Monitor Monitor search process (A). Monitor current status (B).	Exam the search process (A). Check the current status (B).	Review the search history (A). Check where a user is in the navigation process (B).
Keep Records Keep records of metadata of an item(s).	Keep records of metadata of an item(s) before accessing it/them.	Keep records of citation of an item. Bookmark the URL of a site.
Access Access a specific item (A). Access items with common characteristics (B). Access an area/location (C).	Get access to an item(s) based upon the location of an item(s).	Link to a specific site (A). Link to a collection (B). Access the Help section (C).
Organize Organize items with common characteristics.	Sort out a list of items with common characteristics.	Sort the results by relevancy or publication date.

continued on following page

Table 8.3. continued

Evaluate		
Evaluate correctness of an item (A). Evaluate specificity of an item (B). Evaluate usefulness of an item(C). Evaluate fitness of an item (D). Evaluate duplication of an item (E). Evaluate the authority of an item (F).	Assess the correctness of an item(s), specificity of an item, usefulness an item(s), fitness of an item, duplication of an item(s) or authority of an item. Evaluate to make sure different types of "finding" intentions are satisfied.	Make sure an item is the one a user is looking for (A). Double check whether the item has the specific information a user is looking for (B). Check whether each item is worth keeping (C). Pick up the best item(s) from all the useful ones (D). Check whether an item is a duplicate of another one that was read or used before (E). Check whether an item is the authentic one (F).
Obtain		
Obtain specific information (A). Obtain part of the item (B). Obtain a whole item(s) (C).	Get hold of specific information, part of the item, or a whole item(s).	Write down the stock quote of a company (A). Copy several pages of an article (B). Download a video file (C).
Disseminate		
Disseminate to a specific person (A). Disseminate to a group of people (B).	Distribute or circulate information to a person or a group of people.	E-mail a retrieved image to a friend (A). Send a retrieved article to a listserve (B).

nine new types of entities instead of a general information resource identified in the original work. As part of interactive intentions, while entities refer to types of things that users intend to acquire or work on, attributes specify the traits/elements of these entities. In digital environments, information resource is no longer the only entity available. In order to effectively retrieve information, users have to interact with data/information, knowledge, concept/term, format, item/objects/site, process/status, location, system, and humans. Tables 8.4 and 8.5 present dimensions of interactive intentions and types of entities with definitions and examples.

Dimensions of Retrieval Tactics

While intentions and their associated entities with attributes constitute interactive intentions, methods and their associated entities with attributes represent retrieval tactics. Methods refer to the techniques users apply to interact with data/information, knowledge, concept/term, format, item/objects/site, process/status, location, system and humans. The types of methods include scanning, specifying, manipulating, tracking, selecting, comparing, extracting, acquiring, consulting, and trial-and-error. In the author's previous works (Xie, 2000, 2002), searching contains all the activities related to the identification of related items from collections of IR systems. However, the pre- and post-searching of management of concepts and process is missing. Therefore, manipulating is added to represent query formulation, reformulation,

Table 8.4. Dimensions of interactive intentions

Types of Intentions	Entities	Attributes
Identify Learn Explore Create Modify Monitor Organize Access Keep records Evaluate Obtain Disseminate	Data/information	Specific Common General Undefined
	Knowledge	Domain knowledge System knowledge Information retrieval Knowledge
	Concept/term	Broad Narrow Synonym Parallel
	Format	Different forms of terms Syntax/commands
	Item/object/site	Meta-information Part of item A whole item A series of items with common characteristics A database/collection
	Process/status	Search process or status
	Location	An area A section
	System	Types of systems Features Structure
	Human	Professionals Experts Friends Colleagues

and system customization. Table 8.6 presents the types of methods with definitions and examples. The same types of entities and attributes of interactive intentions are also the dimension for retrieval tactics. The integration and combination of these two dimensions characterizes the 11 retrieval tactics employed by users: scanning, manipulating, specifying, tracking, selecting, surveying, comparing, extracting, acquiring, consulting, and trial-and-error tactics. Table 8.7 presents the dimensions and examples of retrieval tactics.

Dimensions of Information-Seeking Strategies with Examples

Researchers have pioneered work in the area of dimensions of information-seeking strategies. Belkin and Cool (1993) proposed a multifaceted classification of information-seeking strategies based on four "behavioral" dimensions, which consists

Table 8.5. Types of entities with definitions and examples

Types of Entities	Definitions	Examples
Data/information	Facts	Stock quotes, etc.
Knowledge	Information about system, information retrieval and domain of the search topic	System knowledge, domain knowledge, information retrieval knowledge
Concept/term	Ideas or notions	Interactive information retrieval, digital libraries, etc.
Format	Different forms of terms or commands	Abbreviation of an association, error corrections, etc.
Item/object/site	An article or a thing or a Web site containing information	A journal, a video file, a Web site, etc.
Process/status	Information retrieval process or status	Search history, browsing path, etc.
Location	A defined area/location of an item(s)	URL of a site, call number of a book, etc.
System	Different types of systems or system features	Google, help, etc.
Human	Human serving as a resource	A librarian, a friend, a colleague, etc.

Table 8.6. Types of methods with definitions and examples

Types	Definitions	Examples
Scan	Look through an item or a series of items quickly.	Look at, look through, flip through, etc.
Manipulate	Manage different concepts and their combinations, system settings, etc.	Reformulate queries by applying synonyms; Customize display of retrieved results.
Specify	State search statements.	Identify authors for searching; identify title for searching; identify subjects for searching, etc.
Track	Follow meta-information to get to specific location, specific page, specific information, etc.	Follow, turn to a specific page, trace, etc.
Select	Pick up an item among a series of items or from a location.	Enter a number, pull out, pick up, choose, etc.
Survey	Review search process or examine current status.	Check search history, check current status, etc.
Extract	Take out key information.	Take out keywords from an article
Compare	Identify some information from different items and make a comparison.	Make a comparison, associate, relate, compare, etc.
Acquire	Write down, copy specific or meta-information or check out items, etc.	Take notes, copy, check out, etc.
Consult	Direct questions to a human or help system.	Ask questions, talk to, seek advice, consult, etc.
Trial-and-Error	Figure out something, especially system functions or system structures by trying different possibilities/approaches without following specific instructions.	Wander around, try, play around, etc.

of the goal of the interaction, method of interaction, mode of retrieval, and types of resources interacted with. They suggested that this could represent a space of possible information-seeking strategies within an information-seeking episode. Chang (1995) focused on one type of information-seeking strategy, browsing, and further identified the underlying common dimensions of browsing: scanning, resource, goal, and object. Based on these four dimensions, she classified five themes and nine patterns of browsing.

Both of these studies have considered user subgoal as one of the dimensions, but they did not further explore the relationships between user goals and other dimensions of information-seeking strategies. Furthermore, their identification of methods and entities of interaction is limited. Even though it is clear that the users' goals are strong determiners of their information behaviors, researchers still understand very little about the range and nature of interactive intentions and even less about how they relate to information-seeking strategies.

Based on the empirical studies of interactive information retrieval in a variety of digital environments, the author enhanced her previous work about dimensions of information-seeking strategies, which consist of intentions, method, entities, and attributes of interactions (Figure 8.2). Because interactive intentions are the goals for the interactions, the strategies can be divided into 12 types of information-seeking strategies (Table 8.8). In the table, intention, method, and entities are represented by bold, italics, and underlining, respectively.

Information-Seeking Strategies: Products of Plans and Situations

Information-seeking strategies are constituted by interactive intentions and retrieval tactics. Twelve types of information-seeking strategies are the products of levels of user goals. Concurrently, these strategies are also affected by other planned and situational aspects. The plan-situational model of interactive information retrieval illustrates how plans and situations codetermine the selection of information-seeking strategies, to be more specific, the selection of interactive intentions and retrieval tactics in the information-seeking process.

From the cognitive point of view, Newell and Simon (1972) assume that action is a form of problem-solving, where the actor's problem is to find a path from some initial state to a desired goal state, given certain conditions along the way. The *planned model* approach views information-seeking behaviors as continuous and interrelated actions that are all part of a goal-related plan. This approach attempts to understand information-seeking behavior in relation to general plans and goals. Plans are affected by levels of user goals/tasks, dimensions of tasks, and the social-organizational context users are interacting with as well as the users' personal information infrastructures.

Vera and Simon (1993) further emphasized that plans influence human actions in two ways: first, plans may be used to determine what initial (present) action will lead

Table 8.7. Dimensions of retrieval tactics

Types of methods	Entities	Attributes
Scan Specify Manipulate Consult Select Survey Track Trial-and-error Compare Extract Acquire	Data/information	Specific Common General Undefined
	Knowledge	Domain knowledge System knowledge Information retrieval knowledge
	Concept/term	Broad Narrow Synonym Parallel
	Format	Different forms of terms or Syntax
	Item/object/site	Meta-information Part of item A whole item A series of items with common characteristics A database/collection
	Process/status	Search process or status
	Location	An area A session
	System	Types of systems Features Structure
	Human	Professionals Experts Friends Colleagues

toward desired goals; second, plans may be used to establish a set of "landmarks" that are subgoals along the route to some distant goal. If we apply Vera and Simon's perspective to information retrieval, then plans influence information-seeking behavior in three ways: first, plans are goal directed, so they may be used to establish a set of intentions or subgoals along the route to accomplish their current search goals; second, plans may be used to determine corresponding information-seeking strategies that lead toward desired goals/tasks; third, plans also help in monitoring the search process to adjust the original plan.

In contrast to the cognitivist view represented in the plan model approach, Suchman (1987) proposes an alternative perspective, or *theory of situated action*, drawn from recent developments in the social sciences. This approach posits that the coherence of action is not adequately explained by either preconceived cognitive schema or institutionalized social norms. To be more accurate, the organization of situated action

Table 8.8. Types of information-seeking strategies with divergent examples

---

Identifying strategy by employing scanning tactics
Identify a database(s) /collection(s) to get started by *scanning* meta-information of a database/collection

Identify information to get started by *scanning* a reference list of relevant items

Identifying strategy by employing specifying and scanning tactics
Identify a database(s) /collection(s) to get started by *specifying* terms *and scanning* meta-information of a database(s) /collection(s)

Identifying strategy by employing scanning and extracting tactics
Identify concepts/terms to continue searching by *scanning* retrieved items *and extracting* terms

Identifying strategy by employing consulting tactics
Identify information to continue searching by *consulting* a human

---

Learning strategy by employing consulting tactics
Learn system feature or system structure by *consulting* a human or system help features

Learning strategy by employing trial & error tactics
Learn system features by *trial and error* system features

Learning strategy by employing surveying tactics
Learn domain knowledge by *surveying* descriptors of retrieved results

Learning strategy by employing manipulating tactics
Learn information retrieval skills by *manipulating* different terms/concepts

Learning strategy by employing scanning tactics
Learn database/collection content by *scanning* meta-information of a database/collection

---

Exploring strategy by employing scanning tactics
Explore a specific item/site by *scanning* an item or site

Explore items with common characteristics by *scanning* a collection

Explore items without pre-defined criteria by *scanning* an area

---

Creating search statement strategy for a known item by employing specifying tactics
Create search statement for a known item by *specifying* metadata of the item

Creating search statement strategy for a known item by employing consulting tactics
Create search statement for a known item by *consulting* a human

Creating search statement strategy for items with common characteristics by employing specifying tactics
Create search statement for items with common characteristics by *specifying* terms and their relationships

Creating search statement strategy for specific information by employing specifying
Create search statement for specific information by specifying terms and their relationships

---

continued on following page

Table 8.8. continued

Modifying search statement strategy for a known item by employing manipulating tactics
Modify search statement for a known item by manipulating metadata of the item
Modify search statement for a known item by manipulating format of the item's metadata

Modifying search statement strategy for items with common characteristics by employing manipulating tactics
Modify search statement for items with common characteristics by *manipulating* terms of search statements
Modify search statement for items with common characteristics by *manipulating* formats of search statements

Modifying search statement strategy for items with common characteristics by employing tracking tactics
Modify search statement for items with common characteristics by *tracking* meta-information of retrieved items

Modifying search statement strategy for specific information by employing manipulating tactics
Modify search statement for specific information by *manipulating* terms of search statements
Modify search statement for specific information by *manipulating* formats of search statements

Modifying search statement strategy for specific information by employing consulting tactics
Modify search statement for specific information by *consulting* a human

---

Monitoring strategy by employing surveying tactics
Monitor search process by *surveying* search history of the process
Monitor search status by *surveying* current location

Organizing strategy by employing manipulating tactics
Organize retrieved items by *manipulating* retrieved items based on different criteria

---

Accessing strategy by employing tracking tactics
Access a specific item, items with common characteristics, or an area/location by *tracking* meta-information

Accessing strategy by employing consulting tactics
Access a specific item, items with common characteristics, or an area/location by *consulting* a human

Accessing strategy by employing trial & error tactics
Access a specific item, items with common characteristics, or an area/location by *trial & error* system features

---

Evaluating strategy by employing scanning and comparing tactics
Evaluate correctness, usefulness, fitness, duplication or authority of items by *scanning* and *comparing* meta-information of items

Evaluating strategy by employing specifying and scanning tactics
Evaluate specificity of an item by *specifying* and *scanning* the item

Evaluating strategy by employing specifying and tracking tactics
Evaluate the authority of an item by *specifying* meta-information & *tracking* meta-information of the item

---

Keeping record strategy by employing acquiring tactics
Keep record of meta-information of a site by *acquiring* (Bookmark) meta-information of a site

Keeping record strategy by employing extracting tactics
Keep record of meta-information of an item by *extracting* meta-information of an item

---

continued on following page

Table 8.8. continued

Obtaining strategy by employing acquiring tactics **Obtain** specific <u>information</u> by a*cquiring (write down)* specific <u>information</u> **Obtain** part of the <u>item</u> by *acquiring(copy)* part of the <u>item</u> **Obtain** a whole <u>item(s)</u> by *acquiring (download)* a whole <u>item</u>
Disseminating strategy by employing specifying tactics **Disseminate** <u>information</u> to a specific person by *specifying* email address of a <u>person</u> **Disseminate** <u>an item</u> to a group pf people by *specifying* the listerve of the <u>group</u>

is an emergent property of moment-by-moment interactions between actors and the environment that they are interacting with.

The nature of an activity can be missed if the particular contingent details of the environment a user is interacting with are neglected. Not only planning but situated elements influence the information-seeking process. Information-seeking strategies reflect the interactions between a user and the system as well as between a user and the social-organizational context with which he or she is interacting. To be more specific, they are affected by the environment the user is interacting with, the information object provided by the IR system, and the computational capabilities of the IR system that a user is interacting with via interfaces of the IR system.

Both planned model and theory of situated action have their limitations as well as their contributions. Goal-directed information-seeking behavior is often considered as part of a plan. However, the inherent uncertainty and interactiveness of IR also determines the situational aspect of information-seeking activity. "Situated action" emphasizes the situational aspect of IR. Information-seeking strategies are the products of both planned and situational aspects. Furthermore, there is no clear boundary between

Figure 8.2. Dimensions of information-seeking strategies

planned aspects and situational aspects. While plans cannot predict the moment-by-moment change of situations as Suchman (1987) claimed, most plans are not specifications of fixed sequences of actions; instead, they are strategies that determine each successive action as a function of current information about the situation, as argued by Vera and Simon (1993).

To some extent, planned and situational aspects are intertwined with each other. For example, information-seeking requires users to apply their personal information infrastructures, such as their general cognitive abilities, knowledge skills in relation to the problem/task domain, knowledge and skills in general, knowledge and skills specific to a system, and knowledge and skills regarding information-seeking. Users' knowledge also includes a set of plans for different situations with a set of interactive intentions and associated retrieval tactics. More important, these plans represent users' conscious and unconscious actions toward familiar and unfamiliar situations. Users normally employ their personal information infrastructure to: (1) represent their problems/tasks; (2) establish a set of subgoals/subtasks to fulfill the overall goals/tasks; and (3) develop techniques and strategies to seek required information. At the same time, users' personal information infrastructures are also developed during the information-seeking process when users gain knowledge and skills in order to adapt to different situations and solve problems. Derived from users' knowledge and skills, information-seeking strategies are the stratification of their experiences according to relevance and typicality.

Therefore, information-seeking strategies are the products of plans and situations. The information retrieval process is determined by both planned and situational aspects.

Dimensions of Plans and Situations

Information-seeking strategies are codetermined by plans and situations. The question is how to define the dimensions of plans and situations. Integrating how plans and situations affect human actions, the author further applies them to interactive IR and extends the dimensions of plans and situations to answer the following questions:

- What leads to a plan? Levels of user goals/tasks, personal information infrastructure, and social-organizational context all help define a plan.
    - Levels of user goals/task determine user plans. The dimensions of leading search goals/work tasks define the work tasks in terms of stages of the task, timeframe, and the nature of the task (the structuredness of task, users' familiarity with the task, and situations of the tasks). The user goals/task structure also depicts dimensions of search tasks: origination of tasks, types of tasks, and domain of tasks. These dimensions assist users consciously and unconsciously in selecting appropriate plans for their tasks and, at same time, monitor the IR process.

- ∘ Users' domain knowledge, system knowledge, information-retrieval knowledge, and cognitive styles assist users in determining their actions and plans under different circumstances.

- ∘ The social-organizational context in which the interaction takes places defines the priority and limitations of what users can do in their formation of plans and selections of information-seeking strategies in the retrieval process.

- What is a plan? A plan is a user's arrangement to complete a task. It goes beyond the fixed actions for a desired goal.

- What are the elements of a plan? A plan needs to answer the following questions:

  - ∘ What to do first? It refers to users' first interactive intention and its associated retrieved tactics. In general, it could be the information resources/system that users select to use or interact with first.

  - ∘ How to achieve the goal/task? It includes a set of subgoals or interactive intentions that users have to accomplish in order to achieve the current search goal or search task. It consists of a set of plans that correspond to different types of situations or interactive intentions. More important, the plan also contains arrangements about how to monitor the retrieval process.

  - ∘ When to stop? It is related to users' decisions about when they quit their retrieval process after obtaining complete information, enough information, partial information, or just by frustration.

These dimensions are identified and validated in a recent study by the author (Xie, 2006).

Correspondingly, dimensions of situations can be summarized to answer the following questions:

- What leads to a situation? A situation is the product of interactions between users and IR systems. Situations arise within each social-organizational context (Sonnenwald, 1999). Under the social and organizational context and driven by their levels of goals and tasks, users apply their own information infrastructure to interact with IR systems via interfaces of these systems. Users' interactions with IR systems, especially the objects presented by the systems, leads to the situation in the interactive IR process.

- What is a situation? There is no agreement on the definition of situation. "Definitions vary across individual, social, and environment levels of analysis" (Cool, 2001, p. 7). In the context of interactive IR, a situation is a user's perception of a specific moment based on his/her evaluation of the interaction with an IR system and his/her plan.

- What are the elements of situations? In other words, what are the factors that affect users' perception of a specific moment? Based on an empirical study of users' interactions with an OPAC, Hert (1997) identified the following situated elements: elements associated with users (knowledge, attitudes, expectations, emotions, etc.), elements associated with the problem (subject area, specific requirement, point in the process, group projects or not), elements associated with system response (nature of retrieved sets, status messages, features of individual entries). In the planned-situational model of interactive IR, the outcomes of user-system interactions, which include the results of users' interaction with objects provided by the system, and the outcomes of users' interaction with its interface and its computational capabilities, as well as users' plans, are the major components of a situation. Users' perception of a specific time-space is the result of the assessment of their plans based on the outcomes of interactions with IR systems.

This discussion of dimensions of plans and situations demonstrates the inseparable relationships between the two. On the one hand, a plan contains strategies to deal with different situations rather than a fixed sequence of actions. On the other hand, users' perception of a situation reflects their assessment of their plans based on the consequences of their interactions with an IR system.

Shifts in Current Search Goals and Information-Seeking Strategies: Determination of Situations

Determination of Situations: Precursors of the Shifts

The interplay between planned and situational aspects leads to shifts in current search goals/search tasks and shifts in information-seeking strategies. The results of the previous study by the author (Xie, 2000, 2002) indicate that in the information-seeking process, users' long-term goals, normally do not change. Rarely do their leading search goals change. However, users quite often change their original current search goals, interactive intentions, and retrieved tactics within an information-seeking episode in order to achieve their higher-level user goals/tasks. Different levels of shifts constitute the information-seeking process. Some of the shifts are just follow-ups, while they are the result of plans and situations. Three levels of shifts emerged: (1) current search goal shifts; (2) interactive intention shifts; and (3) retrieval tactic shifts. All these changes can be classified and represented by different patterns. Because shifts of current search goals did not occur as often as information-seeking strategies, and they are limited in terms of whether and how these shifts occur, the author concentrates on the discussion of shifts in interactive intentions and retrieval tactics.

According to Schutz and Luckmann (1973), "The course of life is a series of situations" (p. 113). They identified two types of determination of situations: (1) routine situation and (2) problematic situation. In a "routine situation," the situation can be determined sufficiently with the aid of habitual knowledge. All unknown elements of the situation can be routinely defined, and the situation is not problematic. In the context of IR, a plan is formed based on a user's levels of goals, his/her knowledge and skills, and the resources of a set of interactive intentions and associated retrieval tactics. After assessing the plan and current situation in routine situations, as planned, a user normally moves to the next interactive intention, and selects its corresponding retrieval tactics to fulfill his/her interactive intention.

Not all situations can be routinely determined, however. In a "problematic situation," after correlating the elements of situations with his/her knowledge and plans, a user's knowledge is not clear enough, sure enough, or broad enough to handle the situation. Further clarification of the open elements of the situation is required. Unlike routine situations, users must either rearrange their old knowledge or acquire new knowledge and skills to clarify their present situations. According to Kelly (2006), context defines problematic situations. In the context of IR, the situational aspects have impacts on which facets of knowledge and skills are brought to bear, modifications and rearrangements of the set of interactive intentions and retrieval tactics, and a clearer definition of levels of user goals. Accordingly, an adjusted plan is formed to shift information-seeking strategies. To be more specific, a user might select another retrieval tactic in order to accomplish the current interactive intentions or select the next interactive intention and appropriate retrieval tactics. The problematic situations might also lead to shifts in current search goals.

A third type of situation, which can be named "disruptive situation," emerges in the context of interactive IR. In disruptive situations, users do not encounter any problems, but they are distracted in the process of fulfilling their original current search goals/ search tasks. For example, they might see something that holds their interest that is not relevant to their current search goals/tasks. They explore the new interest for a while, and then come back to their original current search goals/tasks. On the level of current search goal shifts, users have to apply their personal information infrastructure, go back to their leading search goal/work task, change their current search goals/search task, and adjust their plan for the selection of associated information-seeking strategies. On the level of interactive intention shifts, users have to apply their personal information infrastructure to go back their plan for the next appropriate interactive intentions and its corresponding retrieval tactics in order to accomplish their original current search goals/search tasks.

Types of Current Search Goal Shifts

Both planned and situational aspects influence whether users shift their current search goals as well as how they shift their current search goals. On the one hand, leading search goals determine whether users can shift their current search goals, and, more important, shifts in current search goals are also limited by the scope of leading search goals. Concurrently, the dimensions of work tasks might also affect whether and how users shift current search goals. On the other hand, outcomes of user-system interactions also determine whether users have to shift their current search goals, and how they can shift. For example, the results of interaction can generate more interesting results on a related topic, which might lead to the change in current search goals. At the same time, the interaction results can also yield unsatisfactory results, which might lead to a problematic situation, forcing users to change their current search goals.

Based on the interaction process and results, the typical shifts in current search goals can be classified into two types: opportunistic shifts derived from disruptive situations and alternative shifts derived from problematic situations. Opportunistic shifts occur when users see other, more interesting, information by serendipity in the process of achieving their current search goals. Therefore, they move from the current search goal to a related current search goal. For example, a user is looking for information about how people search the Internet (current search goal) in order to write a research proposal for Introduction to Information Science class (leading search goal). In the searching process, she finds some articles about digital references. This new topic is related to another class that she is taking. Therefore, she decides to change her current search goal to the new one for the time being.

Alternative shifts occur when users have to shift their original current search goals to new current search goals because the interaction results cannot produce satisfactory results to accomplish the original current search goals. For example, a Web designer for a news agency needs to find pictures of a politician for the Web page. He cannot find it after searching the picture in different types of IR systems, including digital libraries. However, the page has to be made available to the public within a couple of hours. Therefore, he decides to find a picture of the politician with other people as an alternative one. In general, dimensions of work tasks influence what information-seeking strategies users would apply and how they would apply. This case indicates that the timeframe of the work task also influences whether users change their current search goals. In general, alternative shifts in current search goals are associated with generalizing search tasks or with changing from one aspect to another aspect of the search tasks. It seems the pattern of alternative shifts is from specific to common or general.

Not all the current search goals can be shifted, especially when they are constrained by their leading search goals. For example, in a corporate setting, an engineer has to find information about an old model of equipment because he has to use that information to repair the equipment. Even though the interaction results did not generate useful information, he has to try different approaches to fulfill this goal. He cannot change his current search goal if that is essential in order to repair the equipment. Compared to self-generated tasks, assigned search tasks normally require the user to try his/her best to achieve the current search goals because people who work on the self-generated tasks have more knowledge about their leading searching goals than people who work on the assigned tasks.

Table 8.9. Types of interactive intention shifts

Types of Situations	Continuing Original Interactive Intention	Discontinuing Original Interactive Intention
Routine	N/A	type I intention shifts (planned shifts)
Disruptive	type II intention shifts (opportunistic shifts)	N/A
Problem	type III intention shifts (assisted shifts)	type IV intention shifts (alternative shifts)

Types of Interactive Intention Shifts

As discussed above, shifts in information-seeking strategies occur on two levels: level-one shifts in retrieval tactics and level-two shifts in interactive intentions. Two factors play important roles in defining shifts in interactive intentions: 1) types of situations derived from user-system interactions, and 2) whether a user continues or discontinues his/her original interactive intention after he/she finishes the new intention. Table 8.9 presents four types of interactive intention shifts. In routine situations, users either accomplish or discontinue their original interactive intention. The definition of the disruptive situation determines whether users have to continue their original interactive intentions after the disruption. Therefore, types of interactive intention shifts are not applicable for users who continue their original interactive intentions in routine situations and users who discontinue their original interactive intentions in disruptive situations.

Type I intention shifts occur when the previous interactive intentions are achieved without any problem, allowing users to follow their original plans and select the next interactive intentions. Strictly speaking, these follow-up shifts are just planned transitions. Therefore, type I intention shifts can be called **"planned shifts."** For example, a user was looking for Martin Luther King's "I have a dream" speech. After he found the item, he started to access and evaluated it to see whether it was the one he was looking for, and then obtained the item and disseminated it to a friend. In this case, **obtaining an item and disseminating an item are planned shifts from accessing an item and evaluating the authority of an item.**

Of the four types of shifts, planned shifts are the most frequently occurring shifts in the information retrieval process. Planned shifts happen among different types of interactive intentions except "learning," because "learning" normally serves as an assisted interactive intention when users have problems in achieving their other interactive intentions.

"Identifying," "exploring," "creating search statements," "modifying search statements," "monitoring," "keeping records," "accessing," "organizing," "evaluating," "obtaining," and "disseminating" follow the logical sequences of search process. Not all of the planned shifts follow the sequences of the search process. People might start with "exploring" instead of "identifying information to get started," and "accessing these items" without going through "creating search statements" and "modify search statements." Sometimes users skip the process of "organizing" when the IR system does not provide that option. At those times, "evaluating" goes right after "accessing."

Planned shifts not only take place among different types of interactive intentions, but also appear within several types of interactive intentions. In "monitoring," monitoring current status could occur after monitoring the search process. In "evaluating," "evaluating fitness of an item" (e.g., evaluating different versions of an item) could only happen after "evaluating each specific item."

Type II intention shifts occur when users shift to other interactive intentions temporarily by serendipity in the process of accomplishing their current interactive intentions. Users normally continue to finish their original interactive intentions after their serendipitous interludes. Therefore, type II intention shifts can be named "**opportunistic shifts**." Opportunistic shifts frequently associate with the "evaluating" process. For example, when one user was "evaluating the relevancy of the retrieved results on Web use," she accidentally saw a story of a summer reading program that she participated in, so she explored the article that interests her. **After she "explored the interesting story," she continued to "evaluate" the article**.

Opportunistic shifts do not happen as often as planned shifts do. "Seeing something by serendipity" is the cause of this type of shift. In the process of "accessing," "evaluating," and "exploring," users might see something by serendipity, and that "something" could lead users to "explore" or "learn."

Type III intention shifts occur while users cannot fulfill their current interactive intentions because of problems derived from the user-system interactions, but they do not abandon their current interactive intentions. Instead, new intentions are introduced to assist them in solving problems. Therefore, type III intention shifts are labeled "**assisted shifts**." These problems normally can be related to interactions with the system features, structure, or search results. For example, in exploring one IR system, a user was confused about its structure, so he decided to learn the system structure first before exploring the system. Here is an example of the problem of interaction results. A user found that the retrieved results were too broad after evaluating the results, so he decided to learn some information retrieval skills before going back to narrow down the search results.

Compared to other types of shifts, assisted shifts are quite focused. Whenever an assisted shift happens, help is needed. In the process of accomplishing almost every type of interactive intention, there is a need to "learn." Consequently, "learning" is the leading interactive intention for assisted shifts.

Among all the assisted shifts, "learning system feature, structure, domain knowledge, information retrieval knowledge, database content, and search process" might be required in the process of achieving "creating search statements," "modifying search statements," and "identify." "Learning system structure and system feature" is needed in "exploring," "accessing," "organizing," and "evaluating." "Learning system feature" could be used to "monitor," "obtain," or "disseminate."

Type IV intention shifts occur when users have to give up their previous interactive intentions because of the problematic situations. Alternative interactive intentions are commonly generated to make up for the failure of the previous ones. Accordingly, type IV intention shifts can be described as **"alternative shifts."** For example, one user was trying to access a specific site, but an error occurred stating that site was not available anymore. She changed her interactive intention from "accessing" to "creating a search statement" in order to find the new URL of the site or items with common characteristics to the one that she was unable to access.

In addition to shifts from "accessing" to "creating a search statement," the typical alternative shifts take place from the interactive intention "create a search statement" to "modify search statement." In addition, there is a potential alternative shift relationship between "exploring" and "create a search statement." Users might need to create a search statement to find a piece of specific information if they cannot explore to find it.

Types of Retrieval Tactic Shifts

As level-two shifts of information-seeking strategies, retrieval tactic shifts are applied for users to fulfill their current interactive intentions. Users are able to change their retrieval tactics by shifting their methods, entities, attributes, or both methods and entities. Methods and entities constitute a variety of retrieval tactics. Thus, four types of shifts of retrieval tactics can be further discussed in their change of dimensions: 1) change of methods, 2) change of entities, 3) change of attributes, and 4) change of both methods and entities. Table 8.10 presents types of retrieval tactic shifts and their associated dimension changes.

The main factor that determines the shifts in retrieval tactics is whether the outcome of the original retrieval tactics is partially successful or unsuccessful. Partially successful outcomes might lead to shifts that supplement the original retrieval tactics,

Table 8.10. Types of shifts and associated dimension changes

Types of shifts	Type I tactic shifts (method shifts)	Type II tactic shifts (entity shifts)	Type III tactic shifts (attribute shifts)	Type IV tactic shifts (method-entity shifts)
Change of methods	X			
Change of entities		X		
Change of attributes			X	
Change both methods and entities				X

and unsuccessful outcomes might lead to the shifts that improve the original retrieval tactics. Concurrently, the partial and unsuccessful outcomes might also lead to shifts in retrieval tactics that serve as alternative tactics of the original tactics. Retrieval tactics shifts occur quite often. They appear almost in the process of achieving every type of interactive intention, particularly, in "creating search statements," "modifying search statements," and "evaluating."

In type I tactic shifts, users only change methods to fulfill their current interactive intentions. Therefore, type I strategy shifts can be called **"method shifts."** For example, a user originally tried to learn the search feature by *trial-and-error*, but he could not figure it out. Therefore, he decided to consult the Help of the system. During that process, as his original retrieval tactics did not work, he shifted his retrieval tactics from trial and error a system feature to consulting system Help. Here is another example: one user changed from scanning meta-information of items to tracking meta-information of items in order to explore items with common characteristics. Methods are changed as supplemental or alternative shifts depending on whether the outcome of the original user-system interaction is partially successful or unsuccessful.

In type II tactic shifts, users do not change methods of retrieval tactics; instead, they change the entities of retrieval tactics. Type II strategy shifts can be named **"entity shifts."** For example, in the process of obtaining information about a summer festival, a user tried to acquire/download the whole item regarding the summer festival, but it failed. Therefore, she acquired/wrote down the specific information instead. Entities, not methods, were changed to improve or used as an alternative tactic for the user's original retrieval tactic.

In type III tactic shifts, users cannot accomplish their interactive intentions by applying their original retrieval tactics, and they have to change the attributes of entities. Type III strategy shifts can be labeled **"attribute shifts."** For example, in evaluating the "usefulness of an item," a user scanned the meta-information of an item. She thought it was a relevant item, but was not sure how comprehensively the item covered the subject in which she was interested, so she glanced through the whole item and confirmed that it was an useful item for her. In this case, the user changed her retrieval tactics from scanning meta-information of an item to scanning general information of the whole item. In this example, the new retrieval tactic serves as a supplement tactic for the user's original retrieval tactic.

In type IV tactic shifts, users might change both methods and entities to replace their previous retrieval tactics. Therefore, type IV tactic shifts are characterized as **"method-entity shifts."** For example, in order to find items on security requirements for boarding an airplane, a user modified the search statement by first manipulating concepts/terms in an IR system. She then consulted a human for further modification of the statements. In this case, she shifted both methods and entities of the original retrieved tactic. Consulting a human is the frequently used alternative retrieval tactic for manipulating concepts/terms and trial-and-error a system.

Figure 8.3. Levels of shifts and factors affecting these shifts

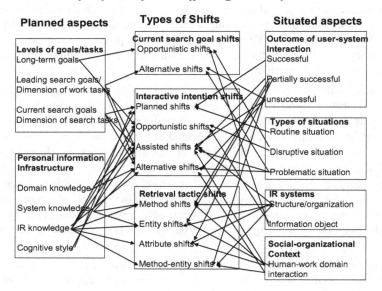

To sum up, users have to change their current search goals/search tasks and informa-tion-seeking strategies in their information retrieval process because of the impact of planned and situational aspects. Users normally first shift their retrieval tactics in order to accomplish their interactive intentions. If that does not work, users then change their interactive intentions in order to fulfill their current search goals/search tasks. Occasionally users also have to shift their current search goals in order to achieve their leading search goals/work tasks. In general, users do not change their long-term goals and leading search goals/work tasks. Figure 8.3 presents the levels of shifts and factors affecting these shifts.

Factors Affecting Shifts in Current Search Goals/Search Tasks and Information-Seeking Strategies

The shifts in current search goals, interactive intentions, and retrieval tactics do not occur randomly. Instead, they are led by the factors that affect these changes. As discussed in the previous sections, both situational and planned aspects influence the change of current search goals and the selection of information-seeking strategies; therefore, they are responsible for the shifts in current search goals, interactions in-tentions, and retrieval tactics. The author would like to discuss how the planned and situational aspects direct the changes, especially the changes in interactive intentions and retrieval tactics.

Planned Aspects

Planned aspects refer to goal- and task-related factors. Levels of user goals and associated dimensions of work tasks and search tasks play essential roles in determining whether and how users change their goals/intentions or retrieval tactics. Comparatively speaking, long-term goals have less impact on the selection of information-seeking strategies and their shifts. Leading search goals/work tasks drive users to search. In other words, users have to search for information in order to accomplish their leading search goals. Leading search goals influence the alternative shifts in current search goals, as users can only change current search goals within the scope of leading search goals. The dimensions of work tasks and search tasks affect users' shifts in interactive intentions. For example, the timeframe of the work task might determine whether users need to have alternative or assisted shifts. At the same time, routine tasks might lead to more planned shifts, while new tasks might require more assisted or alternative shifts.

Users' personal information infrastructure helps them form a plan for their information seeking and retrieving. Their knowledge and resources assist users in shifting their interactive intentions and retrieved tactics to fulfill their current search goals when they encounter problems. To be more specific, users' knowledge about the IR system that they are interacting with, such as system features and system structure, is the key factor for assisted shifts and alternative shifts of interactive intentions. In addition, system knowledge might also lead to some method and entity shifts of retrieved tactics. Users' knowledge about the subject area that a user is looking for, such as terminologies, key experts, and key publications in one subject area, might lead to assisted and alternative shifts in interactive intentions as well as to attribute shifts in retrieved tactics. Users' information retrieval knowledge consists of users' experience and knowledge about how to search for information. It has been shown to be an important factor in determining planned as well as other shifts in interactive intentions, and, more importantly, in determining all the shifts of retrieval tactics. At the same time, users' cognitive styles also affect their ways of interaction with IR systems.

Situational Aspects

Situational aspects are mainly related to IR systems, the information objects stored in these systems, and the social-organizational context that users interact with. More important, situational aspects are related to the outcomes of these interactions. The outcomes of user-system interactions are the precondition for the shifts in interactive intentions and retrieved tactics. The successful outcomes account for the planned shifts in interactive intentions, because users can follow their plans to change from one interactive intention to another. The partial successful outcomes might lead to different types of shifts in retrieval tactics, because users have to change to another tactic to achieve their success. The unsuccessful outcomes force users to come up with assisted and alternative shifts in interactive intentions as well as different types of shifts in retrieved tactics.

Information objects are the information that users interact with via interfaces of IR systems. Information objects include both information derived from information objects stored in the IR systems and messages generated by different retrieval mechanisms of IR systems. Examples of information objects are: a list of retrieved results from an IR system, descriptors, full-text articles, a suggested message or error message generated by the IR system, a video file, and so forth. While interaction results determine the outcomes of the interactions, they affect almost every type of shifts in current search goals, interactive intentions, and retrieved tactics. Especially, information objects that users interact with are the key factors that lead to opportunistic shifts in current search goals and interactive intentions.

Each IR system has its uniqueness in terms of its interface, search mechanisms, organizational structure, collections, and so forth. If a user interacts with an unfamiliar IR system or unfamiliar feature of an IR system, he might encounter problems, especially if he applies his mental models of past experiences into the new system or system feature. Therefore, assisted shifts in interactive intentions that help users learn new system features might be needed in these situations. Simultaneously, the uniqueness of each IR system might also direct changes in different types of retrieved tactics in methods, entities, and attributes.

When users interact with IR systems, at the same time, they also interact with the social-organizational context. The social-organizational context defines the environment in which the interactions take place. While social-organizational context does affect users in terms of general norms and culture in information-seeking strategies, sometimes the work domain of the social-organizational context might have changes that create problematic situations. For example, at an organizational level, the restructure of an organization or a merger of two companies might create problems for users. They might need to engage in assisted and alternative shifts of interactive intentions. In addition, they might have to introduce new retrieved tactics by changing methods, entities, or attributes to improve or serve as alternates for the original retrieval tactics.

Summary

Based on the planned model and the theory of situated action derived from the cognitive and social sciences, as well as existing interactive IR models, plus empirical interactive IR studies in different digital environments, the planned-situational model of interactive IR is developed to illustrate the determination of information-seeking strategies and their shifts (products of plans and situations). It highlights levels of user goals/tasks (long-term goals, leading search goals/work tasks, current search goals/search tasks, and interactive intentions) and their representations. It identifies dimensions of information-seeking strategies (methods, entities, attributes), which consist of 12 types of interactive intentions associated with 11 types of retrieved tactics. It shows how users shift their current search goals (opportunity and alternative shifts), interactive intentions (planned, opportunity, assisted, and alternative shifts), and retrieved tactics (method, entity, attribute, and method-entity shifts) during the information-seeking process. More important, the model also identifies the planned and situational factors that affect the shifts in current search goals, interactive intentions, and retrieved tactics.

The planned-situational interactive IR model is developed based on the author's original model (Xie, 2000, 2002). It further enhances the original model in the following ways:

- Integrates the macro context for interactive IR. The new model incorporates the social-organizational context, especially human-work domain interaction, into the original model. The social-organizational context defines the interaction environment for interactive IR.

- Makes the IR system visible in the new model. The new model specifically presents the information objects and the computational mechanisms of the IR system that users are interacting with via interfaces of IR systems as the major components of the model. It clearly characterizes users' interaction partner and its potential impact on the interactions.

- Illustrates the relationships between levels of user goals and levels of tasks and their relationships. The new model presents the levels of tasks corresponding to levels of tasks, and further identifies the dimensions of work tasks and search tasks. The identification of working and search tasks offers insightful information in terms of how levels of goals and tasks affect information-seeking strategies and their shifts.

- Integrates interactive intentions and retrieved tactics together as information-seeking strategies. The new model integrates interactive intentions and retrieval tactics into information-seeking strategies, because interactive intentions are part of the information-seeking strategies.

- Modifies the types of interactive intentions and retrieval tactics based on the new digital environments. It modifies the intentions by adding exploring, creating search statements, modifying search statements, monitoring, and disseminating intentions, as well as deleting finding and locating intentions based on users' interactions with new digital environments. The new model incorporates new methods such as specifying, manipulating, surveying, and extracting as part of the retrieval tactics. It extends the entities from resource to a diverse number of things, such as data/information, knowledge, concepts, items/objects/sites, formats, process, location, system, and human. It also adds the attributes for each of the entities to further define information-seeking strategies.

- Re-examines the shifts in information-seeking strategies. Shifts in information-seeking strategies are re-examined based on the new definitions of information-seeking strategies. In that sense, shifts in information-seeking strategies can be considered on two levels: level-one retrieval tactic shifts and level-two interactive intention shifts. In general, users change their retrieval tactics in order to achieve their current interactive intentions when they encounter problems.

- Analyzes the factors that lead to the shifts in current search goals, interactive intentions, and retrieval tactics. The planned and situational factors are identified and discussed in terms of how they affect different types of current search goals, interactive intentions, and retrieval tactics. The analysis of the planned and situational factors greatly helps researchers understand the patterns of shifts in information-seeking strategies.

Compared with other interactive IR models introduced in Chapter VII, the planned-situational model offers the following new contributions:

- Integrates the macro- and micro-level of interactive IR models. The planned-situational model not only identifies the partners of the interactions—users and IR systems—as well as the social-organizational context that defines the user-system interaction at the macrolevel, but it also illustrates the selection of and shifts in information-seeking strategies in the information retrieval process at the microlevel.

- Applies the plan model and the theory of situated action into interactive IR. The planned-situational model sheds light on the nature of interactive IR that is codetermined by plans and situation aspects. In other words, information retrieval is the product of plans and situations. Plans are not just specifications of fixed sequence of actions, and planed and situational aspects are intertwined with each other.

- Clarifies, through the discussion of the levels of user goals and tasks, the relationships between the two concepts, which are widely used in different contexts and different meanings by researchers. The identification of dimensions of work tasks and search tasks help reveal how levels of goals and tasks affect information-seeking strategies and their shifts, as well as the information retrieval process.

- Characterizes information-seeking strategies through the identification of dimensions of information-seeking strategies and patterns between interactive intentions and associated retrieval tactics. This model demonstrates that people engage in multiple information-seeking strategies in the IR process. More important, users' information-seeking strategies are not unsystematic, and they have their own patterns.

- This model associates the planned and situational factors directly with patterns of shifts in information-seeking strategies. It provides a theoretical understanding of users' information-seeking strategies in terms of both how and why; moreover, it also offers ways that can be implemented into system design to support users' multiple information-seeking strategies and different levels of shifts.

References

Allen, B.L., & Kim, K.S. (2000). Person and context in information seeking: Interactions between cognitive and task variables. Paper presented at the conference Information Seeking in Context. Göteborg, Sweden.

Bates, M. J. (1979a). Information search tactics. *Journal of the American Society for Information Science, 30*(4), 205-214.

Bates, M. J. (1979b). Idea tactics. *Journal of the American Society for Information Science, 30*(5), 280-289.

Bates, M. J. (1990). Where should the person stop and the information search interface start? *Information Processing and Management, 26*(5), 575-591.

Belkin, N. J. (1993). Interaction with texts: Information retrieval as information seeking behavior. In G. Knorz, J. Krause & C. Womser-Hacker (Eds.), *Information retrieval '93: Von der Modellierung zur Anwendung* (pp. 55-66). Konstanz: Universitaetsverlag Konstanz.

Belkin, N. J., Chang, S., Downs, T., Saracevic, T., & Zhao, S. (1990). Taking account of user tasks, goals and behavior for the design of online public access catalogs. In D. Henderson (Ed.), *Proc. of the 53rd ASIS Annual Meeting,* (pp. 69-79). Medford, NJ: Learned Information.

Belkin, N. J., & Cool, C. (1993, March). The concept of information seeking strategies and its use in the design of information retrieval systems. In *Paper presented at the AAAI Spring Symposium on Case-based Reasoning and Information Retrieval*, Stanford, CA.

Bellardo, T. (1985). What do we really know about online searchers? *Online Review, 9*(3), 223-239.

Bhavnani, S. K. (2002). Important cognitive components of domain-specific search knowledge. In E. M. Voorhees & D. K. Harman (Eds.), *The Tenth Text REtrieval Conference, TREC-2001,* (pp. 571-578). Medford, NJ: Information Today.

Bhavnani, S.K., Bichakjian, C.K., Johnson, T.M., Little, R.J., Peck, F.A., Schwartz, J.L., & Strecher, V.J. (2006). Strategy hubs: Domain portals to help find comprehensive information. *Journal of the American Society for Information Science and Technology, 57*(1), 4-24.

Bilal, D. (2002). Perspectives on children's navigation of the World Wide Web: Does the type of search task make a difference? *Online Information Review,* *26*(2), 108-177.

Borlund, P., & Ingwersen, P. (1997). The development of a method for the evaluation of interactive information retrieval systems. *Journal of Documentation,* *53*(3), 225-250.

Broder, A. (2002). A taxonomy of Web search. *SIGIR Forum, 36*(2), 3-10.

Byström, K., & Järvelin, K. (1995). Task complexity affects information-seeking and use. *Information Processing and Management, 31*(2), 191-213.

Callahan, E. (2005). Interface design and culture. *Annual Review of Information Science and Technology, 39*, 257-310.

Chang, S. (1995). *Toward a multidimensional framework for understanding browsing.* Unpublished doctoral dissertation, Rutgers University, New Brunswick, NJ.

Chen, H., & Dhar, V. (1991). Cognitive processes as a basis for intelligent retrieval system design. *Information Processing and Management, 27*(5), 405-432.

Cool, C. (2001). The concept of situation in information science. *Annual Review of Information Science and Technology, 35*, 5-42.

Cothey, V. (2002). A longitudinal study of World Wide Web users' information searching behavior. *Journal of the American Society for Information Science and Technology, 53*(2), 67-78.

D'Alessandro, D., & Kingsley, P. (2002). Creating a pediatric digital library for pediatric health care providers and families: Using literature and data to define common pediatric problems. *Journal of the American Medical Informatics Association, 9*(2), 161-170.

Daniels, P. (1986). *Developing the user modeling function of an intelligent interface for document retrieval systems.* Unpublished doctoral dissertation, The City University, London, England.

Drabenstott, K. M. (2003). Do nondomain experts enlist the strategies of domain experts? *Journal of the American Society for Information Science and Technology, 54*(9), 836-854.

Dumais, S.T., & Belkin, N.J. (2005). The TREC interactive tracks: Putting the user into search. In E.M. Voorhees & D.K. Harman (Eds.), *TREC: Experiment and evaluation in information retrieval* (pp. 123-152). Cambridge, MA: The MIT Press.

Ellis, D. (1989). A behavioral approach to information retrieval system design. *Journal of Documentation, 45*(3), 171-212.

Ellis, D., & Haugan, M. (1997). Modeling the information seeking patterns of engineers and research scientists in an industrial environment. *Journal of Documentation, 53*(4), 384-403.

Fenichel, C. H. (1981). Online searching: Measures that discriminate among users with different types of experience. *Journal of the American Society for Information Science, 32*(1), 23-32.

Fidel, R. (1985). Moves in online searching. *Online Review, 9*(1), 61-74.

Fidel, R. (1991). Searchers' selection of search keys: I. The selection routine: II. Controlled vocabulary or free-text searching: III. Searching styles. *Journal of the American Society for Information Science, 42*(7), 490-527.

Fidel, R., & Pejtersen, A. M. (2004). From information behavior research to the design of information systems: The cognitive work analysis framework. *Information Research, 10(1)*. Retrieved January 4, 2008, from http://informationr. net/ir/10-1/paper210.html

Fidel, R., Pejtersen, A. M., Cleal, B., & Bruce, H. (2004). A multi-dimensional approach to the study of human-information interaction: A case study of collaborative information retrieval. *Journal of the American Society for Information Science and Technology, 55*(11), 939-953.

Ford, N., Miller, D., & Moss, N. (2002). Web search strategies and retrieval effectiveness: An empirical study. *Journal of Documentation, 58*(1), 30-48.

Hackos, J. T., & Redish, J. C. (1998). *User and task analysis for interface design.* New York: John Wiley & Sons.

Harter, S. P. (1983, May 22-25). The online information specialist: Behaviors, philosophies and attitudes. In *ASIS collected papers* (pp. 201-202). Ann Arbor, MI: UMI.

Hawk, W. B., & Wang, P. (1999). Users' interaction with the World Wide Web: Problems and problem solving. In M. M. K. Hlava & L. Woods (Eds.), *Proceedings of the 62nd ASIS Annual Meeting,* (Vol. 36, pp. 256-270). Medford, NJ: Information Today.

Hawkins, D. T., & Wagers, R. (1982). Online bibliographic search strategy development. *Online, 6*(3), 12-19.

Heckhausen, H., & Kuhl, J. (1985). From wishes to action: The dead ends and shortcuts on the long way to action. In M. Frese & J. Sabini (Eds.), *Goal directed behavior: The concept of action in psychology.* Hillsdale, NJ: Lawrence Erlbaum Associates.

Henzinger, M. R., Motwani, R., & Silverstein, C. (2002). Challenge in Web search engines. *ACM SIGIR Forum, 36*(2), 11-22.

Hersh, W., Sacherek, L., & Olson, D. (2002). Observations of searchers: OHSU TREC 2001 interactive track. In E. M. Voorhees & D. K. Harman (Eds.), *The Tenth Text REtrieval Conference, TREC-2001,* (pp. 434-441). Gaithersburg, MD: U.S. Department of Commerce, NIST.

Hert, C. A. (1996). User goals on an online public access catalog. *Journal of the American Society for Information Science, 47*(7), 504-518.

Hert, C. A. (1997). *Understanding information retrieval interaction: Theoretical and practical implications*. Greenwich, CO: Ablex.

Hider, P.M. (2007). Search goal redefinition thru user-system interaction. *Journal of Documentation, 63*(2), 188-203.

Hildreth, C. R. (1997). The use and understanding of keyword searching in a university online catalog. *Information Technology and Libraries, 16*(2), 52-62.

Hirsh, S. G. (1997). How do children find information of different types of tasks? Children's use of the science library catalog. *Library Trends, 45*(4), 725-745.

Hölscher, C., & Strube, G. (2000). Web search behavior of Internet experts and newbies. In *Proceedings of the Ninth International World Wide Web Conference on Computer Networks: The International Journal of Computer and Telecommunications Networking*, (pp. 337-346). Amsterdam, The Netherlands: North-Holland.

Hoppe, H. U., & Schiele, F. (1992). Towards task models for embedded information retrieval. In P. Bauersfeld, J. Bennett, & G. Lynch (Eds.), *Proceedings of the Conference on Human Factors in Computing Systems*, (pp. 173-180). New York: ACM Press.

Howard, H. (1982). Measures that discriminate among online users with different training and experience. *Online Review, 6*(4), 315-326.

Hsieh-Yee, I. (1993). Effects of search experience and subject knowledge on the search tactics of novice and experienced searchers. *Journal of the American Society for Information Science, 44*(3), 161-174.

Ingwersen, P. (1996). Cognitive perspectives of information retrieval interaction: Elements of a cognitive IR theory. *Journal of Documentation, 52*(1), 3-50.

Ingwersen, P., & Järvelin, K. (2005). *The turn: Integration of information seeking and retrieval in context*. Dordrecht, The Netherlands: Springer.

Kelly, D. (2006). Measuring online information seeking context: Part 1: Background and method. *Journal of the American Society for Information Science and Technology, 57*(13), 1729-1739.

Kim, K. S., & Allen, B. (2002). Cognitive and task influence on Web searching behavior. *Journal of the American Society for Information Science and Technology, 53*(2), 109-119.

Kuhlthau, C. (1991). Inside the search process: Information seeking from the user's perspective. *Journal of the American Society for Information Science, 42*(5), 361-371.

Lazonder, A. W., Biemans, H. J. A., & Wopereis, I. G. J. H. (2000). Differences between novice and experienced users in searching information on the World Wide Web. *Journal of the American Society for Information Science and Technology, 51*(6), 576-581.

MacMullin, S. D., & Taylor, R. S. (1984). Problem dimensions and information traits. *The Information Society, 3*(1), 91-111.

Marchionini, G. (1995). *Information-seeking in electronic environments*. Cambridge, U.K.: Cambridge University Press.

Marchionini, G., Dwiggins, S., Katz, A., & Lin, X. (1993). Information seeking in full-text end-user-oriented search-systems –the roles of domain and search expertise. *Library and Information Science Research, 15*(1), 35-69.

Markey, K., & Atherton, P. (1978). *ONTAP: Online training and practice manual for ERIC database searchers*. Syracuse, NY: ERIC Clearinghouse on Information Resources.

Mayyappan, N., Foo, S., & Chowdhury, G.G. (2004). Design and evaluation of a task-based digital library for the academic community. *Journal of Documentation, 60*(4), 449-475.

Newell, A., & Simon, A. (1972). *Human problem solving*. Englewood Cliffs, NJ: Prentice Hall.

Oldroyd, B. K., & Citroen, C. L. (1977). Study of strategies used in online searching. *Online Review, 1*(4), 293-310.

Palmquist, R. A., & Kim, K. S. (2000). Cognitive style and online search experience on Web search performance. *Journal of the American Society for Information Science and Technology, 51*(6), 558-567.

Pejtersen, A. M., & Fidel, R. (1998, March). A framework for work-centred evaluation and design: A case study of IR on the Web. In *Paper presented at the MIRA Workshop,* Grenoble. Retrieved January 4, 2008, from http://www.dcs.gla.ac.uk/mira/workshops/grenoble/fp.pdf

Pennanen, M., & Vakkari, P. (2003). Students' conceptual structure, search process and outcome while preparing a research proposal. *Journal of the American Society for Information Science and Technology, 54*(8), 759-770.

Rasmussen, J., Pejtersen, A. M., & Goodstein, L. P. (1994). *Cognitive systems engineering*. New York: John Wiley & Sons.

Rieh, S. Y. (2002). Judgment of information quality and cognitive authority in the Web. *Journal of the American Society for Information Science and Technology, 53*(2), 145-161.

Rose, D. E., & Levinson, D. (2004). Understanding user goals in Web search. In S. I. Feldman, M. Uretsky, M. Najork, & C. E. Wills (Eds.), *Proceedings of the Thirteenth Annual World Wide Web Conference,* (pp. 13-19). New York: ACM Press.

Salton, G., & McGill, M. (1983). *Introduction to modern information retrieval*. New York: McGraw-Hill.

Saracevic, T. (1997). The stratified model of information retrieval interaction: Extension and applications. In C. Schwartz & M. E. Rorvig (Eds.), *Proceedings of the 60th Annual Meeting of the American Society for Information Science,* (Vol. 34, pp. 313-327). Medford, NJ: Information Today.

Schacter, J., Chung, G. K. W. K., & Dorr, A. (1998). Children's Internet searching on complex problems: Performance and process analyses. *Journal of the American Society for Information Science, 49*(9), 840-849.

Schutz, A., & Luckmann, T. (1973). *The structure of the life world.* Evanston, IL: Northwestern University Press.

Shiri, A. A., & Revie, C. (2003). The effects of topic complexity and familiarity on cognitive and physical moves in a thesaurus-enhanced search environment. *Journal of Information Science, 29*(6), 517-526.

Shute, S. J., & Smith, P. J. (1993). Knowledge-based search tactics. *Information Processing and Management, 29*(1), 29-45.

Slone, D. J. (2002). The influence of mental models and goals on search patterns during Web interaction. *Journal of the American Society for Information Science and Technology, 53*(13), 1152-1169.

Soloman, P. (1993). Children's information retrieval behavior: A case analysis of an OPAC. *Journal of the American Society for Information Science, 44*(5), 245-264.

Sonnenwald, D. H. (1999). Perspectives of human information behaviour: Contexts, situations, social networks, and information horizons. In D. K. Allen, & T. D. Wilson (Eds.), *Exploring the Contexts of Information Behaviour: Proceedings of the Second International Conference on Research in Information Needs, Seeking and Use in Different Contexts,* (pp. 176-190). London: Taylor Graham.

Suchman, L. A. (1987). *Plans and situated actions: The problems of human-machine communication.* Cambridge University Press.

Sutcliffe, A. G., Ennis, M., & Watkinson, S. J. (2000). Empirical studies of end-user information searching. *Journal of the American Society for Information Science and Technology, 51*(13), 1211-1231.

Toms, E. G., Kopak, R. W., Bartlett, J., & Freund, L. (2002). Selecting vs. describing: A preliminary analysis of the efficacy of categories in exploring the Web. In E. M. Voorhees & D. K. Harman (Eds.), *The Tenth Text REtrieval Conference, TREC-2001,* (pp. 653-662). Gaithersburg, MD: U.S. Department of Commerce, NIST.

Vakkari, P. (2000a). Cognition and changes of search terms and tactics during task performance: A longitudinal study. In *Proceedings of the RIAO 2000 Conference,* (pp. 894-907). Paris: CID.

Vakkari, P. (2000b). Relevance and contributory information types of searched documents in task performance. In N. J. Belkin, P. Ingwersen, & M.-K. Leong (Eds.), *Proceedings of the 23rd Annual International ACM SIGIR Conference on Research and Development in Information Retrieval,* (pp. 2-9). New York: ACM Press.

Vakkari, P. (2001). A theory of the task-based information retrieval process. *Journal of Documentation, 57*(1), 44-60.

Vakkari, P. (2003). Task-based information searching. *Annual Review of Information Science and Technology, 37*, 413-464.

Vakkari, P., & Hakala, N. (2000). Changes in relevance criteria and problem stages in task performance. *Journal of Documentation, 56*(5), 540-562.

Vakkari, P., Pennanen, M., & Serola, S. (2003). Changes of search terms and tactics while writing a research proposal. *Information Processing and Management, 39*(3), 445-463.

van Rijsbergen, C. J. (1979). *Information retrieval* (2nd ed.). London: Butterworths.

Vera, A. H., & Simon, H. A. (1993). Situated action—a symbolic interpretation. *Cognitive Science, 17*(1), 7-48.

Vicente, K. J. (1999). *Cognitive work analysis: Toward safe, productive, and healthy computer-based work.* Mahwah, NJ: Lawrence Erbaum Associates.

Wang, P., Hawk, W. B., & Tenopir, C. (2000). Users' Interaction with World Wide Web resources: An exploratory study using a holistic approach. *Information Processing and Management, 36*(2), 229-251.

Wildemuth, B. M., & O'Neill, A. L. (1995). The "known" in known-item searches: A pilot study. *College and Research Libraries, 56*(3), 265-281.

Wood, F., Ford, N., Miller, D., Sobczyk, G., & Duffin, R. (1996). Information skills, searching behavior and cognitive styles for student centered learning: A computer assisted learning approach. *Journal of Information Science, 22*(2), 79-92.

Xie, H. (2000). Shifts of interactive intentions and information-seeking strategies in interactive information retrieval. *Journal of the American Society for Information Science and Technology, 51*(9), 841-857.

Xie, H. (2002). Patterns between interactive intentions and information-seeking strategies. *Information Processing and Management, 38*(1), 55-77.

Xie, H. (2003). Supporting ease-of-use and user control: Desired features and structure of Web-based online IR systems. *Information Processing and Management, 39*(6), 899-922.

Xie, H. (2006). Understanding human-work domain interaction: Implications for the design of a corporate digital library. *Journal of the American Society for Information Science and Technology, 57*(1), 128-143.

Xie, H., & Cool, C. (2000). Ease-of-use vs. user control: An evaluation of Web and nonWeb interfaces of online databases. *Online Information Review, 24*(2), 102-115.

Yu, H., & Young, M. (2004). The impact of Web search engine on subject searching in OPAC. *Information Technology and Libraries, 23*(4), 168-180.

Yuan, W. (1997). End-user searching behavior in information retrieval: A longitudinal study. *Journal of the American Society for Information Science, 48*(3), 218-234.

Chapter IX

Illustration and Validation of the Interactive IR Framework

Overview of the Empirical Study

Objective of the Study

In order to illustrate and validate the planned-situational interactive IR model, I conducted an empirical study. This study was a pilot of a large-scale study, discussed in the summary of this chapter, that focuses on the investigation of how people seek and retrieve information in their research proposal writing process. The objective of the study is particularly concerned with whether multiple information-seeking strategies were applied and shifts in information-seeking strategies occurred in users' information-seeking and -retrieving process. This study addressed the following research questions:

1.   What are users' levels of goals/tasks and their representation?
2.   What are users' personal information infrastructures?

3.   What is the social-organizational context for users' information seeking and retrieving?

4.   What types of IR systems do users access and what types of influences do these systems have?

5.   What are the types of information-seeking strategies employed by users?

6.   Do users shift their current search goals and information-seeking strategies in the information-seeking and -retrieving process? If yes, how?

7.   What are the factors that lead to different levels and types of shifts?

This research helps us understand the nature of information seeking and retrieving, in particular, the nature of interactive IR. Applying emprical data to examine the major components of the planned-situational interactive IR model and their interactions effectively assists us to validate and illustrate this model. The major contribution of this study is that it investigates users' dynamic information-seeking processes related to their work and search tasks instead of a snapshot of an information-seeking activity. The emprical data further enrich and enhance the interactive IR framework. In addition to this study, I also incorporate some related studies to validate and ilustrate the planned-situational interactive IR model.

Methodology

Twenty-one subjects were recruited from the School of Information Studies at the University of Wisconsin-Milwaukee (UWM). These subjects were students in a class in which they were required to write a research proposal as a final project. The data collection process lasts about a semester (about three months). The data were collected from the following means:

1.   The subjects were instructed to fill out a prequestionnaire that consisted of their demographic information and their past experiences in information seeking and retrieving.

2.   The subjects were instructed to keep a diary of the information-seeking and -retrieving process for writing their research proposals. Each diary records the following information: research proposal topic, search topic, the time spent on each of the information resources, his/her interaction with each of the information resources, types of problems encountered, how he/she solved the problems, results of his/her interactions, his/her next steps, and so forth.

3.   After the subjects were done with information seeking and retrieving, they were instructed to fill in the postquestionnaire, which included the changes or lack of changes in their seach topics and associated reasons; their assessment

of each information resource in terms of accessibility, frequency of use, and satisfaction level; and the types of problems they encountered and how they solved the problems. Most important, they were also asked to provide information related to their application of different types of information-seeking strategies and associated reasons in their information-seeking and -retrieving process for writing their research proposals.

In this study, real users with real problems were employed. Moreover, data were collected in real settings. The information-seeking and -retrieal process was captured in diaries by the subjects themselves. This is one of the effective ways to capture users' behaviors in the information-seeking and -retrieving process unobtrusivley. Therefore, the study offers invaluable information for researchers to understand the interactions between users and different types of IR systems and other types of information resources.

Both qualitative and quantitative data collected from the pre- and post-questionnaires and from the diaries were analyzed. Quantitative data were tallied and analyzed for descriptive analysis. Qualitative data were analyzed by using open coding (Strauss & Corbin, 1990), which is the process of breaking down, examining, comparing, conceptualizing, and categorizing. The examples of coding categories and their relationships are discussed in the following sections.

Levels of User Goals and Tasks and their Representation

The author developed four levels of hierarchical goals based on Daniels' (1986) classification of goals (long-term goals, leading search goals, current search goals, and interactive intentions). This hierarchical user goal structure has been applied and verified in several empirical studies. In her study of Web searching in the home environment, Rieh (2004) applied the user goal structure and found that users were engaged in all four levels of goals: long-term goals (gain knowledge, problem solving, communication, curiosity, entertainment, professional achievement, and help other people), leading search goals (prepare for an event, prepare for online class, plan for vacation, buy house goods, keep up with news, share information with others, etc.), current search goals (look for papers, look for recipes, look for artists, look at stocks, check for available flights, etc.), and interactive intentions (locate, find, read, view, compare, verify, evaluate, etc.). She concluded that users at home sought for diverse goals than people in work places and in libraries.

These four levels of goals were also verified in Lin and Belkin's (2005) experiment. Accordingly, personal interests are one example of longterm goals. Goals to which a searcher's information problem derives from is an example of a leading search goal. Four types of goals (formulating questions, answering questions, monitoring the pools of questions, and fictionalizing questions) in their original model of Multiple Information Seeking Episode (MISE) are representations of current search goals. Interactive intentions (such as identifying, learning, etc.) account for factors in the dimensions of problematic situations, information problems, and the information-seeking process. In this study, user goals and tasks were rather straightforward. The subjects' leading search goal or work task was to write a research proposal. Their current search goal or search task varied depending on each subject and the stages in his or her research process. The longterm goal for all of them was to pursue a graduate or undergraduate degree.

As discussed in Chapter VIII, dimensions of the work tasks can be categorized as stages of the tasks, timeframe of the task, and nature of the task. In order to write their research proposals, the subjects of this study went through several stages, which can be characterized as prefocus, formulation, and postfocus, as identified by Vakkari and his associates (Pennanen & Vakkari, 2003; Vakkari, 2000a, 2000b, 2001; Vakkari & Hakala, 2000; Vakkari, Pennanen, & Serola, 2003). Compared with the results presented by Vakkari and his associates, the results of this study focus more on the application of multiple information-seeking strategies and shifts in information-seeking strategies at different stages.

In the prefocus stage, subjects mainly tried to identify some information to get started by consulting the instructors of their classes and librarians. In addition, to get started, they tried to identify references from articles that were available to them. They also changed search topics frequently to see whether they could find enough useful information as well as whether they could cognitively engage in these topics for their research proposals. Hence, they frequently shifted their current search goals. At the formation stage, they were pretty much settled with the topics of their research proposals. Accordingly, they searched and browsed their selected search topics in online databases, Web search engines, OPACs, and digital libraries based on their preferences. At the post-focus stage, they used more specific terms, as well as more Boolean operators and advanced features of IR systems. They engaged in more retrieval tactic shifts at this stage. Examples of different levels and types of shifts are presented in the section "Shifts in Current Search Goals and Information-seeking Strategies."

The timeframe of the work task for this study was not urgent compared with other types of tasks, because theoretically the subjects had about 3 months in which to write their research proposals. Most of the subjects started their information seeking at the early stage of research proposal writing (two months before the deadline), and they had sufficient time to look for information. The average subject spent about 278 minutes searching for information; the range was from 40 minutes to 690 minutes.

Some subjects worked on the proposal only 1 month before the deadline, so it was more urgent for them to find related information. It is interesting to note that the two subjects who spent the least time (40 and 50 minutes) started 1 month before the deadline, and the subject who spent the most time (690 minutes) started 3 months before. In addition, the subject who started early also accessed more information resources/IR systems than the two subjects who started later. Because not all subjects record the starting date for their information seeking and -retrieving in their diaries, a more detailed analysis cannot be done in this study.

The nature of work task reveals that writing a research proposal is a complex task in which users needs to engage in genuine decision making, as classified by Byström and Järvelin (1995). At the same time, there were also new tasks, identified by Xie (2006), because these subjects were new in the library and information science field even though some of them had worked on a research paper before. The results echo those reported in Xie's (2006) previous work that more subjects planned for their searches and their plans included more information for the new type of tasks compared with other types of tasks, such as routine and typical tasks. About 12 of 21 subjects stated that they planned to some extent for their information seeking in general; nine of them did not plan. However, all 21 subjects stated that they planned for their information-seeking and -retrieving for this research proposal. In addition, they also tried to identify information for getting started by consulting human resources or from some available items. Examples of identifying strategies are presented in Table 9.5.

As to dimensions of search tasks, they were all self-generated, which is why subjects had more flexibility in shifting their current search goals. However, the domain of the task was defined in library and information science. These subjects were newcomers in the area. Even though they tried to find research topics that they were interested in, they did not have sufficient knowledge to look for the information needed for their research proposals. That is why 14 of 20 subjects changed or modified their research topics. Subjects had to come up with search tasks that fell within the area of library and information science. In terms of the nature of tasks, these subjects mainly tried to find documents for their research proposal with some common characteristics. In that sense, this dimension imposed a similar influence on every subject's information-seeking and -retrieving process.

Personal Information Infrastructure

Not all users in the study were the same. They brought their own domain knowledge, system knowledge, and information retrieval knowledge to their information-seeking and -retrieving process. In addition, in the process, they also exhibited their own cognitive and search styles. The subjects offered their opinions regarding the reasons for their unsuccessful searches in the past (Table 9.1). Lack of topic knowledge, system knowledge, and information retrieval knowledge accounted for 47.6%, 23.3%, and 19% of their unsuccessful searches, respectively. That echoes Marchionini's (1995) statement that users' personal information infrastructures affect their information-seeking process. In Table 9.1, 9.2, 9.3, and 9.4, the number of subjects is 21.

For this study, subjects could choose any topic for the research proposal as long as it was related to library and information science. In that case, they might have some domain knowledge of the topic for which they sought information. Their system knowledge could be reflected in their frequency of system use (Table 9.2). Among different types of electronic IR systems, subjects were most familiar with Web pages and Web search engines, which more than 90% of them either used daily or often. About half of the subjects at least used online databases and OPACs often. They were less familiar with digital libraries. As to information retrieval knowledge, their frequency of information searching and level of success for information searching (Table 9.3 and Table 9.4) revealed that majority of them (85.7%) searched for information daily or often, and 80.9% of them were extremely or somewhat more successful in their searches.

Even though each subject is different, all have one thing in common: Their knowledge structure does have impact on how they seek and retrieve information. In

Table 9.1. Reasons for unsuccessful searches (multiple answers available per subject)

Lack of topic knowledge	Lack of system knowledge	Lack of IR skills	Poor system design	Poor system coverage	Information Overload	Others
47.6%	23.3%	19.0%	23.3%	28.5%	28.5%	28.5%

Table 9.2. Frequency of system use

Types of systems	Never use	Rarely use	Occasionally use	Often use	Use daily
Web pages				14.3%	85.7%
Web search engines			4.8%	23.8%	71.4%
Online databases		14.3%	38.1%	47.6%	
OPACs		14.3%	23.8%	47.6%	14.3%
Digital libraries	38.0%	28.6%	28.6%	4.8%	

Table 9.3. Frequency of searching for information

	Never	Rarely	Occasionally	Often	Daily
Frequency			14.3%	9.5%	76.2%

Table 9.4. Level of success in searching for information

	Not at all	A little	Somewhat	Somewhat more	Extremely
Level of success			19.0%	57.1%	23.8%

discussing typical problems that they encountered during the information-seeking process, some of them expressed their problems as lacking domain knowledge, in particular related to finding the right terms for the search topic. For example, subject 2 stated, "Problems I had involved determining the right search terms to use to find information on my topic. Terms I thought were valid were being utilized to express different concepts. I tried using various terms and attempted to use subject heading lists of keyword searching."

As to system knowledge, unfamiliarity with IR systems is a problem. Subject 15 discussed the problem and its solution: "unfamiliarity in database/page, utilize help." IR knowledge is much more complicated. How to express their information needs, how to formulate queries, and how to specify their searches are the typical problems encountered by users. As subject 3 explained, "Don't know how to articulate my information needs, don't know where to look for information. Don't know how to formulate search query, trial and error." "[the problem is] narrowing search for a particular format. No results cause me to look elsewhere," subject 4 added.

Of course, user knowledge of the domain of the search topic, the IR system, and information retrieval are interrelated. More then half of the subjects had the problem of not finding an appropriate number of relevant results, as stated by subject 1: "My typical problem was not enough literature on my topic." "The typical problems I have are either not getting enough results or getting too many. To solve this, I then go back and use different keywords in my search or sometimes use the thesaurus of the database to refine my search," added 23. A related problem is finding relevant information. Subject 11 complained, "My most common problem is finding information that I think is relevant. The best way to avoid this is to know what I want before I start searching, and to use the thesaurus on databases and OPAC's." Subject 16 echoed, "During the search process, it was difficult to find relevant articles, especially given the ambiguity of the search term (peer to peer/p2p). Eventually, relevant descriptors popped up." These problems can be caused by lacking of different types of knowledge; they can be solved by applying the three types of knowledge together. In order to address these problems, researchers have designed different tools to enhance user knowledge. For example, Bhavnani et al. (2006) developed a domain portal named Strategy Hub to guide novice users to find comprehensive and accurate information in the health care area.

Social-Organizational Context

As subjects of this study were homogenous in their social and cultural backgrounds, the focus is put on the work domain analysis (Fidel & Pejtersen, 2004) stated in chapter 8. Table 9.5 presents dimensions of work domain for this study. The dimensions of work domain identify the goals and constraints, priorities, general functions, work processes, and physical objects of the university, the school, and the course that requires subjects to achieve their work tasks, writing research proposals. In order to write research proposals, they had to look for information. They had to take the following steps in relation to finding relevant information for the research proposal: identify stages of the proposal writing; identify search tasks, look for information from external or internal information resources, evaluate/validate information, and apply relevant information to write the proposal.

The university and the school offer a variety of printed and electronic resources for students. At the same time, they could also access other information resources

Table 9.5. Dimensions of work domain

Dimensions	Descriptions
Goals and constraints	Educate students to be information professionals; need skills to conduct research; need skills to retrieve information; financial limits for the availability of printed and electronic resources; not all students are trained in how to seek and retrieve information.
Priority	Develop human resources; discover and disseminate knowledge; offer a variety of information resources and services; train students to be able to effectively retrieve information and incorporate the information into their works.
General function	Develop curriculum; offer classes; provide printed and electronic resources; purchase and develop technology to facilitate information access.
Work process	Identify stages of a work task; identify a search task, look for information from external or internal information resources; evaluate/validate information; apply relevant information to write a research proposal.
Physical resources	Instructors; librarians; classmates; colleagues; friends; electronic resources; printed materials.

available to them. Moreover, instructors, librarians, their classmates, their colleagues, and their friends were the human resources they could also access and consult. However, not all printed and electronic resources were available to them because the financial limits of the university. In other words, they were limited to the available printed and electronic resources. In addition, not all the students were trained in information seeking and retrieving. Their domain, system, and information retrieval knowledge varied. The interactions between actor and work domain consisted of task activities, decision activities, and strategy activities, which are further discussed in the sections related to task dimensions, plans and situations, information-seeking strategies, and different levels and types of shifts.

IR Systems

In general, OPACs, online databases, Web search engines, and digital libraries are the most popularly accessed electronic IR systems. The subjects in this study used different types of IR systems depending on their tasks. Because this work task was more academically-oriented, online databases were the major choice for them. Just as subject 2 stated, "Depends on information need. For schoolwork I usually use an online database through UWM's library Web site; for personal use, I typically use Google first. I feel with online databases my results will be more academic; with a search engine like Google, I feel I will more likely access the information I'm searching for." "For research, scholarly databases, because they're more in depth and less unwanted junk is recalled. For fast facts, Wiki and Google because they're fast and easy," subject 22 explained. Some of the subjects chose what they were familiar with. Subject 15 said, "Search engines or databases, they're what I'm most familiar with."

The major IR systems that subjects selected for this study included the following: 1) Online databases, mainly online databases subscribed to by UWM, such as Ebscohost, Library Literature & Information Science databases, Web of knowledge, Eric, etc.; 2) Web search engines, such as Google Scholar, etc.; 3) OPACs, such as PatherCat, WorldCat, etc.; 4) Web pages, such as the American Library Association (ALA) site, Online Computer Library Center (OCLC) site, and so forth. Users interacting with IR systems are actually interacting with the cognitive structures of the designers and developers involved in the interface, system, and content-building process, as suggested by Ingwersen and Järvelin (2005).

In this study, the design of IR systems affected users' information-seeking strategies in the following ways: first, the design of overall user interface could lead to more applications of certain strategies and fewer of others. Of course, users had to search for information in their IR process. An alternative approach was to browse to find what they needed. While most of the IR systems have search options, not all of them have browsing functions, in particular, in OPACs, some Web search engines, and online databases. Under these circumstances, the subjects had to create search statements and modify search statements instead of browsing. They did find an alternative way to browse when they could not browse in OPACs. Subject 18 illustrated her browsing strategy: "I browsed the stacks near the call numbers that corresponded to things I found in the catalog. I found several additional materials that way."

Second, the availability or unavailability of certain features suggested whether users could engage in certain strategies. In accessing information, some IR systems offer direct links to help users "find documents like this one." "I linked the authors from the citations to other pertinent articles that they wrote on the subject that I was writing my proposal about," subject 19 described his strategy. However, subject 22 could not apply this strategy because "I didn't find anything in the databases to be able to link to them. Otherwise I would have." Not every IR system offers monitor functions, such as search history. When users used systems that did not have monitor functions, they might not be able to monitor their searches. For example, subject 8 commented, "I've just never used this function of a database. I don't know if it is available to me." Another, subject 7, complained that by monitoring the search herself, she might lose her train of thought: "During my searching, I tend to get distracted and follow links, then maybe go back, maybe not. When I find something I like, I may jot it down or save it to a file. I find that if I try to document my entire string, I lose my train of thought and the momentum of the search."

Third, the design of specific features of IR systems and their availability also affected the effectiveness of the application of certain strategies. The majority of subjects sorted their results. However, they did not use only the sort function offered by IR systems. Instead, they manually sorted their results based on their own criteria. For example, according to subject 1, "I sorted my results by publication type, specifically looking for scholarly journals or peer-reviewed journals." Subject 12 sorted the results based on specific categories for writing the literature review part of the research proposal: "When I was getting ready to write my literature review, I organized the articles that I had based on certain subjects and how they would best answer my research questions." Subject 4 offered more detailed sorting categories: "I separated the results by the points I was attempting to make in the literature review, that is, reading prowess, Harry Potter material, proliferation of genre, etc." Every user had to evaluate his or her search results. However, the existing IR systems did not effectively support this strategy. In general, users checked the title and abstract of an article to determine its relevance and usefulness, but that is not enough. According to subject 2, "In using the abstract, I helped determine the usefulness of items. Often times I could not be sure if an article was useful until I viewed the full text." "I scanned the abstract, but also I scanned the article itself. Sometimes the abstract didn't give me all the information I needed to determine if I could use an article or not," subject 24 agreed.

Fourth, users' experiences in using IR systems also influenced whether they applied and how they applied different types of strategies. Within all the strategies, learning was affected the most. Some of the subjects did not use help because of their past experiences. Subject 2 presented the typical statement: "Don't remember using these types of features, not having much luck with them before...." "I do not use these features too often because of the bad experiences I have had with them in the past," echoed subject 19. Others had concerns with the current Help feature. Subject 9 explained the reason, "Generally trial and error, considered using help feature to find truncation operation, (? Or *), but just tried both. Help feature takes too long to go through."

Fifth, the information objects stored in IR systems that users interacted with in general might have determined the outcome of the current strategy, which, in turn, might have affected their choices of next strategy. After evaluating the results, users decided their next strategy based on the outcome of the evaluation. This study revealed several possible applied strategies following the evaluation strategy: 1) obtain an item(s), part of the item, or specific information about the item if evaluation outcome is successful; 2) access items that share some similar characteristics with the evaluated item(s) by linking to them if the evaluation outcome is successful or partially successful; 3) monitor the search process or learn new knowledge or database/collection content if the outcome of the evaluation is unsuccessful or partially successful; 4) identify information/concepts/term/item/site to create new search statement if the outcome of the evaluation is unsuccessful or partially successful; 5) create new search statement or modify the original search statement if the outcome of the evaluation is unsuccessful or partially successful. Detailed examples of these strategy shifts are further illustrated in section titled "Shifts in Current Search Goals and Information-Seeking Strategies."

Types of Information-Seeking Strategies

This study demonstrates that users do employ multiple information-seeking strategies in their information-seeking process. They engage in a variety of information-seeking strategies, represented by the 12 types of interactive intentions and 11 types of retrieval tactics. Table 9.6 presents the examples derived from the diaries and postquestionnaires of the study that illustrate the 12 types of information-seeking strategies. In these examples, intentions, methods, and entities are illustrated by bold,

Table 9.6. Examples of information-seeking strategies

Identifying is applied in the beginning of the information-seeking and -retrieving process to get started or in the middle of the process to continue finding more information. Subjects of this study employed different types of retrieval tactics in order to achieve identifying intention.

Identifying strategy by employing scanning tactics
Identify information (related to evaluating digital libraries) to get started by *scanning* an item (Power-Point file from a guest speaker of the class) (S7)

Identifying strategy by employing scanning and extracting tactics
Identify information (specific authors and terminologies) to get started by *scanning* a series of personal items (several articles from previous classes) and *extracting* terms and other information (author names) (S24)

Identifying strategy by employing consulting tactics
Identify database(s) to get started by *consulting* a human (via virtual reference of a university library) (S12)

Identifying strategy by employing consulting tactics
Identify metadata of items (title and author of articles) to get started by *consulting* a human (the instructor of the class) (S8)

Identifying strategy by employing tracking tactics
Identify metadata of items (citations of articles) to continue searching by tracking metadata of a specific item (references of an article) (S8)

Learning is an essential strategy when users encounter problems. In order to learn different types of knowledge, the subjects of this study had two options: consult a human or consult a system Help feature and figure things out themselves.
Learning strategy by employing consulting tactics
Learn system knowledge (how to truncate ? or *) by *consulting* system (Help) feature (S9)

Learning strategy by employing trial & error tactics
Learn system knowledge by *trial and error* with different formats of truncation (? or *) (S9)

Learning strategy by employing consulting tactics
Learn domain knowledge (better search terms) by *consulting* system features (thesaurus) (S12)

Learning strategy by employing manipulating tactics
Learn information retrieval skills by *manipulating* formats of terms (teen or teenager and library or librarian) (S14)

Learning strategy by employing scanning tactics
Learn content of a database by *scanning* meta-information of a database (description of Web of Knowledge) (S24)

continued on following page

Table 9.6. continued

Exploring is an alternative strategy for creating search statements, and it is also a supplemental strategy for creating and modifying search statements. In this study, subjects mainly explored items with common characteristics because they had some idea of what they were trying to find when they looked for information.

Exploring strategy by employing scanning tactics
Explore to find <u>items</u> with common characteristics (relevant articles) by *scanning* a series of <u>items</u> (special issue of a journal) (S2)

Explore <u>items</u> with common characteristics (senior and teenagers use Internet) by *scanning* content of <u>sites</u> (Web site) (S5)

Explore <u>items</u> with common characteristics (school library media research) by *scanning* metadata (index) of a <u>site</u> *(*ala.org) (S2)

Explore <u>items</u> with common characteristics (the explosion of fantasy genre, post Harry Potter publications) by *scanning* a section (reading section) of a <u>location</u> (a public library) (S4)

Creating search statements is essential in the information-retrieval process. The nature of the work task determines that the subjects of this study were more likely to look for items with common characteristics; therefore, creating search statement strategies were applied mostly to items with common characteristics in this study. Specifying and consulting are the retrieval tactics associated with creating search statements.

Creating search statement strategy for items with common characteristics by employing consulting tactics
Create search statement for <u>items</u> with common characteristics (whether library use increases academic performance for suburban and urban high school students) by *consulting* a <u>human</u> *(*have a virtual chat with a librarian) (S13)

Creating search statement strategy for items with common characteristics by employing specifying tactics
Create search statement for <u>items</u> with common characteristics by *specifying* a <u>term</u> (self-check machines) (S1)

Creating search statement strategy for a known item by employing specifying tactics
Create search statement for known <u>items</u> (articles cited a specific author) by *specifying* metadata of the <u>items</u> (cited author of the items) (S22)

continued on following page

Table 9.6. continued

Similar to creating a search statement strategy, modifying a search statement strategy was also applied in this study, mostly for items with common characteristics. Manipulating, tracking, and specifying were the major retrieval tactics corresponding to modifying search statements.

Modify search statement strategy for items with common characteristics by employing tracking tactics
Modifying search statement for <u>items</u> with common characteristics by *tracking* meta-information of retrieved <u>items</u> (descriptor: libraries—automation and checkout) (S1)

Modify search statement strategy for items with common characteristics by employing manipulating tactics
Modify search statement for <u>items</u> with common characteristics by *manipulating* <u>terms</u> of search statements (from "libraries—automation and checkout" to "libraries—automation and self-check") (S1)

Modify search statement for <u>items</u> with common characteristics (on whether international collaboration and global librarianship were published in US journals) by *manipulating* <u>terms</u> of search statements (different combinations of the terms "international," "global," and "librarian") (S18)

Modify search statement for <u>items</u> with common characteristics (on whether international collaboration and global librarianship were published in US journals) by *manipulating* <u>formats</u> of search statements (different combinations of formats of the terms "international," "global," and "librarian") (S18)

Modify search statement strategy for items with common characteristics by employing specifying tactics
Modify search statement for <u>items</u> with common characteristics (urban high school students and their use of libraries) by *specifying* meta-information of retrieved <u>items</u> (specify publication date from 2000-2007) (S13)

Although it is important to monitor the search process, only one subject checked search history. Many of them had to manually monitor the process by reviewing their own notes of what they had done because not all IR systems have that feature. Surveying tactics were mainly applied for monitoring search process and status.
Monitoring strategy by employing surveying tactics
Monitor search <u>process</u> (history of search queries) by *surveying* search history of the <u>process</u> (check the saved search history function in a database) (S24)

Monitor search <u>process</u> and <u>status</u> (where I have been and what I have done) by *surveying* search history of <u>process</u> and current <u>status</u> (review my notes for each step of searching) (S12)

Organizing is an effective approach for users to sort their retrieved results. Existing IR systems only offer a few options for users to organize their results. Subjects had to manually organize the results based on the themes and usefulness of the articles. Manipulating tactics were employed to organize retrieved items.
Organizing strategy by employing manipulating tactics
Organize retrieved <u>items</u> by *manipulating* retrieved <u>items</u> based on publication date (S9)
Organize retrieved <u>items</u> by *manipulating* retrieved <u>items</u> based on whether they are scholarly journals or peer-reviewed journals (S1)
Organize retrieved <u>items</u> by *manipulating* retrieved <u>items</u> based on the usefulness of the articles (S19)

Organize retrieved <u>items</u> by *manipulating* retrieved <u>items</u> based on different themes of the literature review for the research proposal (S4)

continued on following page

Table 9.6. continued

Accessing is essential for users to get to the actual information they need. In this study, subjects either used the system feature to link to an electronic item if it was available or tried to gain access to an item(s) at a physical location. Subjects tried to access a specific item or a location by employing track-ing tactics.

Accessing strategy by employing tracking tactics

Access a specific <u>item</u> by *tracking* meta-information of the <u>item</u> (link to the full text of an article) (S2)

Accessing an <u>area/location</u> (journal section of a library) by *tracking* meta-information of an <u>area/loca-tion</u> (call number starting with Z) (S18)

Every retrieved item needs to be evaluated for its usefulness or relevance, but existing IR systems do not facilitate the evaluation process. In this study, subjects spent quite some time assessing each item, mainly by scanning the meta-information of an article, such as title, author, abstract, and so forth. It seems that their work tasks determined whether they mainly looked for scholarly articles for the litera-ture review part of the research proposal; therefore, the usefulness of the articles is the major criteria that they applied to evaluate retrieved items. Of course, when they tried to assess whether a specific item is what they were looking for, they also had to assess the correctness of the item. Scanning tactics played a major role in evaluating the usefulness and correctness of items.

Evaluating strategy by employing scanning tactics

Evaluate usefulness of <u>items</u> by *scanning* meta-information of <u>items</u> (scan the titles and abstracts of articles) (S8)

Evaluate usefulness of <u>items</u> by *scanning* meta-information of <u>items</u> (look at the titles, subject terms, abstract, and date of publication of articles) (S9)

Evaluate usefulness of <u>items</u> by *scanning* the whole <u>items</u> (view the full text of articles) (S2)

Evaluating strategy by employing specifying and scanning tactics

Evaluate correctness of an <u>item</u> (citation of an article) by *specifying* and *scanning* the meta-informa-tion of the <u>item</u> (find and check the author and title of the article) (S24)

Keeping records assists users in accessing information. The meta-information of items was what subjects tried to keep records of. Acquiring and extracting were the retrieval tactics used for keeping records.

Keeping records strategy by employing acquiring tactics

Keep records of meta-information of an <u>item</u> by *acquiring* meta-information of the <u>item</u> (e-mail myself the citation) (S9)

Keep records of meta-information of a <u>site</u> (containing the article needed) by *acquiring* (Bookmark) meta-information of a <u>site</u> (add the URL to the favorite folder) (S3)

Keeping records strategy by employing extracting and acquiring tactics

Keep records of meta-information of an <u>item</u> by *extracting* and *acquiring* meta-information of an <u>item</u> (identify and write down the citation information) (S13)

Keep records of meta-information of a <u>site</u> by *extracting* and *acquiring* meta-information of the <u>site</u> (identify and write down the URL of the site) (S7)

continued on following page

Table 9.6. continued

When users find what they are looking for, they need to obtain specific information, part of the item, or a whole item for further reading or use. E-mailing, saving/downloading, writing down, printing, and copying were the most popularly applied acquiring methods for subjects of this study to obtain information.

Obtaining strategy by employing acquiring tactics

Obtain specific <u>information</u> (relevant information for literature review of the research proposal) by a*cquiring (write down)* specific <u>information</u> (notes) (S19)

Obtain a series of <u>items</u> (articles) by *acquiring (save and print)* a series of <u>items</u> (the articles) (S2)

Obtain an <u>item</u> (an article) by *acquiring (copy)* the <u>item</u> (the article) (S8)

Obtain a series of <u>items</u> (articles) by *acquiring (copy)* a series of <u>items</u> (the articles) (S18)

Obtain an <u>item</u> (an article) by *acquiring (e-mail to myself)* the <u>item</u> (the article) (S23)

In this study, disseminating strategies were mainly applied when subjects worked as a group on the research proposal. Subjects used the e-mail system as the dissemination tool. As nobody sent any articles to the whole class, therefore, specifying the listerve of the group was not applied in this study.

Disseminating strategy by employing specifying tactics

Disseminate <u>items</u> (articles) to members of a group by *specifying* e-mail addresses of two <u>people</u> (S9)

italics, and underlining, respectively. Other researchers also identify different types of information-seeking strategies. For example, after investigating user behavior in the thesaurus-enhanced systems, Blocks, Cunliffe, and Tudhope (2006) described a model of information searching in controlled vocabulary enhanced systems which illustrates the basic search process. The search process starts from identifying concepts via free text terms, mapping them to controlled terms, constructing a query, executing the query and evaluating the results. These steps match some of the major interactive intentions identified from this study. However, this model concentrates on the query formulation process without considering other interactive intentions, such as learning, accessing, organizing, and so forth.

Dimensions of Plans and Situations

Dimensions of Plans

A plan is a user's arrangement for completing a task. It goes beyond the fixed actions for a desired goal. Users do have plans for their information seeking and retrieving even though not all of them are aware of their plans. In this study, subjects were asked about their plans for information seeking and retrieving for their research proposals. Based on the responses, their plans can be divided into the following categories. (1) The majority of their plans focused on the information resources that they would access. Subject 8 described her plan: "I am going to search card catalog and library/information science-related databases for information related to my proposal. I will also use works cited from sources I find useful in order to find more related resources." (2) Some of the plans also included the order of the information resources that they planned to use. Subject 18 further listed the steps taken to access different types of resources: "(a) online research, databases, (b) catalog search and shelf browsing, (c) reading, (d) asking people (informants) questions/ interviews, (e) information synthesis, new facets/questions/ideas to research, and back to a." (3) Some of their plans consisted of strategies they would apply. Here is subject 3's strategy: "Start general, see what is interesting, focus my topic, formulate hypothesis." "My plan is to use as many information-seeking strategies as possible. Start with the ones that I know and then branch out. Seek help when necessary," said subject 19 in discussing his plan. (4) The plans of several subjects even consisted of their arrangements for changing original search topics. "I'm going to look into a topic I'm interested in, first looking on the open Web and then for databases and libraries. After a lot of this, I'll change my topic at the last minute," said subject 20 about predicting his research process. To sum up: users' plans provided the answers for the following questions discussed in Chapter VIII: (1) what to do first, and (2) How to achieve the goal/task? Interestingly, the subjects of this study did not offer explicit answers about when to stop even though, consciously and unconsciously, they had their plan.

This study did not specifically explore what led to a plan. However, this study indicates that levels of user goals/tasks, users' personal information infrastructure, and social-organizational context do affect the formation of plans. Comparing the subjects' general plans for information seeking and retrieving with their plans for looking for information for research proposal writing, the author found that latter ones are more specific than the former ones. For example, here is a general plan for subject 2: "This typically depends on the type of information I am searching for. If my search is academic, I am more likely to plan, at least mentally, the databases or resources I intend to search. I also have an idea of the terms or limiters I may wish to use. Often with personal searches, it is more in-the-moment searches that are unplanned or unexpected queries that I search." Another interesting finding is that even though nine of the subjects stated they did not plan for general situations, everyone had their plans for their information seeking and retrieving for their research proposals. At the same time, their personal information infrastructure influenced their plans mainly by the resources they planned to use and strategies they planned to apply. Of course, social-organizational context also affects their plans because many of them intended to start with UWM library catalogues and online databases available at UWM.

Dimensions of Situations

A situation is a user's perception of a specific moment based on his/her evaluation of his/her interaction with an IR system and his/her plan in the context of interactive IR. The types of situations were mainly identified from the subject's diaries and postquestionnaires. Their situations were directed by the user-system interactions within the social and organizational context. Users have to assess their levels of goals and tasks, and then apply their own personal information infrastructure to deal with different types of situations. Detailed discussion of the planned and situational factors that define the situations is presented in the section "Factors Affecting Shifts in Current Search Goals/Search Tasks and Information-seeking Strategies."

Three types of situations emerged from this study that validated the types of situations presented in the planned-situational model: planned situation, problematic situation, and disruptive situation. In routine situations, subjects could handle the situations by applying their habitual knowledge. Routine situations determined the planned shifts in current search goals and interactive intentions. In problematic situations, subjects had to rearrange their existing knowledge or apply new knowledge to clarify their situations. Problematic situations led to alternative shifts in current search goals and assisted and alternative shifts in interactive intentions as well as different types of retrieval tactic shifts. In disruptive situations, subjects were distracted by something interesting to them in the process of achieving their current search goals. Disruptive situations were mainly responsible for the opportunistic shifts in current search goals and interactive intentions. The examples of how subjects shifted at different levels and different types are discussed in detail in the section "Shifts in Current Search Goals and Information-seeking Strategies."

It is interesting to note that plans and situations are intertwined with each other. Different users have different plans for different types of situations. That is why a user's situation is also defined by his/her plan. At the same time, to what extent a user has to change his/her plan is also determined by the situation that he/she encounters. Based on a quasi-experiment, Ng (2002) found that the degree of plan deviation decreased along with change from problematic to nonproblematic situation.

Shifts in Current Search Goals and Information-Seeking Strategies

Types of Current Search Goal Shifts

As stated in the previous chapter, users' long term goals and leading search goals/ work tasks generally don't change; their current search goals/search tasks do change as the results of their interaction with different types of IR systems and the social-organizational context. Of course, changes of current search goals depend on how leading search goals/work tasks are defined. In this study, the leading search goal/work task for the subject was to write a research proposal on library and information science. In that sense, if a subject changed his/her search topics, as long as these topics were within the coverage of library and information science, he/she still did not change the work task. Instead, he/she changed the current search goals/search tasks. However, users might change or modify their work tasks in their information-searching process. Pharo (2004), in an empirical study, reported that examples of change of parts of work-task goals were found because of the lack of relevant resources. The current study validated the two types of shifts in current search goals/search tasks: alternative shift and opportunistic shift. Within the 19 responses, 13 of the subjects made changes to their original current search goals. Only six of them did not make changes to their current search goals during their information-seeking and -retrieving process.

Alternative shifts occurred when subjects had problems finding enough useful information on the topic or when they encountered problematic situations. These types of shifts accounted for the majority of current search goal shifts in this study. For example, subject 8 started with searching for disabilities and library services. Then she and her group members each explored different ideas, such as how the Patriot Act affects library services, in particular, censorship and libraries, and so forth. While they could find some general information related to these topics, they could not find specific information related to their topics. In other words, there was not enough information to be found for the literature review part of the proposal. Based on their interests, they decided to come up with an alternative current search goal/search task: services for immigrants in public libraries.

Subject 20 also changed his current search goal/search task for the same reason, lack of information. He first tried to find information related to computer use in public libraries, in particular, monitoring techniques in relation to library size. But many relevant retrieved results were not full-text. As it was close to the final submission date, he was not willing to go with the search task because he was unlikely to use interlibrary loan services. Then he got an idea for a new topic from a different class. He searched for information related to benchmarks and ratings in strategic planning for libraries in several online databases, a Web search engine, and the ALA Web site, and he found enough related information.

Some of the alternative shifts are interrelated in terms of their topics for the search tasks. Subject 13 started from the relationship between frequency of library use and students' performance at school. She tried her searches in a couple of databases available at UWM, but her searches only led to a number of book reviews instead of articles and research studies. The results she came up with had more to do with librarians in urban areas than students' library use. She also found some articles related to reading performance. Then she chatted with a librarian from a university library via virtual chat. Still she did not obtain the information for her original search task. Then she changed the search task to why urban high school student use or do not use libraries and possible ways to attract them to the library. After searching Google and several online databases, she found what she was looking for.

Opportunistic shifts occurred when subjects found something interesting in the process of achieving their original current search goals/search tasks. At that time, they encountered disruptive situations. Subject 11 was initially interested in finding information regarding visually impaired users' use of OPACs. She searched several online databases and e-mailed librarians for the blind for more information. However, when she reviewed the retrieved documents and information provided by the librarians, she found that visually impaired users don't use OPACs. At the same time, she did find articles related to the information seeking of visually impaired users quite interesting. Therefore, she shifted her original search task to information seeking of visually impaired users. Strictly speaking, this is a combination of opportunistic and alternative shift, because the retrieved results simultaneously forced the subject to change and offered her an opportunity for the new search task.

Planned shifts occurred when subjects did not actually shift their search tasks; instead, they modified their original search tasks. These shifts occur as part of the plan. Two types of planned shifts were derived from the data: clarified shift and supplement shift.

Clarified shift refers to a shift that narrows down the original search task. It is part of the plan that users have in mind. They normally start with a broad search task, and then narrow it down in the search process. Subject 3 narrowed down her topic from museums, to something with museums, and finally to how digital libraries of museums affect museum attendance. When she started talking to the instructor of the class to get advice, she intended to narrow down the topic from museums to something on museums. After having a couple of ideas, she searched the Library and Information Science and Technology Abstract available on the UWM site. Reviewing the search results, she decided to narrow down her search task to digital libraries in museums and how they affect museum attendance. Then she searched and explored more online databases for this modified search task.

Supplement shift refers to a shift to offer more information for the original search tasks. For example, subject 15 started with searching for information on prison libraries and censorship from a variety of online databases. In the process of reviewing the retrieved results, she found that access to information went hand in hand with the topic of censorship in prison. In addition, she thought that adding this new aspect would help deepen her research. That new aspect was added to the search task. These two types of planned shifts in current search goal can be accounted for by the two types of goal change identified by Hider (2006): goal clarification and new information. In the clarified shift, the information objects that the subject interacted with assisted her in clarifying her current search goal. In the supplemented shift, new information derived from user-system interactions helped the subject to search for new information.

Types of Interactive Intention Shifts

In order to achieve their current search goals, users have to shift their information-seeking strategies, which consist of shifts at two levels: types of interactive intention shifts and types of retrieval tactic shifts. As stated in Chapter VIII, there are four types of interactive intention shifts. Type I interactive intention shifts are planned shifts in routine situations. Users have to fulfill multiple interactive intentions in order to accomplish their current search tasks. The results of this study demonstrated that planned shifts were the most frequently occurring shifts. In general, users might go through the following search process: "identifying," "creating search statements," "modifying search statements," "keeping records," "accessing," "organizing," "evaluating," "obtaining," and "disseminating." However, there are changes or omissions of some of the steps for a variety of reasons. For example, subject 15 searched prison libraries and censorship in Library Literature & Information Science database. After the search, she accessed the 280 results. She did not organize the results because the database offered its default organization (sort by publication date). After displaying the results, she started to evaluate the usefulness of these articles by browsing them. In the above example, accessing items with common characteristics are the planned shifts for creating a search statement; evaluating items with common characteristics is the planned shift for accessing items with common characteristics. Organizing intention was omitted.

Type II interactive intention shifts (opportunistic shifts) occur when users see something serendipitously in disruptive situations. They then temporarily move from their current interactive intentions. Because of the limitation of diaries, the subjects in this study did not record anything that was not related to their research proposal. Therefore, the author could not find examples of strictly speaking opportunistic shifts. The diary data did reveal some of the opportunistic shifts that were related to their original search topics. For example, in evaluating the retrieved results on urban high school student use of the library, subject 13 found that the digital divide is an interesting issue. She started to explore the issue of the digital divide and then continued to evaluate those retrieved articles for their usefulness for her research proposal. Sometimes the opportunistic shifts in interactive intentions might also lead to the opportunistic shifts in current search goals. In the example discussed concerning the opportunistic shift of current search goals, subject 11 first shifted her interactive intentions from evaluating to exploring. When she found that the new topic was more interesting, she shifted her current search goals.

Type III interactive intention shifts (assisted shifts) occur when new interactive intentions are introduced to assist users to achieve their original interactive intentions. These shifts happen when users encounter problematic situations. "Learning" is the key interactive intention for assisted shifts, because users need help at that time. For example, in the process of creating search statements, subject 9 did not know how to truncate in ERIC. She tried both ways to learn how to create search statements by using the proper truncation symbols: trial and error and check Help features. In this example, she tried to learn system knowledge (truncation symbol) by trial and error and consulting the Help feature of the online database. That helped her create search statements afterwards. Subject 24 intended to search archives and information retrieval in one of the library and information science databases, but the search did not yield any relevant results. He had to browse the subject heading listings to find "information storage & retrieval systems—Archival material" as a usable subject heading. In this case, learning domain knowledge and system knowledge are the assisted shifts for modifying search statements.

Type IV interactive intention shifts (alternative shifts) occur when users try to make up their original interactive intentions under problematic situations. "Modifying search statements" can be the alternative shifts in "creating search statements" when users encounter problems. For example, in searching Google, subject 1 first created the search statement "resources used by teachers," but no relevant results were found. Then she tried "teacher resources actually used," and still no luck. Finally she had to modify her search statement to "Wisconsin education," then she found what she needed. Of course, if a user plans to modify search statements and knows how to proceed, then these shifts can be planned shifts. "Exploring" is also a frequently occurring alternative shift for "creating searching statements" or "modifying search statements." For example, after searching for information related to "young adult" and research with different variations of the terms, subject 2 found too many results in online databases and they were not relevant. She decided to browse subject headings instead of searching for keywords in an OPAC, and she found a couple of useful sources.

Types of Retrieval Tactic Shifts

Four types of shifts are involved in retrieval tactic shifts: change of methods, change of entities, change of attributes, and change of both methods and entities. The outcome of the original retrieval tactics, in particular partially successful or unsuccessful outcomes, mainly affects the shifts in retrieval tactics. In method shifts, users change their methods in the process of achieving their current interactive intentions. In the example of the assisted shift in interactive intentions discussed above, subject 9 tried to learn how to use truncation for creating a search statement by trial and error and by consulting the Help feature of an online database. In this example, "consulting" a Help feature is a shift in method for a "trial and error" system feature. "Consulting" is an alternative method for "trial and error" in this case.

In entity shifts, users change the entities of their retrieval tactics in order to accomplish their current interactive intentions. In this type of shift, users might keep the same method. In this study, subject 18, in the process of modifying a search statement for items with common characteristics (on the issue of whether international collaboration and global librarianship were published in US journals), changed from manipulating terms of search statements (different meaning of "international," "global," "librarian") to manipulating formats of search statements (different formats of "international," "global," "librarian"). In this case, "formats" is an alterative entity for "terms" of search statements in modifying search statements.

In attribute shifts, users change the attributes in order to achieve their current interactive intentions. They might keep the same method and same entity in their attribute shifts. For example, subject 24 first scanned meta-information (abstract) of an item (an article) in evaluating the usefulness of the item. However, he was not sure whether the article was useful because the abstract did not give him all the information he needed to determine whether he could use the article. Therefore, he also scanned the whole item. In this example, "whole" is a supplemental attribute for the "meta-information" of an item in evaluating the usefulness of the item.

In method-entity shifts, users change both methods and entities in order to fulfill their current interactive intentions. For example, subject 1 intended to modify her search statement for items with common characteristics by tracking the meta-information of retrieved results (descriptor: libraries—automation and checkout), but she did not find enough useful information. Then she modified her search statement for items with common characteristics by manipulating search terms (from "libraries—automation and checkout" to "libraries—automation and self-check"). In this example, "manipulating search terms" is a supplemental shift for "tracking meta-information of retrieved results."

One thing to be noted for this study is that the subjects conducted successive searches for their research proposals because this project lasted several months. In this respect, the current study echoes that of Spink, Wilson, Ford, Foster, and Ellis (2002), who also observed that users shifted their information-seeking strategies during and between their successive searches.

Factors Affecting Shifts in Current Search Goals/ Search Tasks and Information-Seeking Strategies

Types of shifts in current search goals, interactive intentions, and retrieval tactics are influenced by both planned and situational aspects, as discussed in Chapter VIII. This study offers specific examples to illustrate how planned and situational aspects lead to different types of shifts. For ease of understanding, the author discusses the planned and situational aspects based on the examples offered in the above sections.

Planned Aspects

Levels of user goals and dimensions of work tasks and search tasks are the leading planned aspects that affect different types of shifts. Within levels of user goals, leading search goals normally do not change, but they do have impact on shifts in current search goals because, after all, the achievement of current search goals is to fulfill leading search goals. Leading search goals determine whether shifts in current search goals are acceptable. No doubt, planned shifts in current search goals are within the scope of the leading search goals. Leading search goals mainly define the range of alternative shifts in current search goals. When subject 8 could not find enough useful information regarding disabilities and library services, and how the Patriot Act affects library services, she had to make an alternative shift in search task (find information related to services for immigrants in public library) which had to be related to library and information science as required for the research proposal. The influence of user goals on search pattern was also detected by Slone (2002, 2003). The results of her study indicated that users who sought for educational goals were more motivated, they accessed every search tool available, and they were more persistent, while users who sought for personal use goals applied few search approaches, and it was easy for them to quit.

As to dimension of tasks, changes of current search goals in general occur in their early stages when users still are exploring the potential topics of the research proposal. Changes of current search goals are also related to the timeframe of the task. The subjects in this study had about 3 months to prepare for their research proposal, and most of them started their searching for information in early March and early April, with an average of 278 minutes spent on finding useful information. They had more time to survey different topics of the search task. Their academic-oriented task determined that they needed to collect scholarly articles, which made it difficult for them to obtain useful information. That also led to more alternative shifts in current search goals.

Users' personal information infrastructure also plays a key role in determining shifts in current search goals, in particular, their personal interest and domain knowledge. In the examples of shifts in current search goals, subjects' personal interests and domain knowledge determined what new topics they chose to select. Even in planned shifts, they selected the topics they were interested in narrowing down or adding. Subject 3 narrowed down the topic from "museum" to "how digital libraries affect museum attendance," which was codetermined by the information that she interacted with and her personal interest and knowledge of the topic. In addition, subjects' lack of system and information retrieval knowledge led to alternative shifts in current search goals because of their failure to find useful information,

This study indicates that users' personal information infrastructure is the main planned aspect of shifts in interactive intentions and retrieval tactics. Specifically, subjects' information retrieval knowledge and system knowledge defined assisted shifts and alternative shifts. In the four examples of assisted shifts and alternative shifts in interactive intentions, system knowledge and information retrieval knowledge affected the shifts in two ways. On the one hand, the subjects' lack of knowledge mainly or partially led to the problematic situations (subject 9 unable to truncate, subject 2 dealing with too many results, and subject 24 and subject 1 unable to find useful information). On the other hand, their knowledge, as well as their cognitive styles, also guided them to take the assisted or alternative shifts (introducing "learning" by subject 9, "modifying search statements" by subject 1, and "exploring" by subject 24 and subject 2). In the example of subject 24, domain knowledge also assisted him to select "information storage & retrieval system—Archival material" as a subject heading.

Comparatively speaking, the subjects' information retrieval skills and their cognitive styles were mainly responsible for the shifts in retrieval tactics, which included shifts in methods, entities, attributes, and methods-entities. In all the examples of retrieval tactic shifts, the subjects' information retrieval skills guided them to the shifts, for example, from trial and error to consulting in method shift (S9), from terms to formats in entities shifts (S18), from meta-information to whole (S24), and from tracking retrieved results to manipulating search terms (S1).

Situational Aspects

The outcomes of user-system interactions are the major situational aspects for different types of shifts in current search goals, interactive intentions, and retrieval tactics. To be more specific, the outcomes of interactions are the basis for these types of shifts. The outcomes of interactions can be classified into three categories: successful, partially successful, and unsuccessful. In general, successful outcomes lead to planned shifts in interactive intentions. For example, when subject 15 successfully created a search statement, she accessed the retrieved results. After she successfully accessed the retrieved results, she started to evaluate each retrieved item.

Partially successful outcomes normally account for the majority of shifts in retrieval tactics. For example, in entity shifts, subject 18 changed from manipulating terms to manipulating formats of search statements because she only found some information by applying the former tactic. In attribute shifts, subject 24 changed from scanning the meta-information of an item to a whole item because she was not sure of the usefulness of the article. In a method-entity shift, subject 1 used manipulating search terms as a supplemental shift for tracking the meta-information of retrieved results because she did not find enough information.

Unsuccessful outcomes are the driving force for users to choose alternative shifts in current search goals, assisted and alternative shifts in interactive intentions, and some of the retrieval tactic shifts. In the examples of assisted shifts in interactive intentions, subject 9 did not know how to truncate in ERIC, and subject 24's search did not yield any results. They had to come up with assisted shifts. For the same reason, subject 9 had to change the method of her retrieval tactics. In the examples of alternative shifts in interactive intentions, both subjects 1 and 2 did not find any relevant results. These unsuccessful outcomes forced them to take alternative shifts.

The information objects of IR systems that users interact with consist of information stored in these systems as well as messages presented to users via the interfaces of these systems. This study demonstrates that the information retrieved by the subjects were mainly responsible for the planned and opportunistic shifts in current search goals and opportunistic shifts in interactive intentions. In the examples of planned shifts in current search goals, after reviewing the retrieved results from their search, subject 3 further specialized her search task from "museum" to "impact of digital library on museum attendance," and subject 15 added "access to information" to her original search task, "prison libraries and censorship." In the example of opportunistic shift in current search goals, subject 11 found articles related to the information seeking of visually impaired users when she looked for information regarding visual impaired users' use of OPAC, and that led to the opportunistic shift. In the example of opportunistic shift of interactive intentions, subject 13 found that the digital divide was quite interesting and explored the issue in the process of evaluating the retrieved items related to high school students' use of libraries. Anderson (2005) found that users look for and use triggers in their interactions with information objects to assess the relevance and usefulness of texts and their representations. This study further reveals that these triggers could also lead to different levels and types of shifts.

Users can access different types of IR systems in different digital environments. Moreover, different systems offer different designs and different features. It is impossible for users to get familiar with all of the systems. Even though users normally try to use IR systems that they are familiar with, they still need to learn different features. In the example of assisted shift of interactive intentions, subject 9 tried to learn how to truncate in ERIC in order to create a search statement. Learning system knowledge, domain knowledge, and information retrieval knowledge are the major components of assisted shifts. The influence of IR systems on shifts is also identified by other studies. After analyzing transaction logs, Hider (2007) concluded that the nature of the IR system influences search goal redefinition. In particular, the availability of abstract and hyperlinking descriptors have an impact on search goal redefinition.

Finally, social-organizational context defines the user-system interaction. In this study, subjects were limited by the IR system/resources that were available to them. They mainly accessed the online databases subscribed to by the university library. In addition, they also tried to use publicly available Web search engines and digital libraries. Because this work task (writing a research proposal) was the assignment for an introductory class, many subjects did not have sufficient domain knowledge, system knowledge, and information retrieval knowledge, which led to some of the alternative shifts in current search goals, assisted and alternative shifts in interactive intentions, and different types of retrieval tactic shifts discussed above.

As it turned out, instructors of the school and librarians in the library were the main human resources available for the subjects. These human resources were used for the assisted and alternative shifts in retrieval tactics. For example, subject 7 first got started identifying information (related to evaluating digital libraries) by scanning an item (PowerPoint file from a guest speaker of the class) but could not access the information. She then consulted the instructor of the class to help her get started by identifying something from the references of an article provided by the instructor. In this example, "consulting human" is an alternative shift for "scanning an item" for "identifying something to get started."

For ease of illustration, individual planned and situational aspects are highlighted for their roles in different levels and different types of shifts. In actuality, shifts in current search goals, interactive intentions, and retrieval tactics are codetermined by both planned and situational aspects. These identified planned and situational factors correspond to Hert's (1997) situated elements related to users, the problem, and the system response. This study identifies more factors related to levels of user goals and dimensions of tasks and their impact on defining and clarifying situations.

Summary

In this chapter, the planned-situational model is illustrated and validated by applying an empirical study conducted by the author. By collecting prequestionnaire, diary, and postquestionnaire data from 21 subjects who had to look for information in order to write their research proposals, this study offers examples to demonstrate the essentials of the model:

- The subjects of this study did apply multiple information-seeking strategies in their information-seeking and -retrieving process. The study indicated that subjects engaged in every type of identified information-seeking strategy discussed in Chapter VIII.

- Furthermore, the subjects also had to shift their current search goals and their information-seeking strategies because of the planned and situational aspects. As their leading search goal/work task was required as part of the assignment, they changed their current search goals, mainly their search topics, and their information-seeking strategies in order to write their research proposals.

- Levels of user goals/ tasks, dimensions of user goals/tasks, and users' information infrastructure were the major planned aspects that influenced shifts in current search goals, interactive intentions, and retrieval tactics. Because of their work task, the subjects' current search tasks were more related to looking for items with common characteristics. Many subjects in this study did not have sufficient domain, system, and information retrieval knowledge to seek information, because they were in their first semester of the program taking an introductory class.

- Outcomes of user-system interactions, IR system design and structure as well as its collection, and the social-organizational context were the key situational aspects that affected shifts in current search goals, interactive intentions, and retrieval tactics.

- Both planned and situational factors defined the types of situations that users encountered and led to different levels and types of shifts.

This study helps understand and confirm the planned-situational interactive IR model. Its strengths can be summarized into the following aspects: 1) These subjects had the same work task, and it was easy for the author to examine unique patterns of applied information-seeking strategies, shifts in current search goals and information-seeking strategies, and associated planned and situational factors; 2) It is a longitudinal study. The data collection process went about 3 months, which provided more detailed information regarding the subjects' information seeking and retrieving during the research proposal writing process; and 3) Multiple data were collected in natural settings. Subjects could look for information in any locations and search any systems at any time. The data derived from questionnaires and diaries corroborate each other.

Of course, this study also has its weaknesses. First, the sample size and one type of work task limit the generalizability of the study. More subjects with different demographic characteristics and who engage in different types of work tasks need to be recruited. Second, while diaries are able to record the information-seeking process unobtrusively, not all subjects offered detailed information. Some of them mainly concentrated on recording the strategies in relation to creating search statements and modifying search statements, and less on other types of strategies. It was the subject who decided what information and how much information he/she would record, even though they were all given the same diary forms and instructions.

In order to enhance this study, the author currently works on a project to recruit more subjects representing general users of different types of IR systems with various ethnic backgrounds, education and literacy levels, computer skills, occupations, and other demographic characteristics. Subjects will be asked to keep an "information interaction diary" for two weeks to record their information-seeking and -retrieving activities related to the tasks that they have to achieve within those 2 weeks. The diary will cover their tasks/goals, their associated information-seeking problems, the information resources used, their information-seeking strategies applied, the outcome of each applied information-seeking strategy, the problems occurred, the resolutions taken, and so forth. More structured and instructional diary forms will be sent to users to guide them in recording as detailed information as possible.

In addition, these subjects will be invited to come to a research lab to search for information for two of their own information problems. They will be instructed to "think aloud" during their information retrieval process. Their information retrieval process will be captured by Morae, which is a usability testing software that not only records users' movements but also captures their "think aloud' during their information retrieval process. By showing not just "what" actions the user takes but also "why" and "how," Morae helps us to have a complete and accurate understanding of user needs and behaviors. Researchers will also observe and take notes during the search process. By integrating both diary and log data, we can have a better understanding of users' information-seeking and -retrieving processes. It is the author's hope that this project will further validate and enhance the planned-situational interactive IR model.

References

Anderson, T. D. (2005). Judgements in the context of scholarly research. *Information Research, 10*(2), 226.

Bhavnani, S. K., Bichakjian, C. K., Johnson, T. M., Little, R. J., Peck, F. A., Schwartz, J. L., et al. (2006). Strategy hubs: Domain portals to help find comprehensive information. *Journal of the American Society for Information Science and Technology, 57*(1), 4-24.

Blocks, D., Cunliffe, D., & Tudhope, D. (2006). A reference model for user-system interaction in thesaurus-based searching. *Journal of the American Society for Information Science and Technology, 57*(12), 1655-1665.

Bystrom, K., & Järvelin, K. (1995). Task complexity affects information-seeking and use. *Information Processing and Management, 31*(2), 191-213.

Daniels, P. (1986). *Developing the user modeling function of an intelligent interface for document retrieval systems.* Unpublished doctoral dissertation, the City University, London, England.

Fidel, R., & Pejtersen, A. M. (2004). From information behavior research to the design of information systems: The cognitive work analysis framework. *Information Research, 10(1).* Retrieved January 5, 2008, from http://informationr. net/ir/10-1/paper210.html

Hert, C. A. (1997). *Understanding information retrieval interaction: Theoretical and practical implications.* Greenwich, CO: Ablex.

Hider, P. (2006). Search goal revision in models of information retrieval. *Journal of Information Science, 32*(4), 352-361.

Hider, P. M. (2007). Search goal redefinition through user-system interaction. *Journal of Documentation, 63*(2), 188-203.

Ingwersen, P., & Järvelin, K. (2005). *The turn: Integration of information seeking and retrieval in context.* Heidelberg: Springer.

Lin, S. J., & Belkin, N. (2005). Validation of a model of information seeking over multiple search sessions. *Journal of the American Society for Information Science and Technology, 56*(4), 393-415.

Marchionini, G. (1995). *Information-seeking in electronic environments.* Cambridge, U.K.: Cambridge University Press.

Ng, K. B. (2002). Toward a theoretical framework for understanding the relationship between situated action and planned action models of behavior in information retrieval contexts: Contributions from phenomenology. *Information Processing and Management, 38*(5), 613-626.

Pennanen, M., & Vakkari, P. (2003). Students' conceptual structure, search process, and outcome while preparing a research proposal: A longitudinal case study. *Journal of the American Society for Information Science and Technology, 54*(8), 759-770.

Pharo, N. (2004). A new model of information behaviour based on the Search Situation Transition schema. *Information Research, 10*(1), 203.

Rieh, S. Y. (2004). On the Web at home: Information seeking and Web searching in the home environment. *Journal of the American Society for Information Science and Technology, 55*(8), 743-753.

Slone, D. J. (2002). The influence of mental models and goals on search patterns during Web interaction. *Journal of the American Society for Information Science and Technology, 53*(13), 1152-1169.

Slone, D. J. (2003). Internet search approaches: The influence of age, search goals, and experience. *Library and Information Science Research, 25*(4), 403-418.

Spink, A., Wilson, T. D., Ford, N., Foster, A., & Ellis, D. (2002). Information seeking and mediated searching study: Part 3. Successive searching. *Journal of the American Society for Information Science and Technology, 53*(9), 716-727.

Strauss, A., & Corbin, J. (1990). Basics of qualitative research: Grounded theory procedures and techniques. Newbury Park: Sage.

Vakkari, P. (2000a). E-cognition and changes of search terms and tactics during task performance: A longitudinal study. In *Proceedings of the RIAO 2000 Conference,* (pp. 894-907). Paris: C.I.D.

Vakkari, P. (2000b). Relevance and contributory information types of searched documents in task performance. In N. J. Belkin, P. Ingwersen, & M.-K. Leong (Eds.), *Proceedings of the 23rd Annual International ACM SIGIR Conference on Research and Development in Information Retrieval,* (pp. 2-9). New York: ACM Press.

Vakkari, P. (2001). Changes in search tactics and relevance judgments when preparing a research proposal: A summary of the findings of a longitudinal study. *Information Retrieval, 4*(3-4), 295-310.

Vakkari, P., & Hakala, N. (2000). Changes in relevance criteria and problem stages in task performance. *Journal of Documentation, 56*(5), 540-562.

Vakkari, P., Pennanen, M., & Serola, S. (2003). Changes in search terms and tactics while writing a research proposal: A longitudinal case study. *Information Processing and Management, 39*(3), 445-463.

Xie, H. (2006). Understanding human-work domain interaction: Implications for the design of a corporate digital library. *Journal of the American Society for Information Science and Technology, 57*(1), 128-143.

Chapter X

Implications of the Planned-Situational Interactive IR Model

Theoretical Implications: Understanding the Nature of IR

The planned-situational model of interactive IR not only clarifies some of the important issues of information retrieval but also sets up a foundation for researchers to further explore the nature of interactive IR.

Clarification of Important Concepts

The terms "information need," "problematic situation," "anomalous state of knowledge," "goal" or "user goal," and "task," "work task," or "search task" have been widely used in IR literature, but the definitions of these terms are still ambiguous. The structure of levels of user goals/tasks helps clarify the relationship among the information need, goal, task, and interactive intention. The structure of levels of goals/tasks confirms that one level of user goal/task cannot account for the influence of user goal/task on information retrieval. Interactive intentions are the products of levels of user goals/tasks. A user's information need cannot be discussed on an abstract level. Instead, it corresponds to levels of user goals/tasks. Long-term goals and leading search goals define the work tasks that lead users to seek information. Therefore, information need comes from long-term goals and leading search goals/ work tasks. At the same time, information need is represented by current search goals/search tasks and further enriched, modified, or changed by a set of interactive intentions that emerge in the information retrieval process.

"Problematic situation" (Wersig, 1979) and "anomalous state of knowledge" (Belkin, 1980) are considered as driving forces for information retrieval. In that sense, "problematic situation" and "anomalous state of knowledge" emerge in the process of achieving their leading search goals or work tasks. In that process, users encounter a problem, and they do not have enough knowledge to deal with it. Therefore, they need to look for information to assist them in solving the problem. In most of the situations, they cannot clearly express their problems, and they have to clarify their thoughts or knowledge in the process of information retrieval.

User goal and task have been used interchangeably in IR research. As discussed in Chapter VIII, user goal is used to represent levels of goals, for example, intention (Belkin et al., 1990; Broder, 2002; Chang, 1995; Rose & Levinson, 2004), current search goal (Hert, 1996, 1997) and leading search goal (Slone, 2002). At the same time, tasks are named for work tasks (Fidel, Pejtersen, Cleal, & Bruce, 2004; Kim & Allen, 2002; Kuhlthau, 1991; Vakkari, 2001) and search tasks (Bilal, 2002; Ford, Miller, & Moss, 2002; Kim & Allen, 2002; Schacter, Chung, & Dorr, 1998; Shiri & Revie, 2003; Sutcliffe, Ennis, & Watkinson, 2000). Work tasks are introduced to distinguish between tasks and search tasks (Borlund & Ingwersen, 1997; Ingwersen, 1996; Ingwersen & Järveline, 2005; Vakkari, 2003). Levels of user goal associate user goals to the related tasks. While leading search goals refer to a user's work-task-related goal that leads to a search, current search goals refer to specific results a user intends to obtain, which is the goal of the search task. Interactive intentions are the subgoals that a user has to accomplish in order to achieve his/her current search goals. In that sense, subtasks are comparable to interactive intentions that users have to work on in order to fulfill their search tasks. The dimensions of working and search task clearly define the nature of the tasks and user goals.

Researchers have examined information-seeking strategies from different levels: (1) tactics/moves, such as Bates' (1979a, 1979b) information tactics, Shute and Smith's (1993) knowledge-based search tactics, Fidel's (1991) operational and conceptual moves, Shiri and Revie's (2003) cognitive and physical moves, and so forth; (2) information-seeking strategies, such as concept-oriented strategies (Markey & Atherton, 1978), system-feature-oriented search strategies (Chen & Dhar, 1991), the interaction-related strategies, including "interactive scanning" (Hawkins & Wagers, 1982), browsing strategies vs. analytical strategies (Marchionini, 1995), the plan strategies vs. reactive strategies (Soloman, 1993), and so forth; and 3) patterns, such as Ellis' (1989) information seeking patterns of academic social scientists, Ellis and Haugan's (1997) information-seeking patterns of engineers and research scientists, Kuhlthau's (1991) model of the information search process, and so forth. The planned-situational model of interactive IR is established based on the research of different levels of information-seeking strategies. However, the identification of information-seeking strategies in the model goes beyond the query formulation and reformulation; instead, it further covers multiple information-seeking strategies that users engage in the information-seeking process. Moreover, multiple dimensions of information-seeking strategies are explored to understand the nature of IR in terms of not only how users act but also under what circumstances these strategies are applied.

Nature of Interactive IR: Products of Plans and Situations

Information retrieval is to find desired information from a database. However, there are a couple of problems associated with the IR process. First, the problem is that the information a user is looking for is not an isolate information request; instead, it relates to levels of user goals and tasks. It is associated with the long-term goal that a user has to achieve in the long run, and it is part of the leading search goal or work task that he/she has to accomplish within the short timeframe. The dimensions of work task determine the scope of retrieved information. To be specific, the stage of the task determines what information a user is trying to find; the timeframe of the task decides the process of information retrieval; the structuredness of the task, the user's familiarity with the task, and the situation of the task direct how the desired information is retrieved. In addition, the information retrieval process also links to the social-organizational context in which the interaction takes place.

Second, the information a user is looking for cannot be easily expressed or defined. Information need or "anomalous state of knowledge" can only be clarified by users' interactions with systems, including the information objects stored in the systems. Users have to apply their own personal information infrastructure to select appropriate information-seeking strategies from their plans. Information-seeking strategies consist of interactive intentions and corresponding retrieval tactics that are the products of plans and situations. Users engage in multiple information-seeking strategies in the information-seeking and -retrieving process. The interactive IR process is constituted by information-seeking strategies applied in the user-system interaction process. Although user goals have been recognized as the essential factor in determining the structure and nature of information retrieval (Belkin, Cool, Stein, & Theil, 1995; Cool, 1993; Hert, 1997), the planned-situational interactive IR model systematically examines the microlevel of user goal–interactive intentions. Interactive intentions are the subgoals that users have to fulfill in order to accomplish their current search goals/search tasks, and they are the products of levels of user goals as well as situational elements. In the information retrieval process, users have to choose suitable interactive intentions to achieve their current search goals/search tasks. The complexity of the information retrieval process—the interaction process between user and system—requires users to employ multiple information-seeking strategies to accomplish their current search goals/search tasks. Furthermore, information-seeking strategies can be characterized by the integration and combination of 12 types of interactive intentions and 11 types of retrieval tactics. Not limited by query formulation and reformulation, interactive intentions can be grouped into 12 types: identifying, learning, exploring, creating, modifying, monitoring, accessing, organizing, evaluating, keeping records, obtaining, and disseminating. Examples of information-seeking strategies are: learning system features by trial-and-error system features, exploring items with common characteristics by scanning meta-information of retrieved results, creating a search statement for a known item by specifying the metadata of the item, monitoring the search process by surveying the search history, organizing search results by manipulating retrieved results based on different criteria, and so forth.

Third, users have to interact with IR systems to find their desired information. However, the interaction process is dynamic rather static. Researchers recognize that users do not follow the same information-seeking goal or apply the same information-seeking strategy in the information-seeking process. Bates' (1989) "berrypicking" process, Belkin's (1996) episode model of information seeking, Saracevic's (1996) stratified interaction model, Spink's (1997) interactive feedback, and shifts in problems/stages/strategies/focus investigated by Robins (2000), Olah (2005), Spink and Wilson (1999) and Xie (2000, 2002) all confirm the dynamic IR process. This model reveals that user goals not only change but also change on several levels. This is the first model that actually examines how users shift their goals in the information-seeking and -retrieving process. Although users' leading search goals/work tasks seldom change, their goals in relation to their search tasks (current search goals), their subgoals in relation to how to solve their information problems (interactive intentions), and their retrieval tactics do change in the information-seeking and -retrieving process.

Furthermore, this model identifies patterns of different levels of shifts, and suggests that these shifts do not happen randomly. In the process of fulfilling their leading search goals, users might change their current search goals/search tasks. In the process of accomplishing their current search goals, users have to change their information-seeking strategies at two levels: either change their retrieval tactics or change their interactive intentions during user-system interactions. However, all these changes do not happen by accident; instead, they can be classified and represented as, for example, opportunistic and alternative shifts in current search goals, and planned, opportunistic, assisted, and alternative shifts in interactive intentions. Different types of interactive intention shifts are classified depending on three types of situations (routine, disruptive, and problematic) and whether a user continues his/her original interactive intention. Shifts in retrieval tactics can be summarized as method, entity, attribute, and method-entity shifts. Shifts in interactive intentions and retrieval tactics are the products of planned and situational aspects. The discussion of shifts in current search goals, interactive intentions, and retrieval tactics enables researchers to understand what constitutes the information-seeking and -retrieving process.

Practical Implications: Implications for Interactive IR System Design

The limitations of "planned model" from a cognitive point of view and "situated action" derived from recent developments in social science discussed in Chapter VIII also affect their applications to system design. The former is constrained by limitations on the designer's ability to predict any user's actions, the latter by limitations on the design of an information retrieval system for general users. This model recommends an "interactive approach," which takes account of both "planned model" and "situated action." This approach suggests an interactive IR system to support users' multiple types of interactions and shifts in information-seeking strategies. The design of interactive IR systems also needs to balance user and system role in the information retrieval process. Moreover, an interactive Help mechanism is essential for users to effectively interact with IR systems.

Supporting Multiple Types of Information-Seeking Strategies

The 12 types of interactive intentions represent different interactive intentions occurring within the process of achieving different current search goals/search tasks and leading search goals/work tasks. The only differences are that the order and frequency of the interactive intentions might occur differently in fulfilling different types of user goals/tasks. The reason for these differences is that the information retrieval process is interactive, and it is the product of both plans and situations. To be more specific, interactive intentions and retrieval tactics are the products of hierarchical levels of user goals/tasks, plans and situations, and they also defined by interactions between user-system and user-social-organizational context.

It is impractical to identify the sequences of interactive intentions and information-seeking strategies within a specific type of current search goal because of the interplay between planned and situational aspects. Despite the changes in the order and frequency of different interactive intentions in the process of accomplishing current search goals/search tasks, the occurrences of interactive intentions can be identified. Each type of interactive intention has its own corresponding retrieval tactics, and templates can be implemented to an IR system to support different types of interactive intentions based on the most frequently applied information-seeking strategies for each type of interactive intention.

Users need support in formulating queries as well as other forms of interaction. Twelve types of interactive intentions represent 12 types of interactions. If an IR system supports 12 types of interactive intentions, it also supports multiple types of interactions. In addition to query formulation and reformulations, users need IR systems to facilitate them to:

- Identify a collection/database/system to get started, identify some personal leads to get started, or identify information/concepts/items/site from the retrieved results to continue searching. *Scanning different types of personal materials* is the retrieval tactic applied for "identifying information to get started." **Suggestion**: set up a personal working space, provide access to users' personal leads, and allow them to browse and link to these personal leads, such as a URL suggested by an expert, a file containing the article read by the user, and so forth. At the same time, highlighting the key information of a collection/database or allowing users to search for relevant collections and databases helps users effectively scan the meta-information of the collection/database and select the right ones to search. In addition, the outcomes of the user-system interaction always lead to new leads to search. It is important for the IR system to make it easier for users to scan and track the meta-information of the search results. In other words, it is useful to make every part of the meta-information to be linkable.

- Learn system features, structure, domain knowledge, and IR knowledge. *Consulting experts/peers or system Help, scanning meta-information*, and *trial-and-error* are the frequently used retrieval tactics for "learning." **Suggestion**: provide a context-sensitive Help mechanism to assist users to get "right to the question" answer for their questions of system function, system structure, domain knowledge, and information retrieval knowledge, because users sometimes have problems expressing their problems. In addition to the table of content or index, the Help mechanism should offer hyperlinks of information and examples of how to use different system features, because most of the time users either do not have time to read instructions or do not understand the instructions. The system should offer immediate access to the location information of any items as well as information about general system structure and the structure of any databases. Previous research (Cool & Xie, 2004; Xie & Cool, 2006) has demonstrated that users prefer visual information to text information in Help mechanisms; therefore the above information should be better communicated to users via interactive tutorials or demonstrations.

- Explore specific items/sites, items with common characteristics, and items without predefined criteria. Different *scanning tactics* are applied for exploring. **Suggestion**: provide browsing mechanisms with different access points for users to effectively access to information from different channels, such as different subjects, different formats, different time, different geographical locations, different authors, and so forth, to help users find what they are interested in.

- Create search statements and modify search statements for a known item, items with common characteristics, and specific information. *Specifying the known information of the item* is used for "creating search statements for a known item." *Manipulating the metadata of the item* and *manipulating the format of the item's metadata* are the retrieval tactics applied for modifying search statements for a known item. The problem with this type of interaction is that users do not always have complete information for a known item, and sometimes they only have vague and partial information for an item. **Suggestion**: provide a browsing mechanism of partial search, such as partial title, partial author, and so forth; provide other options for characteristics of a known item, such as image or text, date range, length of an item, and so forth. *Specifying different terms and their relationships* is a frequently applied retrieval tactic for "creating search statements for items with common characteristics." *Manipulating the metadata of the retrieved item, manipulating different terms and their relationships* and *manipulating different formats of terms* are the retrieval tactics applied for modifying search statements for items with common characteristics. **Suggestion**: provide positive feedback mechanisms, such as offering "documents like marked;" more important, allow users more control about what they like about a specific document, so they are able to select key terms, a paragraph, the author, even a chart from the document, and so forth. *Specifying specific terms and their relationships* is one of the information-seeking strategies employed for "creating search statements for specific information." *Manipulating the metadata of the item* and *manipulating format of the item's metadata* are the common retrieval tactics applied for modifying search statements for specific information. It is a challenge for users to come up with specific queries to search for specific information. **Suggestion**: allow experienced users to construct complicated queries to find relevant documents containing specific information; allow novice users to use natural language queries for their searches.

- Monitor the search process or current status. Monitoring strategies are applied by employing *surveying search history* and *surveying current location tactics*. In order to effectively retrieve information, it is essential to know the search process and current status. **Suggestion**: offer search history or search path for users; more important, make it visible when needed, and invisible when not needed.

- Organize retrieved items. In digital environments, users apply organizing strategies by employing *manipulating retrieved items* tactics based on different criteria. **Suggestion**: provide more options for users to organize the retrieved results, for example, author, subject themes, scholarly works, journal, and so forth; offer visual displays based on the subject areas of the retrieved results.

- Access a specific item, access items with common characteristics, or access an area/location. *Tracking meta-information* is a popular tactic for users to **"access an item(s)/location." Suggestion**: provide direct links to guide users easily to access the item(s)/location. An alternative approach is to provide a visual map for users to access items with common characteristics or an area/location.

- Evaluate information/item in terms of its usefulness, correctness, specificity, duplication, fitness, or authority. *Scanning and comparing tactics, specifying and scanning tactics,* and *specifying and tracking tactics* are the retrieval tactics employed for different types **of "evaluating." Suggestion**: recommend different display or summary options for different types of evaluation with meta-information and search terms highlighted for users to evaluate usefulness, correctness, specificity of an item; design a comparing mechanism that facilitates users to compare two or more documents for duplication, fitness, or authority; apply the techniques used to test the integrity of the Web documents to test the authority of retrieved documents. Further, allow users to search for key terms within the text displayed, and so forth.

- Keep a record of the meta-information and search process or status and obtain specific information, part of the information, or a whole item. *Different acquiring tactics* are the frequently used strategies for **"keeping records and obtaining." Suggestion**: provide easy access to search history and search results with meta-information highlighted as well as copying, downloading, saving, and printing options for users to keep track of their searches and obtain information/item(s), and further integrate these features into their personal working space or personal desktop.

- Disseminate items/objects/sites to a specific person or a group of people. When users find useful information, they might need to send it to one specific person or a group of people. A variety of *specifying tactics* such as specifying an e-mail address, specifying the listserve of a group, and so forth, are needed in applying disseminating strategies. **Suggestion**: offer different options for users to copy, save, download, and print as well as e-mail or post the information/item/object/site to a person or a listserve or a Web site from his/her address book. That again requires the integration of the dissemination features to a user's personal working space or personal desktop.

Balancing Ease-of-Use and User Control: System Role and User Involvement and Feedback Mechanisms

Designing an interactive IR system needs to take into consideration that not all users are same. The planned and situational aspects determine the nature of IR, or the process of user-system interaction. Information retrieval is interactive, and interaction requires that both the user and the system play different roles in performing different tasks (Beaulieu, 2000). While some users prefer ease-of-use IR systems, others also desire more control in the interaction process. One crucial issue related to ease-of-use and user control is which/who does what in the information retrieval process. Hix and Hartson (1993) claim that it is a cooperative task between a user and the system in using an interactive system. In that sense, decisions must be made about which/who does what. As early as in 1990, Bates raised essential questions for the design of an IR system, "What capabilities should we design for the system, and what capabilities should we enable the searcher to exercise" (p. 576)? She called for the need to delegate clear responsibilities for system and user involvements. While Bates (1990) focused on the discussion of both the user and system involvements from different levels of search activities, the author of this book tries to associate the system and the user involvement with the effective interaction in the information retrieval process.

The success of user-system interaction depends on the collaboration of both partners. Brajnik, Mizzaro, Tasso, and Venuti, (2002) argued that neither the user nor the system could solve information problems individually, and they proposed a collaborative coaching approach where users are in charge of search sessions while systems offer suggestions. However, users and systems do not play the same roles in applying different types of information-seeking strategies. White and Ruthven (2006) pointed out that it is important to understand what users would like to control and what they would be willing to allow systems to control. Applying Bates' (1990) framework to system involvement, they tested the three systems that offered different levels of support for tactics and stratagems: the Manual system suggested search activities when requested, the Assisted system always offered search activities, and the Automatic system provided automatic Help. They concluded that users would like to take responsibility for query reformulations and selection retrieval strategies, but they would allow systems to make relevance judgments for them. The author concluded in an empirical study (Xie, 2003) that user involvement focuses on how to make conceptual judgments and decisions while system role concentrates on how to enhance users' knowledge structures and help users make a variety of judgments and decisions. The planned-situational model clearly illustrates the generally applied information-seeking strategies in the IR process. Not all the strategies require the same involvement of users and systems, however; users and systems play different roles in applying different information-seeking strategies. Figure 10.1 presents user involvement and system role required in applying the 12 types of information-seeking strategies. Six types of information-seeking strategies in which systems play major roles are presented in italics.

Users are mainly responsible for identifying, exploring, learning, creating search statements, modifying search statements, and evaluating strategies. Identifying information to get started or continue searching requires users to identify search leads before or during the searching process. At that time, by applying their personal information knowledge, they have to associate the potential leads with their levels of user goals/tasks and their social-organizational context to make decisions about whether the leads are relevant or useful for them to pursue. Although exploring does not always have a purpose, what users choose to explore and view is also related to their levels of goals/tasks and their personal interests. Consciously and unconsciously they have to make judgments about what to view, how to view, and to what extent they view. When users have to learn different types of knowledge, they decide what information they need to fill in the gap. Strategies for creating and modifying search statements require users to come up with concepts and their relationships to represent their information need. The query formulation and reformulation process helps clarify users' anonymous state of knowledge as well as helps them deal with the impact of situational factors. It is a challenging task and time-consuming work for users to assess the correctness, specificity, usefulness fitness, duplication and authority of an item. The assessment is a decision-making process in which users match the item with their current search goal/search task, compare and select the most relevant and useful items from the results, remove the duplication from the selected items, and judge the authenticity of an item.

Figure 10.1 User involvement and system role required in applying ISS

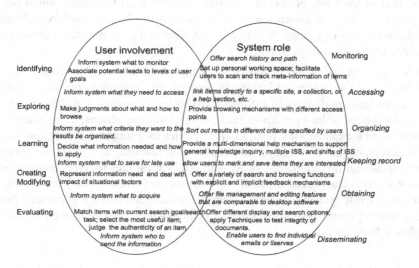

Simultaneously, IR systems can mostly handle the monitoring, accessing, organizing, keeping records, obtaining, and disseminating strategies. IR systems need to offer search history and search path for users. Keeping records of metadata of an item(s) should not be users' work; instead, IR systems need to allow users to easily mark what they are interested in and, further, create mechanisms for users to easily access them or save items for later usage. IR systems can facilitate accessing strategies by linking users directly to a specific site, a collection, or a Help section. IR systems can sort out the retrieved results or the collection by certain criteria that users prefer, such as relevancy, publication dates, formats, and so forth. File management and editing features are essential for obtaining strategies. Moreover, these features should be comparable to other desktop software that users are familiar with. Finally, IR systems can offer flexible formats for items and enable users to bring in or help them find individual e-mail address or liserves to facilitate disseminating strategies.

Even though users and IR systems are responsible for different types of strategies, the accomplishment of these strategies still needs collaboration by both systems and users. For the strategies where users take the leading roles, IR systems can facilitate the judgment and decision-making as suggested in the above "supporting multiple information-seeking strategies" section. Belkin (2000) well explained the relationships in the example of query reformulations. According to him, users would like to take control over system recommendation for query reformulation as the main task, but they are fine with the system suggesting terms as a subsidiary task as long as they can select terms suggested by the system. Without the support of IR systems, users cannot effectively apply these strategies. For the strategies that IR systems are mainly responsible for, users also have to be involved. Users need to inform IR systems what they want to monitor, keep a record of, or access; which criteria they would like to organize the collection or retrieved results; which item, part of the item, or specific information they need to obtain; which person or group they want to disseminate the results to; and whether they have addresses for these persons or groups. Without the involvement of users, IR systems cannot accomplish these strategies at all.

Most important, users and IR systems need to communicate with each other. On the one hand, users need to inform IR systems of their intentions and levels of user goals/tasks and shifts in information-seeking strategies. On the other hand, IR systems need to let users know the outcomes of their actions, their status, error messages with explanations, results conveyed in a meaningful way, suggestions for their moves, explanation of system structure and features, and so forth. Comparatively speaking, it is easier for systems to covey messages to users because users cannot always clearly describe their information need and what they really want. In that sense, while systems can provide explicit statements or ways of presentation to users about systems' responses, systems need to solicit explicit as well as implicit feedback from users.

Explicit feedback about users' interactive intentions and the dimensions of their work tasks and search tasks, for example, timeframe of the task, and so forth, can be sought in a variety of ways, including multiple choices, direct input, yes/no questions, and so forth. Concurrently, IR systems can also solicit implicit feedback by tracking users' tactics or moves and by providing positive and negative feedback. White and Ruthven (2006) applied an unobtrusive approach by monitoring users' interactions with the representation of top-ranked documents to assist users in selecting terms to represent their information needs. By monitoring retrieval tactics that correspond to interactive intentions, IR systems can better support multiple types of information-seeking strategies. The outcome of users' actions and whether they continue their original interactive intentions are the determining factors for shifts in interactive intentions. By tracking the outcomes of users' information-seeking strategies and types of interactive intentions with corresponding retrieval tactics, IR systems can help users effectively shift their information-seeking strategies.

Because users cannot always express their needs clearly, feedback mechanisms are essential for them to convey what they want implicitly. User feedback is affected by both situational and planned factors, and users are effectively promoting user-system interactions. Based on the outcomes of the previous interactions and levels of goals/tasks, a user applies his/her personal infrastructure to make decisions about the selection of the next information-seeking strategy to interact with an IR system. To some extent, any information-seeking strategies that users apply to interact with IR systems represent the feedback that they would like to convey to the systems. It seems that it is not enough for users to just select a relevant document; more important, users need to be able to specify what parts/elements of the item/results that they are really interested in. Spink (1997) identified five types of interactive feedback: content relevance, term relevance, magnitude, tactical review, and term review. These five types of feedback well represent the types of feedback occur in the user-system interaction.

User feedback, especially relevance feedback, is also related to the system design. Researchers have conducted a series of studies of relevance feedback in TREC. Different approaches of relevance feedback have been explored: automatic query expansion (Beaulieu, Fowkes, Alemayehu, & Sanderson, 2000; Robertson, Walker, & Beaulieu, 1999, 2000), term selection (Belkin et al., 2001), and passage/summary feedback (Alexander et al., 2001; Belkin et al., 2002; Yang, Maglaughlin, Meho, & Summer, Jr., 1999; Yang, Maglaughlin, & Newby, 2001). In addition, while positive feedback tells systems to look for items with similar terms, paragraphs, images, and so forth, negative feedback allows users to remove the terms that they are not interested in and make the results more focused. Researchers have explored both positive and negative feedback in TREC 6 and TREC 7 (Belkin et al., 2001). Not all IR systems provide similar feedback mechanisms. The better feedback mechanisms that an IR system offers, the more effectively users can interact with the IR system. However, explicit feedback imposes a cognitive burden on users, and it is not always the one that users prefer or that is most effective (Belkin et al., 2001; Yang et al., 2001). White and Ruthven's (2006) finding echoed the TREC findings that users would allow systems to make relevance judgments for them because they preferred systems that unobtrusively track user interaction to systems that required explicit user involvement. Implicit feedback approaches—such as identification of relevance by recording queries, documenting views, and redisplaying query results—and their relative timing and summary requested by users, were demonstrated to be performed better than explicit feedback (Vogt, 2001; White, Jose & Ruthven, 2002).

Creating Interactive Help Mechanisms

IR systems permit timely access to electronic information. However, the IR process is dynamic, and the user-system interaction process is not only an information-seeking and -retrieving process, but to some extent, it is also the process by which users clarify their information need. To make things worse, IR systems are all constructed somewhat differently, and that creates a difficult situation for users who must learn how to use each unique system. The great promise of IR systems, that of effective access to information, will go unrealized if people cannot learn to use them effectively. A long history of research in information science tells us that people repeatedly use the same searching tactics and strategies that they first learn. Far less is known about how people respond to new searching environments; the types of problems and Help-seeking situations they encounter, and the strategies they employ to resolve these situations. Without such knowledge, supportive Help mechanisms cannot be developed, and the design of IR systems will proceed in a manner that will not equally benefit people at all levels of computer experience, intelligence, problem-solving ability, learning style, literacy, and other important variables. The central argument is that research is needed to better understand design principles that will lead to the development of better, more supportive interactive Help systems for the general public.

Much of the existing research on Help use has focused on the evaluation of existing Help features and users' use or nonuse of Help in IR systems. After examining the Help facilities of 16 interactive IR systems, Trenner (1989) concluded that "Help" in IR systems is often inadequate, and the reason for that is that Help is a low priority in the development of these systems. According to Nahl (1999), novice searchers are the main users of Help mechanisms. Slack (1991) studied the effectiveness and use of online Help features in five different OPACs, and she found that even though the Help feature was utilized by one-third of the novice users, it did not assist the users in their Help-seeking situations. It has been suggested that utilizing natural language searching abilities may improve a user's interaction with the Help feature. However, a study reported by Kreymer (2002) found that although natural language may be useful for average end-users during some parts of the searching episode, overall, when using system Help, the results vary widely and are generally not very effective.

Research has demonstrated that the existing Help in IR systems cannot satisfy users' needs. Houghton (1984) identified the types of assistance offered in online Help systems: command, help and error assistance, prompting, online tutors, and online documentation. However, it is not enough just to offer these assistances. The question is what types of Help users need in terms of their structure and content. Because users may encounter complicated Help use situations, Hellman (1989) suggested representing the organizational context in a support system by constructing a context database. The context database covers information about task flows, task-connected information objects, and so forth. Elkerton and Palmiter (1991) demonstrated that the goal-oriented and procedural structure of the Help system is more effective in initial information retrieval for novice users of HyperCard users. Brajnik et al. (2002) have developed a conceptual framework of "collaborative coaching" between users and IR systems, stressing the importance of interaction in the design of intelligent Help mechanisms.

A study was conducted by the author and her associate (Cool & Xie, 2004; Xie & Cool, 2006) to examine some of the issues described above. Results of this research further demonstrate the importance of developing better interactive Help mechanisms to support people using IR systems of all kinds. The major finding of the study is that while people generally view Help systems as important, they find these systems to be lacking in usefulness in a variety of areas, and they tend to use Help mechanisms infrequently. The analysis of reasons given for not using IR Help points to general inadequacies in the interactive capabilities of these systems as partners in help-seeking situations. Based on the interactions between users and IT personnel in information technology problem-solving, Kim (2005) described a collaborative problem-solving model that has implications for the design of Help systems in IR systems. The model consists of nine steps: describing background, identifying problem, contact/attempting contact, explaining problem, analyzing problem, suggesting solution, implementing solution, solving problem, and post-acting.

Help seeking, especially learning to use the Help systems of an IR system, can be viewed as a multidimensional information behavior insofar as it is one of the multiple information-seeking behaviors that people engage in during episodes of information searching with the goal of interacting with information (Cool, 2006). Within the existing research, limited attention has been given to theoretically clarifying the concept of Help seeking as it relates to information behavior generally, and to information searching more particularly. Research and development in this area has largely proceeded without attention to the precursors of help-seeking behaviors within the context of IR (Jansen, 2005).

Previous studies have shown that Help systems are not very effective in helping end-users, especially novice users, who are trying to learn how to use new IR systems. One of the primary reasons for the limited helpfulness of most Help systems is that they are modeled after traditional noninteractive models, and as such have not evolved into interactive Help partners that can more effectively assist people in help-seeking situations. Another reason is that the modes of interaction and dialogue structures best suited to these users' needs have not been well researched. In order to improve Help mechanisms in this direction, we need more research to better understand the help-seeking situations people encounter during episodes of information searching, the strategies they employ in such situations, and the help-seeking dialogues that can best respond to them. The planned-situational model provides insights into situations that users have to deal with and strategies that they have to apply in their interactions with IR systems.

One important issue is that a Help mechanism is not just a Help button. A Help mechanism relates to the overall design of the interface of an IR system, especially its structure and features. A Help mechanism can involve three types of Help: explicit, context-sensitive, and implicit. Here explicit Help refers to features that clearly labeled "Help," such as Help button, FAQ, and so forth. The formats of explicit Help can be visual display, demo, snapshots, FAQ, and so forth. Context-sensitive Help refers to the assistance offered to users at specific time for specific situation. Context-sensitive Help normally requires users to communicate with IR systems, and dialog is the main format for the system to solicit information and offer advice and suggestions. Implicit Help refers to the assistance provided without the clear label of Help. Different types of design features imply different types of support for users, such as browsing feature, searching feature, organizing feature, linking feature, tracking feature, and so forth.

A good Help mechanism needs to assist users to become familiar with the systems that they are interacting with, the topic domain of the information that they are looking for, and the IR skills that they need to interact with IR systems. More important, it needs to help users to deal with different situations that they encounter during user-system interactions. To be specific, a good Help mechanism needs to support users when they intend to 1) learn general knowledge of IR systems, domain of the search topics, and information retrieval; 2) apply multiple types of information-seeking strategies; and 3) shift their information-seeking strategies. Figure 10.2 presents how a Help mechanism fulfills the three types of support.

When users interact with IR systems for a specific information problem, they need to have knowledge of the IR system, the domain knowledge of that information problem, and information retrieval skills to interact with IR systems. An IR system should provide explicit help of general knowledge to users about the system to assist them in getting started or in the retrieval process. For users, it is important to present the knowledge base visually in different domains related to the collections of an IR system; this will help them understand the knowledge structure and related concepts/terms of the domain of which the information problem is embedded. The effective way for users to gain general knowledge of IR systems is to be offered

Figure 10.2 Three types of support in a help mechanism

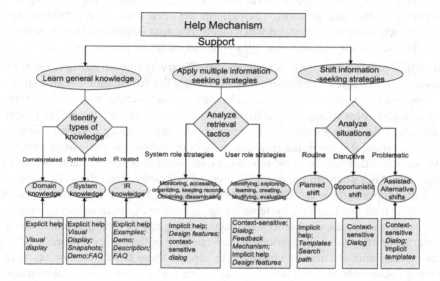

a visual demonstration of the system knowledge map including system structure, specific features, general and specific commands, and so forth. Frequently Asked Questions (FAQ) is another effective tool for presenting system knowledge information. As to the information retrieval skills, the system should provide examples of the most frequently applied information-seeking strategies, demonstrations and descriptions of how to convey their needs and requests to systems, how to deal with problematic situations, and so forth. These can also be presented in FAQ. Explicit help is mainly offered for users to learn general knowledge about the system, domain, and information retrieval.

It is not enough for users to have just general knowledge about systems, domain, and IR skills. Users need support and guidance in applying multiple information-seeking strategies during the information retrieval process. In order to provide better help, IR systems can offer explicit guidance in retrieval tactics for each of the interactive intentions and the relationships among the interactive intentions in general Help. By providing templates and instructions for different types of interactive intentions, users can quickly select appropriate retrieval tactics to accomplish their interactive intentions. At the same time, users cannot always explicitly express their interactive intentions, and IR systems also need to analyze users' retrieval tactics to infer their interactive intentions. Based on the discussion in Chapter VIII, each type of the interactive intentions corresponds with several types of retrieval tactics. For example, users apply identifying strategy by employing scanning and selecting tactics, exploring strategy by employing tracking tactics, organizing strategy by employing manipulating tactics, evaluating strategy by employing scanning and comparing tactics, and so forth. The patterns between interactive intentions and retrieval tactics can aid IR systems when identifying user intentions. How to support multiple information-seeking strategies is discussed in the previous section.

The critical part of how a Help mechanism can effectively support multiple informa-tion-seeking strategies is to provide help to enhance the information-seeking strate-gies applied by the users. As discussed in the previous section, users and systems play different roles in applying different strategies. Users play the major role in strategies of identifying, exploring, creating, modifying, learning, and evaluating. In supporting these strategies, the Help needs to focus on how to enable users to make a decision; in other words, to provide what users need in order to effectively make a decision. After analyzing and inferring users' interactive intentions, IR systems can better support them by offering context-sensitive Help to communicate with users about their needs and the systems' suggestions. For example, context-sensitive Help can ask users about whether they want to bring any of their personal leads to get started or offer some suggestions at the beginning of the retrieval process. Feed-back mechanisms can also be employed to support these strategies. For example, "finding documents like this one" is an effective tool for users to find documents with common characteristics. Implicit feedback approaches based on the systems' observation of user behaviors without imposing a cognitive load on users are pre-ferred by users. In addition, designing useful features as part of the implicit Help, such as browsing, searching, organizing, viewing, and so forth, supports users' decision-making processes.

IR systems take the main responsibility in supporting users' monitoring, accessing, organizing, keeping records, obtaining, and disseminating strategies. Implicit Help with different design features, such as features for organizing results, linking docu-ments, managing and editing files, offering a variety of formats, sending information to different individuals or groups, and so forth, greatly enhances the effectiveness of these strategies. Simultaneously, it is insufficient to just offer users system features; context-sensitive Help is also required for the systems to interact with users about when, what, and how to access, organize, keep records, obtain, and disseminate.

Users need the support most when they encounter problems. Problematic situations require users to apply new knowledge and skills to solve the problems. Problematic situations are highly related to the outcomes of user-system interactions and the information objects that users interact with via the interfaces of IR systems. If the outcomes are partially successful or unsuccessful, then users might need help in assisting their original information-seeking strategies or introducing alternative information-seeking strategies. Even if the outcome is successful, users might still need to shift their information-seeking strategies. The information that users interact with, including retrieved results derived from IR systems or messages presented by IR systems, and so forth, also lead users to new situations. Analysis of situations—which is the key for supporting a shift in information-seeking strate-gies—involves analysis of the last action and its outcome. The major situations that the planned-situational model highlights are the situations that lead to four types of shifts in information-seeking strategies: planned shifts, opportunistic shifts, assisted shifts, and alternative shifts.

Because shifts in information-seeking strategies occur on two levels, shifts in in-teractive intentions and shifts in retrieval tactics, the author concentrates on how systems can be designed to support different levels of shifts. Even though both plan and situational aspects codetermine shifts in information-seeking strategies, shifts in interactive intentions and retrieval tactics do not occur randomly. There are pat-terns of shifts in interactive intentions and retrieval tactics. The model illustrates four types of shifts in interactive intentions based on whether problems occurred in achieving the current interactive intention and whether a user continues his/her original interactive intention after he/she completes the new intention. In addition, four types of retrieval tactic shifts are identified based on the change of dimensions of retrieval tactics in order to supplement, improve, or serve as an alternative for the original tactic. Users need interactive IR systems to offer them guidance through different shifts. Based on the analysis of situations, four types of shifts occur in three types of situations:

- Routine situations lead users to planned shifts. As planned shifts in interactive intentions are part of plans, each level of a planned shift has its own struc-ture. In addition, these shifts are highly related to the success of the previous interactive intentions. **Suggestion**: Incorporate templates of how to achieve frequently occurring leading search goals and current search goals, embed the most frequently occurring planned shifts in interactive intentions into the templates as default settings, and guide users smoothly through their planned shifts when they successfully accomplish their interactive intentions. Implicit Help is useful for these types of situations.

- Disruptive situations guide users to opportunistic shifts. Because opportunistic shifts in interactive intentions occur when users see something by serendip-ity, the environment, the system, or the information users are interacting with might lead to this type of shift. **Suggestion**: It is difficult to predict types of opportunistic shifts, but the interactive IR systems need to enable users to explore their new interactive intentions. Most importantly, IR systems should be able to guide users back to their original intentions after finishing their opportunistic shifts. Communicating with users about whether they need to go back to their original interactive intentions and keeping a record of what a user has done and allowing him/her to go back to his/her original intention are essential for this type of shift. Context-sensitive Help is desired for disruptive situations.

- Problematic situations turn users to assisted shifts. Because assisted shifts in interactive intentions happen when users have problems in achieving their interactive intentions, "learning" has to be introduced in order to solve the problems in the process of fulfilling the original interactive intention. **Suggestion**: When there are problems in the information-seeking process, interactive IR systems need to detect or inquire about the reason of the failures, and further provide context-sensitive Help mechanisms to facilitate assisted shifts.

- Problematic situations might also direct users to alternative shifts. Alternative shifts in interactive intentions are the outcomes of failing to accomplish users' original interactive intentions. In general, making up for the failure accounts for the alternative shifts. **Suggestion**: When users have to quit their previous intentions because of an error, IR systems need to provide guidance. For example, if a user fails to access an item, he/she needs to change from "accessing" to "creating a search statement" to find that item or items with common characteristics. When users decide to abandon their previous intentions, interactive IR systems could lead users to change their intentions. In order to support this type of shift, the Help mechanism needs to offer context-sensitive Help to interact with users to solicit information regarding their levels of goals and dimensions of tasks to further suggest alternative shifts.

In addition to shifts in interactive intentions, shifts in information-seeking strategies also involve shifts in retrieval tactics. In the process of fulfilling a current interactive intention, users might encounter problems by applying one specific retrieval tactic. While they can change the interactive intention at that time, they can also just change the retrieval tactic. Four types of retrieval tactic shifts are identified: changing methods, entities, attributes, and method-entity. Shifts in retrieval tactics are highly correlated with the outcomes of user-system interactions by applying the original tactic; therefore, interactive IR systems need to solicit feedback from users in terms of their interaction outcomes. If the outcome is partially successful or unsuccessful, then the system should facilitate the change of method, entity, attribute, or method-entity by providing suggestions of possible methods, entities, and attributes that users might be able to apply to achieve their current interactive intentions. Moreover, the IR system should recommend retrieval tactics that are useful to supplement, improve, or serve as an alternate for the original retrieval tactic. The typical retrieval tactics for each interactive intention can be implemented into the system to guide users.

In the process of information retrieval, users encounter problems, and they need the Help mechanisms of these IR systems to assist them in identifying their Help problems, locating the desired Help information related to their problems, and understanding the provided information that will help them solve their problem. In order to support users' help-seeking process, we need to understand more about the precursors that lead to help seeking. In other words, what brings people to seek help? What are the similarities and differences between help-seeking and general information seeking? Furthermore, we need to identify patterns of the problematic situations that users encounter and help-seeking behaviors that they exhibit. It seems that users' evaluation of the Help mechanism of an IR system is related to their evaluation of the IR system. At the same time, their use of the Help mechanism of an IR system is also associated with their use of the IR system. It is interesting to further investigate the relationships between the evaluation of the Help mechanisms of IR systems and the evaluation of the IR systems, and the relationships between their use of IR systems and their use of Help mechanisms of the IR systems.

Implications for Interactive IR System Evaluation: Multi-Dimensional Evaluation Framework

The objective of evaluating interactive IR systems is to examine how users and IR systems interact in the interactive IR process. While the traditional approach concerns IR system performance, the user-oriented approach takes into account the interactions between users and IR systems. It is important to come up with a multidimensional evaluation framework to guide the evaluation process. To be more specific, the objective of interactive IR system evaluation needs to:

• Assess the interactive IR system performance
• Assess the interface usability and organizational usability
• Assess the interactive process between users and IR systems

This section presents a multidimensional framework (Figure 10.3) for interactive IR system evaluation based on the planned-situational interactive IR model.

Evaluation of Interactive IR System Performance

Relevance criteria are essential for the evaluation of traditional IR systems as well as for the evaluation of interactive IR systems. The question is how to measure relevance in the environment of interactive IR. The dynamic nature and multidimensional assessment of the user-oriented relevance judgment pose challenges for relevance measurement in interactive IR. Researchers have realized the inadequacy of the binary measurement of relevance; Spink, Greisdorf, and their associates have conducted a series of studies to identify relevance in different regions and levels

Figure 10.3 Multidimensional framework for interactive IR system evaluation

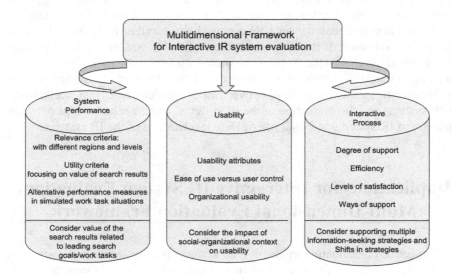

from not relevant, partially not relevant, partially relevant, to relevant (Greisdorf & Spink, 2001; Spink & Greisdorf, 2001; Spink, Greisdorf, & Bateman, 1998). Greisdorf (2003) further illustrated the multistages of relevance evaluation with topicality, pertinence, and utility of retrieved items. According to him, not relevant, partially not relevant, partially relevant, and relevant correspond closely to not on topic, not pertinent, not useful, and useful. In Web search engine environments, while precision cannot be measured by the traditional approach because of the best match results, precision was calculated based on the relevance judgments for the first 10 (Chu & Rosenthal, 1996) or 20 items (Ding & Marchionini, 1996). In addition, it is a challenge to evaluate the precision and recall of multimedia systems, such as image retrieval systems. If the calculation of precision and recall is based on both the text and image, the results of these two modals might not correspond with each other (Srihari & Zhang, 1999). It is important to evaluate the system performance of multimedia systems by integrating all the multimodal data. It is another challenge to evaluate the precision and recall of cross-language information retrieval systems because users look for information in unknown languages. According to Oard (2001), mean average precision is an inappropriate measure for interactive CLIR systems because that is based on an implicit assumption that users are able to understand the documents well enough for the identification of relevant ones.

Relevance is not the only measurement for interactive IR system performance. Based on an empirical study, Su (1992, 1994) found that the best evaluation measurement for interactive IR system performance is the value of search results. This value is highly correlated with users' satisfaction with search results and their satisfaction with the precision of the results. The importance of precision and recall depends on the tasks that users intend to accomplish. After reviewing Web search engine evaluation, Su (2003a) further identified five evaluation criteria with 16 performance measures: relevance criteria including the precision ratio of relevant and partially relevant hits based on the first 20 hits as well as the user's relevance vs. the system's relevance ranking, efficiency criteria measured by search time and number of search queries submitted, utility criteria in terms of value of search results, user satisfaction criteria with response time, search interface, online document, output display, interaction, precision, time saving and user's judgment of overall success, and connectivity with valid links. Her study (Su, 2003b) on user satisfaction criteria echoes other researchers' criteria identified in the previous study except that users also consider their affective feelings during their interaction with search engines as a key criterion. Considering the uniqueness of the interactive environments, Borlund and his colleagues (Borlund, 2000, 2003; Borlund & Ingwersen, 1998) introduced two performance measures to replace the traditional relevance measures: relative relevance and ranked half-life indicator. Relative relevance measures the degree of agreement between system output relevance and the user's judgment of the retrieved output. Nonbinary values can be applied to the relative relevance judgments. The ranked half-life indicator considers the algorithmic rank position and the assigned relevance values of retrieved output. These two measures convert the traditional relevance concept into a multidimensional and dynamic concept.

In addition to the criteria discussed above, researchers also emphasize the importance of recognizing relevance change over time, and these changes may occur within one interactive session (Dunlop, 2000; Mizzaro, 1998). The planned-situational interactive IR model indicates that it is crucial to assess the value of the search results toward the accomplishment of the leading search goals/work tasks because the current search goals/search tasks might change in the process of user-system interaction. On the one hand, users clarify their current search goals/search tasks by interacting with IR systems. On the other hand, users might compromise their current search goals/search tasks because of the situational factors. Even though their current search goals/search tasks might change in the retrieval process, their leading search goals/work tasks normally do not change. Therefore, the value of the search results should not be limited to the current search goals/search tasks; more important, the value should be judged in terms of to what extent and how the search results assist users in fulfilling their leading search goals/work tasks (the degree of support and ways of support for leading search goals/work tasks). Concurrently, efficiency also needs to measure the time users spend in achieving their current search goals/search tasks.

Evaluation of Interface Usability and Organizational Usability

Usability studies account for the essential part of the evaluation studies of interactive IR systems. Usability studies have been conducted to either recommend design principles or improve the existing design. For example, Fox et al. (1993) developed a prototype of a digital library based on a usability study of an interface. Nielsen (1993) clearly specifies the five usability attributes: learnability, efficiency, memorability, errors, and satisfaction. Most of the research has focused on the interactive features and interfaces of IR systems on efficiency and user satisfaction. Comparing interactive interface with another interactive interface or a noninteractive one is an effective and frequent evaluation approach. Beheshti, Large, and Bialek (1996) compared user preference on a browsable graphic interface simulating book shelves with a text-based OPAC, and users preferred the graphical interface for its intuitiveness and less cognitive load. Dennis, Bruza, and McArthur (2002) compared three interactive search paradigms of a query-based search engine, a directory-based search engine, and a phrase-based query recommendation-assisted search engine by measuring time, relevance, and cognitive load. Borgman et al., (2001) evaluated the Alexandria Digital Earth Prototype for use in undergraduate education by comparing the experimental group and control group to identify the useful components of the simulation and assess learning outcomes. Bishop et al. (2000) explored the extent, nature, purpose, and importance of use of a digital library testbed compared to other systems, viewing behavior, and user satisfaction. The perspectives from users are essential for the evaluation of interactive IR systems, in particular, their usability. Crudge and Johnson (2004) tested and demonstrated that repertory grid technique is suitable for eliciting evaluative constructs from users for the evaluation of usability and the performance of search engines.

In general, usability attributes cover the key assessment of the usability of interface and features. Usability is highly correlated to how IR systems can support both ease-of-use and user control and how IR systems facilitate the communication between users and IR systems. As discussed in the planned-situational model, users have different personal information infrastructures, and they have different needs and requirements in their interactions with interfaces of IR systems. While some of them like the ease-of-use of interfaces or features, others might prefer the control they can have. Researchers (Xie, 2003; Xie & Cool, 2000) concluded that users desired both ease-of-use and user control. In that sense, evaluation of the usability of interfaces should extend to what extent IR interfaces support both ease-of-use and user control (the degree of support for ease-of-use and user control) and in what ways IR interfaces support both ease-of-use and user control. A related issue is user involvement and system role, especially how users and IR systems communicate with each other. IR systems need to enable users to inform systems about their intentions and levels of user goals/tasks, and they also need to convey to users action outcomes, status, error messages with explanation, moves or strategy suggestions, system structure explanations, and so forth. Because users cannot always express their information need, it is crucial for IR systems to solicit information from users in a variety of ways. The evaluation of IR systems should also include users' satisfaction level about how IR systems communicate with users, and, more important, how IR systems solicit explicit feedback and infer implicit feedback from users.

Lamb (1995) argued that usability should not be limited to interface usability and that content usability, organizational usability, and interorganizational usability are also imperative. Kling and Elliott (1994) modeled players in the design and use of a university digital library. They defined four dimensions of organizational usability: the physical proximity and social restrictions on using the system, the level of compatibility of files in different systems, the possibility of integrating the system into a person or group's work, and the availability of training and help to users. Elliott and Kling (1997) further identified dimensions of organizational usability into three levels, individual, organizational, and environmental, based on Markus and Rubey's (1983) conceptualization of organizational validity. Applying Kling and Elliott's (1994) model, Davies (1997) developed a model to represent how different groups of stakeholders of a university electronic library had their impact on the development of a digital library. Following Davies' (1997) model, Xie and Wolfram (2002) illustrated three types of interactions of players engaged in the unique environment of state digital libraries. Influenced-based interactions reveal different needs, experiences, and expectations of the players and how they affect the coverage, content, and formats of digital libraries. Activity-based interactions involve tangible services extended by one entity to another, which comprise promotion and training. Communication-based interactions highlight the communication process of feedback.

In the planned-situational model, users interact with IR systems within certain social-organizational contexts. Users especially interact with work domain in those contexts. All the players involved in the development and use of IR systems interact with each other. The evaluation of interactive IR systems also needs to assess the organizational usability of IR systems. Elliott and Kling's (1997) three levels of organizational usability can be applied to the evaluation of interactive IR systems. On the individual level, to what extent and in what ways can IR systems be integrated into work? On the organization level, to what extent and in what ways do organizational structure, norms, and social organizations of computing affect IR system use? On the environmental level, what is the work/life ecology?

Evaluation of the Interactive Process between Users and IR Systems

While the majority of the research has focused on interactive IR system evaluation, in particular usability studies, very few studies have explored the evaluation of interactive processes between users and systems. Dillon (2001) called for the need to evaluate user-system interactions beyond usability. He further proposed measures for evaluating user experience at three levels: process, outcome and affect, which are related to what a user does, attains and feels. He concluded that the best way to assess interaction quality is to measure user experience.

It is crucial to evaluate the system performance to see whether a system provides relevant and useful information for users to achieve their tasks. However, users' evaluation of an IR system is not only affected by the search results; more important, it is also influenced by their experience in the interaction process. There are a couple of reasons in terms of why users prefer systems that facilitate their interactions over those systems that only provide relevant results.

First, users' affective feelings are related to the interaction process. Su's study (2003b) of user satisfaction criteria indicated that users consider their affective feelings during their interaction with search engines as an important criterion. In general, users' affective modes associate with usefulness of search results as well with their experience in the interaction process. Users' frustration with IR systems normally leads to unsuccessful interactions with IR systems.

Second, user-system interactions determine the efficiency and success of the system performance. The planned and situational model considers users' information-seeking strategies as the products of planned and situational actions. In order to fulfill their task efficiently, users need support in applying multiple information-seeking strategies; moreover, they need support when they encounter different situations. Without system support, users are unable to effectively interact with IR systems in the information retrieval process.

Third, the user-system interaction process represents the dynamic change and clarification of information need and possible changes in current search goal/search task under different situations. As discussed in Chapter VIII, users' long-term goals and leading search goals/work tasks normally do not change in the information retrieval process. However, their current search goals or work tasks might change in different situations in order to accomplish their leading search goals or work tasks. That might also lead to changes in users' perception of the relevance and usefulness of documents. Bruce (1994) came up a method for users to articulate their cognitive schema by tracking users' situational relevance estimation at different phases of IR interaction, such as problem state, system interaction, and document interaction. By evaluating how IR systems support the interaction process, researchers can have a clearer picture of whether and how users compromise or clarify their current search goals/search tasks in the interactive retrieval process; in other words, to what extent IR systems effectively support users in achieving their levels of user goals/tasks.

Fourth, the interactive nature of multimedia IR and CLIR raises more problems for the evaluation of Multimedia IR and CLIR systems. Belkin (1995) considered this as the most significant characteristic of multimedia IR from the evaluation perspective. Users switch from recognition to specification and scanning instead of searching in the multimedia environment. With all the challenges musical retrieval facing, Downie (2003) stressed the multiexperiential challenge. The experience of music varies with different individuals, according to their moods, situations, and circumstances. When users search for information in a language they don't have competency, they need more guidance from the system to formulate and reformulate queries as well as making sense of the search results (Gey, Kando, & Peters, 2005). That is why it is essential to evaluate the user-system interaction process and associated changes of goals at different levels.

Both quantitative and qualitative approaches need to be applied to the evaluation of user-system interactions. IR systems need to support users' interactive intentions, with corresponding retrieval tactics applied in the interactive IR process. These measurements can be generated based on the above discussion:

1. Degree of support. This measures to what extent IR systems support users to achieve each interactive intention.

2. Efficiency. This measures how much time users spend in achieving each interactive intention.

3. Levels of satisfaction. This measures to what extent users are satisfied with IR system support in accomplishing interactive intentions.

4. Ways of support. This reveals in what ways IR systems support users in fulfilling their interactive intentions.

Interactive IR systems need to support multiple information-seeking strategies as well as shifts in information-seeking strategies in the interactive IR process. The measurements for IR systems supporting the fulfillment of interactive intentions can also be applied to IR systems supporting shifts in information-seeking strategies:

1. Degree of support. This measures to what extent IR systems support users in different levels of shifts.

2. Efficiency. This measures how much time users spend achieving different levels of shifts.

3.   Levels of satisfaction. This measures to what extent users are satisfied with IR system support of their different levels of shifts.

4.   Ways of support. This uncovers the ways IR systems help users in fulfilling their different levels of shifts.

Integrating Multidimensional Criteria for the Evaluation of Interactive IR Systems

In evaluating interactive IR systems, multi-dimensional criteria need to be applied altogether. Evaluation cannot be limited to system performance; the usability of the system and the extent to which the system supports interactive processes also need to be assessed. Furthermore, as Ellis (1996) argued, the quantification measurement of information retrieval research limits the theoretical and methodological development; qualitative methods also need to be applied in information retrieval interaction.

As discussed in the planned-situational model, the overall objective of users' interaction with IR systems is to find useful information in order to achieve their levels of user goals/tasks. A task-oriented evaluation approach is essential for assessing system performance, usability, and how the system facilitates user-system interactions. Hersh, Pentecost, and Hickam (1996) stressed the importance of the task-oriented evaluation approach, which consists of measurement of success in terms of answering questions, user certainty in answering questions, time to answer questions, ability to find relevant articles, and satisfaction with interface, because IR systems need to enable users to solve their information problems. However, the task-oriented evaluation approach cannot be limited just to search tasks, because search tasks might change in the process of user-system interactions. In addition, users work on search tasks in order to achieve their work tasks.

The objective of IR system evaluation is not only to identify the advantages and disadvantages of each individual system but also to identify the best system among a group of IR systems. The question is how to evaluate and compare different interactive IR systems. Interactive TREC studies have contributed significantly to research on interactive IR system evaluation, especially for the evaluation and comparison of interactive IR systems in terms of methodology, experiment design, and reporting techniques by enabling researchers to share the same tasks, document collections, evaluation methods, and experience. More important, although the evaluation focuses on system performance comparison, it also extends to the usability of specific interactive features of these systems, the process of users' interaction with these features, and why users like or dislike these features by applying log analysis, verbal protocol analysis, and questionnaires. For example, Belkin et al. (2001) found in TREC 8 that users preferred a local context analysis system over a relevance feedback system because searchers have to expend more effort to use relevance feedback. In TREC 9, searchers chose to enter new search terms rather than use the relevance feedback option based on short summaries of documents because they did not understand the feedback mechanism (Alexander et al., 2001). Because of the limitation of the setting, assigned tasks, and convenience sample, many of the TREC studies did not yield to statistically significant results. However, user preference does show what users prefer and why they prefer it. For example research showed that users preferred implicit feedback to explicit feedback because they wanted to apply the least amount of effort in the information retrieval process (White et al., 2002).

However, TREC studies also have their own limitations. In general, evaluation of interactive IR systems requires real users with real problems in real settings. The lab setting, assigned tasks, and convenience sample pose problems in evaluating interactive IR systems. By integrating two evaluation approaches together, Borlund (2003) proposed a hybrid approach for assessing the dynamic nature of information needs and relevance in experimental settings. Based on Ingwersen's communication models (Ingwersen, 1992, 1996) and Byström and Järvelin's (1995) work task concept, Borlund (2003) suggested the simulated work tasks situation to develop a simulated information need for users to interpret individual information need as in real life. The situation also enables users to judge situational relevance. The recommendation for the application of simulated work tasks situations consists of the following requirements:

- Apply simulated work task situations as well as real information needs in the same tests;
- Design simulated task situations to fit to the information environment and the tested subjects;
- Apply either both simulated work task situations and simulated situations or only simulated work task situations; and
- Permute the order of search jobs.

As part of the model, he suggested alternative performance measures: relative relevance and the ranked half-life introduced by Borlund and Ingwersen (1998). The performance measures consider relevance as a multidimensional and dynamic concept. However, the two measures are limited only to the evaluation of system performance even though the simulated task situations take into consideration both users' work and search tasks. The evaluation also needs to extend the evaluation to the interface and organizational usability of IR systems as well as to how IR systems support the interactive information retrieval process. In order to evaluate interactive IR systems at multidimensional levels, we need to take into consideration the evaluation criteria discussed above on system performance, interface usability and organizational usability, and the interactive process between users-systems. At the same time, the employment of simulated task situations enables the evaluation and comparison of multiple interactive IR systems.

Summary

The chapter summarizes the theoretical and empirical implications of the planned-situational model. One of the key contributions of the model is to clarify and integrate some of the key concepts in interactive IR research. While information needs, problematic situations, anomalous state of knowledge, and user goals and tasks are the driving forces for information retrieval, they are used interchangeably in IR research. However, the definitions of these concepts are still ambiguous. The structure of levels of user goals/tasks illustrates the relationships among these concepts. Higher levels of user goals/tasks lead to lower levels of user goals/tasks. Interactive intentions are the subgoals/subtasks that users have to accomplish in order to achieve their higher levels of user goals/tasks. Moreover, the multidimensional information-seeking strategies identified by the model represent research on different levels of information-seeking strategies, and extend to multiple information-seeking strategies that users engage in the interactive IR process that are not limited to query formulations and reformulations.

The main theoretical contribution of the model is that it enables researchers to understand the nature of interactive IR. It is a challenge for people to retrieve useful information to solve their information problems. The planned-situational model presents the factors related the plans and situations that users encounter during their interactions with IR systems and the social-organizational context in which the interactions occur. Levels of user goals/tasks and their dimensions affect the way that users interact with IR systems and the scope of the information they intend to retrieve. The identification of multiple interactive intentions with corresponding retrieved tactics represents multiple information-seeking strategies. Multiple information-seeking strategies are the products of plans and situations. Users apply their information infrastructure to select appropriate information-seeking strategies in different situations. The dynamic interaction process requires users to shift their levels of user goals and information-seeking strategies. This is the first interactive IR model that illustrates levels of shifts in current search goals, interactive intentions, and retrieved tactics. Furthermore, the model also identifies the actual patterns of shifts occurring at the different levels that comprise the information-seeking process.

Practically, the planned-situational model provides suggestions for how to design interactive IR systems to support multiple information-seeking strategies. The template of each type of interactive intention, with its own associated retrieval tactics, can be implemented into interactive IR systems to guide users in fulfilling their interactive intentions. More important, the model provides guidance in terms of how to support ease-of-use and user control, because users have different knowledge structures and different requirements in interaction with IR systems. A related issue is how to assign different roles between users and systems in terms of who is doing what in the interactive IR process. Not all the information-seeking strategies identified by the model require the same involvement of user and systems. While users take leading roles in identifying, exploring, learning, creating, modifying, and evaluating strategies, systems mainly deal with the monitoring, accessing, organizing, keeping records, obtaining, and disseminating strategies. Simultaneously, users need to convey to IR systems their levels of user goals and their interactive intentions; IR systems need to inform users about the status of their actions, explanation of error messages, retrieved results, suggestions for information-seeking strategies, and so forth. Interactive IR systems need to solicit explicit feedback and infer implicit feedback from users because users cannot always clearly express their information needs.

Information retrieval systems are not all designed same. Thus, it is also a challenge for users to express their information needs, so an interactive Help mechanism is needed in order for users to effectively interact with IR systems. The planned-situational model calls for the need to create multi-dimensional Help mechanisms to support users in learning general knowledge of IR systems, searching topics, and information retrieval; to support users in applying multiple information-seeking strategies; and to support users in shifting their information-seeking strategies. System knowledge maps enable users to understand system structure and features as well as commands. Creating a knowledge base for different domains allows users to enhance their knowledge of the domain of their information problems. The most frequently applied information-seeking strategies can guide users in gaining information retrieval skills.

In order to support multiple information-seeking strategies, templates and instructions for different types of interactive intentions need to be provided to users. The patterns between user interactive intentions and retrieval tactics can be implemented for IR systems to infer user intentions. Context-sensitive Help and feedback mechanisms are needed for both user- and system-oriented strategies. Analysis of situations assists IR systems in supporting shifts in information-seeking strategies, which are comprised by shifts in interactive intentions and shifts in retrieval tactics. Three different situations lead to the four types of shifts in interactive intentions. Implicit Help and templates are mainly offered in routine situations. Context-sensitive Help and dialog mechanisms are employed in disruptive situations. At the same time, both context-sensitive and implicit Help are needed in problematic situations. In addition, interactive IR systems also need to facilitate four types of retrieval tactic shifts, in particular changing methods, entities, attributes, and methods-entities. To sum up, a Help mechanism is not just a Help button, and it associates with the overall design of the IR system.

The planned-situational model calls for the need to develop a multidimensional evaluation framework to evaluate interactive IR systems. This framework requires the assessment of interactive IR system performance, the assessment of the usability of the interface or features and organizational usability, and, more important, the assessment of the interactive process between users and IR systems. In evaluating system performance, relevance measurement needs to go beyond the binary measures and be extended to different regions and levels. The value of the search results toward the achievement of leading search goals/work tasks is the key measure of system performance because users might change their current search goals/search tasks in the retrieval process, but they generally do not change their leading search goals/work tasks. In addition to traditional usability attributes, organizational usability also needs to be assessed, especially to what extent and in what ways IR systems can be integrated into users' work. To what extent and in what ways do the organizational structure, norms, and social organization of computing affect IR system use? What is the work ecology? This model emphasizes the importance of IR systems supporting the user-system interaction process. The evaluation of how IR systems support the interactive process focuses on how interactive IR systems support multiple information-seeking strategies as well as shifts in information-seeking strategies during the interactive retrieval process. The measurements have both quantitative and qualitative components, including degree of support, efficiency, level of satisfaction, and ways of support.

The planned-situational model not only provides guidance in developing criteria for the evaluation of interactive IR systems, but also assesses the approaches applied in the evaluation of interactive IR systems. The task-oriented approach can connect the evaluation of system performance, usability, and user-system interaction to how interactive IR systems support users in accomplishing their levels of user goals/tasks. However, the task-oriented approach is not enough to evaluate and compare different interactive IR systems. TREC studies offer methodology, experiment design, and report techniques in evaluating interactive IR systems. The unnatural settings, assigned tasks, and convenience sample in TREC studies might not lead to significant statistical results. Borlund's (2003) proposal for simulated work task situations enables users to associate the situations with their real information needs. Furthermore, the proposal creates opportunities for users to compare different interactive IR systems in terms of system performance, usability, and users-systems interaction under the same conditions.

References

Alexander, N., Brown, C., Jose, J., Ruthven, I., & Tombros, A. (2001). Question answering, relevance feedback, and summarization: TREC-9 interactive track report. In E. M. Voorhees & D. K. Harman (Eds.), *The Ninth Text REtrieval Conference (TREC-9),* (pp. 523-532). Gaithersburg, MD: U.S. Department of Commerce, NIST.

Bates, M. J. (1979a). Information search tactics. *Journals of the American Society for Information Science, 30*(4), 205-214.

Bates, M. J. (1979b). Idea tactics. *Journal of the American Society for Information Science, 30*(5), 280-289.

Bates, M. J. (1989). The design of browsing and berry-picking techniques for the online search interface. *Online Review, 13*(5), 407-424.

Bates, M. J. (1990). Where should the person stop and the information search interface start? *Information Processing and Management, 26*(5), 575-591.

Beaulieu, M. (2000). Interaction in information searching and retrieval. *Journal of Documentation, 56*(4), 431-439.

Beaulieu, M., Fowkes, H., Alemayehu, N., & Sanderson, M. (2000). Interactive Okapi at Sheffield-TREC-8. In E. M. Voorhees & D. K. Harman (Eds.), *The Eighth Text REtrieval Conference, (TREC-8)* (pp. 689-698). Gaithersburg, MD: U.S. Department of Commerce, NIST.

Beheshti, J., Large, V., & Bialek, M. (1996). PACE: A browsable graphical interface. *Information Technology and Libraries, 15*(4), 231-240.

Belkin, N. J. (1980). Anomalous states of knowledge as a basis for information retrieval. *Canadian Journal of Information Science, 5,* 133-143.

Belkin, N. J. (1995). Strategies for evaluation of interactive multimedia information retrieval systems. In I. Ruthven (Ed.), *MIRO 95, Proceedings of the Final Workshop on Multimedia Information Retrieval.* Glasgow, Scotland: Springer.

Belkin, N.J. (1996). Intelligent information retrieval: Whose intelligence? In J. Krause, M. Herfurth, & J. Marx (Eds.), Harausforderungen an die Informationswirtschaft. Informationsverdichtung, Informationsbewertung und Datenvisualisierung, *Proceedings of the 5th International Symposium for Information Science (ISI '96),* (pp. 25-31). Konstanz: Universitätsverlag Konstanz.

Belkin, N. J. (2000). Helping people find what they don't know. *Communications of the ACM, 43*(8), 58-61.

Belkin, N. J., Chang, S., Downs, T., Saracevic, T., & Zhao, S. (1990). Taking account of user tasks, goals and behavior for the design of online public access catalogs. In D. Henderson (Ed.), *Proceedings of the 53rd ASIS Annual Meeting,* (pp. 69-79). Medford, NJ: Learned Information.

Belkin, N. J., Cool, C., Jeng, J., Keller, A., Kelly, D., Kim, J., et al. (2002). Rutgers' TREC 2001 interactive track experience. In E. M. Voorhees & D. K. Harman (Eds.), *The Tenth Text REtrieval Conference, TREC-2001,* (pp. 465-472). Gaithersburg, MD: U.S. Department of Commerce, NIST.

Belkin, N. J., Cool, C., Kelly, D., Lin, S. J., Park, S. Y., Perez-Carballo, J., et al. (2001). Iterative exploration, design and evaluation of support for query reformulation in interactive information retrieval. *Information Processing & Management, 37*(3), 403-434.

Belkin, N. J., Cool, C., Stein, A., & Theil, U. (1995). Cases, scripts and information seeking strategies: On the design of interactive information retrieval systems. *Expert Systems with Applications, 9*(3), 379-395.

Bilal, D. (2002). Perspectives on children's navigation of the World Wide Web: Does the type of search task make a difference. *Online Information Review, 26*(2), 108-177.

Bishop, A. P., Neumann, L. J., Star, S. L., Merkel, C., Ignacio, E., & Sandusky, R. J. (2000). Digital libraries: Situating use in changing information infrastructure. *Journal of the American Society for Information Science, 51*(4), 394-413.

Borgman, C. L., Gilliland-Swetland, A. J., Leazer, G. H., Mayer, R., Gwynn, D., Gazan, R., et al. (2001). Evaluating digital libraries for teaching and learning in undergraduate education: A case study of the Alexandria Digital Earth Proto Type (ADEPT). *Library Trends, 49*(2), 228-250.

Borlund, P. (2000). Experimental components for the evaluation of interactive information retrieval systems. *Journal of Documentation, 56*(1), 71-90.

Borlund, P. (2003). The IR evaluation model: A framework for evaluation of interactive information retrieval systems. *Information Research, 8*(3). Retrieved January 7, 2008, from http://informationr.net/ir/2008-2003/paper2152.html

Borlund, P., & Ingwersen, P. (1997). The development of a method for the evaluation of interactive information retrieval systems. *Journal of Documentation, 53*(3), 225-250.

Borlund, P., & Ingwersen, P. (1998). Measures of relative relevance and ranked half-life: Performance indicators for interactive IR. In R. Wilkinson, B. Croft, & C. V. Rijsbergen (Eds.), *Proceedings of the 21st ACM SIGIR Conference on Research and Development of Information Retrieval,* (pp. 324-331). Melbourne, FL: ACM Press.

Brajnik, G., Mizzaro, S., Tasso, C., & Venuti, F. (2002). Strategic help in user interfaces for information retrieval. *Journal of the American Society for Information Science, 53*(5), 343-358.

Broder, A. (2002). A taxonomy of Web search. *SIGIR Forum, 36*(2), 3-10.

Bruce, H. W. (1994). A cognitive view of the situational dynamism of user-centered relevance estimation. *Journal of the American Society for Information Science, 45*(3), 142-148.

Byström, K., & Järvelin, K. (1995). Task complexity affects information-seeking and use. *Information Processing and Management, 31*(2), 191-213.

Chang, S. (1995). *Toward a multidimensional framework for understanding browsing.* Unpublished doctoral dissertation, Rutgers University, New Brunswick, NJ.

Chen, H., & Dhar, V. (1991). Cognitive processes as a basis for intelligent retrieval system design. *Information Processing and Management, 27*(5), 405-432.

Chu, H., & Rosenthal, M. (1996). Search engines for the World Wide Web: A comparative study and evaluation methodology. In S. Hardin (Ed.), *Proceedings of the 59th ASIS Annual Meeting,* (pp. 127-135). Medford, NJ: Information Today.

Cool, C. (1993). Information retrieval as symbolic interaction: Examples from humanities scholars. In S. Bonzi, J. Katzer, & B. H. Kwasnik (Eds.), *Proceedings of the ASIS Annual Meeting,* (Vol. 30, pp. 247-277). Medford, NJ: Information Today.

Cool, C. (2006, June). Human information behavior in the help-seeking process: Implications for the design of interactive automated help functionalities in digital libraries. In *Paper presented at the Libraries in the Digital Age*, Dubrovnik, Croatia.

Cool, C., & Xie, H. (2004). How can IR help mechanism be more helpful to users? In L. Schamber & C. L. Barry (Eds.), *Proceedings of the 67th ASIST Annual Meeting,* (pp. 249-255). Medford, NJ: Information Today.

Crudge, S.E., & Johnson, F.C. (2004). Using the information seeker to elicit construct models for search engine evaluation. *Journal of the American Society for Information Science, 55*(9), 794-806.

Davies, C. (1997). Organizational influences on the university electronic library. *Information Processing and Management, 33*(3), 377-392.

Dennis, S., Bruza, P., & McArthur, R. (2002). Web searching: A process-oriented experimental study of three interactive search paradigms. *Journal of the American Society for Information Science and Technology, 53*(2), 120-133.

Dillon, A. (2001). Beyond usability: Process, outcome and affect in human-computer interactions. *Canadian Journal of Library and Information Science, 26*(4), 57-69.

Ding, W., & Marchionini, G. (1996). A comparative study of Web search service performance. In S. Hardin (Ed.), *Proceedings of the 59th ASIS Annual Meeting,* (Vol. 33, pp. 136-142). Medford, NJ: Information Today.

Downie, J. S. (2003). Music information retrieval. *Annual Review of Information Science and Technology, 37,* 295-340.

Dunlop, M. (2000). Reflections on Mira: Interaction evaluation in information retrieval. *Journal of the American Society for Information Science, 51*(14), 1269-1274.

Elkerton, J., & Palmiter, S. L. (1991). Designing help using a GOMS model: An information retrieval evaluation. *Human Factors, 33*(2), 185-204.

Elliott, M., & Kling, R. (1997). Organizational usability of digital libraries: Case study of legal research in civil and criminal courts. *Journal of the American Society for Information Science, 48*(11), 1023-1035.

Ellis, D. (1989). A behavioural model for information retrieval system design. *Journal of Information Science, 15*(4/5), 237-247.

Ellis, D. (1996). The dilemma of measurement in information-retrieval research. *Journal of the American Society for Information Science, 47*(1), 23-36.

Ellis, D., & Haugan, M. (1997). Modeling the information seeking patterns of engineers and research scientists in an industrial environment. *Journal of Documentation, 53*(4), 384-403.

Fidel, R. (1991). Searchers' selection of search keys: III. Searching styles. *Journal of the American Society for Information Science, 42*(7), 515-527.

Fidel, R., Pejtersen, A. M., Cleal, B., & Bruce, H. (2004). A multidimensional approach to the study of human-information interaction: A case study of collaborative information retrieval. *Journal of the American Society for Information Science and Technology, 55*(11), 939-953.

Ford, N., Miller, D., & Moss, N. (2002). Web search strategies and retrieval effectiveness: An empirical study. *Journal of Documentation, 58*(1), 30-48.

Fox, E. A., Hix, D., Nowell, L. T., Brueni, D. J., Wake, W. C., Heath, L. S., et al. (1993). Users, user interfaces, and objects-envision: A digital library. *Journal of the American Society for Information Science, 44*(8), 480-491.

Gey, F. C., Kando, N., & Peters, C. (2005). Cross-language information retrieval: The way ahead. *Information Processing and Management, 41*(3), 415-431.

Greisdorf, H. (2003). Relevance thresholds: A multi-stage predictive model of how users evaluate information. *Information Processing and Management, 39*(3), 403-423.

Greisdorf, H., & Spink, A. (2001). Median measure: An approach to IR systems evaluation. *Information Processing and Management, 37*(6), 843-857.

Hawkins, D. T., & Wagers, R. (1982). Online bibliographic search strategy development. *Online, 6*(3), 12-19.

Hellman, R. (1989). User support: Revealing structure instead of surface. *Behaviour and Information Technology, 8*(6), 417-436.

Hersh, W., Pentecost, J., & Hickam, D. (1996). A task-oriented approach to information retrieval evaluation. *Journal of the American Society for Information Science, 47*(1), 50-56.

Hert, C. A. (1996). User goals on an online public access catalog. *Journal of the American Society for Information Science, 47*(7), 504-518.

Hert, C. A. (1997). *Understanding information retrieval interaction: Theoretical and practical implications.* Greenwich, CO: Ablex.

Hix, D., & Hartson, H. R. (1993). *Developing user interfaces: Ensuring usability through product and process.* New York: John Wiley & Sons.

Houghton Jr., R. C. (1984). Online help systems: A conspectus. *Communications of the ACM, 27*(2), 126-133.

Ingwersen, P. (1992). The user-oriented IR research approach. *Information retrieval interaction: Chapter 5* (pp. 83-122). London: Taylor Graham.

Ingwersen, P. (1996). Cognitive perspectives of information retrieval interaction: Elements of a cognitive IR theory. *Journal of Documentation, 52*(1), 3-50.

Ingwersen, P., & Järvelin, K. (2005). *The turn: Integration of information seeking and retrieval in context.* Dordrecht, The Netherlands: Springer.

Jansen, B. J. (2005). Seeking and implementing automated assistance during the search process. *Information Processing and Management, 41*(4), 909-928.

Kim, S.-J. (2005). Collaborative interaction behaviors in an information technology problem-solving context: Cognitive movements of the helper and the helped. *Journal of Information Science, 31*(6), 483-495.

Kim, K. S., & Allen, B. (2002). Cognitive and task influence on Web searching behavior. *Journal of the American Society for Information Science and Technology, 53*(2), 109-119.

Kling, R., & Elliott, M. (1994). Digital library design for organizational usability. *SIGOIS Bulletin, 15*(2), 59-70.

Kreymer, O. (2002). An evaluation of help mechanisms in natural language information retrieval systems. *Online Information Review, 26*(1), 30-39.

Kuhlthau, C. (1991). Inside the search process: Information seeking from the user's perspective. *Journal of the American Society for Information Science, 42*(5), 361-371.

Lamb, R. (1995). Using online Information resources: Reaching for the *.*'s. In F. M. Shipman, R. Furuta, & D. M. Levy (Eds.), *Proceedings of Digital Libraries '95, The Second Annual Conference on the Theory and Practice of Digital Libraries,* (pp. 137-146). Austin, TX: Department of Computer Science, Texas A&M University.

Marchionini, G. (1995). *Information-seeking in electronic environments*. Cambridge, U.K.: Cambridge University Press.

Markey, K., & Atherton, P. (1978). *ONTAP: On-line training and practice manual for ERIC database searchers*. Syracuse, NY: ERIC Clearinghouse on Information Resources.

Markus, M. L., & Robey, D. (1983). The organization validity of management information systems. *Human Relations, 36*(3), 203-226.

Mizzaro, S. (1998). How many relevances in information retrieval? *Interacting with Computers, 10*(3), 303-320.

Nahl, D. (1999). Creating user-centered instructions for novice end-users. *Reference Services Review, 27*(3), 280-286.

Nielsen, J. (1993). *Usability engineering*. San Diego, CA: Academic Press.

Oard, D. (2001). Interactive cross-language information retrieval. *SIGIR Forum, 35*(1), 1-3.

Olah, J. (2005). Shifts between search stages during task-performance in mediated information seeking interaction. In B. Wildemuth, M. Crandall, & A. Grove (Eds.), *Proceedings of the 68th ASIST Annual Meeting*. Retrieved January 7, 2008, from eprint.rclis.org

Robertson, S. E., Walker, S., & Beaulieu, M. (1999). Okapi at TREC-7: Automatic ad hoc, filtering, VLC, and interactive track. In E. M. Voorhees & D. K. Harman (Eds.), *The Seventh Text REtrieval Conference (TREC-7)*, (pp. 253-264). Gaithersburg, MD: U.S. Department of Commerce, NIST.

Robertson, S. E., Walker, S., & Beaulieu, M. (2000). Experimentation as a way of life: Okapi at TREC. *Information Processing and Management, 36*(1), 95-108.

Robins, D. (2000). Shifts of focus on various aspects of user information problems during interactive information retrieval. *Journal of the American Society for Information Science, 51*(10), 913-928.

Rose, D. E., & Levinson, D. (2004). Understanding user goals in Web search. In *Proceedings of the Thirteenth Annual World Wide Web Conference*, (pp. 13-19). New York: ACM Press.

Saracevic, T. (1996). Relevance reconsidered'96. In P. Ingwersen & N. O. Pors (Eds.), *Proceedings of CoLIS 2, Second International Conference on Conceptions of Library and Information Science: Integration in Perspective*, (pp. 201-218). Copenhagen: Royal School of Librarianship.

Schacter, J., Chung, G. K. W. K., & Dorr, A. (1998). Children's Internet searching on complex problems: Performance and process analyses. *Journal of the American Society for Information Science, 49*(9), 840-849.

Shiri, A. A., & Revie, C. (2003). The effects of topic complexity and familiarity on cognitive and physical moves in a thesaurus-enhanced search environment. *Journal of Information Science, 29*(6), 517-526.

Shute, S. J., & Smith, P. J. (1993). Knowledge-based search tactics. *Information Processing and Management, 29*(1), 29-45.

Slack, F. E. (1991). *OPACs: Using enhanced transaction logs to achieve more effective online help for subject searching.* Unpublished doctoral dissertation, Manchester Polytechnic, Manchester, UK

Slone, D. J. (2002). The influence of mental models and goals on search patterns during Web interaction. *Journal of the American Society for Information Science and Technology, 53*(13), 1152-1169.

Soloman, P. (1993). Children's information retrieval behavior: A case analysis of an OPAC. *Journal of the American Society for Information Science, 44*(5), 245-264.

Spink, A. (1997). Study of interactive feedback during mediated information retrieval. *Journal of the American Society for Information Science, 48*(5), 382-394.

Spink, A., & Greisdorf, H. (2001). Regions and levels: Measuring and mapping users' relevance judgments. *Journal of the American Society for Information Science and Technology, 52*(2), 161-173.

Spink, A., Greisdorf, H., & Bateman, J. (1998). From highly relevant to not relevant: Examining different regions of relevance. *Information Processing and Management, 34*(5), 599-621.

Spink, A., & Wilson, T. D. (1999). Toward a theoretical framework for information retrieval (IR) evaluation in an information seeking context. In *Proceedings of MIRA 99: Evaluation Framework for Multimedia Information Retrieval Applications,* (pp. 75-92). Scotland: Department of Computing Sciences, University of Glasgow.

Srihari, R. K., & Zhang, Z. F. (1999). Exploiting multimodal context in image retrieval. *Library Trends, 48*(2), 496-520.

Su, L. T. (1994). The relevance of recall and precision in user evaluation. *Journal of the American Society for Information Science, 45*(3), 207-217.

Su, L. T. (2003a). A comprehensive and systematic model of user evaluation of Web search engines: I. Theory and background. *Journal of the American Society for Information Science and Technology, 54*(13), 1175-1192.

Su, L. T. (2003b). A comprehensive and systematic model of user evaluation of Web search engines: II. An evaluation by undergraduates. *Journal of the American Society for Information Science and Technology, 54*(13), 1193-1223.

Sutcliffe, A. G., Ennis, M., & Watkinson, S. J. (2000). Empirical studies of end-user information searching. *Journal of the American Society for Information Science and Technology, 51*(13), 1211-1231.

Trenner, L. (1989). A comparative survey of the friendliness of online "help" in interactive information retrieval systems. *Information Processing and Management, 25*(2), 119-136.

Vakkari, P. (2001). A theory of the task-based information retrieval process. *Journal of Documentation, 57*(1), 44-60.

Vakkari, P. (2003). Task-based information searching. *Annual Review of Information Science and Technology, 37*, 413-643.

Vogt, C. (2001). Passive feedback collection–an attempt to debunk the myth of clickthroughs. In E. M. Voorhees & D. K. Harman (Eds.), *The Ninth Text REtrieval Conference (TREC-9)*, (pp. 141-150). Gaithersburg, MD: U.S. Department of Commerce, NIST.

Wersig, G. (1979). The problematic situation as a basic concept of information science in the framework of the social sciences—a reply to N. Belkin. *New trends in informatics and its terminology* (pp. 48-57). Vinity, Moscow: International Federation for Documentation.

White, R. W., Jose, J. M., & Ruthven, I. (2002). Comparing explicit and implicit feedback techniques for Web retrieval: TREC-10 interactive track report. In E. M. Voorhees & D. K. Harman (Eds.), *The Tenth Text REtrieval Conference, TREC-2001*, (pp. 534-538). Gaithersburg, MD: US Department of Commerce, NIST.

White, R. W., & Ruthven, I. (2006). A study of interface support mechanisms for interactive information retrieval. *Journal of the American Society for Information Science and Technology, 57*(7), 933-948.

Xie, H. (2000). Shifts of interactive intentions and information-seeking strategies in interactive information retrieval. *Journal of the American Society for Information Science and Technology, 51*(9), 841-857.

Xie, H. (2002). Patterns between interactive intentions and information-seeking strategies. *Information Processing and Management, 38*(1), 55-77.

Xie, H. (2003). Supporting ease-of-use and user control: Desired features and structure of Web-based online IR systems. *Information Processing and Management, 39*(6), 899-922.

Xie, H., & Cool, C. (2000). Ease-of-use versus user control: An evaluation of Web and nonWeb interfaces of online databases. *Online Information Review, 24*(2), 102-115.

Xie, H., & Cool, C. (2006). Toward a better understanding of help seeking behavior: An evaluation of help mechanisms in two IR systems. In A. Dillon & A. Grove

(Eds.), *Proceedings of the 69th ASIST Annual Meeting (Vol. 43)*. Retrieved January 7, 2008, from http://eprints.rclis.org/archive/00008279/01/Xie_Toward.pdf

Xie, H., & Wolfram, D. (2002). State digital library usability: Contributing organizational factors. *Journal of the American Society for Information Science and Technology, 53*(13), 1085-1097.

Yang, K., Maglaughlin, K., Meho, L., & Sumner Jr., R. G. (1999). IRIS at TREC-7. In E. M. Voorhees & D. K. Harman (Eds.), *The Seventh Text REtrieval Conference (TREC-7)*, (pp. 555-566). Gaithersburg, MD: U.S. Department of Commerce, NIST.

Yang, K., Maglaughlin, K. L., & Newby, G. B. (2001). Passage feedback with IRIS. *Information Processing and Management, 37*(3), 521-541.

Chapter XI

Conclusions and Future Directions

Conclusions and Contribution of the Book

The emergence of the Internet has allowed millions of people to use a variety of electronic information retrieval (IR) systems, such as digital libraries, Web search engines, online databases, and Online Public Access Catalogues (OPACs). The nature of IR is interaction. Interactive information retrieval is defined as the communication process between the users and the IR systems. However, the dynamics of interactive IR is not yet fully understood. Moreover, most of the existing IR systems do not support the full range of users' interactions with IR systems. Instead, they only support one type of information-seeking strategy: how to specify queries by using terms to select relevant information. However, new digital environments require users to apply multiple information-seeking strategies and shift from one information-seeking strategy to another in the information retrieval process.

The objective of this book has been to develop a theoretical framework for interactive IR by integrating a variety of theories and empirical studies on interactive information retrieval. This book contributes significantly to research on interactive information retrieval not only by providing a theoretical framework for understanding the nature of IR but also by offering implications for the design and evaluation of interactive IR systems. The major contributions of the book include:

1.   The development of a theoretical framework for interactive IR in digital environments, especially the discussion of information retrieval as the products of plans and situations. The uniqueness of the planned-situational model is that it accounts for the social-organizational context in which user-system interactions take place and users' information infrastructures as they apply to user-system interactions, as well as the dynamic information retrieval process signified by shifts in information-seeking strategies. This model identifies the nature of information retrieval as interaction that is codetermined by plans and situations. Levels of user goals/tasks, in particular their relationships and dimensions of work and search tasks, are the driving forces for information retrieval. In addition, the situational factors, such as the outcomes of user-system interactions and the information objects that users interact with, determine the information retrieval process in terms of how and why users shift their current search goals/search tasks and information-seeking strategies. The model further connects planned and situational factors to patterns between the microlevel of user goal—interactive intentions—and retrieval tactics and the patterns of shifts in information-seeking strategies.

2.   The integration of existing theoretical frameworks on user-oriented IR across multiple disciplines. This framework is created based on the following theoretical works:

   a.   The macrolevel interactive IR models (Belkin, 1993, 1996; Ingwersen, 1992; Ingwersen & Järvelin, 2005; Saracevic, 1996, 1997). Ingwersen's cognitive model, Belkin's episode model of interaction with texts, and Saracevic's stratified interaction model consider the nature of IR as the process of users' interaction with IR systems. This is the foundation for the framework. The macrolevel interactive IR models identify the major elements involved in the interactive IR process and factors affecting the interactive IR process. However, these models cannot provide detailed information about specific processes or issues, and moreover they cannot identify the patterns between information-seeking strategies and factors that lead to different types of information-seeking strategies.

   b.   The microlevel of interactive IR models complements the macrolevel of interactive IR models to focus on one specific issue of interactive IR that the macrolevel of interactive IR models fail to investigate. The microlevel of interactive IR models explores the driving force of information retrieval: Vakkari's task-based IR process (Vakkari, 2000a, 2000b, 2001,

2003; Vakkari & Hakala, 2000; Vakkari, Pennanen, & Serola, 2003), the dynamic of the information retrieval process (Bates' berrypicking model, 1989), a specific component of IR (Spink's model of interactive feedback, 1997), one type of user-system interaction (Wang, Hawk & Tenopir's model of user-Web interaction, 2000), and the relationship between IR interaction and information-seeking process (Hert, 1997). Microlevel interactive IR models offer insightful information on specific issues and process, but they also need to be connected to the macrolevel of information retrieval and be able to apply to different settings. In addition, Pharo and Järvelin's search situation transition method is an effective tool to analyze interactive IR (Pharo, 2002, 2004; Pharo & Järvelin, 2004).

c.   The "planned model" and "situated action" (Newell & Simon, 1972; Suchman, 1987; Vera & Simon, 1993; Hert, 1997; Xie, 2000, 2002). While the "planned model" derived from cognitive science considers information-seeking behaviors as a goal-directed plan, "situated action" based on social science views information-seeking behaviors as the result of moment-by-moment interactions among a user, a system, and the environment. Both approaches have their limitations. Information-seeking strategies are the products of both plans and situations.

d.   User goals/tasks and information-seeking strategies. The research on user goals and information-seeking strategies (Belkin et al., 1990; Belkin, Marchetti, & Cool, 1993; Chang, 1995; Hert, 1996, 1997) has highlighted the driving force for information retrieval. However, previous research only examined one level of user goal and its relationship to information-seeking strategies. Adapted from Daniels' (1986) classification of goals, the author constructs the hierarchical structure of user goals. At the same time, the author illustrates the relationships between levels of user goals and levels of tasks and identifies the dimensions of work and search tasks. Furthermore, the author illustrates how levels of goals/tasks affect the selection of information-seeking strategies and shifts in information-seeking strategies.

3.   The comprehensive literature review of the empirical studies of interactive IR in a variety of digital environments, such as OPACs, online databases, Web search engines, and digital libraries. For each of the digital environments, the review covers background and history, current development, challenges for users, research overview, and, more importantly, the interaction studies. Interaction studies are organized based on the research in each environment. The review discusses the key elements in interactive IR research from the impact of task, knowledge structure on interactive IR, different levels of information-seeking strategies, system role, user involvement in interactive IR, interactive

cross-language IR, interactive multimedia IR, and the evaluation of interactive IR systems.

4. The discussion of the theoretical implications of the planned-situational model of interactive information retrieval. The theoretical implication of the model is two-fold. First, it proposes a new approach for researchers for understanding the nature of IR in that users engage in multiple information-seeking strategies, and they have to shift their information-seeking strategies under different situations during the information retrieval process. This model considers issues brought up by both the macro- and micro-level of interactive IR models. This the first model that examines the shifts in information-seeking strategies and, further, associates planned and situational factors to the patterns of shifts in current search goals/search tasks and shifts in information-seeking strategies. Second, the model sheds light on some of the essential concepts in interactive IR research. Different levels of user goals and tasks are often used without differentiation. This model highlights the levels of user goals and their corresponding levels of tasks, and further illustrates the dimensions of work and search tasks that influence their information-seeking strategies. In the process of achieving leading search goals and work tasks, users may encounter problems, and the problematic situations and anomalous state of knowledge force users to gain new knowledge by looking for information to assist them solving their problems. Information-seeking strategies have been investigated on different levels, from tactics and moves to patterns, but these studies mostly focus on the types of information-seeking strategies related to query formulation and reformulation. The planned-situational model presents multiple information-seeking strategies that users apply in the IR process as well as dimensions of information-seeking strategies; this offers an in-depth view of the nature of information retrieval.

5. The discussion of the implication of planned-situational model to the design of interactive IR systems. The model provides guidance for interactive IR system design in the following aspects: 1) Support multiple types of information-seeking strategies in the information retrieval process; 2) support different types of shifts in information-seeking strategies; 3) balance ease-of-use and user control in system design for different levels of user groups; 4) delegate system role and user involvement in applying different types of information-seeking strategies in the IR system design; 5) support user-system communication by soliciting explicit and implicit feedback from users; and 6) offer a multidimensional help mechanism to assist users learning general knowledge of domain search topics, IR systems and information retrieval, applying multiple information-seeking strategies, and facilitating shifts in information-seeking strategies.

6. The development of a new framework for the evaluation of interactive IR systems. The planned-situational model specifies the roles that interactive IR systems need to play in user-system interactions. In that sense, the frame-

work for evaluation emphasizes the assessment of the interactive IR system performance, as well as the usability of the interface, or features, and the organizational usability. While system performance focuses on the value of search results in terms of the extent to which it helps users achieve their leading search goals/work tasks and the importance of introducing different regions and levels of relevance judgment, the usability evaluation concentrates on users' satisfaction level with regard to how interfaces support ease-of-use and user control and organizational usability at the individual, organizational, and environmental levels. More important, the framework calls for the assessment of the support for the interactive IR process that previous research has neglected. The assessment of the support for the interactive process between users and IR systems includes the degree of support, ways of support, levels of satisfaction, and efficiency. The framework also reviews and integrates new approaches for evaluating interactive IR systems from a task-oriented approach to a simulated work-task-situation approach that considers real information needs in the comparison of different interactive IR systems.

Unsolved Problems and Further Research Directions

This section focuses on four of the critical issues in interactive information retrieval that the planned-situational model examines, but where there are still unsolved problems: (1) Theoretically, we need to deal with the problem of whether we can create a one-size-fits-all model to account for all the user-system interactions for a variety of work and search tasks; (2) Practically, we need to fill in the gap between users-oriented study and system-oriented design, and further design interactive IR systems to facilitate effective user-system interactions; (3) At the same time, we also need to examine the unique characteristics of interactive multimedia IR and cross-language IR, and further explore how to design and effectively evaluate interactive multimedia IR and cross-language IR systems; (4) Finally, we need to develop a framework for the evaluation of interactive IR models. For each of the issues, the discussion concentrates on: (1) What has been discussed in the model; (2) What are the unsolved problems; and (3) What needs to be investigated further? In addition, questions related to interactive IR are also raised for further research.

One-Size-Fits-All Model?

The planned-situational model takes account of both the macrolevel and microlevel interactive IR models. On the one hand, it covers the major components involved in the interactive IR process from levels of user goals/tasks, personal information infrastructure, the social-organizational context, IR systems, user-IR system inter-actions, and planned and situational factors. On the other hand, it also identifies multiple information-seeking strategies and shifts in information-seeking strategies in the information retrieval process. Shifts in information-seeking strategies are at the center of the model. At the same time, the model further discusses the system role and user involvement in users' applying multiple information-seeking strategies and the creation of an interactive help mechanism to support users to gain general domain, system and information retrieval knowledge, to apply multiple informa-tion-seeking strategies, and to shift from one strategy to another.

The author explored the original model in general library use environments (Xie, 2000, 2002). The author expanded and enhanced the model based on interactive studies in different digital environments; moreover, this model was also validated and tested in an empirical study investigating how people sought and retrieved information in their research proposal writing process. Nonetheless, the planned-situational model still needs to be tested and validated in different digital environments. Further research needs to examine users' information-seeking strategies in general IR environment involving a variety of work and search tasks related to users' work and personal information needs across different types of IR environments. The implication of the model, especially the allocated different roles that systems and users play, has been explored in online database environments (Xie, 2003); more research needs to look into the implications of the planned-situational model for different aspects or issues of interactive IR. That also raises an issue for further research: whether we can have a one-size-fits-all-model to account for all the issues in interactive IR or whether we need different interactive IR models to illustrate various issues and aspects in the interactive IR process.

The Gap between Users-Oriented Study and System-Oriented Design

Researchers and designers of IR systems normally belong to two different camps. One problem of the user-oriented approach is that these studies normally stay as studies, and they are not further implemented into operational system design. This book is strengthened by representing user-system interactions from both user elements and system components and by further offering design guidelines. These guidelines include how to design interactive IR systems to support multiple information-seek-ing strategies and shifts in information-seeking strategies, how to make users and systems collaborate together in the information retrieval process, and how to build an interactive help mechanism to facilitate users' interactions with IR systems.

However, design principles are just suggestions. Simultaneously, it is more valu-able for researchers to engage in discussion and collaboration with designers to create prototypes of interactive IR systems that implement the suggested design principles. By testing the prototype of interactive IR systems, researchers can have a better understanding of the extent to which the prototype system can support users effectively retrieving information. Further, researchers can convince designers to work more closely with the researchers of interactive IR to design new interactive IR systems and improve the existing IR systems to support effective IR interactions. That potentially also poses a challenge in terms of how to convert the results of user studies into the structure and features of system design.

Complexity of Interactive Multimedia IR and CLIR

It is not easy for users to effectively retrieve text information. It is even more complicated for them to search for multimedia information. This book incorporates some of the representative research in interactive multimedia IR and CLIR; it uncovers the unique problems of these types of IR and proposes suggestions. For example, De Vries (2001) highlighted the complexity involved in conducting multimedia search tasks, such as being unable to express the nonverbal aspects of multimedia need, in particular emotional and aesthetic values. He proposed the design of a system to facilitate an iterative search process for users to recognize and compare that instead of describing it. In his review of music information retrieval, Downie (2003) identified the challenges facing music information retrieval. In addition to the multirepresentational challenge, multicultural challenge, and multidisciplinarity challenge, he also emphasized the multiexperiential challenge. The experience of music varies with different individuals, and the experience also changes depending on a person's mood, situation, and circumstances. That poses challenges for music IR systems to serve users' needs and adapt to their uses. Smeaton (2004) also emphasized the importance of understanding user needs and relevance criteria in searching digital video. However, he also pointed out that is difficult to focus on users because of the complexity and multifaceted of video information. Rui, Ortega, Huang, and Mehrotra (1999) suggested the incorporation of the two paradigms of visual IR together: one paradigm based on text only and another based on visual information only, and further incorporated users into the IR system loop. Relevance feedback was recommended for effective multimedia IR.

Users experience uncertainty in their IR process. Cross-language IR adds another layer of uncertainty for users when they have to deal with unknown languages. Gey, Kando, and Peters (2005) pointed out that users need much more support in formulating queries and selecting relevant documents. However, users also intend to favor the simplest interactions in CLIR when they are fine with their retrieved documents (Petrelli et al., 2004; Petrelli, Hansen, Beaulieu, & Sanderson, 2002; Petrelli, Levin, Beaulieu, & Sanderson, 2006). In addition, users' search tactics vary and are more complicated for query reformulations when under the manual condition compared with the automatic condition (Dorr et al., 2004). Research has also demonstrated that users exhibit some unique information-seeking behavior for multilingual IR (Zhang et al., 2007).

Research in multimedia IR and CLIR reveal that multimedia IR and CLIR are more complicated than text and English IR. The exploratory research in these areas is not enough for us to have a complete picture of how users interact with information and IR systems in multimedia IR and CLIR environments. More research needs to involve real users with real problems in real settings in order to discover the nature of multimedia IR and CLIR interaction. It is also important to further identify the similarities and differences among different types of retrieval to investigate whether it is feasible to develop an integrated interactive IR model.

The Evaluation of Interactive IR Models

There are no standard criteria for evaluating interactive IR models. In general, it is important for an interactive IR model to provide a better understanding of the nature of IR, especially the interactions between users and systems during the IR process. Simultaneously, it is also essential for the model to offer guidelines for the design of new interactive IR systems and to improve the existing IR systems to support effective and efficient user-system interactions. Saracevic (1996) identified the key characteristics that interactive IR models need to have:

- Provide different types of interactive processes and their relationships during IR process;
- Identify main elements and variables involved in the interactive IR process;
- Associate interactive IR models with HCI research;
- Be able to evaluate interactive IR; and
- Be able to be tested scientifically.

Research is ongoing in terms of how to evaluate or test interactive IR models. These models cannot be just tested in one environment; instead, they need to be tested in a variety of environments, including real users with real problems in real settings. Only by doing that can different types interactive processes, major elements, and variables involved in the interactive IR process be identified and tested, and interactive IR models modified and enhanced. Interactive IR is a very complicated process; it involves users and their knowledge applied in the interaction process, the levels of goals and tasks driving them to seek information, the social-organizational context in which the interactions take place, and the IR systems as partners and facilitators of the interactions. It is essential to apply an interdisciplinary approach for the development of interactive IR models. As a result, interdisciplinary research also needs to be applied to the evaluation of interactive IR models. The ultimate test of interactive IR models can only be accomplished after the design of actual interactive IR systems based on these models and the evaluation of users' interaction with these systems in real settings.

Further Research Directions and Related Questions

The book reviews interactive studies in different digital environments, and integrates the theoretical frameworks of user-oriented studies, as well as macro- and micro-levels of interactive IR models, and further develops the planned-situational interactive IR model to account for the nature of IR, in particular, the interactive IR process. Further research directions and related questions can be summarized as follows:

- Understand how users with diverse knowledge structures and demographic backgrounds interact with IR systems for a variety of work and search tasks in different environments, further implementing the results of studies into the development of interactive IR models. In order to represent the interactive IR process, interdisciplinary research—such as users' cognitive processes and information-seeking strategies (cognitive science, psychology, social science), user-system interaction via interface (HCI, communication theory), and IR system design (computer science, engineering)—needs to be integrated in developing interactive IR models. The objective of user studies is to maximally portray the complete picture of user-system interactions under diverse circumstances. Moreover, the results of the studies need to offer concrete examples or design principles for the design of interactive IR systems. Specifically, further research needs to explore the following questions:

  - Do different types of users exhibit different types of behaviors or strategies? Are there any patterns that can be identified for different types of users?

  - Under what circumstances do users change their levels of user goals/tasks and information-seeking strategies? What are the most important factors among the factors that determine the shifts in information-seeking strategies?

  - What are the patterns of shifts in levels of user goals/tasks and information-seeking strategies?

  - How can the protocols of user-system interactions in the information-seeking and retrieving process be characterized for system design?

- It seems that it might not be feasible to develop a one-size-fits-all interactive IR model. Simultaneously, the model will lose the context if it only focuses on one issue or problem. One solution is to integrate macro- and micro-level interactive IR by highlighting specific issues or problems under the major components and structure of the macrolevel of interactive IR. Specific questions for further research should include:

  ○ Can we have a one-size-fits-all model to account for all the issues in interactive IR, or do we need different interactive IR models to illustrate various issues and aspects of the interactive IR process?

  ○ How can we best represent the macro- and micro-level of interactive IR?

- Acknowledging the complexity of interactive multimedia IR and cross-language IR is far from enough. The extra layer of uncertainty in these IR environments requires users to engage in more interactions and need more support from IR systems in their information-seeking and retrieving process. Further research should look into the following questions:

  ○ What are the unique information seeking or searching behaviors exhibited by users in nontext and nonEnglish IR environments?

  ○ How can user-system interactions in nontext and nonEnglish IR environments be characterized?

  ○ What types of support do users need in interactive multimedia IR and CLIR?

- The value of interactive IR models cannot be realized if they are not tested with actual interactive IR systems. The ultimate test for any IR model is to test its application in actual system design and use. The existing problem of application is mainly caused by the lack of communication between the two camps. One way to break the stalemate is to promote communication between researchers and system designers. More important, researchers of interactive studies need to offer concrete protocols for designers to implement into the system design or to work closely with designers to develop a workable protocol. One approach that can be applied is to offer design principles that support multiple information-seeking strategies and different types of shifts in user goals/tasks and information-seeking strategies, as discussed in Chapter X. More research is needed to offer different prototypes to support or facilitate multiple information-seeking strategies and shifts in information-seeking strategies, and to further validate/test and identify the best prototype system for actual design. In addition, current research on interactive IR systems has explored personalization/ customization (Perugini & Ramakrishnan, 2003) and visualization options (Leide, Large, Beheshti, Brooks, & Cole, 2003) as well as the design of IR systems or features for different types of users. The problem is how to accommodate users who prefer interfaces that are easy to use or that enable them to have more control. Further research should extend to the following questions:

○   How can the gap between user-oriented study and system-oriented design be filled in? What effective approaches can be applied to encourage researchers and designers to work together?

• How can protocols for user-system interactions be identified and further implemented into interactive IR system design in such a way that user-system interactions for diverse user goals/tasks in diverse environments are facilitated?

• How can different roles that users and systems play in their interaction process be allocated?

• How can IR systems be designed that balance ease-of-use as well as user control?

• Finally, the evaluation of interactive IR systems and evaluation of interactive IR models need to be further researched. As to the evaluation of interactive IR systems, a multidimensional evaluation framework, including system performance, usability, and the user-system interaction process, is discussed in Chapter X. However, the measurements for these three aspects are still not in agreement. Far less work has been done in evaluating interactive IR models. Further research needs to work on the following questions:

• What measurements should be applied to assess system performance, usability, and the user-system interaction process?

• How can interactive IR systems be evaluated incorporating information from real users with real problems in real settings?

• What are the criteria needed to evaluate interactive IR models?

References

Bates, M. J. (1989). The design of browsing and berry-picking techniques for the online search interface. *Online Review, 13*(5), 407-424.

Belkin, N. J. (1993). Interaction with texts: Information retrieval as information seeking behavior. In G. Knorz, J. Krause, & C. Womser-Hacker (Eds.), *Information retrieval '93: Von der Modellierung zur Anwendung* (pp. 55-66). Konstanz: Universitaetsverlag Konstanz.

Belkin, N.J. (1996). Intelligent information retrieval: Whose intelligence? In J. Krause, M. Herfurth, & J. Marx (Eds), Harausforderungen an die Informationswirtschaft. Informationsverdichtung, Informationsbewertung und Datenvisualisierung,

Proceedings of the 5th International Symposium for Information Science (ISI '96), (pp. 25-31). Konstanz: Universitätsverlag Konstanz.

Belkin, N. J., Chang, S., Downs, T., Saracevic, T., & Zhao, S. (1990, November). Taking account of user tasks, goals and behavior for the design of online public access catalogs. In D. Henderson (Ed.), *Proceedings of the 53rd ASIS Annual Meeting*, (pp. 69-79). Medford, NJ: Learned Information.

Belkin, N. J., Marchetti, P. G., & Cool, C. (1993). BRAQUE: Design of an interface to support user interaction in information retrieval. *Information Processing and Management, 29*(3), 325-344.

Chang, S. (1995). *Toward a multidimensional framework for understanding browsing*. Unpublished doctoral dissertation, Rutgers University, New Brunswick, NJ.

Daniels, P. J. (1986). *Developing the user modeling function of an intelligent interface for document retrieval systems*. Unpublished doctoral dissertation, The City University, London, U.K.

De Vries, A. P. (2001). Content independence in multimedia databases. *Journal of the American Society for Information Science and Technology, 52*(11), 954-690.

Dorr, B. J., He, D., Luo, J., Oard, D. W., Schwartz, R., Wang, J., & Zajic, D. (2004). Comparative evaluation of multilingual information access systems. In *iCLEF 2003 at Maryland: Translation Selection and Document Selection*, (pp. 435-449). Heidelberg: Springer-Verlag.

Downie, J.S. (2003). Music information retrieval. *Annual Review of Information Science and Technology, 37*, 295-340.

Gey, F.C., Kando, N., & Peters, C. (2005). Cross-language information retrieval: The way ahead. *Information Processing & Management, 41*(3), 415-431.

Hert, C. A. (1996). User goals on an Online Public Access Catalog. *Journal of the American Society for Information Science, 47*, 504-518.

Hert, C. A. (1997). *Understanding information retrieval interaction: Theoretical and practical implications*. Greenwich, CO: Ablex.

Ingwersen, P. (1992). *Information retrieval interaction*. London: Taylor Graham.

Ingwersen, P., & Järvelin, K. (2005). *The turn: Integration of information. Seeking and retrieval in context*. Heidelberg: Springer-Verlag.

Leide, J. E., Large, A., Beheshti, J., Brooks, M., & Cole, C. (2003). Visualization schemes for domain novices exploring a topic space: The navigation classification scheme. *Information Processing and Management, 39*(6), 923-940.

Newell, A., & Simon, A. (1972). *Human problem solving*. Englewood Cliffs, NJ: Prentice Hall.

Perugini, S., & Ramakrishnan, N. (2003). Personalizing interactions with information systems. *Advances in Computers, 57*, 323-382.

Petrelli, D., Hansen, P., Beaulieu, M., & Sanderson, M. (2002). User requirement elicitation for cross-language information retrieval. *The New Review of Information Behaviour Research, 3*, 17-35.

Petrelli, D., Hansen, P., Beaulieu, M., Sanderson, M., Demetriou, G., & Herring, P. (2004). Observing users-designing clarity: A case study on the user-centred design of a cross-language retrieval system. *Journal of the American Society for Information Science and Technology, 55*(10), 923-934.

Petrelli, D., Levin, S., Beaulieu, M., & Sanderson, M. (2006). Which user interaction for cross-language information retrieval? Design issues and reflections. *Journal of the American Society for Information Science and Technology, 57*(5), 709-722.

Pharo, N. (2002). *The search situation and transition method schema: A tool for analysing Web information search processes.* Tampere, Finland: Tampere University Press (Doctoral dissertation. Acta Universitatis Tamperensis, 871). Retrieved January 6, 2008, from http://acta.uta.fi/pdf/951-44-5355-7.pdf

Pharo, N. (2004). A new model of information behaviour based on the search situation transition schema. *Information Research, 10*(1), 203. Retrieved January 6, 2008, from http://informationr.net/ir/10-1/paper203.html

Pharo, N., & Järvelin, K. (2004). The Search Situation and Transition method: A tool for analyzing Web information search processes. *Information Processing and Management, 40*(4), 633-654.

Rui, Y., Ortega, M., Huang, T. S., & Mehrotra, S. (1999). Information retrieval beyond the text document. *Library Trends, 48*(2), 455-474.

Saracevic, T. (1996). Modeling interaction in information retrieval (IR): A review and proposal. In S. Hardin (Ed.), *Proceedings of the American Society of Information Science, 33*, 3-9.

Saracevic, T. (1997). The stratified model of information retrieval interaction: Extension and applications. In *Proceedings of the 60th Annual Meeting of the American Society for Information Science, 34*, 313-327.

Smeaton, A. F. (2004). Indexing, browsing and searching of digital video. *Annual Review of Information Science and Technology, 38*, 371-407.

Spink, A. (1997). Study of interactive feedback during mediated information retrieval. *Journal of the American Society for Information Science, 48*, 382-394.

Suchman, L.A. (1987). *Plans and situated actions: The problems of human-machine communication.* Cambridge University Press.

Vakkari, P. (2000a). Cognition and changes of search terms and tactics during task performance: A longitudinal study. In *Proceedings of the RIAO 2000 Conference,* (pp. 894-907). Paris: CID.

Vakkari, P. (2000b). Relevance and contributory information types of searched documents in task performance. In *Proceedings of the 23rd Annual International ACM SIGIR Conference on Research and Development in Information Retrieval,* (pp. 2-9). New York: ACM Press.

Vakkari, P. (2001). A theory of the task-based information retrieval process. *Journal of Documentation, 57*(1), 44-60.

Vakkari, P. (2003). Task-based information searching. *Annual Review of Information Science and Technology, 37,* 413-64.

Vakkari, P., & Hakala, N. (2000). Changes in relevance criteria and problem stages in task performance. *Journal of Documentation, 56,* 540-562.

Vakkari, P., Pennanen, M., & Serola, S. (2003). Changes in search terms and tactics while writing a research proposal: A longitudinal case study. *Information Processing & Management, 39,* 445-463.

Vera, A. H., & Simon, H. A. (1993). Situated action–a symbolic interpretation. *Cognitive Science, 17*(1), 7-48.

Wang, P. Hawk, W. B., & Tenopir, C. (2000). Users' interaction with World Wide Web resources: An exploratory study using a holistic approach. *Information Processing and Management, 36*(2), 229-251.

Xie, H. (2000). Shifts of interactive intentions and information-seeking strategies in interactive information retrieval. *Journal of the American Society for Information Science, 51*(9), 841-857.

Xie, H. (2002). Patterns between interactive intentions and information-seeking strategies. *Information Processing & Management, 38*(1), 55-77.

Xie, H. (2003). Supporting ease-of-use and user control: Desired features and structure of Web-based online IR systems. *Information Processing & Management, 39*(6), 899-922.

Zhang, P., Plettenberg, L., Klavans, J. L., Oard, D. W., & Soergel, D. (2007). Task-based interaction with an integrated multilingual, multimedia information system: A formative evaluation. In *Proceedings of the 2007 Conference on Digital Libraries,* (pp. 117-126). New York: ACM Press.

About the Author

Iris Xie is an associate professor in the School of Information Studies at the University of Wisconsin-Milwaukee. Her research interests and expertise focus on information seeking and retrieving, in particular interactive information retrieval between users and IR systems and its implications for the design and evaluation of a variety of IR systems in the digital age. Dr. Xie won the dissertation award from the Association for Library and Information Science Education (ALISE) in 1999. She is the principal investigator on many research grants awarded by different agencies, which include the Institute of Museum and Library Services (IMLS), Online Computer Library Center (OCLC), ALISE, and so forth. She has a strong record in publishing refereed articles and presenting at international conferences in the field of library and information science.

Index

A

alternative shifts 248
anomalous state of knowledge (ASK)
     hypothesis 5
attribute shifts 249
automatic query expansion 161

B

balancing ease-of-use 302
Bates' berrypicking approach 198
Belkin's ASK hypothesis 5
Belkin's episode model 188

C

cognitive work analysis (CWA) 15, 225
compromised need 4
conscious need 3
creating interactive help mechanisms 306
cross-language information retrieval
     (CLIR) 171, 340
current search goal shifts, types 244, 281

D

Dervin's sense-making approach 8
digital libraries, challenges for users 121
digital libraries, current developments 120
digital libraries, definition and types 118
digital libraries, evaluation criteria 136
digital libraries, usability studies 130
digital libraries, usage patterns 126
digital library environments, interactive IR
     116–152
dimensions of plans 278
dimensions of situations 280
dimensions of work tasks 220

E

Ellis' model of information-seeking behav-
     ior 197
entity shifts 249
explicit feedback vs. passive/implicit feed-
     back 163

F

factors affecting shifts in current search
     goals 286

formalized need 4

H

Hert's IR interaction 201

I

information-seeking strategies 236
information-seeking strategies, dimensions 228
information-seeking strategies, shifts 281
information-seeking strategies, types 273
information retrieval (IR) systems 334
information search process (ISP) 10
Ingwersen's cognitive model 184
integrated IS&R research framework 185
interaction studies 124
interactive intentions, dimensions 231
interactive intention shifts, types 246, 283
interactive IR, nature of 296
interactive IR framework 215–262
interactive IR in digital environments, nature 215
interactive IR models 183–214
interactive IR system design, implications 298
interactive IR system performance, evaluation 313
interactive multimedia information retrieval 134
interactive multimedia IR, complexity 340
interactive studies, types 158
interactive track, overview 156
interactive track environments 153–182
IR systems 226, 271

K

knowledge structure, impact 99
knowledge structure of users 66
knowledge structure on search success, effect 40
Kuhlthau's information search process (ISP) approach 10

M

macro-level of interactive IR models 204

method-entity shifts 249
micro-level of interactive IR models 204
microlevel of interactive IR models 197
multidimensional model of user-Web interaction 203
multimedia IR, patterns 96

O

one-size-fits-all model? 338
online database environments, interactive IR 53–82
online databases, challenges for users 58
online databases, current developments 56
online databases, definitions 54
online databases, interaction studies 61
online help 127
online industry, major elements 54
online IR systems, evaluation criteria 71
online public access catalog (OPAC) environments, interactive IR 29–52
online public access catalogues (OPACs) 334
OPAC, challenges for users 34
OPAC, evaluation studies and usability testing 41
OPAC, interaction studies 36
OPAC, research overview 35
OPAC, strategies/behaviors and affecting factors 38
OPACs, current developments 33
OPACs, definition and types 30

P

passage feedback 162
personal information infrastructure 223, 267
Pharo's search situation and transition method 204
planned-situational interactive IR model 216
planned-situational interactive IR model, implications 294–333
public access catalogue extension (PACE) 41

Q

query formulation and reformulation 160
query length 164

R

relevance feedback 161
retrieval tactics, dimensions 233
retrieval tactic shifts, types 285

S

Saracevic's stratified interaction model
    192
searchers' knowledge vs. the impact of the
    dimensions of tasks 158
search strategies levels 63
search tactics and strategies 165
social-organizational context 225, 270
Spink's model of interactive feedback 201
static text 154
stratified interaction model 192
streaming text 154

T

Taylor's levels of information need ap-
    proach 3
Text REtrieval Conference (TREC)
    153–182
type III intention shifts 247
type II intention shifts 247
type I intention shifts 246
type IV intention shifts 248

U

University of Wisconsin-Milwaukee
    (UWM) 264
user-oriented approaches 2
user-oriented IR research approaches 1–28
users-oriented study and system-oriented
    design, the gap 339

V

Vakkari's theory of the task-based IR pro-
    cess 199
visceral need 3

W

Web search engine environments, interac-
    tive IR 83–115
Web search engines, challenges for users
    87
Web search engines, current developments
    85
Web search engines, definitions and types
    84
Web search engines, evaluation criteria
    101
Web search engines, interactions studies
    90
Web search engines, research overview 89
Wilson's information seeking context ap-
    proach 12